THE SECOND WORLD WAR

Twentieth-Century Wars
General Editor: Jeremy Black

Published titles

Gerard DeGroot	*The First World War*
Peter Lowe	*The Korean War*
Spencer C. Tucker	*The Second World War*

Forthcoming

D. George Boyce	*The Falklands War*
Ritchie Ovendale	*The Gulf War*

Twentieth-Century Wars
Series Standing Order ISBN 0-333-77101-X

You can receive future titles in this series as they are published. To place a standing order please contact your bookseller or, in the case of difficulty, write to us at the address below with your name and address, the title of the series and the ISBN quoted above.

Customer Services Department, Macmillan Distribution Ltd
Houndsmill, Basingstoke, Hampshire RG21 6XS, England

THE SECOND WORLD WAR

Spencer C. Tucker

palgrave
macmillan

This book is dedicated to Malcolm 'Kip' Muir, Jr

First published 2004 by
PALGRAVE MACMILLAN
Houndmills, Basingstoke, Hampshire RG21 6XS and
175 Fifth Avenue, New York, N.Y. 10010
Companies and representatives throughout the world

PALGRAVE MACMILLAN is the global academic imprint of the Palgrave Macmillan division of St. Martin's Press, LLC and of Palgrave Macmillan Ltd, Macmillan® is a registered trademark in the United States, United Kingdom and other countries. Palgrave is a registered trademark in the European Union and other countries.

ISBN 0–333–92093–7 paperback
ISBN 0–333–92092–9 hardback

This book is printed on paper suitable for recycling and made from fully managed and sustained forest sources.

A catalogue record for this book is available from the British Library.

A catalogue record for this book is available from the Library of Congress.

10   9   8   7   6   5   4   3   2   1
13   12   11   10   09   08   07   06   05   04

Typeset by Cambrian Typesetters, Frimley, Surrey
Printed in China

Contents

Maps

Preface

World War II is in many ways the 'favorite war.' Today it is seen as the 'good war,' pitting the forces of good in a life-and-death struggle against evil and, at least in Adolf Hitler, the Devil Incarnate. After a decade of giving in to the demands of the dictators, the Western powers finally went to war to prevent brutal fascist regimes from dominating the world. World War II was also one of the greatest conflagrations in world history, waged across the globe and on land, in the air, on the sea, and under the sea. The stakes were enormous, and in the end the United States, Britain, the Soviet Union and their many allies prevailed, defeating the principal Axis powers of Germany, Italy, and Japan, and their associates.

In retrospect, the outcome seems almost inevitable, although few saw it that way at the time. In the first several years of the war it seemed impossible to predict an Allied victory, and the men and women who risked everything to join the resistance to Nazism in the early years deserve our special thanks for moral and physical courage in the face of seemingly insurmountable odds. In the end the resistance goal of defeating Fascism was realized, though not its hope for a new Europe cleansed of its old pathologies. Soon the world was locked in a new struggle known as the Cold War. Fortunately, for much of the world at least, this new conflict was not a shooting war.

My intention in writing this book is to provide a clear overview of events leading up to World War II, of the war itself, and of its aftermath. It is impossible to cover everything in a single volume with a severe word limitation, but I have endeavored to treat the causes of the war, the military strengths and weaknesses of the warring powers, and the pivotal battles and important weapons systems. I also deal with the major diplomatic and military decisions and milestones of the conflict, such as the decision to employ the atomic bomb; and the reasons why the war evolved as it did. I provide a view of life on the home fronts; and, finally, I examine the immediate aftermath of the war and its important effects, the peace settlement, and origins of the Cold War.

Order of battle statistics vary widely, and exact casualty figures are even more elusive. For the sake of consistency, unless otherwise noted casualty figures have come from R..Ernest Dupuy and Trevor N. Dupuy, *Harper's Encyclopedia of Military History*. I have also used extensively, as a statistical source, J. C. B. Dear and M. R. D. Foot's *The Oxford Companion to World War II*.

I am greatly indebted to the Virginia Military Institute for its support of my writing activities and to the following colleagues who read all or part of the manuscript and made many helpful suggestions and comments: Walter Boyne, Brigadier General Charles Brower IV, Timothy Dowling, John Fredriksen, Jack Greene, Eric Osborne, Rear Admiral Ret. Hirama Yoichi, Malcolm Muir Jr, Priscilla Roberts, Stanley Sandler, Don Thomas, H. P. Willmott, and David Zabecki. I am also appreciative of the fine work of my copyeditor, Penny Simmons.

I am particularly indebted to Malcolm 'Kip' Muir Jr. We have been good friends since 1982, when we both attended a military history workshop at the US Military Academy, West Point. 'Kip' graciously allowed me to sit in on his course on World War II when he was a visiting professor at VMI in 2002. It was a pleasure to observe a master teacher at work, and some of his fine lecture material has found its way into this book.

I am grateful both to my cadet research assistants Lawton Way and Shelley Cox, who helped track down many small facts and citations, and to my mapmaker Donald S. Frazier for the seven maps in this volume. I also acknowledge the patience and forbearance of my wife Beverly over the long hours I have spent in research and writing this book. Beverly also read the manuscript and made many useful stylistic suggestions.

Spencer C. Tucker

Maps

Map 1   *Europe, September 1938*

Map 2   *The German invasion of France and the Low Countries, May 10 to June 25, 1940*

Map 3   *The German invasion of the Soviet Union (Operation BARBAROSSA)*

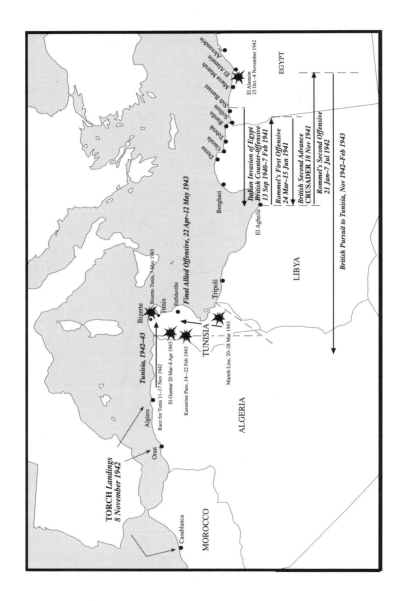

Map 4   *The war in North Africa*

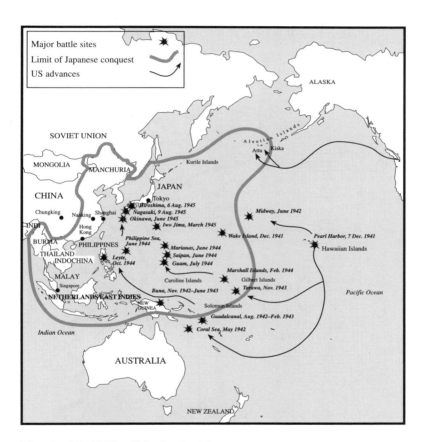

Map 5   *World War II in the Pacific*

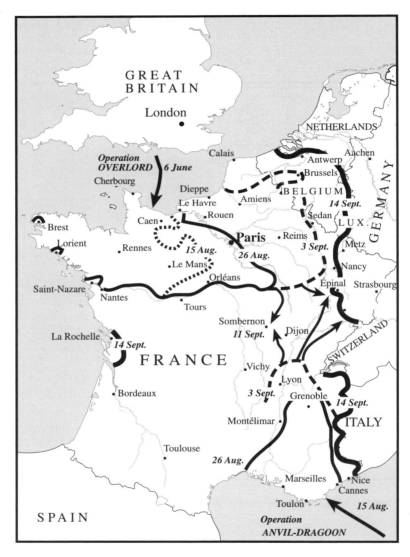

Map 6   *France, 1944*

Map 7   *Europe, 1945*

1

The Road to War, 1931–1939

On September 1, 1939, German forces invaded Poland. Two days later, Britain and France declared war on Germany. Thus began World War II, the most wide-ranging and costly conflict in human history, ultimately involving virtually every major power and region.

Some historians actually date the war in 1937, with the Japanese invasion of China. Japanese official histories begin with 1931, when Japan's military overran Manchuria. Perhaps an even more accurate place to begin, however, is with World War I. The First World War exacted a horrible human cost, destroyed the existing power structure of Europe and toppled all the Continental empires, wiped out much of the accumulated capital of Europe, and stimulated unrest in the colonial areas of the world. No statement concerning its effects seems too extreme. It was simply the most important single event of the twentieth century.

In January 1919 representatives of the victorious Allied or Entente powers met in Paris to impose peace terms on the defeated Central powers. These treaties, all named for Paris suburbs, collectively make up the Paris peace settlement: Versailles with Germany, St Germain with Austria, Trianon with Hungary, Neuilly with Bulgaria, and Sèvres (later superseded by the Treaty of Lausanne, Switzerland) with Turkey.

The centerpiece of the settlement, the Versailles Treaty, is often depicted as a piece of French villainy that was too harsh on Germany and sowed the seeds of revenge that led to World War II. This pattern was not without precedence. It is worth noting another (preliminary) peace of Versailles, that of 1871 when, following the Franco–Prussian War (1870–71), German Chancellor Otto von Bismarck imposed a truly harsh settlement on France. Unlike the 1919 settlement, Bismarck saw to it that the 1871 settlement was enforced. France had to cede all of Alsace and most of Lorraine and pay an indemnity of 5 billion francs,

2.5 times the cost of the war to Germany, and Prussian troops occupied northeastern France until the indemnity was paid. The 1919 Treaty of Versailles was the worst of all possible worlds – too harsh to conciliate but too weak to destroy. It was also not enforced and this, rather than its severity or lack thereof, made possible a renewal of the struggle.

The Paris peace settlement was drafted chiefly by Britain, France, and the United States. German leaders claimed they had assumed the November 1918 armistice would lead to a true negotiated settlement. Yet in March and May 1918, when they were winning the war, the Germans had imposed settlements on Russia and Romania, treaties that set new standards for the punitive treatment of a vanquished foe. In the Treaty of Brest-Litovsk Russia lost most of its European territory, up to a third of its population, and three-quarters of its iron and coal production. It was also required to pay a heavy indemnity. In the Treaty of Bucharest, Romania had to cede considerable territory as well as grant Germany a 90-year lease on its oil fields.[1]

Far from being dictated by French Premier George Clemenceau as many Americans came to believe, the Paris peace settlement of 1919 was largely the work of British Prime Minister David Lloyd George and US President Woodrow Wilson. They repeatedly blocked proposals advanced by Clemenceau. The irony here is that the British and American leaders prevented a settlement that, although punitive, might indeed have brought actual French and Belgian security and prevented war in 1939.

The most novel creation of the conference was undoubtedly the League of Nations; Wilson insisted that the conferees discuss it first. Clemenceau did not place much stock in a league but he did support the French plan that called for mandatory membership and an independent military force. The Anglo-American plan that was adopted relied primarily on moral suasion; its strongest weapon was the threat of sanctions. Clemenceau saw such an organization as itself a threat to French security as many people would believe that the League of Nations would resolve international problems.[2]

The most contentious issue at the peace conference, and arguably its most important, was that of French and Belgian security. Some matters were easily resolved. Alsace and Lorraine were returned to France, and Belgium received the border enclaves of Eupen and Malmédy. France was granted the coal production of the Saar for 15 years in compensation for Germany's deliberate destruction of French mines at the end of the war. The Saar itself was placed under League of Nations' control with its inhabitants to decide their future at the end of the period.

A storm of controversy broke out over the issue of the Rhineland, the German territory west of the Rhine River. France wanted the Rhineland taken from Germany and made into one or more independent states that would maintain a permanent Allied military presence to guarantee that Germany would not again strike westward. Lloyd George and Wilson worked to prevent Clemenceau from securing this. Believing that wars end with the shooting and already seeking to disengage their nations from Continental commitments, Lloyd George and Wilson saw taking the Rhineland from Germany as 'an Alsace-Lorraine in reverse.' They also wanted to end the Allied military presence on German soil as soon as a peace treaty was signed.

These considerable differences were resolved when Clemenceau agreed to yield on the Rhineland in return for an Anglo-American Treaty of Guarantee, whereby Britain and the United States promised to come to the aid of France should Germany again strike west. The Rhineland would remain part of the new German Republic but was to be permanently demilitarized, along with a belt of German territory east of the Rhine 50 kilometers (30 miles) deep. Allied garrisons would remain for only a limited period: the British would occupy a northern zone for five years, the Americans a central zone for ten, and the French a southern zone for 15 years. Unfortunately for France, the pact for which it traded away national security never came into force. The US Senate refused to ratify the Treaty of Guarantee, and the British government claimed its acceptance was contingent on American approval. Many Frenchmen now believed the peace had been lost.

Germany forfeited some other territory in addition to that yielded to Belgium and France. It lost northern Schleswig to Denmark and a portion of Silesia and the Polish Corridor to the new state of Poland. The latter two cessions were justified along lines of ethnicity. A corridor of former German territory allowed Poland access to the sea, but it also separated East Prussia from the remainder of Germany. The corridor became a major rallying point for German nationalists. The Western Allies rejected doing away with it and relocating the German population from East Prussia, a policy followed (although not with official sanction) at the end of World War II. Germans keenly felt their territorial losses, even though these did not materially alter German power. Before it began its march of territorial conquest in 1938, Germany was still the most powerful state in central and western Europe.

The Treaty of Versailles sharply limited Germany in both the size and nature of its military establishment. The new German army, the *Reichswehr*, was restricted to 100,000 men serving 12-year enlistments.

It was denied heavy artillery, tanks, and military aviation, and its General Staff was to be abolished. The navy was limited to six pre-dreadnought battleships, six light cruisers, 12 destroyers, and no submarines. Right from the beginning the Germans violated these provisions. The General Staff remained, although under another name and clandestinely. The *Reichswehr* became an elite, cadre force capable of rapid expansion, while Germany maintained equipment that was to have been destroyed and worked out arrangements with other states to develop new weapons and train military personnel.

Other major provisions of the settlement included Article 231, the so-called 'war guilt clause.' It fixed blame for the war on Germany and its allies and was the justification for reparations, which were fixed at $33 billion in 1920, well after Germany had signed the treaty on June 28, 1919. British economist John Maynard Keynes claimed reparations were a perpetual mortgage on Germany's future and that there was no way the Germans could pay them. His conclusions were challenged later by Frenchman Étienne Mantoux, who pointed out that Germany had the resources to pay the sums demanded and ultimately spent more money in rearming than the amount of the reparations. In any case Germany, unlike France in 1871, made no real effort to pay.[3]

It was the new German democratic government of the Weimar Republic and not the Kaiser or the army, which had been responsible for the decisions that led to the defeat, that bore the shame of Versailles. Many Germans believed the lie spun by the political right (and the army) that their nation had lost the war only because of the collapse of the home front.

Collectively, the breakup of the Austro-Hungarian Empire and the peace treaties following the war created a number of new states in Central Europe, most notably Poland, but also Czechoslovakia and Yugoslavia. Setting the boundaries of the new Polish state proved difficult, especially in the east; it was not until December 1919 that a commission headed by Lord Curzon drew that line. Neither the new Polish government nor the Russians recognized it, however. Romania was greatly enlarged, with the chief addition being Transylvania, which was taken from Hungary. The principal loser at the peace conference, Hungary, was left with only 35 percent of its prewar area. The reduced states of Austria and Hungary were now confronted by Yugoslavia, Czechoslovakia, and Romania. The latter three, the so-called 'Little Entente,' allied to prevent a resurgence of their former masters. They came to be linked with France through a treaty of mutual assistance between that nation and Czechoslovakia.

Many, particularly the French, were unhappy with the peace settlement. French Marshal Ferdinand Foch, who had led the Allied armies to victory, declared that the peace had been 'lost.' He predicted that Germany would strike again in a generation.[4]

The Allied solidarity of 1918 soon disappeared. When the peace treaties were signed, the United States was already withdrawing into isolation and Britain was disengaging from the Continent. This left France alone among the Great Powers to enforce the peace settlement. Yet France was weaker in terms of population and economic strength than Germany, even given the latter's 1919 losses. In effect it was left up to the Germans themselves to decide whether they would abide by the treaty provisions, and this was a blueprint for disaster.

The German government deliberately adopted obstructionist policies, and by 1923 it had halted major reparations payments. French Premier Raymond Poincaré decided to act. Poincaré believed that if the Germans were allowed to break part of the settlement, the remainder would soon unravel. In January 1923 French troops supported by Belgian and Italian units entered the Ruhr, the industrial heart of Germany. Chancellor Wilhelm Cuno's government adopted a policy of 'passive resistance,' urging the workers not to work and promising to pay their salaries. The German leaders thereby hoped to secure sufficient time for the United States and Britain to force France to depart. Although pressure was forthcoming, Poincaré refused to back down, and the result was catastrophic inflation in Germany.

The mark had already gone from 4.2 to the dollar in July 1914 to 8.9 in January 1919, largely in consequence of Berlin avoiding the policy of heavier taxes favored by the Western Allies during the war. It then tumbled precipitously because of deliberate government policies. By January 1920 the mark was 39.5 to the dollar; in January 1921, 76.7; in January 1922, 191.8. Then came the French occupation and the ruinous policy of paying workers' salaries for their patriotic idleness. In January 1923 it was 17,972, but by July it was 353,412; in August it hit 4,620,455; and in November, when the old mark was withdrawn in favor of a new currency, the mark was 4.2 trillion to the dollar. This economic chaos wiped out the German middle class, many of whom lost faith in democracy. It would be an important factor in bringing Adolf Hitler to power a decade later.[5]

Seemingly, Poincaré had won, as Germany agreed to pay reparations under a scaled-down schedule. French troops withdrew from the Ruhr in 1924. Although Frenchmen generally approved of Poincaré's action, they also noted its high financial cost and the opposition of Britain and the United States. These factors helped bring the left to power in France in 1924, and it reversed Poincaré's go-it-alone approach. The new German government of Chancellor Gustav Stresemann also announced a policy of living up to its treaty obligations. 'Fulfillment' and 'conciliation' replaced 'obstruction' and brought the Locarno Pacts of 1925, by which Germany voluntarily guaranteed its western borders as final and promised not to resort to war with its neighbors and to resolve any disputes through arbitration. Poincaré's action was the last independent French military action between the wars, but for a half-decade calm prevailed internationally.

By the 1930s the national boundaries were still basically those agreed to in 1919. Italy, Germany, and Japan were not satisfied with this situation, however. These 'revisionist' powers risked war to bring about change. The 'status quo' powers of France, Great Britain, and the United States saw no benefit in changing conditions, but they were also unwilling to risk war to defend the 1919 settlement. They stood by as, bit by bit, the dissatisfied powers dismantled the peace settlement. From the Japanese invasion of Manchuria in 1931 to the beginning of war in Europe in 1939, military might was employed by those powers desiring to upset the status quo but not by those who sought to maintain it. Western leadership and resolve seemed paralyzed. This was partly in consequence of the heavy human cost of World War I. France alone had lost 1,397,800 dead or missing in the conflict. Including wounded, 73 percent of French combatants had been casualties.[6]

France could not sustain another such bloodletting. Its military doctrine came to be summed up in the phrase, 'Stingy with blood; extravagant with steel.' If war came, France expected to fight on the defensive, relying on artillery and a defensive belt stretching along the frontier from Switzerland to Belgium. Begun in 1929 and named for Minister of War André Maginot, this line was never intended as a puncture-proof barricade. But while it actually met the test in World War II and diverted the Germans to the north, the line also helped limit the French military to a defensive mind set.[7]

By the 1930s attitudes toward the Great War had changed. In Germany many people thought their nation had not lost the war militarily, but had been betrayed by communists, leftists, pacifists, and Jews – the 'November Criminals' as Hitler called them. Many people, especially in Britain and the United States, came to believe that the Central powers had not been responsible for the war, that the conflict had been a mistake with little or nothing gained, and even that the settlement had been too hard on Germany.

In Britain the costs of World War I had also been heavy. British Empire military casualties totaled 908,371 killed and 2,090,212 wounded (34 percent of forces mobilized). There was also sympathy in influential upper-class circles for fascist doctrines and dictators who were seen as opponents of Communism. Winston Churchill went out of his way to praise Italian dictator Benito Mussolini. The British government avoided Continental commitments and its leaders came to embrace 'appeasement,' the notion that meeting the more legitimate demands of the dictators would obviate the need for war. Prime Minister Neville Chamberlain (1937–40) was the principal architect of this appeasement policy. There was also great concern in Britain, as elsewhere, over the possible air bombardment of cities in any future war. The previous British prime minister, Stanley Baldwin, gloomily predicted, 'the bomber will always get through. The only defence is offence, which means you have to kill more women and children more quickly than the enemy if you want to save yourselves.'[8]

The United States had been one of the few powers actually to benefit from the war. At modest cost in terms of human casualties (its military battle deaths were 50,585, only 3 percent of the force), it emerged from the struggle as the world's leading financial power. Yet Americans were dissatisfied with their involvement in European affairs; they believed they had been misled by wartime propaganda and that the arms manufacturers, the so-called 'merchants of death,' had drawn the nation into the war to secure their sales to the Allied powers. In the 1920s and 1930s the United States followed a rigid neutrality, and Congress passed legislation preventing the United States from loaning money or selling arms to combatants in a war. Unfortunately, such well-intentioned legislation benefitted the aggressor states, which were already well-armed, and handicapped their victims. In his first administration President Franklin D. Roosevelt (1933–45) understood the threat that aggression posed to the world community, but most Americans eschewed involvement in world affairs.

The Soviet Union was also largely absorbed in its internal affairs. Following World War I Russia underwent a frightful civil war as the communist 'Reds,' who had seized control in November 1917, battled to stay in power against the opposition 'Whites' supported by the Western Allies. By the end of 1920 the Reds had pushed the Whites off Russian soil. Efforts by the government to introduce communist economic practices only heightened the chaos and famine. Vladimir Ilyich Lenin reversed course in his New Economic Policy of 1921, noting that it was 'easier to change the policy than the peasants,' and gradually the economy began improving. By 1929 Josef Stalin, who took power after Lenin's death in 1924, was firmly in control. Stalin pushed the collectivization of agriculture that brought the deaths of millions, but he also pursued the industrialization essential for modern warfare.

In his foreign policy Stalin was a revisionist in that he did not accept the new frontiers in Eastern Europe as final. Particularly vexing to him was the creation of Poland, which had been partially carved from former Russian territory. Russia subsequently lost additional lands to Poland with the 1921 Treaty of Riga following defeat in the 1920 Russo–Polish War. After 1933 and Adolf Hitler's accession to power, Stalin grew especially concerned about Germany, for the German *Führer* (leader) had clearly stated his opposition to Communism and his intention of bringing large stretches of eastern Europe under German control. Hitler had written in *Mein Kampf*:

> If land was desired in Europe, it could be obtained by and large only at the expense of Russia, and this meant that the new Reich must again set itself on the march along the road of the Teutonic Knights of old, to obtain by the German sword sod for the German plow and daily bread for the nation.[9]

Stalin became interested in collective security, and People's Commissar for Foreign Affairs Maksim Litvinov (1930–39) pursued an internationalist course. In 1934 the USSR joined the League of Nations. While working to strengthen the Soviet Union's ties to the rest of the world, however, Stalin was carrying out unprecedented actions against his own people.

The total number of people 'repressed' during the Stalin era came to around 40 million, with half of these killed. The so-called 'Great Terror' consumed virtually all the old guard Bolshevik leadership and, importantly for World War II, most of the senior army officers. The executed included 3 of 5 marshals; 13 of 15 army commanders; 8 of 9 fleet admirals and admirals grade I; 50 of 57 corps commanders; and 154 of 186 divisional commanders. Undoubtedly, the purges claimed the most aggressive, outspoken officers. Certainly, no military establishment could experience such losses and be effective, and the consequences were most keenly felt in 1941 when the Germans invaded the Soviet Union. Among those perishing was army commander Marshal Mikhail Tukhachevsky, who had foreseen the German operational concept for an invasion of the Soviet Union and developed a counter to it. The Great Terror seems to have been motivated by Stalin's own paranoia and determination to hold on to power. Paradoxically, throughout his long years in power Stalin feared his own people far more than he did threats from abroad.[10]

By the late 1930s many Western leaders distrusted the Soviet Union to the point that they hoped German strength could be directed east against it, and Nazism and Communism would destroy one another. Thus, despite the fact that the Kremlin was willing to enter into arrangements with the West against Germany and Japan, no effective coalition was forged and the events of the decade took course largely ignoring the Soviet Union.

The chain of events that culminated in the September 1939 German invasion of Poland began in Asia in 1931, when Japan seized Manchuria. Japan had been one of the chief winners in World War I, for at little cost it had secured the German colonial possessions in Asia – the islands north of the equator, and cessions in China. Riding the crest of an ultra-nationalist wave, Japanese leaders sought to take advantage of European and US weakness occasioned by the world economic depression and the continuing upheaval in China to rectify what they regarded as an accident of geography, a profound disadvantage in terms of natural resources. The Japanese sought access to resources not only in Manchuria, but also in Mongolia, China, and south Asia.

Although Japan had many of the trappings of a democracy, it was not one. Emperor Hirohito, nominal head of state (1926–1989) and commander of the armed forces, was no mere figurehead. Well-briefed on the expansionary moves of his military and generally embracing its views, he proved unwilling to stand up for his convictions or to take any action that might have altered the course of events. What mattered to Hirohito was preserving the imperial system with himself as its head. After World War II the US government, which enlisted Hirohito to help govern Japan during the occupation, deliberately played down his role leading to and during the war.[11]

In Japan the army and navy departments were independent of the civilian authorities and had the right to approach the emperor directly. Dating from 1936 the ministers of war and navy had to be serving officers and this gave the military a veto over public policy, as no government could be formed without its concurrence. Army leaders had little sympathy for parliamentary rule and for civil government, and in the 1930s they dominated the government and occasionally resorted to political assassinations, even of prime ministers.

On the night of September 18, 1931, Japanese staff officers of the elite Kwantung Army in southern Manchuria set off an explosion near

the main line of the South Manchuria Railway near Mukden and blamed
the act on nearby Chinese soldiers. The Japanese military then took
control of Mukden and began the conquest of all Manchuria. Tokyo had
been presented with a *fait accompli* by its own military, but it supported
the action.

The Japanese held that they had acted only in self-defense and
demanded that the crisis be resolved through direct Sino-Japanese nego-
tiation. China, however, appealed the matter to the League of Nations,
the first major test for that organization. The League Council, though,
was reluctant to embark on tough action against Japan without the assurance of collaboration by the United States, which was not forthcoming.
The British also opposed drastic action. Without British and American
agreement, the League could do little. Consequently, the Council merely
called on China and Japan to withdraw their troops from the area of
conflict. Japan ignored this, continuing its military operations.

In late October the League again called on Japan to evacuate the territory it had occupied, but Tokyo refused. In January 1932 the United
States responded with the so-called 'Stimson Doctrine.' Named for
Secretary of State Henry L. Stimson, it called for non-recognition of any
arrangement violating the Pact of Paris (Kellogg-Briand Pact) of 1928
that had outlawed aggressive war. In February 1932 Japan proclaimed
the 'independence' of Manchuria in the guise of the new state of
Manchukuo, headed by former Chinese Emperor Henry Pu-Yi, previously deposed in 1912. A protocol that September established a Japanese
protectorate over Manchukuo.

A Special Assembly of the League led to the establishment of the
Lytton Commission, named for its chairman, Edward Robert Bulwer, First
Earl Lytton. The commission spent several months visiting Japan, China,
and Manchukuo but concluded that no plan would be acceptable to both
China and Japan. Its final report of October 1932, however, largely exon-
erated China and condemned the Japanese invasion as not justified by
'self-defense.' It concluded that only the presence of Japanese troops
made Manchukuo possible and recommended establishment there of an
autonomous government under Chinese sovereignty that would recognize
Japan's special economic interests. The commission then urged that all
League members continue non-recognition of Manchukuo.

On February 24, 1933, the League Assembly approved the report and
the Stimson doctrine of non-recognition. Of 42 member states, only
Japan voted 'No.' Never before had such a universal vote of censure
been passed against a sovereign state. The Japanese delegation then
walked out, a step heartily endorsed by the Japanese press. On March

27, Tokyo gave notice of its intention to withdraw from the League (according to the League Covenant two years' notice was required).[12]

Manchukuo was larger than France and Germany combined, but in March Japanese troops added to it the province of Jehol. Early in April they moved against Chinese forces south of the Great Wall to within a few miles of Beijing (Peking) and Tianjiu (Tientsin). In May Chinese forces evacuated Beijing, then under the authority of pro-Japanese Chinese leaders. The latter concluded the T'ang-ku truce with Japan, which required Chinese troops to be withdrawn south and west of a line running roughly from Tianjin to Beijing. Japanese troops withdrew north of the Great Wall, creating a demilitarized zone administered by Chinese friendly to Japan. The Chinese government concluded that, for the present, Manchuria was lost.

Had the great powers been able to agree on a policy and acted militarily, Japan would have been forced to withdraw from its conquests. Such a war would have been far cheaper than fighting a world war later, but the global economic depression and general Western indifference to the plight of Asians precluded such sacrifice. A worldwide financial and commercial boycott in accordance with Article 16 of the Covenant might also have compelled Japanese withdrawal, but this too was beyond Western resolve. It is now clear that the failure to enforce collective security was a fateful blunder. Other states with similar aspirations took notice.

Germany was next to take advantage. Adolf Hitler, who came to power in January 1933 by legal means, now precipitated a series of crises, playing on Western fears and taking advantage of the narrow nationalist approach of most Western leaders. Repeated Western surrenders to Hitler's demands only whetted his appetite for expansion.

In October 1933 Hitler withdrew Germany from both the League of Nations and the ongoing international disarmament conference meeting in Geneva. These steps marked a reversal of Stresemann's earlier policies. In response, in June 1934 the Soviet Union, Poland, and Romania mutually guaranteed their existing frontiers. That September the Soviet Union further identified itself with the status quo by joining the League of Nations.

In November 1933 France became alarmed when Poland accepted Hitler's offer of a non-aggression pact. Poland had already signed such a pact with Moscow in 1932. Poland clearly was hedging its bets, and new French Foreign Minister Louis Barthou undertook a series of visits to France's eastern allies to bolster ties. He also sought military pacts with Italy and the Soviet Union. The problem lay in bringing London

along. Although Britain had promised at Locarno in 1925 that it would
defend France and Belgium in the event of German attack, it had refused
to make any such pledge regarding Central and Eastern Europe.

While these events were in progress, on July 25, 1934, Austrian
Nazis, acting with the tacit support of Berlin, attempted to seize power
in Vienna in order to achieve *Anschluss*, or union with Germany. Other
cabinet members escaped, but Chancellor Engelbert Dollfuss's decision
to remain at his post cost him his life. Ultimately, Austrian authorities
put down the *putschists* without outside assistance, although on learning
of events Italian dictator Benito Mussolini, who considered Austria
under his influence, ordered troops to the Brenner Pass.

Hitler had initially expressed pleasure at the *putsch*, but when news
arrived of its failure he washed his hands of it. There was in fact little he
could have done as Germany, still largely unarmed, was in no position
to oppose Italy. Hitler expressed regret at the Dollfuss murder, recalled
his ambassador who had promised the *putschists* asylum, and assured
the world that Germany had no role in the failed coup.[13]

The attempted Nazi takeover of Austria was clearly a setback for
Hitler. Secure in French support, that September Mussolini met with
new Austrian Chancellor Kurt von Schuschnigg in Rome and announced
that Italy would defend Austrian independence. A French pact with Italy
rested on agreement with Yugoslavia, and on October 9, 1934, King
Alexander of Yugoslavia arrived at Marseilles for discussions with the
French government. He was met on the dockside by Barthou, but there
the two men were assassinated by Croatian terrorists. The plot was led
by Ante Pavelich, who in 1941 became premier of the Nazi puppet
'Kingdom of Croatia.'

This event was a great embarrassment for France, although Barthou's
successor, Pierre Laval, did secure the pact with Italy. The January 1935
French-Italian accords called for joint consultation and close cooperation between the two powers in Central Europe and reaffirmed the independence and territorial integrity of Austria. They also recommended a
multilateral security pact for Eastern Europe. In secret provisions Italy
promised to support France with its air force in the event of a German
move in the Rhineland, and France agreed to provide troops to aid Italy
if the Germans should threaten Austria. France also transferred land to
the Italian colonies of Libya and Eritrea, and Laval promised Mussolini
that France would not oppose Italy realizing its colonial ambitions.
Laval may have given Mussolini a more unambiguous approval, but, in
any case, *Il Duce* (the leader) thereafter behaved as if he had France's
approval to wage aggressive war.[14]

Laval decided not to put up a fight for the Saar, and only a week after the Rome Accords, with Hitler declaring the Saar to be his last territorial demand in Europe (the first of many such statements), Saarlanders went to the polls. On January 13, 1935, they voted nine to one to rejoin Germany and, on March 1, the League Council formally returned the Saar to German control.

Only two weeks later, on March 16, Hitler proclaimed the rearmament of Germany. Secret rearmament had been underway for some time, including an air training center at Lipetsk, gas warfare school at Torski, and a tank school at Kazan, all in the Soviet Union; but Hitler now announced publicly that the Reich would reintroduce compulsory military service and increase the army to more than 500,000 men. He justified this by the fact that the Allies had not disarmed.[15]

Paris, London, and Rome protested but did nothing to compel Berlin to observe its treaty obligations. In April 1935 Laval, Prime Minister Ramsay MacDonald of Britain, and Mussolini met at Stresa on Lake Maggiori and formed the so-called 'Stresa Front,' agreeing 'to oppose unilateral repudiation of treaties that may endanger the peace' ('of Europe' being added at Mussolini's request). On May 2 France and the Soviet Union signed a five-year pact of mutual assistance in the event of unprovoked aggression against either power. The French, however, refused to agree to a military convention that would have coordinated their military response to any German aggression.[16] On May 16 the Soviet Union and Czechoslovakia signed a similar mutual assistance pact, but the USSR was not obligated to provide armed assistance unless France first fulfilled its commitments.

Britain took the first step in the appeasement of Germany, in the process shattering the Stresa Front. On June 18, 1935, London signed a naval agreement with Germany that condoned its violation of the Versailles Treaty. In spite of having promised Paris in February that it would take no unilateral action toward Germany, London concluded an arrangement that permitted the Reich to build a surface navy up to 35 percent that of Britain, in effect a force larger than the navies of either France or Italy. It also allowed Germany 45 percent of the Royal Navy in submarines, specifically prohibited Germany by the Treaty of Versailles. British leaders were not worried. The Royal Navy had only 50 submarines and that would mean the Germans could build only 23. Also, the British were confident that asdic, later known as sonar, would enable them to detect submarines out to a range of several thousand yards, and that they would thus be able to sink German submarines at whim. The Anglo-German Naval Agreement was, of course, another postdated German check. It was also the first occasion when any power sanctioned Germany's misdeeds and it cost Britain the displeasure of its ally France.

On October 3, 1935, believing with some justification that he had Western support, Mussolini invaded Ethiopia (Abyssinia). Long-standing border disputes between Italian Somaliland and Ethiopia provided the excuse. The Italians had built up their military strength in the Horn of Africa, and the invasion was no surprise. Mussolini's goal was to create a great Italian empire in Africa and to avenge Italy's defeat by the Ethiopians at Adowa in 1896. The outcome of the Italo–Ethiopian War was a foregone conclusion. Ethiopia was completely outclassed militarily, especially in the air, where the *Regia Aeronautica* enjoyed a virtual monopoly. The latter conducted a variety of missions, including aerial resupply. The Italians also intercepted Ethiopian radio communications, and the *Regia Aeronautica* employed poison (mustard) gas. In May 1936 Italian forces took Addis Ababa and Mussolini proclaimed the king of Italy as the emperor of Ethiopia.

On October 7, 1935, the League of Nations had condemned Italy, the first time it had branded a European state an aggressor. But British Foreign Secretary Sir Samuel Hoare and French Foreign Minister Pierre Laval worked behind the scenes in the infamous Hoare-Laval Proposals to broker away Ethiopia to Italy in return for Italian support against Germany. A public furor erupted in both their countries when this became known, and both men were forced to resign. Ultimately the League voted to impose sanctions, but not on oil, which would have brought an Italian withdrawal. The argument against this sanction was that Italy could always turn to the United States, which was not bound by League decisions. In the end, even those ineffectual sanctions that had been voted were lifted. Italy, like Japan, had gambled and won, and another blow had been dealt to collective security.

Probably the seminal event on the road to World War II occurred in early 1936, when Hitler remilitarized the Rhineland. On March 7, 1936, 22,000 German troops, armed with little more than rifles and machine guns, marched into the Rhineland, in defiance of the Treaty of Versailles but also of the Locarno Pacts, which Germany had voluntarily negotiated. Hitler timed the operation to occur while France was in the midst of a bitterly contested election campaign that brought the leftist 'Popular Front' to power.

Incredibly, France had no contingency plans for such an eventuality. Army Chief of Staff General Maurice Gamelin told the Cabinet that the choices were to do nothing or total mobilization. The French intelligence services grossly overestimated the size of the German forces in the operation and believed Hitler's claims that the *Luftwaffe* had achieved parity with the French *Armée de l'Air*. In reality the two groups of obsolete biplane Arado Ar 65, Ar 68, and Heinkel He 51 fighter aircraft that Germany put aloft lacked guns and/or synchronization gear to enable them to fire through their propellers. Had French aircraft appeared, their only recourse would have been to ram! The only *Luftwaffe* aircraft capable of reaching London, the Junkers Ju 52, could not have flown there carrying bombs and returned. But then this was not a real issue, as the *Luftwaffe* had few bombs available, perhaps at most several hundred. In a vain cover for its own inaction, Paris appealed to Britain for support, but Foreign Secretary Anthony Eden made it clear that Britain would not fight for the Rhineland, which was after all German territory. Speaking for the Cabinet, Eden announced in the House of Commons that, while Germany's action was 'inexcusable' as a breech of a freely signed international treaty, it in no way implied a hostile threat to France.[17]

Had the French acted, their forces would have rolled over the Germans and it probably would have been the end of the Nazi regime. Hitler himself recalled, 'We had no army worth mentioning . . . If the French had taken any action, we would have been defeated; our resistance would have been over in a few days. And what air force we had then was ridiculous. A few Junker 52s from Lufthansa, and not even enough bombs for them.'[18]

Acquisition of the Rhineland was immensely important for Germany. It provided a buffer for the Ruhr and a venue for invading France and Belgium. The action also had another important effect, for on October 14 Belgian leaders denounced their treaty of mutual assistance with France and again sought security in neutrality. Germany promptly guaranteed the inviolability and integrity of Belgium so long as it abstained from military action against Germany.

Almost immediately after the German remilitarization of the Rhineland another international crisis erupted, this time in Spain, where civil war began on July 18, 1936. The issue centered on whether Spain would follow the modernizing reforms of the rest of Western Europe or maintain its traditional structure. The Republic, installed only in 1931, stood for public education, land reform, and separation of Church and State. Spanish traditionalists, including the great landowners and the Catholic Church, opposed such reform. When the Republicans won a narrow victory in the elections of 1936, the traditionalists, known as the Nationalists, took to arms.

The Republicans had the navy, air force, and a minority of the army. The Nationalists controlled the bulk of the army, including its elite units. Although this is by no means certain, the Republicans would probably have won the civil war had Spain been left alone to decide its fate. Certainly, the conflict would have ended much sooner. But Spain was not left alone. Germany and Italy intervened early. Both powers provided critical air support that allowed the airlifting of 13,000 Nationalist troops and half a million pounds of equipment across the Straits of Gibraltar from Morocco to Nationalist-held territory in Spain, in effect the first large-scale military airlift.

Germany even formed an air detachment, the *Kondor Legion* of 6000 men with 100 aircraft, to fight in Spain. In all 19,000 men and 350 aircraft served in the *Kondor Legion* in the course of the war. It proved a key factor in the ultimate Nationalist victory. The Germans also tested their latest military equipment under combat conditions, developed new fighter tactics ('the finger four' formation), and learned the necessity of close coordination of air and ground operations, along with the utility of dive-bombing. Italy also provided important naval support and sent three divisions of troops, 2000 artillery pieces, and 750 aircraft. Ultimately, more than 100,000 Italians fought in Spain.[19]

Surprisingly, the Western democracies cut the Spanish Republic adrift. France initially sent some arms but, under heavy British pressure, reversed its stance. British leaders came up with a non-interventionist policy. Although all the Great Powers promised to abide by it, only the Western democracies did so. This agreement, which made it impossible for the Republicans to obtain the arms they needed to counter fascist forces deploying the latest weapons and tactics, was probably the chief factor in their defeat.

Among major powers only the Soviet Union and Mexico assisted the Republic. Stalin apparently hoped for a protracted struggle entangling the Western democracies and Germany at the other end of the Continent. In any case, he demanded that the Republic pay for its aid in gold. During the course of the war the Soviet Union sent some 3000 personnel, 800 aircraft, and tanks and artillery. This included first-line Soviet aircraft, such as the Polikarpov I 16 fighter and Tupolev SB 2 twin-engined bomber. Eventually this Soviet aid permitted the Spanish communists, not a significant political factor in 1936, to take over the Republican government. Finally, in March 1939, Nationalist forces, led by General Francisco Franco, entered Madrid and by April hostilities ended. Some 600,000 Spaniards died in the fighting; the Nationalists executed another 200,000 people after the war and it is likely that a similar number died of starvation and disease.[20]

The Western democracies emerged very poorly from the test provided by the Spanish Civil War. Although tens of thousands of foreign volunteers had fought in Spain, most of these for the Republic, the governments of the Western democracies had done little, and many doubted whether there was will left in the West to defend democracy. Internationally, the major effect of the fighting in Spain was to bring together Germany and Italy. On October 25, 1936, they agreed to cooperate in Spain, to collaborate in matters of 'parallel interests,' and to work to defend 'European civilization' against Communism. Thus was born the Rome–Berlin Axis. On November 25 Germany and Japan signed the Anti-Comintern pact to oppose activities of the Comintern (Third International), created to spread Communism. Germany and Japan also signed a secret agreement the same day that provided that if either state was the object of an unprovoked attack by the Soviet Union then the other would do nothing to assist the USSR. On November 6, 1937, Italy joined the Anti-Comintern Pact.

Shortly afterward, Mussolini announced that Italy would not assist Austria against a German attempt to consummate *Anschluss*. Italy also withdrew from the League of Nations, and it recognized Manchukuo as an independent state in November 1937. Germany followed suit in May 1938. By 1938 the Great Powers were dividing into two antagonistic groups. Given their close cooperation during peace, it is ironic that the Axis powers utterly failed to do so in war.

Japan, meanwhile, continued to strengthen its position in the Far East, asserting its exclusive right to control China. Tokyo declared that the Western presence in China threatened the peace of Asia. It demanded an end to Western loans and military advisors to China and threatened the use of force if such aid continued. In 1935 Japan began encroaching upon several of China's northern provinces. The Chinese government at Nanjing, headed by Generalissimo Jiang Jieshi (Chiang Kai-shek), initially pursued a policy of appeasement *vis-à-vis* the Japanese, but students and the Chinese military demanded action. The Chinese communists expressed a willingness to cooperate with the Nationalist government and place their armies under its command if Nanjing would adopt an anti-Japanese policy. The rapid growth of anti-Japanese sentiments in China and the increasing military strength of the Nationalists were disturbing to Japanese military leaders, who sought to establish a pro-Japanese regime in China's five northern provinces.

On the night of July 7, 1937, a clash occurred west of Beijing between Japanese and Chinese troops. Later that month, after Nanjing rejected a Japanese ultimatum, the Japanese invaded the coveted northern provinces. In a few days they had occupied both Tianjin and Beijing, and by the end of the year Japan had extended its control into all five Chinese provinces north of the Yellow River. In mid-December Japan also installed a new government in Beijing. Japan never declared war against China, however, which enabled it to avoid US neutrality legislation and to purchase raw materials and oil. But it also allowed Washington to send aid to China.

The fighting was not confined to North China, for in August 1937 the Japanese attacked the great commercial city of Shanghai. Not until November, after three months of hard fighting involving the best Nationalist troops, did the city fall. Japanese forces then advanced up the Yangtse and in December they took Nanjing, where they committed wide-scale atrocities.[21]

As scholars have since noted, Japan developed a collective amnesia over its actions at Nanjing and its atrocities in the war through South Asia in general. The Chinese say that Japan has a long history and short memory. This Japanese avoidance of responsibility stands in sharp contrast to German attempts to come to terms with the Holocaust, and it has affected relations with China and the Republic of Korea to the present.[22]

During their effort to clear the Yangtse River of all Western shipping, on December 12, 1937, Japanese forces attacked a US Navy gunboat, the *Panay*. It was clearly identified as an American warship, and the details of its movements had been provided to the Japanese by the Americans. Three other American ships belonging to an oil company were also bombed and sunk, and four British vessels were shelled. Strong protests from Washington and London brought profuse apologies from Tokyo. The Japanese falsely claimed they had not been aware of the nationality of the ships, and they stated their readiness to pay compensation and give guarantees that such incidents would not be repeated. Washington and London accepted the amends, but events served to convince Tokyo that it had little to fear from Western intervention.

China again appealed to the League of Nations, which condemned Japan anew. But the West failed to act by withholding critical supplies and financial credits to Japan. Again collective security failed. By the end of 1938 Japanese troops had taken the great commercial cities of Tianjin, Beijing, Shanghai, Nanjing, Hankow, and Canton; and the

Nationalists were forced to relocate their capital to the interior city of Chungking, which Japan heavily bombed. In their desperation the Chinese demolished the dikes on the Yellow River, costing hundreds of thousands of lives and flooding much of northern China until 1944.

Japan was also confronting the Soviet Union. Fighting began in 1938 between Japanese and Soviet troops in the poorly defined tri-border area where Siberia, Manchukuo, and Korea meet, normally referred to as Changkufeng. Although no state of war was declared, significant battles were fought, especially at Changkufeng Hill in 1938 and Nomonhan/Khalkhin Gol in 1939. The former ended on August 10, 1938, with Soviet forces still holding the hill. Nomonhan/Khalkhin Gol, fought from May to September 1939, commenced with a Japanese attack. General Georgi K. Zhukov then mounted a counter-offensive of three divisions and five brigades. The fighting involved several hundred aircraft.

A cease fire in September preempted a planned Japanese counter-attack, and the dispute between Japan and the USSR was resolved by treaty in June 1940. Each side suffered about 18,000 casualties, but the battles had an importance that far outweighed these figures. The fighting undoubtedly influenced Stalin's decision to sign a non-aggression pact with Germany that August. It also gave Tokyo a new appreciation of Soviet fighting ability and helped in 1941 to influence Japanese leaders to strike not north into Siberia, but against the easier targets of the European colonial possessions of Southeast Asia.[23]

In the West, by 1938 the situation was such as to encourage Hitler to embark upon his own territorial expansion. Mussolini was now linked with Hitler, and France was again experiencing ministerial instability. In Britain 'appeasement' was at full force, so much so that in February 1938 Eden, a staunch proponent of collective security, resigned as foreign secretary.

Austria was Hitler's first step. On February 12, 1938, Austrian Chancellor Kurt von Schuschnigg traveled to Berchtesgaden at Hitler's insistence to meet with the German leader. Under heavy pressure Schuschnigg agreed to appoint Austrian Nazi Arthur Seyss-Inquart as minister of the interior and other Austrian Nazis as ministers of justice and foreign affairs. On March 9, in an attempt to maintain his nation's independence, however, Schuschnigg announced a plebiscite on the issue of *Anschluss* to be held in only four days, hoping that the short interval would not allow the Nazis to mobilize effectively.

Hitler was determined that no plebiscite be held, and on March 11 Seyss-Inquart presented Schuschnigg with an ultimatum demanding his resignation and postponement of the vote under threat of invasion by German troops, already mobilized on the border. Schuschnigg gave in, canceling the plebiscite and resigning. Seyss-Inquart then took power and invited in the German troops 'to preserve order,' although they had already crossed the frontier.

Had it been ordered to fight, the small Austrian Army might have given a good account of itself. Germany would have won, of course, but its military was hardly ready for war and a battle might have dispelled some rampant myths about the German military. Indeed, hundreds of German tanks and vehicles of the German Eighth Army broke down during the drive toward Vienna.[24]

On March 12 Hitler returned to his boyhood home of Linz, and on the next day the German government declared Austria to be part of the Reich. On March 14 perhaps a million Austrians gave Hitler an enthusiastic welcome to Vienna. France and Britain lodged formal protests with Berlin, but that was the extent of their reaction. After the war Austrian leaders denied culpability for their association with the Third Reich by claiming that their country was the first victim of Nazi aggression.[25]

The *Anschluss* greatly strengthened Germany's position in Central Europe. Germany was now in direct contact with Italy, Yugoslavia, and Hungary, and it controlled virtually all the communications of southeastern Europe. Czechoslovakia was almost isolated and its trade outlets were at German mercy. Militarily, Germany outflanked the powerful western Czech defenses. It was thus not surprising that, despite Hitler's pledges to respect the territorial integrity of Czechoslovakia, he should next seek to bring that state under his control.

In Austria Hitler had added 6 million Germans to the Reich, but another 3.5 million lived in Czechoslovakia. Germans living there had long complained about discrimination in a state that had only minority Czechs, Germans, Slovaks, Hungarians, Ukranians, and Poles. In 1938, however, Czechoslovakia had the highest standard of living east of Germany and was the only remaining democracy in Central Europe.

Strategically, Czechoslovakia was the keystone of Europe. Bismarck had stated that whoever controlled 'the Bohemian bowl' controlled Europe. Czechoslovakia had a military alliance with France, and it had a well-trained 400,000-man army and the important Skoda munitions complex at Pilsen, as well as strong fortifications in the west. Unfortunately for the Czechs, the latter were in the *Erzegeberge* (Ore Mountains) bordering the Bohemian bowl, where the population was almost entirely German. Also, from the German point of view, it could now be said that Bohemia-Moravia, almost one-third German in population, protruded into the Reich. Hitler now pushed the past demands of Konrad Henlein's *Sudetendeutsch* (Sudeten German) Party to relieve legitimate complaints into outright separation of the German regions from Czechoslovakia and their union with Germany.

In May 1938, during key Czechoslovakian elections, German troops massed on the border and threatened invasion. Confident in French support, the Czechs mobilized their army. Both France and the Soviet Union had stated their willingness to go to war to defend Czechoslovakia, and in the end nothing happened. Hitler then began construction of fortifications along the German frontier in the west. Called by the Germans the West Wall, it was clearly designed to prevent France from supporting its eastern allies.

Western leaders, who believed they had just averted war, now pondered whether Czechoslovakia, which had been formed only as a consequence of the Paris Peace Conference, was really worth a general European war. British Prime Minister Neville Chamberlain concluded that it was not. In July he offered to send Lord Runciman to Prague as a mediator, which the Czech government accepted. On September 7, based on Runciman's suggestions, Prague offered Henlein practically everything that the Sudeten Germans demanded, short of independence.

A number of knowledgeable Germans were alarmed over events. They knew Germany was not ready for war and were certain that Hitler was leading their state to destruction. During August and early September 1938 several opposition emissaries traveled to London with messages from the head of the *Abwehr* (German military intelligence) Admiral Wilhelm Canaris and Chief of the German General Staff General Ludwig Beck. They warned London of Hitler's intentions and urged a strong British stand. Beck even pledged, prior to his resignation in mid-August, that if Britain would agree to fight for Czechoslovakia he would stage a *putsch* against Hitler. Nothing came of these warnings, as London was firmly committed to appeasement.[26]

By mid-September Hitler was demanding 'self-determination' for the Sudeten Germans and threatening war if it were not granted. Clearly, he was promoting a situation to justify German military intervention. France would then have to decide whether to honor its pledge to Czechoslovakia. If it chose to do so, this would bring on a general European war.

In this critical situation Chamberlain asked Hitler for a personal meeting, and on September 15 he flew, for the first time in his life, to Germany and met with Hitler at Berchtesgaden. There Hitler informed him that the Sudeten Germans must be able to unite with Germany and that he was willing to risk war to accomplish this. London and Paris now decided to force the principle of self-determination on Prague. On September 19 they demanded that the Czechs agree to an immediate tránsfer to Germany those areas more than 50 percent German. When Prague asked that the matter be referred to arbitration, as provided under the Locarno Pacts, London and Paris declared this unacceptable. The Czechs, they said, would have to accept the Anglo-French proposals or bear the consequences alone.

The British and French decision to desert Czechoslovakia resulted from many factors. The populations in both countries dreaded a general war, especially with air attacks, for which neither nation believed itself adequately prepared. Britain had begun to rebuild the Royal Air Force (RAF) only the year before. In August 1938 Chief of Staff of the French Air Force General Joseph Vuillemin was given a 'tour' of *Luftwaffe* facilities, in which planes were flown around from one field to another to give the illusion of greater numbers; and test aircraft were touted as already in production. Vuillemin gave the French government a gloomy assessment of France's prospects against such a force, as the Germans knew through phone taps of the French embassy.

Both Chamberlain and French Premier Éduard Daladier feared the destruction of their capitals by the much-touted *Luftwaffe*. They also believed they would be fighting alone. Western leaders did not believe they could count on the USSR, the military of which was still reeling from the deadly purges. In France and especially in Britain there were also influential individuals who viewed Nazism as a bulwark against Communism. As stated earlier, they hoped that if Hitler could be diverted eastward and enmeshed in a war with the Soviet Union, Communism and Fascism might destroy one another.

Chamberlain, who had scant experience in foreign affairs, hoped to reconcile differences in order to prevent a general European war. He strongly believed in the sanctity of contracts and, despite evidence to the contrary, could not accept that the leader of the most powerful state in Europe was a blackmailer and a liar. But the West also suffered from a moral uncertainty. In 1919 it had touted 'self-determination of peoples,' and by this Germany had a right to all it had hitherto demanded. The transfer of the Sudetenland to the Reich did not seem too high a price to pay for a satisfied Germany and a peaceful Europe. Finally, there was the powerful impact of Hitler's statements that once his demands upon Czechoslovakia had been satisfied, he would have no further territorial ambitions in Europe.

Under heavy British and French pressure, on September 21 Czechoslovakia accepted the Anglo-French proposals. The next day Chamberlain again traveled to Germany and at Godesberg in the Rhineland so informed Hitler. To Chamberlain's surprise Hitler upped the ante, demanding that all Czech officials be withdrawn from the Sudeten area within ten days and that no military, economic, or traffic establishments be damaged or removed.

Hitler's demands led to the most serious international crisis in Europe since 1918. On September 24 Prague informed London that Hitler's demands were absolutely unacceptable. Their rapid implementation would create panic among the Czech population and not allow Prague time to organize any effective means of military defense. London and Paris agreed with the Czech position and decided not to pressure Prague to secure its acceptance. It thus appeared that Hitler might have to carry out his threat to use force and that a general European war might ensue.

In these circumstances, President Roosevelt made a direct appeal to Hitler, urging an international conference. On September 28 Mussolini talked to Hitler and secured his agreement for such a meeting. Perhaps Hitler's acceptance was prompted in part by the unenthusiastic reception Berliners accorded to a German motorized division moving through Berlin on September 27, which left Hitler in a rage.[27]

Chamberlain, Daladier, and Mussolini then repaired to Munich to meet with Hitler on September 29. No representative of Soviet Russia was invited and Czechoslovakia itself was not officially represented. There were no real negotiations, the object being simply to give Hitler the Sudetenland and avoid war.

At Munich Hitler was on his worst behavior, treating Chamberlain in the most brusque and peremptory fashion. After the conference Hitler vowed that he would attack and destroy the British and the French. It was an astonishing reaction to his diplomatic triumph and it shows clearly that Hitler believed he had been cheated out of a military victory.[28]

The Munich agreement, dated September 30 but actually signed just after midnight, gave Hitler everything he demanded: evacuation would take place during October 1–10 under conditions arranged by an international commission, which would also determine plebiscite areas. Early on the morning of October 1, 1938, German troops marched across the frontier, and two days later Hitler made a triumphal entry into Eger, the unofficial capital of the Sudeten Germans.

Other nations of Central Europe also jumped in. Poland demanded, and received, an area around Teschen of some 400 square miles with a population of 240,000 people, only 100,000 of whom were Poles, and, in November, Hungary secured some 4800 square miles of Czechoslovakia with about a million people.

In retrospect, and psychological and morale factors notwithstanding, it would have been better for the West to have fought Germany in September 1938 rather than capitulating at Munich. The line-up against Germany might have included the Soviet Union and Poland, but, even discounting them, the German Army would have been forced to fight against France and Britain, as well as Czechoslovakia. Hitler's claims to the contrary, Germany was not ready for war in September 1938. The *Luftwaffe* had 1230 first-line aircraft, including 600 bombers and 400 fighters, but nearly half of this number was earmarked for use in the East, leaving the rest too thinly stretched over the Reich frontier to counter any serious offensive by the French Air Force and RAF. The *Luftwaffe* also was short of bombs. Worse, only five fighting divisions and seven reserve divisions were available to hold eight times that number of French divisions.

Britain itself was far from ready, its rearmament program having begun only the year before. France had many more artillery pieces than Germany, but was weak in the air. According to one estimate France had only 250 first-quality fighters and 350 bombers out of perhaps 1375 front-line aircraft, but France could have counted on 35 well-armed and well-equipped Czech divisions, backed by substantial numbers of artillery and tanks, and perhaps 1600 aircraft.[29]

Later, those responsible for the Munich débâcle advanced the argument that it bought a year for the Western democracies to rearm. Winston Churchill stated that British fighter squadrons equipped with modern aircraft rose from only five in September 1938 to 26 by July 1939 (and 47 by July 1940), but he also noted: 'The year's breathing space said to be "gained" by Munich left Britain and France in a much worse position compared to Hitler's Germany than they had been at the Munich crisis.'[30]

The September 1938 crisis had far-reaching international effects. Chamberlain and Daladier were received with cheers at home, the British prime minister reporting that he believed he had achieved 'peace in our time.' But the agreement effectively ended the French security system. Poland, Romania, and Yugoslavia now had to question French commitment. The always-suspicious Stalin was further alienated from the West. He expressed the view that Chamberlain and Daladier had surrendered to Hitler in order to facilitate Germany's *Drang nach Osten* ('Drive to the East') and precipitate a war between Germany and the

Soviet Union. For the German resistance to Hitler, Munich was also a disaster. Even the most diehard of plotters realized that the opportunity to eliminate Hitler had vanished.

Despite Hitler's assurance that the Sudetenland was his last territorial demand in Europe, events soon proved the contrary. The day after Munich, Hitler told his aides that he would annex the remainder of the country at the first opportunity. Within a few months Hitler seized upon the internal situation in Czechoslovakia to his advantage. In March 1939 he threw his support to the leader of the Slovak Popular Party, Josef Tiso, who sought complete independence for Slovakia. On March 14 Slovakia and Ruthenia declared their independence. That same day Hitler summoned elderly Czech President Emil Hácha to Berlin. After subjecting him to lengthy and tiring ceremonies, Hácha was allowed to meet with Hitler and Reichsmarschall Hermann Göring at 1:00 a.m. the next day. Then Göring threatened the immediate destruction of Prague by the *Luftwaffe* unless Moravia and Bohemia were made Reich protectorates. German bombers, he alleged, were awaiting the order to take off. Hácha signed, and that same day, March 15, Nazi troops occupied what remained of Czechoslovakia. The Czech lands became the 'Protectorate of Bohemia and Moravia,' while Slovakia became a vassal state of the Reich with little more independence than Bohemia-Moravia.[31]

Thirty-five highly trained and well-equipped Czech divisions disappeared from the anti-Hitler order of battle. Hitler had also eliminated what he had referred to as 'that damned airfield,' while the output of the Skoda arms complex would now supply the Reich's legions. In Bohemia and Moravia the *Wehrmacht* absorbed 1582 aircraft, 2000 artillery pieces, and sufficient equipment to arm 20 divisions. The Germans also secured there nearly a third of the tanks they deployed in the west in spring 1940. Between August 1938 and September 1939 Skoda produced nearly as many arms as all British arms factories combined.[32]

Hungarian troops crossed into Ruthenia and incorporated it into Hungary. Then, on March 21, Germany demanded from Lithuania the immediate return of Memel, with its mostly German population. Lithuania had received the Baltic city after World War I to gain access to the sea. The Lithuanian government had no recourse but compliance, and on March 23 Hitler arrived in Memel on board the battleship *Deutschland*.

Hitler's seizure of the rest of Czechoslovakia clearly demonstrated that his demands were not limited to Germans and were rather determined by the need for *Lebensraum*. His repudiation of the formal pledges given Chamberlain at Munich also convinced the British that they could no longer trust Hitler. Indeed, Britain and France responded with a series of guarantees to the smaller states now threatened by Germany. Clearly, Poland would be the next pressure point, as the German press stepped up charges of Polish brutality against the German minority.

On March 31 Great Britain and France extended a formal guarantee to support Poland in the event of a German attack. At the eleventh hour, and under the worst possible circumstances with Czechoslovakia lost and the Soviet Union alienated, Britain had changed its Eastern European policy and agreed to do what the French had sought in the 1920s. Mussolini took advantage of the general European situation to strengthen Italy's position in the Balkans by occupying Albania. On April 8 Italian troops occupied Scutari and Tirana, King Zog fleeing into Greece. An Albanian constituent assembly then voted to offer the crown to King Victor Emmanuel of Italy. On April 13 Britain and France extended a similar guarantee to defend Greece and Romania.

The Western powers began to make belated military preparations for the inevitable war, and they worked to secure a pact with the Soviet Union. Unfortunately, the guarantee to Poland gave the USSR protection on its western frontier, virtually the most it could have secured in any negotiations.

On April 28 Hitler in a speech to the Reichstag reiterated earlier demands for the Baltic port city of Danzig and insistence that Germany receive extraterritorial rights in the corridor. On May 5 Poland rejected these demands and suggested a common guarantee of the existence and rights of the Free City. Warsaw pointed out that Poland already allowed German citizens to travel across the Corridor without customs or passport formalities.

On May 23 Hitler met with his leading generals at the Reich Chancellory. He reviewed Germany's territorial requirements and the need to resolve these by expansion eastward. War, Hitler declared, was inevitable:

> Danzig is not the object of our activities. It is a question of expanding our living-space to the east, of securing our food-supplies, and of settling the Baltic problem .... There is no question of sparing Poland and we are left with the decision: To attack Poland at the first suitable opportunity.
>
> We cannot expect a repetition of the Czech affair. There will be war.[33]

Poland had to be isolated so there would be no simultaneous conflict with France and Britain, but if this occurred, 'it will be better to attack in the west and incidentally to settle Poland at the same time.'[34]

The same month Britain and France initiated negotiations with the Soviet Union for a mutual assistance pact. The Soviets noted that the Western powers sent low-level delegations to talk with them and that they traveled to the USSR by ship. Although negotiations continued until August, these failed to produce agreement. One of the major reasons for this was the attitude of the Poles.

Poland, Latvia, Lithuania, and Estonia were all unwilling to allow Soviet armies within their borders, even to defend against German attack. Many in these countries feared the Soviets more than the Germans, and Polish leaders refused to believe that Hitler would risk war with Britain and France. But, in consequence of the 1920 Russo–Polish War, Poland's eastern border extended almost to Minsk, and the Russians thought that the French and British wanted them to take the brunt of the German attack. The Poles also had an exaggerated sense of their own military power. Indeed, the Polish general staff planned, in the event of war, to invade Germany. Probably up to 1937 or 1938 the Poles might have even taken Berlin, but German rearmament ended that possibility. In any case, the Anglo-French negotiators refused to sacrifice Poland and the Baltic states to Stalin the way they had handed Czechoslovakia to Hitler.

While the Kremlin had been negotiating more or less openly with Britain and France, it had concurrently sought an understanding with Germany, even to the point of Stalin dispatching personal emissaries to Berlin. Stalin held equal suspicion for all foreign non-communist powers, be they totalitarian or non-totalitarian, aggressive or passive. His preoccupation was power and what was in the best interest of the Soviet Union.[35]

On March 10, 1939, addressing the Eighteenth Party Congress of the Soviet Union, Stalin said that the USSR did not intend to 'pull anyone else's chestnuts out of the fire.' He thus signalled to Hitler his readiness to abandon collective security and negotiate an agreement with Berlin. Within a week Hitler had annexed Bohemia and Moravia, confident that the Soviet Union would not intervene. Another consideration was that Stalin himself faced the potential of war on two fronts, owing to the threat from Japan in the Far East. Japanese pressure on Mongolia and the Maritime Provinces may well have played a significant role in predisposing Stalin to make his pact with Hitler.

On May 3, 1939, Stalin gave further encouragement to Hitler when he dismissed Commissar for Foreign Affairs Litvinov and appointed

Vyacheslav Molotov in his place. Litvinov was both a champion of collective security and a Jew. Hitler later told Mussolini that the dismissal of Litvinov made fully evident the Kremlin's wish to transform its relations with Germany. At the end of May the German Foreign Office informed its Moscow embassy that Berlin wanted to make 'a certain degree of contact' with the Kremlin. This began the process that would culminate in the Nazi-Soviet pact. Stalin made all the major negotiating decisions, including inviting German Foreign Minister Joachim von Ribbentrop to Moscow.

Ribbentrop arrived in the Soviet capital on August 23 and concluded final negotiations with Stalin personally. The Soviet-Nazi agreement was signed that night. It consisted of an open ten-year non-aggression pact, but there were two secret protocols, which did not become generally known until Rudolf Hess revealed them during proceedings of the International Tribunal at Nuremberg. These secret arrangements, not publicly acknowledged by the Soviet Union until 1990, partitioned Eastern Europe between Germany and the Soviet Union in advance of the German invasion of Poland, for which Hitler was now in effect receiving Stalin's permission. Any future territorial rearrangement of the area would involve a sharing of territory. The Soviet sphere included eastern Poland, the Romanian province of Bessarabia, Estonia, Latvia, and Finland. Lithuania went to Germany, although a month later Hitler traded it to Stalin in exchange for further territorial concessions in Poland. In addition a trade convention accompanying the pact provided that Russia would supply vast quantities of raw materials to Germany in exchange for military technology and finished goods. This economic arrangement was of immense help to Germany early in the war, as Churchill later made clear to Stalin.

Stalin drew Ribbentrop aside and told him that he personally guaranteed that the Soviet Union would not betray its partner. Although Hitler's and Stalin's interests coincided over Poland, Stalin failed to understand the danger of the alliance. Certainly, he expected that Hitler would face a protracted war in the West that would allow the Soviet Union time to rebuild its military. All indications are that Stalin welcomed the pact with Germany, while he regarded the subsequent wartime alliance with Britain and the United States with fear and suspicion. All this becomes understandable when one realizes that Stalin's primary concern was with the internal stability of the Soviet Union.[36]

The Nazi-Soviet Non-Aggression Pact was like a thunderbolt upon the world community. Communism and Nazism, supposed to be ideological opposites on the worst possible terms, had come together; a generation more versed in ideology than power politics was dumb-founded.

On August 22 Hitler summoned his generals and announced his intention to invade Poland. Neither Britain nor France, he said, had the leadership necessary for a life-and-death struggle: 'Our enemies are little worms,' he said, 'I saw them at Munich.' British and French arma-ment did not as yet amount to much. Germany, therefore, had much to gain and little to lose for the Western powers probably would not fight. In any case, Germany must accept the risks and act with reckless reso-lution.[37]

The German invasion of Poland, set for August 26, actually occurred on September 1. The delay was brought by Italy's decision to remain neutral. Prompted by his foreign minister and son-in-law Galeazzo Ciano, Mussolini lost faith in a German victory. Ciano proposed that Mussolini tell Hitler that Italy would enter the conflict only if Germany would agree to supply certain armaments and raw materials. The Germans then rescinded their plans on August 25, and engaged in fren-zied discussions. The next day Mussolini asked for immediate delivery of 170 million tons of industrial products and raw materials, an order impossible for Germany to fulfill.[38]

Hitler then asked that Mussolini maintain benevolent neutrality towards Germany and that he keep secret the decision to remain neutral and indeed continue military preparations so as to fool the English and French. Mussolini agreed. The weight of Italy in the Axis combination was so slight that it took only a few days for Germany to reset its mili-tary plans and go it alone. On September 1, following false charges that Polish forces had crossed onto German soil and killed German border guards – an illusion completed by the murder of concentration camp prisoners who were then dressed in Polish military uniforms – German forces invaded Poland. World War II had begun.[39]

2

The Axis Triumphant, 1939–1940

The German conquest of Poland

On September 1, 1939, the military balance appeared to favor Hitler's opponents. The ground forces of Poland, France, and Britain outnumbered those of Germany by three to two, although some French and British troops remained overseas to meet imperial commitments.

Polish Marshal Edward Śmigły-Rydz commanded 280,000 men in 6 armies of 30 infantry divisions, 11 cavalry brigades, and 2 mechanized brigades. An additional three million Poles had undergone some military training. Reserves would bring the regular divisions up to full strength and held the potential of 15 more divisions, but much of the army's military equipment was of World War I vintage.

In September 1939 Great Britain had 1,270,000 men under arms: 180,000 in the Royal Navy and Royal Marines, 897,000 in the army, and 193,000 in the Royal Air Force (RAF). Conscription had been introduced in April 1939 but the army only numbered five regular infantry divisions in addition to 16 Territorial Army divisions being organized. One mobile (later armored) division was in the process of formation. A good proportion of the British Army was overseas at the outbreak of war, including Egypt and Palestine. In India many of the Indian brigades had one British battalion. Most of the British formations were largely untrained and underequipped.

Many observers regarded the French Army as the world's most powerful, although in September 1939 France's population was only about half that of Germany. It was organized into 94 divisions, including 63 infantry, 7 motorized infantry, 3 light mechanized, and 5 cavalry. France employed conscription to build the largest possible reserve and it also relied on a large number of non-metropolitan troops. In September 1939 the French had 3200 tanks, more than the Germans and many of better quality. The problem for France was not so much equipment as tactical doctrines governing its use. Senior commanders had learned their trade in World War I and did not understand the implications of changes in military technology for tactics and strategy. The French High Command rejected the new theories of armor warfare; it continued to view tanks in World War I terms as operating in support of infantry, employed in small penny-packets rather than massed and functioning as entire divisions.

Some forward-thinking French officers, most notably Lieutenant Colonel Charles de Gaulle, argued for change. De Gaulle sought a larger professional force formed on speed and maneuverability around armor divisions with organic artillery, motorized infantry, and air support. There is no indication that anyone on the French Army Council showed more than a passing interest in De Gaulle's important book, *Vers l'armée de metier* (1934). De Gaulle and British military reformers and armor advocates Major Basil H. Liddell Hart and Major General J. F. C. Fuller actually taught their counterparts in Germany about armored doctrine, and the German panzer divisions were modeled along the lines envisioned by the Western military reformers.[1]

In Britain, France, and the United States military non-conformity was discouraged. The British Experimental Mechanised Force was disbanded, as was the Amphibious Warfare School. Victors in war tend to rest on their laurels, while it is the defeated and the outgunned powers that seem chiefly interested in military innovation. In the air the Allies were at serious disadvantage. Given varying definitions for 'serviceable,' 'combat ready,' and 'front line,' precise statistics are elusive, but the RAF, the best prepared of any of the Allied air forces, had around 3600 serviceable aircraft, of which perhaps 1900 were combat-ready.[2]

British fighter assets were totally inadequate, as the RAF had chosen to concentrate on strategic bombing. Air power advocates championed strategic bombing in order to justify an independent air force. 'Father of the Royal Air Force' Marshal Hugh Trenchard sold this approach to the British government as an effective means of policing the empire. Certainly, these men had little interest in fighters and virtually none in ground support aviation. Such an approach made some sense in the early 1930s when bombers and fighters were of about the same speed and had no means of identifying high-flying bombers prior to their arrival over target, but it was nullified by improvements in fighter speed and performance, backed by ancillary developments in integrated warning systems, especially radar, against air attack. By September 1939 the

British had some fine fighter aircraft, but no real understanding of close air support.

In September 1939 the French *Armée de l'air* had perhaps 1400 aircraft, but two-thirds of these were obsolete. Although the Polish Air Force (*Lotnictwo Wojskowe*) counted 1900 aircraft, it deployed just slightly more than 400, including 159 fighters (15 squadrons) and 154 bombers. Most of its aircraft, especially fighters, were obsolete. The PZL P 37B, the best bomber in the Polish inventory, was comparable in speed and range to the German Dornier Do 17 and carried the greater bomb load of the Heinkel He 111, but only 36 were operational in September 1939. Poland also had little in the way of anti-aircraft artillery and no early warning system against air attack.[3]

The Poles lacked manufacturing plants, but the French and British had no such excuse for their own lack of modern aircraft. Their problem was allocation of resources and the failure of military leaders to realize the importance of securing control of the air space over the battlefield. Generals who had learned their trade in World War I controlled defense allocations, and they favored traditional ground forces. The French aviation industry therefore continued producing planes at the absurdly low rate of about 40 a month, even into 1940. The French thus produced in a year what they would lose in a week of actual combat. Most French designs were also inferior to the basic German fighter, the Bf 109.

The *Reichsheer* (German Army) counted more than a million men: 98 active and reserve divisions and one cavalry brigade. Including reserves, Germany could call on 2.5 million men, and its army would grow to more than 300 divisions in the course of the war. In September 1939, however, 36 of the 98 divisions were being formed and were untrained. Although strictly disciplined and thoroughly trained, the Germany Army was far from being a totally modern force and as a whole was unready for mobile warfare. The bulk of its active divisions were of World War I pattern, relying on horses. A German infantry division in 1939 required between 4077 and 6033 horses in movement and even panzer divisions utilized them. As late as 1944 an estimated 85 percent of German Army divisions were horse-drawn with very few vehicles.[4]

As with the French, the thinking of the German higher command tended to run along World War I lines. German military reformers, however, recognized the concept of high-speed warfare and, because Germany had lost the last war, army leaders were more willing to give the new ideas a trial. The German reformers also had one great advantage in that Adolf Hitler would make this decision himself. In 1937 Heinz Guderian, the architect of Germany's armored forces, published a book, *Achtung! Panzer!*, advancing his theories of high-speed tank warfare. Unlike many of his senior generals, whose thinking tended to run in the old grooves, Hitler embraced the new theories that were the logical extension of German tactics that had evolved in 1918 combined with new technology. These held special appeal for him because *Blitzkrieg* (Lightning War), as it came to be known in the West, promised decisive quick victory, and a short war was the only war that Germany could reasonably expect to win.

By the war's beginning the German Army fielded a small number of new-type divisions: 6 armored, 4 mechanized ('light'), and 4 motorized infantry. These 14 new-style divisions were only a small proportion of the whole German Army, but in the first nine months of the war they were worth more than the remainder together. Ironically, much of Germany's military equipment was second-rate. The Mark I tank, for example, actually was a 'tankette,' one of the species of experimental training vehicles built by the world's armies between the wars. Germany had some 2900 tanks for the invasion of Poland: 1400 PzKpfw Is with only two machine guns each; 1200 PzKpfw IIs mounting a 20mm gun; 98 PzKpfw IIIs, with an unsatisfactory 37mm gun; and only 211 PzKpfw IVs with a 75mm gun.

The original plan was to equip each German panzer division with 570 tanks. At the time of the invasion each had only about 300, but the success of the Blitzkrieg lay not so much in the equipment as in its employment, and especially the use of combined arms teams with supporting arms as mobile as the tanks. The problem in World War I had been the inability of reserves to close with sufficient speed in an attack once a breach had been opened in the enemy lines. The Blitzkrieg, with its mechanized reserves, greatly compressed the time in favor of the attackers. Guderian also believed in massing tanks rather than dispersing them, and in using these units to achieve fast, sudden breakthroughs at weak points in the enemy lines, without benefit of preliminary bombardment.[5]

Infantry, moving with the tanks in armored vehicles and trucks, and mobile anti-tank guns would provide support for the panzers. The whole idea was to keep moving. Tactical air power formed a key element, especially 'flying artillery' in the form of the Junkers Ju 87 *Sturzkampfflugzeug*, more commonly known as the Stuka. Developed in 1935, this single-engine dive-bomber proved vulnerable to anti-aircraft guns and high-performance fighters, but it was also a highly mobile and accurate artillery platform; and as long as Germany controlled the skies, the Stuka could operate with relative impunity. Thus Liddell Hart noted, 'the German Army achieved its amazing run of victories, not because it was overwhelming in strength or thoroughly modern in form, but because it was a few degrees more advanced than its opponents.'[6] It was truly a case of the sum being greater than its parts.

The German Army was well-trained and superbly led. After 1933 the German schools stressed daily physical activity and in consequence German soldiers were in excellent physical condition. The army's 11-man squads were equipped with the MG34 air-cooled light machine gun. Four men manned the MG34; the remaining seven were armed with bolt-action Mauser rifles. It is a myth that German soldiers were mere automatons, blindly obeying orders from superiors. There was in fact great flexibility in how orders were to be carried out, and German non-commissioned officers (NCOs) exercised more authority and had greater responsibility than in most armies, including that of the United States. German NCOs habitually led in combat, leaving a relatively small number of commissioned officers to plan and direct operations. The German Army also placed emphasis on front-line units and had its best officers forward. The corollary of this is that throughout the war the German Army suffered from logistics problems and was deficient in intelligence capabilities.

The German Army also had too many specialized units, and the military as a whole suffered from the maze of overlapping jurisdictions and inefficiencies that marked the Third Reich at all levels. For example, the army was in competition with the *Waffen SS* (Armed [Fighting] SS), which grew during the war to 38 divisions and had first claim to the best equipment. The *Luftwaffe* had control of everything in the air but little interest in naval aviation. Airborne troops were *Luftwaffe* personnel and the air force also had charge of anti-aircraft artillery. Eventually the *Luftwaffe* even fielded 22 ground divisions, including the Hermann Göring Armored Division. The navy had the equivalent of six divisions. All three services competed for and hoarded scarce raw materials, and there was a maze of intelligence agencies, all of which acted independently and jealously guarded their own findings.

Germany's chief advantage was in the air, for at the start of hostilities Germany had the most powerful air force in the world. The death in 1936 of strategic bomber proponent General Walther Wever brought a shift in emphasis to tactical air power, which remained the case throughout World War II. In September 1939 *Luftwaffe* commander General Hermann Göring commanded more than 3600 front-line aircraft.

The Germans were impressed by US Marine Corps experiments with precision dive-bombing and, as noted, came to embrace this technique;

indeed, all German bombers had to be capable of dive-bombing. This entailed considerable aircraft structural changes with attendant production delays and a diminution in bomb-carrying capacity. The flying weight of the Ju 88 went from six to 12 tons, sharply reducing both its speed and bomb-carrying capacity.[7]

The *Luftwaffe*, the newest of the military services, was also the least professional and suffered the most from promotions not based on merit. During the war it was also the least conscious of communications security. Germany's limitations in the air first became evident during the 1940 Battle of Britain when Göring attempted to wage a strategic bombing campaign with a tactical air force, but it is also true that the German military probably got the best possible use from its air resources. The *Luftwaffe* performed well in Poland and during the invasion of France and the Low Countries in 1940. It was also impressive in the fighting against the Soviet Union, at least until the Battle of Stalingrad.

The Germans also developed some exceptional aircraft. In addition to the Stuka, the Germans had a superb air-superiority fighter in the Bf 109, certainly one of the best all-around aircraft of the war. The E Model of 1939 had a top speed of 342 miles per hour and was armed with 2 x 20mm cannon and 2 x 7.92mm machine guns. With 35,000 manufactured by war's end, the Bf 109 also enjoyed the distinction of having the largest production run of any fighter aircraft in history. It went through a variety of models; by war's end the G model had a top speed of 402 mph.[8]

In 1914 Germany had faced the strategic dilemma of fighting a two-front war and had chosen to concentrate against France first. Thanks to the non-aggression pact, in 1939 Hitler did not have to worry about the Soviet Union to the east. He did have to be concerned about Britain and France attacking in the west while he invaded Poland, but Hitler halfway expected that Britain and France would not fight for Poland. In any case, the German military strategy for Poland was the 1914 Schlieffen Plan in reverse. Germany would leave a weak covering force of just 25 reserve and depot divisions in the west between Aachen and Basel. It would have few artillery pieces, no tanks, and virtually no aircraft. The German forces in the west would be ranged against a French Army nearly four times as large with far more equipment. The Germans could not rely on static defenses, for their West Wall was not yet complete. If France could act quickly, it would be able to relieve German pressure on Poland.[9]

The Poles were confident. They expected to hold out until the French and British mounted a massive offensive against Germany from the west. Allied strategy called for British and French forces to attack Germany from the air immediately, with France launching a ground offensive on the fifteenth day of the war.

Thanks to Belgian neutrality, however, any French effort to relieve pressure on Poland would be largely limited to a 90-mile stretch between the Rhine and the Moselle rivers. The Germans concentrated their defenses there and sowed mines in front of approaches to the West Wall. But because of their reliance on reserves and the need to retrieve artillery from storage, the French would not be able to mount any major offensive action until about September 17. By that date Poland was collapsing, so the French High Command had good excuse for counter-manding the plan.

Germany had the advantage of being able to attack Poland from three directions at once. They committed 1,250,000 men in 45 divisions (other divisions trailed in the second and third echelons but did not see action), 2900 tanks, and more than 1500 aircraft, including 426 fighters and 897 bombers. German ground forces formed two principal flanking groups with a weak center. Colonel General Fedor von Bock commanded Army Group North, consisting of the Third Army in East Prussia and the Fourth Army in Pomerania facing the Polish Corridor. The Third Army would thrust south while the Fourth Army moved southeast; the two would then link up for a drive on Warsaw. Lieutenant General Guderian had charge of XIX Corps, the two panzer and two mechanized divisions in Army Group North. Foreseeing the creation of panzer armies, Guderian wielded these as a single entity in order to take advantage of their mobility. This was not the case in Army Group South, where most of the German panzers were dispersed. The bulk of German strength lay with Army Group South, commanded by Colonel General Karl Rudolf Gerd von Rundstedt, and consisting of the Eighth and Tenth Armies in Silesia and the Fourteenth Army in Slovakia. These armies would drive north, on Warsaw. The Germans thus hoped to trap the bulk of the Polish forces west of the Vistula River and had only weak forces connecting their two army groups and protecting the western approach to Berlin.[10]

The Poles found themselves in a difficult situation geographically. Śmigły-Rydz and his generals did not want to meet the Germans as far east as Warsaw, and so the bulk of Polish forces were dispersed and deployed forward on the frontiers where they could be, and were indeed, cut off and surrounded. Polish forces manned an 800-mile front from Lithuania to the Carpathian Mountains. Such wide dispersal of assets played to German advantage. The Poles were not thinking only of defense; they also formed a special assault group to invade East Prussia.

The Polish offensive doctrine was reflected in the relative equality in numbers of bombers to fighter aircraft in the Polish Air Force.

Also, thanks to British pressure, the Poles delayed their mobilization for two days so as not to provide Germany with a pretext for attacking, and it was not yet completed when the Germans struck. The weather also worked against the Poles. Normally, September is wet but in 1939 it was dry, and the flat Polish plain proved excellent terrain for the German panzers. The Polish military command was highly centralized and relied on telephone communications, which the Germans easily severed. Added to this the ethnic Germans living in Poland provided assistance to the invaders.

German forces, massed on the frontiers before the invasion, started moving into Poland at 4:45 a.m. on September 1. The outcome was clear within a few days. *Luftwaffe* control of the air inhibited Polish mobilization and prevented the Poles from bringing their numbers to bear. German planes ranged far and wide and spread panic by attacking Polish population centers, including Warsaw. German aircraft also attacked Polish roads, railroads, supply dumps, and airfields.

Contrary to myth, the Polish Air Force was not caught on the ground. On August 26 its aircraft had been dispersed and moved to secretly prepared airstrips. Its pilots fought bravely, but it was no match for the *Luftwaffe*. The best Polish formations were cavalry, some of which actually charged German infantry with drawn sabers. Polish morale, however, could not make up for their inferiority in weapons and failure to appreciate the impact of modern firepower on tactics.[11]

The German invasion proceeded like clockwork. Within two days Polish forces in the south were in jeopardy. The speed of the German advance was such that the mobilization of Polish reserves could not keep up with the tactical situation. Polish units were cut off and lost to the defense. By September 7 Army Group South had taken Krakow and was approaching Lodź; the Third and Fourth Armies to the north, meanwhile, linked up and were advancing on Warsaw, the Fourth Army along the right bank of the Vistula. On the 17th, the day that the Soviet Union invaded Poland from the east, elements of Guderian's divisions linked up with armored spearheads of Army Group South. Two days later it was all but over when remnants of 19 Polish divisions and three cavalry brigades, some 100,000 men in all, surrendered to the Eighth Army.

From the start of the war Warsaw had been subjected to indiscriminate terror bombing. On September 13 the Germans announced their intention to bomb cities and Hitler also ordered that civilians be prevented from leaving Warsaw. These decisions sprang from the belief that terror bombing would hasten Polish surrender. Following a stout defense, Warsaw capitulated on September 27 with nearly 150,000 troops taken prisoner. The last organized Polish resistance ceased on October 6.

Meanwhile, the best the French could muster in the west was a token drive in the Saar by nine divisions. Ordered to move only to the outposts of the West Wall, by September 12 the French had advanced a maximum of five miles on a 16-mile front and taken 20 abandoned villages. Casualties were negligible, but the French then halted; and when Warsaw surrendered they began a withdrawal to the Maginot Line, completed on October 4.

German General Siegfried Westphal, then a major serving in the west, recalled his amazement at the failure of the French to take advantage of German weakness:

> During September there was not a single tank on any part of the German Western Front. All in all, the stock of ammunition would have lasted for three days in battle. The Army High Command possessed no serviceable reserve in the rear. All the flying units of the *Luftwaffe* were in service in Poland, leaving only a few reconnaissance planes and obsolete fighters available in the West.
>
> Every expert serving at that time in the Western Army felt his hair stand on end when he considered the possibility of an immediate French attack. It was incomprehensible that no such attack should take place, that the appalling weakness of the German defense should be unknown to the French leaders.[12]

Westphal believed that if the French had undertaken a major offensive, it would have reached the Rhine. Indeed, every staff exercise General Beck had conducted before the war had the French Army accomplishing as much.[13]

Britain also did little. British historian John Terraine observed that the French offensive was 'undoubtedly pathetic, but it does not behove the British to dwell on it; their own Expeditionary Force had not even completed its assembly.'[14] Polish pleas for RAF bombing raids against Germany, agreed to before the war, fell on deaf ears. When queried in the House of Commons about the possibility of an incendiary air strike on the Black Forest, Air Minister Sir Kingsley Wood was appalled: 'Are you aware that it is private property?' he said. 'Why, you will be asking me to bomb Essen next!' The best the British could do was to drop leaflets on Frankfurt, Munich, and Stuttgart, informing the German people of the nature of their country's aggression. Wood described these as an attempt 'to rouse the Germans to a higher morality' and claimed that the 'truth raids' had caused the German authorities 'great irritation.' General Edward Spears, another MP, contemptuously referred to this as 'confetti warfare.'[15]

As previously noted, on September 17 the Red Army, acting under the secret provisions of its pact with Germany and without declaration of war, had invaded Poland from the east. The Poles had few troops to oppose this second invasion, and the Soviets quickly absorbed about a third of Poland (some 130,000 square miles) with a population of 13 million people. This territory was roughly equal to the land lost by Russia as a consequence of the Paris Peace settlement and the Russo–Polish War.

The Polish campaign cost the Germans 16,000 dead and 32,000 wounded. They also lost up to a third of their tanks and aircraft. The Russian cost was fewer than 1000 dead. In contrast, the Poles lost 66,300 killed, 133,700 wounded, and 587,000 taken prisoner (200,000 by the Soviets). Total Soviet casualties were less than 3000.[16]

About 90,000 Polish troops escaped, most into Hungary and Romania. A number subsequently made their way to France and continued the fight, and by May 1940 the Polish Army in exile in France numbered 80,000 men. Polish troops fought in France, Norway, the Western Desert, Italy, and in the 1944 Normandy Campaign. A parachute brigade distinguished itself in Operation MARKET-GARDEN in September 1944, and the 1st Polish Armored Division fought in Normandy and across northwest Europe. Three Polish destroyers, two submarines, a training vessel, and a supply ship made it to Britain, as did 38 merchant ships. Two fighter squadrons manned by Polish pilots provided valuable assistance in the 1940 Battle of Britain.

Poland again disappeared from the map. Germany annexed outright about half the territory it had taken. Poles were then forced out and the area completely Germanized. The remaining territory under German jurisdiction, known as the General Government, which included Warsaw and Krakow, was to be exploited for cheap labor. The day after he became Poland's governor, Hans Frank declared the Poles 'shall become the slaves of the German Reich.' General Franz Halder recorded in his diary on October 18: 'We have no intention of rebuilding Poland . . . . Low standard of living must be conserved. Cheap slaves . . . .'[17]

Einsatzgruppen, special extermination units, moved into Poland to arrest or execute intelligentsia and potential leaders as well as Jews. Throughout German-occupied territory the Nazis imposed harsh and demeaning regulations. The Soviets also imposed a brutal regime in their part of Poland. Ultimately, the Soviets deported some 1.2 million Poles to the Soviet Union. In April 1940, as part of their effort to deprive Poland of its natural leaders, the Soviets executed up to 15,000 Polish officers and intellectuals and buried them in mass graves in the Katyn Forest near Smolensk. The Germans discovered the execution site on their invasion of the Soviet Union and, grateful for anything that would cast attention away from their own horrendous acts, announced the Soviet atrocity to the world. The Kremlin steadfastly denied responsibility and blamed the Katyn Massacre on the Germans. Not until 1990 did Russian leader Mikhail Gorbachev publicly acknowledge his country's guilt.[18]

The Ultra secret

Before Poland had been defeated, it provided an intelligence *coup* for the West. As with all major military powers, the Germans had in the years before the war sought to develop a secure means of military communications. Toward this end they selected a commercial encoding machine known as the Enigma device, developed by German Dr Arthur Scherbius and demonstrated at the International Postal Congress in 1923. By 1928 the German military was using it. Japan also bought the machine.

Enigma resembled a typewriter in appearance, with a series of rotors or wheels, the settings of which could be changed. The device enabled the operator to encode a plain text in any of 150 million possible ways. Understandably, the Germans assumed that messages so encoded were unbreakable. They were mistaken. The Poles understood the German threat, and in 1928 they formed a special cryptography group at the University of Poznan. They also purchased the commercial model of Enigma, and by 1935 they had broken into the German radio codes, information they largely shared with the British and French in 1938. Late that same year, however, the Germans added a sixth rotor, which helped to convince the Poles that the Germans were about to make an aggressive military move. The Poles modified their own machines to keep up with the German advances, and they continued to break into the German codes, but the defeat of their country came too quickly for Enigma to be of utility to them.

On their defeat the Polish codebreakers and their machines were spirited out to France and to England. At Bletchley Park outside of

Buckingham, the British assembled a mix of mathematicians, cryptographers, engineers, and eccentrics, including Alan Turing, regarded as the father of the modern computer. There they continued the work begun by the Poles. By 1940 Bletchley Park had come up with additional devices that, given time, could sort their way through the possible variations of an encoded text. Careless German practices, mostly in the *Luftwaffe*, gave the electro-mechanical devices, called 'bombes,' a head start and greatly shortened the delay between reception and decoding of messages. The changeable settings meant that most messages could not be read in 'real time,' but the information was nonetheless invaluable.

Such intelligence was identified by the codeword of 'Ultra.' As delays in decoding were reduced, many of the Ultra messages proved of great tactical value. It was of the utmost importance that knowledge of the codebreaking be concealed, and perhaps the most remarkable element in the Ultra story is that the choices made concerning its use never betrayed the source. Ultra was never compromised and the Germans continued to believe that their system was secure. The British and Americans shared cryptographic information, especially after the United States entered the war, but Ultra played a key role in most Allied operations, including the 1941 naval Battle of Matapan, the Battle of the Atlantic, the 1942 Allied invasion of North Africa and Battle of El Alamein, and the 1944 Normandy Invasion. Ultra also neatly complemented the double-agent system run by the British. Much of Ultra's importance was simply providing negative information of what the Axis did not know about planned Allied operations. Ultra intelligence diminished by the end of the war, when the fighting was on the Continent of Europe and the Germans used more secure landlines for communication, but it was certainly a key factor in the Allied victory and undoubtedly shortened the war, perhaps by several years. Information on Ultra was not made public until 1974, when Group Captain F. W. Winterbotham published *The Ultra Secret*. Its revelations forced the rewriting of most earlier histories of the war.[19]

The Polish underground also later provided London with other important intelligence information, including the first reports of German V 2 rocket test launchings at Peenemünde. In May 1944 its agents even secured a dud V 2, which the Poles then dismantled and studied. Later a British aircraft collected it from a secret landing strip in Poland and flew it out for further study, enabling the British to calculate rather accurately its range and capabilities.[20]

After the defeat of Poland, Hitler offered peace on a 'forgive-and-forget' basis. Speaking before the Reichstag on October 6, Hitler offered vague peace terms including formation of a new Polish state organized to the satisfaction of Germany and the Soviet Union, return of some colonial possessions to Germany, 'solution and settlement of the Jewish problem,' revival of international trade, and a conference of the leading European states to resolve these matters. The Western Allies rejected this offer to desert their ally in defeat, and the war continued.[21]

The Winter War

Concerned that Germany would turn on the Soviet Union as soon as it had disposed of France and Britain, Stalin now frantically sought to build up the Soviet Union's military strength. On September 1, 1939, the conscription age in the Soviet Union was lowered from 21 to 19, bringing the Red Army up from 1.5 million men in January 1938 to nearly 5.4 million by June 22 1941 and over 592 divisions in wartime.[22]

Also, on September 16 that year Stalin signed a truce with Japan that ended fighting in the Soviet Far East. Stalin particularly feared a future German attack via the Gulf of Finland and sought cover for his second largest city of Leningrad, only 20 miles from the Finnish border on the Karelian Isthmus. He now demanded from Finland much of the isthmus, destruction of all Finnish fortifications there, cession of certain islands in the Gulf of Finland, and a lease of the Hanko peninsula to the west for a Russian naval base. In return he was prepared to cede to Finland more Russian territory than he demanded: 1066 square miles of territory in return for 2134, although the latter was located to the north in East Karelia above Lake Ladoga.[23]

With a population of only 3.7 million people, Finland hardly seemed able to resist Soviet demands. While the Finns were open to some compromise on the issue of Leningrad, they were most upset by Stalin's demand for disarmament and the base on the Hanko peninsula. When Finnish leaders, who believed Stalin was bluffing, refused to yield Hanko after nearly two months of tough negotiations, Stalin ordered the invasion of his neighbor, taking a leaf from Hitler's book in the form of alleged border incidents.

The Soviet–Finnish War, also known as the 'Winter War,' opened on November 30, with the Soviets sending 20 divisions against 16 Finnish. Although the war's final result was a foregone conclusion, it was not one of Stalin's most successful military exploits. Despite its overwhelming superiority in manpower, the Red Army required nearly four months to crush its minuscule opponent. In December the Finns halted the main

Russian thrust across the Karelian Isthmus at the Mannerheim Line, named for Marshal Karl Mannerheim. Finnish morale, equipment, and tactical leadership were all superior to those of the Soviets. The Finns were, of course, fighting for their homeland, but they also showed great ability in improvisation, as with the gasoline bomb in a bottle hurled at Russian tanks and dubbed the 'Molotov cocktail,' by their effective use of ski troops, and even in fitting largely antiquated biplane aircraft with skis to enable them to operate from snow. The chief Russian problems were lack of officer leadership, largely attributable to the Great Purges, poor training, and low morale among the men.

Not until February 1940 could Soviet forces mount an effective assault on the Mannerheim Line. By early March weight of numbers and superior artillery enabled the Soviets to break through the Mannerheim Line and end Finnish resistance, and on the 12th Stalin dictated a peace settlement. Stalin did not annex Finland, or even Helsinki, but he exacted territorial concessions well in excess of those sought before the war. The Finns were forced to yield roughly 25,000 square miles of territory, including the Karelian Isthmus. The war also displaced 500,000 Finns, for virtually all left the territory ceded to the Soviet Union. Although these terms were regarded as harsh by the Finns and Finland's many international supporters, they were mild compared to those the USSR imposed on the other three Baltic countries.

In the case of Finland, Stalin may have been deterred by strong anti-Soviet sentiment that the invasion had aroused throughout the world. Indeed, 11,000 volunteers went to Finland to fight against the Soviets. Britain and France actually considered military intervention against the Soviet Union, including bombing strikes against the Caucasian oil fields and an 'uninvited landing' in Norway as a preliminary step to sending troops to Finland. Seen in retrospect, such a step would have been a disaster for the Allied war effort. Stalin may also have been restrained by desire to keep his options open about a possible alliance with the West against Hitler and to minimize the many disadvantages resulting from the Soviet aggression. One consequence for the Soviet Union of its invasion, expulsion from the League of Nations, was hardly a major blow.

Stalin must bear responsibility for the initial Soviet military failure in Finland. Fresh from his relatively bloodless triumph in Poland, he personally intervened to reject the plan advanced by Chief of Staff Marshal Boris M. Shaposhnikov that entailed a careful build-up and employment of the best Soviet troops, even those from the Far East. Many of the Soviet units were poorly trained, scratch formations. Worse, the Soviet troops were unprepared for winter fighting. Stalin had rebuked Shaposhnikov for overestimating the Finns and underestimating the Red Army. The new plan, worked out on Stalin's orders and confirmed by him, led to the fiasco of the early Soviet defeats, until Shaposhnikov had to remedy the situation.[24]

In the end the Soviets had thrown 1.5 million men – almost half their army in Europe – 3000 aircraft, and nearly as many tanks against Finland. They suffered 230,000 to 270,000 dead – many the result of cold and poor Soviet medical services – and a comparable number of wounded. They also lost 1800 tanks and 634 aircraft. On their side the Finns sustained 25,000 killed and 44,000 wounded, and 62 of the 162 planes of their largely antiquated air force were lost.[25]

One of the war's most important effects was the damage to Soviet military prestige. Many observers now doubted that the Soviet Union was capable of waging a large-scale war, a conclusion Hitler was too quick to draw. Another consequence was Soviet adoption of the Finnish automatic sidearm.[26]

After the German invasion of the Soviet Union in June 1941, Finland waged war against the Soviet Union as a co-belligerent of Germany. In the so-called 'Continuation War', 16 revamped Finnish divisions retook the territory lost earlier to the Soviet Union. Among those then extending congratulations to the Finns for their achievement was US Secretary of State Cordell Hull. Mannerheim issued strict orders that the army not shell Leningrad. In the winter of 1941, when Soviet lines were stretched to the breaking point, a determined Finnish assault would undoubtedly have given the Germans Leningrad, with uncertain consequences for the war in the East. When the tide of war again turned, in June 1944 the Soviets invaded Finland with 450,000 infantry, 800 tanks, and 2000 aircraft. The Finns fought valiantly, but were again forced to sue for peace, signing an armistice in September 1944.[27]

Hitler, meanwhile, was preparing to move west. On November 23, 1939, he called together his military chiefs for a conference at the Chancellory and revealed his goal as nothing short of world domination. He reviewed the early struggles and reminded his generals that few of them had supported his early decisions. He alone had 'the firm will to make brutal decisions.' Hitler claimed he was indispensable. He might be charged with simply wanting to 'fight and fight again.' Hitler did not reject this. Germany's goal was 'a larger *Lebensraum*' and he 'did not organize the armed forces in order not to strike.'[28]

Time was working against Germany. The USSR was not dangerous at the moment; its army would remain ineffective for the next year or two, but it would adhere to the Nazi-Soviet Non-Aggression Pact only as long as it proved beneficial, and Germany could oppose the USSR only when it was free in the West. The Soviet Union was seeking to increase its influence in the Balkans and was striving toward the Persian Gulf, which was also Germany's foreign policy goal. Hitler dismissed US aid to the Allies as not yet important. The moment was favorable, but it might not be so in six months. Hitler ruled out compromise: 'Victory or defeat . . . . I shall attack France and England at the most favorable and earliest moment. Breach of the neutrality of Belgium and Holland is of no importance. No one will question that when we have won.'[29]

While the Germans prepared to strike, all was quiet in the west. Indeed, this period came to be known as the '*Sitzkrieg*,' 'Phony War,' and 'Bore War.' The French manned their Maginot Line and there was bitterness over the attitude of the British toward the war. While France had fully mobilized, Britain had only imposed partial conscription. By October 11 Britain had only four divisions in France, characterized by Churchill as a 'symbolic contribution.' Not until December 9 was the first British soldier killed – a corporal shot on patrol. The Germans also remained quiescent behind their West Wall in the Rhineland. Hardly any air action took place, with both sides reluctant to unleash the bombing of cities.[30]

Allied fear of German air attack had of course been one of the key factors in the Western surrender at Munich in 1938, and British and French authorities were deeply concerned about the bomber. Air power advocates claimed that it alone would decide the war's outcome. Much of their reasoning had taken hold, and British authorities gloomily forecast in early 1939 that 600,000 British civilians would be killed by bombs in the first two months of a war. This led to misdirection of resources in Britain. Five years of war ended up claiming 60,000 British civilians to both bombs and the V 1s and V 2s.[31]

Hitler was less concerned with air strikes on German cities than against its war industries. In his October 9 directive to the armed forces to prepare for an attack in the west, he cited 'the greatest danger' to Germany as 'the vulnerability of the Ruhr.' If this German industrial center were to be struck, 'it would lead to the collapse of the German war economy and thus of the capacity to resist.' Seizure of Belgium and Holland would give German U-boats and the *Luftwaffe* 'a better starting point' and would also serve as a protective barrier for the Ruhr. 'The conduct of the war depends on possession of the Ruhr. If England and France push through Belgium and Holland into the Ruhr, we shall be in the greatest danger.' Hitler set November 12 as the date of the offensive against the west.[32]

Hitler need not have worried. British and French leaders had pressed King Leopold III of Belgium to permit their forces to advance into Belgium to meet a German invasion of that country, but they had no plans of taking the offensive themselves. The Allies had decided on a war of attrition, relying on the economic strangulation of a naval blockade to bring Germany to its knees. A similar blockade had been a major factor in the Allied victory in World War I, but there was a vast difference between the German situations of 1914 and 1939. In World War I both Italy and Russia had been active military opponents of Germany; now both were friendly neutrals. What these two nations could not supply to the Reich from their own production they could purchase abroad, nullifying the effects of an Allied blockade. First Lord of the Admiralty Winston Churchill, a stranger to the word 'inaction,' pressed for indirect approaches that might utilize Britain's naval superiority. His efforts found expression in a scheme to mine the coastal waters of neutral Norway.

High-grade Swedish iron ore was vital to the German war economy, with Germany importing about nine million tons a year. The ore from mines in northern Sweden was shipped from the Swedish port of Luleá at the head of the Gulf of Bothnia, thence through the Baltic to Germany. Between December and April, when the Baltic was frozen, the ore passed by rail from northern Sweden to the northern Norwegian port of Narvik, where it was loaded on ore ships that moved down the coast in Norwegian territorial waters and thence to Germany.[33]

Churchill supported a plan to mine Norwegian waters to force German ships out to sea and allow them to be legally intercepted. Such action would violate Norway's neutrality, but in December and January the British and French cabinets discussed both this and a plan to send an expeditionary force to aid the Finns in their war against the Soviet Union and coincidentally seize the Swedish iron mines. This mad venture would have added the Soviet Union to the list of Allied enemies. These deliberations were soon an open secret.

Initially, Hitler had no intention of opening a new front in northern Europe. The reason was obvious, for on December 17 he set January 14, 1940, as the date for the start of the western offensive. Hitler believed that maintenance of strict neutrality by Norway and Sweden was the best course for Germany, but in February he concluded that the British intended to move against western Norway and that Germany would have to get there first.[34]

On March 13 Soviet and Finnish negotiators signed an agreement ending their war and with it the possibility of Allied intervention in

Finland. British leaders considered this a major setback, given mounting public pressure for some military action. When the Allied Supreme War Council met on March 28, there was considerable demand for deeds. New French Premier Paul Reynaud, who had replaced Édouard Daladier in part from the clamor for action, went on record as favoring mining Norwegian territorial waters. In return he agreed to another Churchill plan, Operation ROYAL MARINE, the mining of the Rhineland waterways. Chamberlain, although not enthusiastic, consented. He too felt the need to do something. The conferees set April 4–5 as the date for the mining operation to halt the iron ore from Narvik. Churchill and others hoped that the Allied intervention in Norway would trigger a German military response that would then allow them to land troops. On April 4 British troops were set to embark, and ships ready to sail to lay the mines and land the troops. Had the Allied operation gone forward as planned, it would have stolen a march on Hitler, whose own invasion of Norway was scheduled for April 9.[35]

Fate, in the form of the French War Committee, interceded. The March 28 conference had agreed that the committee would have to concur with the plans, and it objected to ROYAL MARINE, fearing reprisal German bombing of France. London then balked at the operation against Norway without French approval. Resolving this matter led to postponement of the Norwegian operation until April 8.

The Germans had a rather accurate reading of British intentions. The British, however, failed to appreciate the fact that two could spring a trap, and they discounted intelligence reports of German plans to attack both Denmark and Norway (as a result, after the invasion the British formed the Joint Intelligence Committee). Certainly, the British did not divine the scale of the German operation, which involved virtually the entire German Navy. Even more curiously, the Norwegian government discounted alarming reports and failed to mobilize its forces. Indeed, Norwegian leaders were more concerned about British intentions than those of Germany.[36]

On April 7 an RAF aircraft sighted a German cruiser and seven destroyers 130 miles south of Cape Lindesnes, Norway, heading due north. At 5:00 a.m. on April 8 British destroyers laid a minefield at the entrance of the Vestfjord, north of Bodø, and an hour later British and French ministers delivered a note to the Norwegian government stating the intention of their governments to disrupt the passage of ships carrying 'contraband' through Norwegian territorial waters. Near midnight that day the Norwegian government received reports that 15 German warships had entered Oslo fjord and that other German ships were off

Bergen and Stavanger. The first shots were fired shortly after 4:00 a.m. on April 9 when two nineteenth-century Norwegian guns at the fortress of Oscarborg near Oslo opened fire on the German heavy cruiser *Blücher*. She was subsequently sunk by shore-launched torpedoes. The other German ships in the fjord, including the cruiser *Emden* and pocket battleship *Lützow*, turned back. By then the *Luftwaffe* was active, and it proved the key to German success in the Norwegian campaign. After morning fog had lifted, German transports landed at Oslo's Fornebu airport, disgorging troops who took the city. But the delay occasioned by the fog allowed both the Norwegian government and King Haakon VII to escape.[37]

As reports of German ship sightings in the North Sea arrived, British ships with troops aboard were ordered to return to port, offload the men, and then to steam out again to engage the German warships. The first contact between the two navies occurred quite by accident on April 8 when the British destroyer *Glowworm*, which had separated to look for a man overboard, encountered the German heavy cruiser *Hipper* and four destroyers bound for Trondheim with 1700 troops. Although fatally damaged by gunfire, the *Glowworm* went down fighting by ramming and badly damaging the *Hipper*.[38]

Although the Germans took Denmark in only a day, at a cost of 20 casualties, Norway proved more difficult. The Germans soon gained control of Oslo, Bergen, and Trondheim, as well as airfields on which to base their fighters and bombers. The advantage was immediately obvious, as RAF aircraft working from more distant British bases could not provide adequate cover for the Royal Navy ships and their few obsolete British carrier-based fighters. The *Luftwaffe* pounced on the smaller British ships and drove the Royal Navy out to sea, allowing their troops ashore to consolidate their positions, at least in southern Norway. This worked both ways, of course. On the morning of April 10, 15 Fleet Air Arm Skua bombers, flying from the Orkney Islands at the extreme limit of their range, attacked and sank at Bergen the German light cruiser *Königsberg*, the first major operational warship sunk by air attack in history. Also the British submarine *Truant* torpedoed the German light cruiser *Karlsruhe* in the Kattegat, damaging her so severely that she was scuttled.[39]

On the 9th, 10 large German destroyers entered the long approach to Narvik through Vestfjord undetected by British ships and landed some 2000 troops. The Royal Navy countered with 5 destroyers of the 2nd Destroyer Flotilla under Captain B. A. W. Warburton-Lee. After a difficult passage through snow storms up the Vestfjord, the destroyers reached Narvik at 4:00 a.m. on April 10, forced their way into the harbor, and attacked the unsuspecting Germans. The British sank two of the German ships and damaged three others. But five of the German destroyers escaped detection in nearby fjords and these appeared just as the British force was about to withdraw. Catching the British from both flanks, the German destroyers launched torpedoes that sank one British destroyer and disabled another, driving her ashore; Warburton-Lee was among those killed. Another British destroyer was badly damaged, but the Germans did not press their attack, and she and the other two ships escaped down the fjord to safety. Along the way they sank a German supply ship carrying ammunition.

The Admiralty was determined to finish off the German ships at Narvik, and on 13 April the battleship *Warspite* and nine destroyers were sent to do the job. Most of the German destroyers tried to escape into the fjords, where they were sunk or scuttled. In this Second Battle of Narvik, the Germans lost eight large destroyers and a U-boat, the latter bombed and sunk by a catapult aircraft from the *Warspite*. Two British destroyers were damaged, one heavily.

Although German forces ashore were now isolated and cut off, no Allied land forces were immediately available to capitalize on the situation. Finally, after Allied naval bombardment had failed to bring a German surrender, troops were landed on May 8 and carriers *Furious* and *Glorious* flew off RAF Hurricane fighters to be based on land. The Allies took Narvik on the 28th but mounting aircraft losses, the unsatisfactory situation elsewhere in the country, and the German invasion of France brought evacuation on June 7–8 of the 25,000 troops landed. The following day the Norwegian Army surrendered.

On the evening of June 8, the British aircraft carrier *Glorious* and two destroyers were caught unawares by the German battleships *Scharnhorst* and *Gneisenau* and sunk. The *Glorious* had on board six Swordfish aircraft, but she also had taken on Hurricane fighters, which impeded flight operations. One of the destroyers did manage, however, to damage *Scharnhorst* with a torpedo, and a few days later *Gneisenau* was hit and damaged by a torpedo from a British submarine. Both German capital ships were out of action for six months. All Allied troops evacuated from Vestfjord reached Britain safely. In the engagements at sea off Norway the British also damaged the German pocket battleship *Lützow*.[40]

The Norwegian campaign ruined the German surface navy; it lost 3 cruisers and 10 destroyers, half of the navy total, but Hitler had secured additional food production for the Reich and protection for his northern flank on the Baltic. Most important, the *Kriegsmarine* now had locations for naval bases nearer to the Allied Atlantic convoy routes. From these bases it would launch attacks into the North Atlantic and later the Allied PQ Arctic convoys bound for the Soviet Union.

The Germans set up a puppet state in Norway headed by home-grown Nazi Vidkun Quisling, whose very name became synonymous with traitor. King Haakon VII escaped abroad on June 7 and, after the Allies evacuated Narvik, he set up a government-in-exile in Britain. Most of the country's 4.7 million tons of merchant shipping now passed into Allied hands, an invaluable addition; in 1941 40 percent of foreign tonnage destined for English seaports was Norwegian. By 1944 Hitler had 365,000 of his best troops in Norway, providing security and protecting against invasion, but a serious drain on stretched German resources.[41]

Hitler's invasion of the west

Hitler's next stroke was against France and the Low Countries: the Netherlands, Belgium, and Luxembourg. He believed that defeating France offered the best chance of getting Britain to the peace table. The German attack, originally set for November 12, was repeatedly postponed as a consequence of bitter cold weather and pleas for more time from his generals. On January 10, 1940, the pilot of a German military aircraft flying from Munster to Köln became lost in dense fog and was forced to land near Mechelen-sur-Meuse, Belgium. This single event may have altered history. The passenger, Major Helmut Reinberger, was a staff officer of the 7th Airborne Division carrying top-secret operational plans for the German attack in the west. Reinberger was to have traveled by train but delays led him to fly. Although the two Germans tried to burn the papers, the Belgian police secured the bulk of them. This discovery was but one of a number of indications of a German plan to strike west that caused neutral Belgium to open talks with France and Britain. In any case, when Hitler learned that the invasion plan had been compromised, he abandoned it.[42]

The need to recast the plan now caused the invasion to be delayed until May. The new plan was drawn up by General Erich von Manstein, assisted by Generals Guderian and Walther Model. Known as the Cut of the Sickle (SICHELSCHNITT), it shifted the major effort from central Belgium to just north of the Maginot Line. The northern effort would occur first, drawing the Allies into Belgium. Then the major blow would fall to the south, in the hilly and wooded Ardennes – reputedly impassable for tanks.

The Germans planned to cross the Meuse River and crack the French lines at Sedan, then swing northwest to the Channel and cut off the best British and French divisions, which would have moved into Belgium. General von Bock's Army Group B, charged with invading Belgium and Holland, was downgraded from 37 divisions in the original plan to only 28 in the Manstein plan, and 3 rather than 8 panzer divisions. General von Rundstedt's Army Group A, which was to move through the Ardennes, was upgraded from 17 to 44 divisions, including 7 rather than one armor divisions. At the point of the breakthrough the Germans would outnumber the French, 44 divisions to 9.

The original plan was somewhat similar to the Schlieffen Plan of 1914 and would have followed Allied staff predictions. Its axis of advance would have encountered the best Franco-British forces and might thus have ended in failure. The Allies, at any rate, were certainly confident of success. Other factors apart from the plan working in the German favor were the experiences they had gained in Poland on the movement of massed armor and supply columns, air superiority, and a single nation system facing four separate national armies.[43]

When the campaign for France and the Low Countries began on 10 May 1940, Germany had assembled in the West 2.5 million men in 136 divisions: 118 infantry (41 in reserve), 10 armored, 7 motorized, and 1 cavalry. Only 10 divisions were in the East. The German western force was matched on the ground by a combined Allied force of more than 2 million men in 3 army groups of 138 divisions. France had 94 divisions: 63 infantry, 7 motorized infantry, 3 armored, 3 light mechanized, 5 cavalry, and 13 fortress divisions. Britain had 10 divisions, all infantry, plus other formations. In addition the Netherlands had 10 infantry divisions, and Belgium 23: 19 infantry, 2 cavalry, and 2 partially motorized. There was also one Polish division.[44]

The Allies actually outnumbered the Germans in tanks (perhaps 3600 to fewer than 2500). The mainstay of the German panzer divisions was still the PzKpfw II with a 20mm gun. There were fewer than 350 PzKpfw IIIs with a 37mm gun, and less than 300 PzKpfw IVs mounting a low-velocity 75mm gun. Of the Allied tanks, 310 were British: 210 light and 100 heavy (including 23 new Matildas). The British Matilda and Mark I, and the French Char B-1 all were a match for the best German tanks. The heavy Char B-1 was probably the best tank in any army in 1940. Heavily armored, it had a 47mm gun in a revolving turret; but its primary armament, a 75mm gun, was mounted in the hull, while the primary German tank guns were in turrets. Thus the crew of the Char B-1 had to turn the whole tank to aim and fire the main gun. The French

SOMUA S-35 tank also mounted the high-velocity 47mm gun, which had excellent penetrating power. Despite all the French production delays, there were some 800 Char B-1s and SOMUA S-35s, or more than the German PzKpfw IIIs and IVs. But few of the French vehicles had radios, forcing most crews to communicate by flags; thanks to Guderian, the German tanks were equipped with radio receivers, although only the command tanks had transmitters as well.

The major Allied problem was, however, in tactical employment. French tank tactics were a war behind. The first three French tank divisions did not assemble for training until January 1940, and each had half as many tanks as the panzer divisions they would have to face. The majority of the French tanks along the eastern frontier were split into packets of up to ten tanks apiece to serve as close infantry support.[45]

In their offensive the Germans relied heavily on joint arms, especially air support from their dive-bombers. As in Poland, the Stuka rendered valuable support to the armored and motorized infantry divisions. In sharp contrast, French tank formations lacked the air support critical to a ground victory. Indeed, the Battle for France was lost in the air. Against 1444 German bombers the French and the RAF could send aloft only 830 fighters. These would have to cope with 1264 German fighters, of which more than a thousand were Bf 109s. Overall, the two German air fleets deployed in the west mustered 3226 combat aircraft as well as some 400 Ju 52 troop carriers: 1016 fighters, 1368 bombers, 343 Stuka dive-bombers, and 500 reconnaissance aircraft. The *Armée de l'Air* and the RAF deployed about half that number. The French had 1147 combat aircraft, including 614 fighters, 170 bombers, and 363 reconnaissance aircraft. The RAF had only 416 of its 1873 combat aircraft in France: four fighter squadrons, four bomber squadrons, and five army cooperation squadrons. On May 15 Churchill committed another six fighter squadrons, much to the dismay of head of Fighter Command Air Marshal Hugh Dowding.[46]

The French aircraft were not that much off those of Germany in terms of quality. The Bloch MB 152 (second in numbers only to the Morane-Saulnier MS 406) had entered service only in 1939. Armed with two 20mm cannon and two 7.5mm machine guns, it was a stable gun platform with good maneuverability, but it was also slower than the Bf 109. The principal problem was that there were too few MB 152s – only about 80 were operational at the time of the German invasion. By the end of the battle for France, 270 MB 152s had been lost in action, having shot down 170 German aircraft. The best French fighter, the Dewoitine D 520, was armed with one 20mm cannon and four 7.5mm machine guns. With a top speed of 329 mph, it was roughly comparable to the Bf-109. Its abilities had been demonstrated several weeks before, on April 21, when the French tested one against a Bf 109E that had been forced down undamaged on French soil. The D 520 was similar to the British Spitfire in that it was inferior in speed to the Bf 109 but had a decided edge in maneuverability. During the Battle of France D 520 fighter pilots claimed a 3:1 kill ratio but there were far too few of them at the front for France, only 37 in May 1940 at the start of the battle. Had the campaign gone differently, the D 520 might have been remembered as one of the premier fighters of the war.[47]

The problem for the Allies lay in numbers of aircraft. Although more than 20 months had elapsed since the débâcle of Munich and eight months since the German attack on Poland, on May 10, 1940, the nationalized French aircraft industry was still manufacturing only 60 planes a month. It was a matter of too little, too late. As the French possessed so few fighter aircraft, it might be assumed that they would counter that deficiency in anti-aircraft weapons. But while the *Luftwaffe* had 72 anti-aircraft (AA) regiments, France had five. France was also short of the 25mm and 40mm guns essential to protect infantry from the German dive-bombers. The *Luftwaffe* fielded 9300 guns – 6700 light 20mm and 37mm – and 2600 heavy motorized 88mm anti-aircraft guns. The French had 1500 anti-aircraft pieces, of which only 17 were new 90mm guns.[48]

Resources had been available. What had been lacking was the foresight to expend them properly. Beginning in 1929 the French spent 5 billion francs on approximately 87 miles of the Maginot Line. Not a solid line, it was a series of forts, each of which was within mutually supporting range to provide an interlocking field of fire. Mobile troops protected the intervals. The line's artillery was mounted in 132 retractable and 2533 fixed turrets. The largest guns were 135mm howitzers and there were only 43 of these in the entire line and only 344 artillery pieces in all, a surprisingly small number considering the length of the front. The majority of the guns were relatively light 75mms (169), mounted singly or in pairs, and shorter range 81mm mortars (132). There were no attached AA positions. The Maginot Line was never considered impregnable but was designed to release French manpower and act as a kind of brake, preventing the Germans from exploiting a breakthrough as long as the forts remained intact.[49]

Actually, the line did what it was supposed to in 1940, forcing the Germans northward. Any advantage to the French was, however, more than offset by Belgium's retreat into neutrality, the lack of effective coordination between the French and the British Expeditionary Force

(BEF), and most importantly, the failure of the mobile portion of the French Army. Had the French been thinking offensively, the Maginot Line might have served as a secure base for French thrusts into the Rhineland in September 1939 or in the spring of 1940.

The Allies faced other problems. Their advance into Belgium would cause them to leave prepared and more easily defended positions in order to meet an advancing enemy on territory that had been neutral the day before. There was also the appallingly inadequate French military leadership, especially in 68-year-old army commander General Maurice Gamelin and many of his senior commanders, who tended to think in 1918 terms. Events might also have turned out differently had there been adequate reserves to deal with the German breakthrough. In addition, the principal German thrust in the Ardennes struck an area that was only weakly held by the French. General André-Georges Corap's Ninth Army was expected to hold a front of more than 50 miles, but Corap had only 9.5 divisions: a screen of two light cavalry divisions and a Spahi brigade and seven infantry divisions, only two of which were of regulars. Most of the men were reservists, and older reservists at that, and they were commanded by generals brought back from retirement.

French military intelligence was also dismal. Ample information was available to suggest an impending German offensive in the Ardennes. The failure of French Ninth Army headquarters to determine its magnitude in the face of mounting evidence almost passes belief. The Germans had positioned the largest concentration of armor thus far in war, and the panzer commanders were only too well aware of the lucrative targets presented by the densely packed German columns. The French later attributed their failure in aerial reconnaissance over the Eifel to inferior aircraft and bad weather. Mesmerized by the German assault against the Netherlands in the first three days of the campaign, Gamelin failed to act in the Ardennes. By the morning of May 11, both French and British pilots had reported mounting evidence of what was to unfold there, but no action was taken. The French intelligence service, the Deuxième Bureau, had no idea of true panzer strength. Still, the German advance might have been stopped or delayed had the French sowed mines or even felled trees. But army headquarters had ordered roads in the Ardennes left clear so as not to impede maneuver of horse cavalry, and the French were now forced to contend with tanks and twice the force that had been expected.[50]

On May 10, the same day that the Germans launched their offensive, the British government collapsed. Chamberlain, already under heavy pressure for the Allied failure in Norway, now resigned, and a new government took over headed by Churchill, actually the principal architect of the Norwegian débâcle. Churchill's new coalition government came into office determined to act resolutely. In effect, May 10 was when Britain really went to war.

The German offensive now went forward both north and south. In the north, where Army Group B had responsibility for the attack against the Netherlands, the Germans committed the bulk of their airborne forces (4000 of 4500 men), supported by a 12,000-man light infantry division carried in transport aircraft. Striking 100 miles behind the border, they attacked the Dutch capital of The Hague and key bridges at Rotterdam and other places. Securing the bridges until German mobile forces could come up was essential to the entire offensive. The attack on The Hague was foiled, but the Germans took the key bridges across the Rhine estuary and held them at the surprisingly small cost of only 180 casualties. Among the latter was airborne commander Major General Kurt Student, who suffered a head wound and was sidelined for eight months.

The 9th Panzer Division, the only armored force available, then drove across the Dutch border and linked up with the special forces at Rotterdam on the third day. Near Breda, German advance elements ran into units of General Henri Giraud's French Seventh Army and drove them back toward Antwerp. Queen Wilhemina and her government, meanwhile, escaped by ship to Britain, where they set up yet another government-in-exile. The *Luftwaffe*, which had control of the skies, pounded Rotterdam and reduced much of the business district to rubble as an inducement to speed peace negotiations. The Netherlands, victim of the new warfare, capitulated on May 14, the fifth day of the offensive.[51]

The invasion of Belgium saw an even more spectacular example of the new technique of vertical envelopment. Here General Walther von Reichenau's Sixth Army faced a formidable barrier as, once German forces had crossed into the Netherlands, Belgian defenders would have ample time to blow two key bridges over the Albert Canal. Also barring the way was the formidable bastion of Fortress Eben Emael, the key to securing Belgium. Hitler himself developed the plan, which Reichenau and his chief of staff General Friedrich Paulus greeted with considerable skepticism. To carry out Hitler's plan General Student assigned his remaining 500 paratroopers to take the fort and two bridges over the canal. Eben Emael and its 1200-man garrison was taken with what seemed an impossibly small force of 78 men. Landing directly on top of the fort itself in gliders, the Germans used 56 hollow-charge explosives to blow up its armored turrets and casemates. The tiny attacking force thus secured its objective in only 28 hours. The vital bridges at Veldwezelt and Vrownhoven were also taken by *coup de main*, and by May 11 the Sixth Army was free to advance. Its tanks took Liège the next day.[52]

The Belgian Army retired to the Dyle (River) Line, where it was met by advancing elements of the BEF and General Georges Blanchard's French First Army north of the Sambre River. This plan, developed by Gamelin, left substantial French resources in the Maginot Line and a 100-mile swath of the Ardennes largely uncovered. By May 15 some 35 Allied divisions occupied the Namur-Antwerp area. As elements of German General Georg von Küchler's Eighteenth Army turned south from the Netherlands to threaten the left of the Allied line, alarming reports arrived of the main German drive to the south.

The southern attack went forward simultaneously with the German drive in the north, but the difficult terrain of the Ardennes and calculated delay to draw the best Allied units to the north meant that it was not until May 12 that Rundstedt's Army Group A, spearheaded by Guderian's XIX Panzer Corps, reached the Meuse. The French were handicapped by the fact that General André Corap's Ninth Army and General Charles Huntziger's Second Army had their weakest forces in the Stenay Gap area. The French were stymied by their inability to mount meaningful counterattacks and by the generally poor discipline of their troops in that sector. Desperate, Corap and Huntziger sought to establish a defense along the Meuse, but Corap was slow to move and Huntziger was outflanked.

Early on May 13 Major General Erwin Rommel's 7th Panzer Division of XV Corps began crossing the Meuse at Dinat. Supported by devastatingly accurate Stuka dive-bombing of French artillery positions, the advancing Germans also crossed at Haux and at Monthermé, then expanded their bridgeheads. To all intents and purposes the struggle for France was over on the 15th when the German breakout occurred. Once the German panzer divisions had broken through, the way was clear for them to drive to the English Channel and cut off the main Allied armies in Belgium. Spearheaded by their flying artillery, the panzers surged forward along a 50-mile wide front. Gamelin ordered up reserves and formed a new army, the Sixth under General Robert Touchon, to try to seal the gap. Giraud also took over Ninth Army from the ineffective Corap, but his forces were badly mauled by the Germans on May 17 and Giraud himself was captured. During May 17–19 Colonel de Gaulle scored the only French successes of the battle when he flung his 4th Armored Division in three successive thrusts against the southern flank of the German advance from Laon. Aided by air power, the Germans blunted the Allied attacks and swept on.

Too late, Premier Reynaud dismissed Gamelin as commander of the army, replacing him with General Maxime Weygand, recalled from Syria. Weygand took up his duties on May 19. Two days later the German southern thrust turned northward in three prongs as General Günther von Kluge's Fourth Army, Reichenau's Sixth, and Küechler's Eighteenth pressed from the east against the Belgians, the BEF, and Blanchard's First Army. General Lord Gort, commanding the BEF to the left of the First Army, sent forces south behind the French to try to counter the German thrust at Arras, but Rommel's 7th Division repulsed them on May 21. The Germans reached Abbeville on May 20 and the English Channel the next day. By May 24, the Germans had captured the port of Boulogne and isolated Calais, forcing the BEF to rely on Dunkirk for resupply. Allied forces in Belgium were now cut off from the bulk of the French forces to the south as the Germans relentlessly tightened their ring.

Confusion marked the Allied High Command, Units could not be located and communication was at best tenuous, but there was also the diversity of national interest overtaken by events. In these circumstances, on May 21 Weygand began assembling an effort to cut off the German southern armored column. He ordered Gort to attack south against the German armor thrust while the French struck northward. Churchill seconded this, ordering Gort to attack with 'about eight divisions.' This would have been in effect a last throw of the dice, but poor Allied coordination postponed any effort until May 26 at the earliest, and by that date it was clear to Gort that the Belgians were collapsing. In one of the most important decisions of the war, Gort refused both sets of orders, called off the southward strike, abandoned Arras, and withdrew British forces northwestward to the coast.[53]

Meanwhile, the Belgian Army, which held the Allied left, was steadily ground down under relentless German attacks. Despite promises that his nation would not undertake any such unilateral action, King Leopold III now surrendered his forces without coordinating this decision with the very allies who had not hesitated to come to his nation's rescue. The unconditional surrender of Belgian forces at 4:00 a.m. on May 28 opened a totally undefended 30-mile gap between the BEF left and the sea. Through this the Germans now poured, threatening to cut off the BEF entirely.

Concurrently, Hitler intervened in his first major military blunder of the war. On May 24 he halted the German armored thrust from the south, with the panzers within striking range of the last British escape ports on the Channel, and he kept them in place for three days. This 'stop order' originated with General Rundstedt, who worried that the tanks had covered too much ground too quickly and were overextended, but Hitler made it a firm order. This action saved the BEF and probably enabled Britain to continue in the war. Hitler took this decision in consequence of his own isolation from events; from his headquarters he could not sense the extent of the Allied collapse. He saw the French armies as still intact and assumed their paper strength to be their actual strength. As the Chief of the General Staff, General Halder, noted in his diary, 'The Führer is terribly nervous. He is frightened by his own success, is unwilling to take any risks and is trying to hold us back.' Halder noted, 'every hour is precious,' but Hitler believed that the German advance had gone too well and that a halt would enable concentration of tank strength for the final push and would also allow infantry to come up in support. Their presence would minimize armor losses, and in any case the tanks would be needed in the subsequent drive south to defeat France.[54]

Göring asked Hitler that the task of destroying the British ground forces be left to the *Luftwaffe* and its dive-bombers. He even requested that German panzers be pulled back several miles to leave the area clear for the *Luftwaffe*. The German Air Force had not received much credit for its brilliant efforts in Poland and the western offensive, and Göring believed it could now destroy the escape hatch of Dunkirk and pin the British against the Channel. Hitler concurred.[55]

During the period May 27–June 4 the British carried out an epic evacuation at Dunkirk. Naval commanders hoped to bring off at most 40,000 men; but in Operation DYNAMO they evacuated 364,628 troops, of whom 224,686 were British. All sorts of vessels, many manned by civilian volunteers, participated in the evacuation. RAF fighter pilots, flying from bases in southern England, did what they could and probably made the evacuation possible. British destroyers rescued the most men but they were also the chief targets for *Luftwaffe* attacks, and by the fourth day of the evacuation 10 had been sunk or put out of action. Such losses induced the Admiralty to make the difficult decision to remove all modern destroyers from the operation. The same reasoning limited the number of fighter aircraft available. Head of Fighter Command Air Marshal Dowding refused to sacrifice valuable aircraft in a battle already lost. He believed that his aircraft would be desperately needed for the defense of Britain, certain to be the next target.[56]

The Dunkirk evacuation was aided by bad weather and fires from burning equipment on the beaches. Before it was over the BEF had lost in France more than 68,000 men killed, captured, or wounded, including at least 2000 during DYNAMO itself; RAF Fighter Command lost 106 aircraft and 80 pilots; and Bomber Command an additional 76 aircraft. Of 693 British vessels in the operation, a third (226) were sunk, including six destroyers; 19 other destroyers were put of action. Other nations lost 17 of the 168 vessels taking part. The BEF was forced to abandon in France virtually all its equipment but, thanks to Hitler's ill-timed interference, it escaped largely intact as far as personnel were concerned.[57]

On June 4, as the last British troops were being evacuated, Winston Churchill appeared before Parliament. In his remarks Churchill did not seek to minimize the disaster ('wars are not won by evacuations'), but he said that Britain would continue on, if necessary alone, and he outlined steps being taken to prepare Britain for invasion. Churchill then issued this challenge:

> Even though large tracts of Europe and many old and famous States have fallen or may fall into the grip of the Gestapo and all the odious apparatus of Nazi rule, we shall not flag or fail. We shall go on to the end, we shall fight in France, we shall fight on the seas and oceans, we shall fight with growing confidence and growing strength in the air, we shall defend our Island, whatever the cost may be, we shall fight on the beaches, we shall fight on the landing grounds, we shall fight in the fields and in the streets, we shall fight in the hills; we shall never surrender, and even if, which I do not for a moment believe, this Island or a large part of it were subjugated and starving, then our Empire beyond the sea, armed and guarded by the British Fleet, would carry on the struggle, until in God's good time, the New World, with all its power and might, steps forth to the rescue and liberation of the old.[58]

In Britain the evacuation swept away the 'phoniness' of the war, but the British also falsely believed that they had been betrayed by others. Many were oblivious to the fact that in May 1918 there had been ten times the number of British divisions in France than in May 1940, that the British evacuation had left the French in the lurch, or that the French First Army had held the Germans from the beaches and allowed them to get away. The French troops contested every bit of ground, and ultimately between 30,000 and 40,000 of its 50,000 men were forced to surrender. The First Army's record shows what might have been accomplished had the French been blessed with better leaders and a proper military doctrine.[59]

On June 5 Army Group B struck south from the Somme. It cut through the French Tenth Army and reached the Seine River west of Paris four days later. Although the French managed to make good a surprisingly high proportion of their earlier heavy aircraft losses through US deliveries and increased production, especially of the Dewoitine D 520, much of their army, stunned by developments and unprepared for improvised action, simply disintegrated. On the 10th Rundstedt's Army Group A hit the French Fourth Army east of Paris and broke through at Châlons. That same day the French government abandoned Paris for the Bordeaux in the southwest. On the 13th the government declared Paris an open city to spare it the fate of Warsaw and Rotterdam, and the next day German troops took peaceful possession of the capital.

French Premier Reynaud pleaded with Churchill to send the bulk of the RAF to France to join in the battle. Churchill at first agreed to send six squadrons, but based on Dowding's dire warning to the Air Ministry that he had the equivalent of only 36 squadrons when 52 were deemed necessary to defend Britain, Churchill agreed to a compromise that the planes would operate out of bases in Britain.[60]

On June 12 Weygand concluded that the situation was hopeless and so informed the cabinet. Reynaud refused to adopt the plan advocated by Undersecretary of State for War Brigadier General de Gaulle, appointed to that post only on June 5, for a fighting retreat to a redoubt in Brittany or transfer of the government and armed forces to North Africa. Most of the cabinet members believed that the total occupation of France was inevitable and some urged an immediate armistice, but Reynaud expressed his determination to continue the fight.

On June 10 Mussolini, convinced that the war was all but won, brought his country into the conflict on the German side by invading southeastern France. On paper at least, Italy seemed to have considerable military strength. Thanks to the influence of the air prophet Guilio Douhet, Italy placed great reliance on air power, but given time from design to production for aircraft of some six years, its air force peaked too early. Even in 1934, when he took over as chief of staff of the air force, General Francesco Pricolo complained that the air force, instead of leading the world as Mussolini claimed, was actually 'at the level of a Balkan state.'[61]

The Italian Navy was far more impressive. In June 1940 the *Supermarina* boasted four reconstructed World War I battleships, two new battleships, and two others under construction. It also had a seaplane carrier, 7 heavy cruisers, 12 light cruisers, 57 destroyers, 25 torpedo boats, and 113 submarines. Fuel was a major problem, however.

In June 1940 the Italian Navy had oil sufficient for only nine months of full, continuous operations.[62]

The Italian Army was essentially a light infantry force lacking in *matériel*. In 1940 it numbered 73 divisions (43 infantry; 5 Alpine; 3 light; 2 motorized; 3 armored; 12 'self-transportable,' with a regiment of truck-drawn artillery; 3 militia; and 2 Lybian). Many Italian formations were understrength and much of their equipment was obsolescent or worse. Many, if not most, Italians thought their nation was on the wrong side, and as a result Italian troops were poorly motivated. The men were also indifferently led, with many high officer appointments made on the basis of political reliability. Having said this, many Italian Army units distinguished themselves in fighting in North Africa and the Soviet Union.[63]

Following Mussolini's declaration of war, 32 Italian divisions attacked five French divisions in the Alpes-Maritimes. Despite their great numerical advantage, the Italians made little headway. The Germans derisively turned down Italian pleas for an air-drop of Italian troops behind the French lines to justify bigger Italian claims in the armistice. Italy captured only 13 villages, and in the whole of this Alpine campaign France admitted to 37 soldiers killed and Italy to 631. As Italian Foreign Minister Galeazzo Ciano commented, the armistice came just in time to save appearances before the facts became generally known.[64]

Some combatants thought that the armistice saved Italy from a French invasion. Mussolini blamed his soldiers and the Italian people in general for not being worthy of him. He told his son-in-law, 'It is the material that I lack. Even Michelangelo had need of marble to make statues. If he had only clay he would have been nothing more than a potter. A people who for sixteen centuries have been an anvil cannot become a hammer within a few years.'[65]

French Premier Reynaud had pledged to continue the fight, but he turned down an offer from Churchill, suggested to him by Jean Monnet and De Gaulle, of an 'indissoluble union' of France and Britain. The French armies were fast disintegrating. As other German forces swept west, south, and east, armored columns raced to secure the remaining northern French ports. On June 16, after the Germans had captured Verdun and begun cutting off the Maginot Line from the rear and had also penetrated it in frontal assaults from the north and east, Reynaud was forced to resign and a majority of the cabinet voted to ask Hitler for terms. Reynaud recommended to President Albert Lebrun that he appoint as premier 84-year-old Marshal Philippe Pétain. The World War

I hero had been brought into the government as deputy premier in order to bolster French resolve, but he now supported an immediate armistice.

On June 17 German columns crossed the Loire River and the Germans cut off French units in the Maginot Line. That same day the Pétain government opened negotiations with the Germans and, on June 22, as German forces captured Lyons, Hitler received the French delegates in the very railroad car at Compiègne in which Marshal Foch had announced to the Germans the armistice terms of 1918. Two days later the French signed an armistice with Italy. Fighting ceased on the battlefields of France on June 25. Germany's defeat of France must rank as one of the most important military events of the twentieth century. In the campaign Germany lost 27,000 men, with another 18,000 missing, and 111,000 wounded. Britain suffered 68,000 casualties, Belgium 23,000, and the Netherlands 10,000. France lost 90,000 men dead and 200,000 wounded. Another two million men, 5 percent of its population, were prisoners, not to be released until the signing of a peace treaty. France was divided into occupied and unoccupied zones and its army was reduced to 100,000 officers and men, exactly the figure left to Germany under the terms of the Versailles Treaty in 1919. The navy, almost entirely intact, remained under French control but was to be disarmed in French ports. Hitler later complained that he had made a serious mistake in not demanding that it be turned over to Germany. France also had to pay for the German occupation of three-fifths of its territory.[66]

Paris was included in the German occupation zone so the new French government established itself at Vichy, a resort town in south central France. The new government was frankly totalitarian. Pétain and his advisors believed that Germany had won the war and that, at least for the foreseeable future, France would be under German control. Some, including the opportunistic politician now Premier Pierre Laval, were more proactive and sought open collaboration with the Germans; Laval thought it only a matter of time before Britain itself was defeated. On July 9 French legislators voted to establish an authoritarian government. 'Liberty, Equality, and Fraternity' was banned from official use to be replaced by the Fascist slogan of 'Work, Family, and Fatherland.'[67]

It took something akin to clairvoyance in the dark days of June 1940 to see ahead to a possible Allied victory, but despite seemingly impossible odds a small number of Frenchmen and Frenchwomen vowed to continue the fight and took the lead in forming what became the Resistance. Some made it out of France to Britain. In London, on June 18, young Brigadier General de Gaulle, only a few days before undersecretary of war and the only French military leader of note to make it out, announced over the British Broadcasting Corporation (BBC) the establishment of the Free French. De Gaulle soon secured British military assistance and, ultimately, recognition of his government. The Vichy government sentenced him to death *in absentia*.

Many Frenchmen blamed their nation's military defeat on poor French morale, the communists, or faulty equipment. Others assumed it was inevitable. In fact, the collapse of French morale had come only after the German breakthrough. The defeat was less a matter of equipment than failures in doctrine and leadership and bitter divisions within French society. Historian Guy Chapman noted the absence in France of any military doctrine: 'The excision of the offensive from the regulations had destroyed the facility of initiative. Nothing was left except the passive defensive.'[68]

The French had seen the campaign as a battle of position, the Germans as one of movement. As German Major General Friedrich von Mellenthin observed, the Germans had concentrated their tanks in divisions and developed a theory of high-speed mobile warfare based on surprise and exploitation of circumstances, while the Allies had divided their tanks up along the entire front. Not only had the Allied generals refused to accept the new theory but, worse, they failed to take adequate steps to counteract it. In contrast to their Allied counterparts, German generals led from the front and were thus positioned to take advantage of circumstances. Also the Germans understood the importance of combined arms – tanks, motorized infantry, and artillery all working in tandem – a lesson the British did not learn until well into 1942. German air power had played a key role, as had poor French morale. It is, however, hard to dispute Mellenthin's conclusion that the defeat of France in 1940 was a 'military masterpiece, worthy to rank beside the greatest campaigns of the greatest generals in history.'[69]

Unfortunately for the Germans, their brilliant victory led them to overlook equipment shortages and shortcomings as well as the relatively short distances the Blitzkrieg had encountered in Poland, France, and the Low Countries. It would encounter a very different situation on the steppes of Russia.

Mers-el-Kébir

Churchill feared above all that the Germans would acquire the French fleet. The French government had promised London that it would scuttle its ships rather than see them fall into German hands, but this pledge was not sufficient for Churchill, who also sought a dramatic gesture to convince Washington – where there were many who believed Britain would soon have to give up – that the British were committed to continuing the war. The result was Operation CATAPULT.

Orders went out from Whitehall for CATAPULT to commence on July 3, 1940. Royal Navy commanders were instructed to offer counterpart French commanders the choice of continuing the fight, sailing their ships to neutral ports where they would be disarmed, or scuttling them. If the French refused, the British were to sink the ships. In several locations the operation went well from the British point of view. They acquired, with but one French seaman killed, warships at Portsmouth, Plymouth, and Gibraltar. After difficult negotiations, French ships at Alexandria were interned, as was the case for French warships in the West Indies. This was not the case in Algeria or Dakar. On July 3 at the French naval base of Mers-el-Kébir near Oran, French commander Vice-Admiral Marcel Bruno Gensoul refused compliance with Force H commander Vice-Admiral Sir James Somerville's request, and British battleships *Valiant* and *Resolution* and battle cruiser *Hood* opened fire. The aircraft carrier *Ark Royal* conducted air operations. British gunfire sank the battleship *Bretagne* and forced the beaching of battleship *Provence* to prevent her sinking. British fire also sank several large French destroyers and severely damaged the modern battle cruiser *Dunkerque*. Modern battle cruiser *Strasbourg* reached the sea and made it to Toulon and safety. In the 'battle,' 1297 French seamen died and another 351 were wounded. At Dakar, British aircraft and naval gunfire damaged the uncompleted battleship *Richelieu*.

CATAPULT led to considerable French bitterness toward Britain that lingers even today. Despite what transpired in July 1940, the French government honored its pledge more than two years later. When in November 1942 the Germans tried to seize the bulk of the French Navy, 80 ships assembled at Toulon, the French scuttled 77 of them. CATAPULT made it more difficult for the Allies to rally the French Empire to their side; indeed, the Vichy government now broke off diplomatic relations with Britain and carried out minor air strike against Gibraltar. Still, from the British perspective CATAPULT had been a success. In the operation the British acquired some 130 French ships, including 2 battleships, 4 light cruisers, 8 destroyers, and 5 submarines.[70]

The Germans now dominated the Continent. They were emphatically the senior partner in the German-Italian combination, and they were on good terms with Franco in Spain, while Russia was benevolently neutral. History seemed to repeat itself, for the Germans now controlled almost exactly the geographic area as had Napoleon, and in 1940 as in 1807 only Great Britain remained at war with the would-be Continental conqueror.

The role of the United States

Churchill promised his countrymen nothing but 'blood, toil, tears and sweat.' He pledged implacable war, and to the Americans he said, 'Give us the tools and we will finish the job.' The United States now began to respond.[71]

Even before 1939 the US government had been anything but neutral. President Franklin Roosevelt was convinced that American security was endangered by European events, and he tried to rally national opinion by declaring that the United States might openly assist the Allies without itself fighting, by using measures short of war. In November 1939 American neutrality legislation had been amended with a repeal of the ban on arms sales. Roosevelt described the British Empire as 'the spearhead of resistance to world conquest,' and the United States as 'the great arsenal of democracy.'[72]

Roosevelt was aided in his stance by Wendell Willkie, his Republican opponent in the presidential election of 1940. Also an internationalist, Willkie took a position close to that of Roosevelt. Yet it was the ominous situation in Europe that had convinced Roosevelt to run for a third term, though he faced an American public that was still strongly isolationist and thus proceeded carefully.

Britain now awaited a German attack. When Churchill appealed to Roosevelt for military assistance, the US reaction was immediate and extraordinary. Within days 600 freight cars were on their way to US ports filled with military equipment to be loaded aboard British merchant ships. These included half a million rifles and 900 old 75mm field guns.[73]

On June 15 Churchill made a direct appeal to Roosevelt for 35 old US destroyers. With Germany controlling both the Channel ports and Norway, Britain faced the prospect of German invasion with but 68 destroyers fit for service, a stark contrast to the 433 destroyers the Royal Navy had in service in 1918. Britain's shipping lanes were even more vulnerable to German submarines with the fall of France, and Italy's entry into the war had made the Mediterranean an area of difficult passage. As Churchill put it to Roosevelt, 'We must ask therefore as a matter of life or death, to be reinforced with these destroyers.' Over the next days and weeks, as the number of these warships continued to dwindle, Churchill's appeal grew to 50–60 destroyers. Roosevelt's insistence on proceeding with the aid was taken against the advice of Army Chief of Staff General George C. Marshall and Chief of Naval Operations Admiral Harold Stark, who believed that Britain was doomed and that such a step would leave America militarily naked before new production could materialize.[74]

With American public opinion strongly opposed to US intervention, Roosevelt masked the transfer in a deal, announced in an executive order of September 3, 1940, not subject to congressional approval. Britain received 50 World War I-vintage destroyers in return for granting the United States rights to bases in Newfoundland, Bermuda, and the British Caribbean Islands. Actually, the United States got far more than it gave in the Destroyers for Bases Deal. The destroyers were in wretched condition, some barely making it across the Atlantic. But they were a tremendous morale boost for the British at a critical juncture and Churchill saw this as another step by the United States toward outright participation. Privately, Hitler saw this in much the same light. Anxious to unleash Japan in Asia to occupy the United States, he ordered talks opened with Japan that had culminated in the September 27 Tripartite Pact. The long war, a clash involving continents that would give advantage to nations with superior sea power, drew closer to realization.[75]

3

The Limits of German Power

Britain now appeared to be in grave peril. The bulk of the 12 BEF divisions that had been on the Continent returned to Britain, joining 15 other divisions (six formed only in May), still only partially trained. In early June there was only one properly equipped and trained division, Major General Bernard Montgomery's 3rd, to defend the British Isles. BEF equipment abandoned in France included 120,000 vehicles, 600 tanks, 1000 field guns, 500 anti-aircraft guns, 850 anti-tank guns, 8000 Bren guns, 90,000 rifles, and half a million tons of stores and ammunition. The army had only about 500 artillery pieces and a like number of tanks, half of them light models. There was one tank battalion of 50 infantry tanks, with the remaining tanks scattered at training schools. The fleet was far to the north, away from the *Luftwaffe*. As Churchill put it, 'Never has a great nation been so naked before her foes.'[1]

In contrast, the German Army numbered 114 divisions and 2000 tanks. If its forces could have landed in Britain in the weeks after the Dunkirk Evacuation there would have been little means of stopping them. But Hitler and his military chiefs were caught off guard by the speed of the French defeat and had no plans for a follow-up invasion of Britain. Not until late July did the Germans begin planning for a descent on England, codenamed SEALION (*Seelöwe*). The Naval Staff claimed that sufficient shipping could not be ready before mid-September at the earliest and that convoying the 13 divisions of an invading first wave to Britain would require 155 transports and more than 3000 smaller craft: 1720 barges, 470 tugs, and 1160 motorboats.[2]

Following the late June defeat of France, Hitler postponed any decision regarding Britain, traveling to Paris – his only visit there – to savor his triumph. Hitler had halfway expected that Britain would not go to war in September 1939. He now hoped and expected that the British people, whom he grudgingly admired and assumed to be rational, would sense the inevitable and agree to peace. The war was over and Germany had won. But the British, who to this point had fought the war in almost leisurely fashion, did not agree. Some of his generals did urge Hitler to strike Britain before it could reorganize and build up its strength. Immediately after Dunkirk, *Luftwaffe* General Erhard Milch pleaded with Hitler to send *Luftwaffe* units to take and hold airheads in southern England from which, as in Norway, Stukas and other German aircraft could operate. Milch stated prophetically, 'If we leave the British in peace for four weeks it will be too late.' Hitler was then preoccupied with the campaign in France, and he believed that the British would soon come round.[3]

On June 3 RAF Fighter Command, which had lost more than 400 planes over France, had only 413 serviceable aircraft: 79 Blenheim bombers, 162 Spitfires, 163 Hurricanes, and 9 Defiants. By mid-July it was up to 650 machines. *Luftwaffe* strength at the time in Field Marshal Albert Kesselring's *Luftflotte* 2 and Field Marshal Hugo Sperrle's *Luftflotte* 3 was perhaps 1480 bombers and dive-bombers and 980 fighters, as well as 140 reconnaissance aircraft.[4]

Even when formal orders were issued for SEALION, German preparations were half-hearted. This was in part because of the sheer magnitude of the operation but also because of the formidable nature of the English Channel. A relatively small stretch of water – 21 miles wide at the narrowest point – the Channel can be extraordinarily rough and unpleasant; high seas come up quickly and the water is shallow with rapid current. At its narrowest the Channel is never more than 216 feet deep and for half of the distance across it is under 100 feet deep. The combination of Channel narrowness and lack of depth, as well as an attack on a lee shore in the full force of prevailing winds would make any invasion a formidable undertaking.

In order to prevent any successful lodgement of German forces, Britain would have to commit all available naval and air assets. Thus German command of the air was the necessary prerequisite for any invasion. Göring, to whom this task now fell, was confident. He predicted that a massive three-day *Luftwaffe* effort against British airfields and radar sites would force aloft the remaining RAF planes so they could be destroyed.[5]

Official British dates for the Battle of Britain are July 10 to October 31, 1940.[6] The battle began with *Luftwaffe* aircraft attacking Channel shipping, and here the Stuka proved particularly effective. Beginning on July 10 and continuing until August 7, the *Luftwaffe* conducted fighter sweeps along the Channel approaches and against land targets. The next phase, from August 8–23, saw German attacks near the coast in south

England and strikes against ground installations, radar stations, and the aircraft industry. The final phase of the battle, August 24 to October 31, consisted of attacks on the London area and other targets designed to affect civilian morale. The Germans, however, never achieved their goal of driving the RAF from the skies.

Why did the Germans fail? Göring's lack of leadership was one factor. He wore many hats, including that of oversight over the German war economy, and he was involved in the battle only in fits and starts, often intervening without knowledge of the actual situation. The former World War I ace did not understand the tactical problems his pilots faced, and he attributed *Luftwaffe* losses to a lack of fighting spirit in his pilots, something that did not sit well with the aircrews.[7]

The Germans also believed their own intelligence reports, which consistently overestimated their effectiveness. In fairness, the British had the same problem. But the Germans shifted their attention from radar masts and vector stations to airfields just as they were rendering Fighter Command blind. Raids then moved prematurely from airfields to London and industrial centers. The early shift from attacks against shipping in the Channel approaches was another major blunder.

The British also enjoyed an excellent early warning system composed of signals intelligence, radar, and a ground observation corps. Ultra provided advance warning of some raids. Radar – an acronym for RAdio Detection And Ranging – played a key role. A radar station is basically a radio transmitter sending out an electromagnetic wave, and a receiving unit. When the waves encounter a dense object, such as an aircraft, they are reflected back to the receiver. The elapsed time between the transmission and its receipt provides the range to the target. The British then led the world in radar technology, and one author contends that this enabled the British to win the Battle of Britain and the Allies to win the war. Radar provided advance warning of the size and direction of the German bomber streams, allowing British fighters to scramble and intercept them. The third leg of coastal watchers was also important. Armed with binoculars, observers provided tallies of German aircraft and their types. This British warning system worked to maximize the effectiveness of RAF fighters, which now rose from airfields in Essex, Sussex, and Kent to inflict losses on the Germans of two and three to one.[8]

In addition to radar and codebreaking the British achieved a number of other scientific successes important to the Allied war effort. These included the hollow-charge warhead, which would lead to an anti-tank weapon in the hands of the infantry, and the jet engine. Throughout the war the British also excelled in camouflage and deception. During the Battle of Britain their dummy (Q and K) airfield sites drew a large number of German air strikes, exploding much German ordnance harmlessly.[9]

One great disadvantage for the Germans in the Battle of Britain was the short range of their aircraft. The Bf 109 had a cruising range of only 100 miles and tactical flying time of only 80 minutes. Counting time to target and return, a German pilot had at best 20 minutes over England, forcing many German planes to crash, out of fuel, short of their bases. This short fighter range also prevented German bombers from striking British airfields north of London.[10]

Germany's crash building program before the war also meant that many of its aircraft over Britain in 1940 were more obsolescent than the British fighters they faced (in February 1940 Göring halted developmental work in favor of current production). But the chief problem confronting the Germans was trying to make a tactical air force work at the strategic level. Britain also dramatically increased aircraft production. Between 1939 and 1940 the Germans improved production by 20 percent, the British by 80 percent.[11]

Minister of Aircraft Production Maxwell Aitken, Lord Beaverbrook, oversaw an effort between July and December 1940 that put 4196 damaged British planes back on line. Of aircraft participating in the Battle of Britain, fully a third were repaired machines. The number of aircraft available to Fighter Command continued to increase throughout the battle: 413 on June 3, 602 on June 30, and 675 on August 1. The Germans believed that RAF fighter losses by mid-August had reduced Fighter Command to only approximately 300 aircraft, but the actual figure was twice that.[12]

German twin-engine bombers in the battle included the obsolescent Heinkel He 111, the Junkers Ju 88 (an excellent aircraft, although but few were available), and the Dornier Do 17 (the 'flying pencil' with only a small bomb load). German fighters consisted chiefly of the Bf 109 and twin-engine long-range Bf 110. Designed as a fighter to accompany strategic bombers that were never built, the Bf 110 was no match for the more agile British fighters and had to be withdrawn from daytime use. On the British side Hawker Hurricanes bore the brunt of the battle, but the Supermarine Spitfire with its great maneuverability was one of the best fighters of the war and a match for the Messerschmitts.

German bombers were lightly protected by few machine guns and so required large numbers of fighters as escorts. In 1940, however, only a third of German aircraft produced were fighters. With three or four fighters required for every bomber sent over Britain, this sharply limited the number of bombers that could be utilized. The Germans had also laid great emphasis on dive-bombers, but the Stuka was slow and highly vulnerable to attacks by British Hurricanes and Spitfires. The Germans had to withdraw the Stuka from the battle, and with it went a third of the German bombers.[13]

Luftwaffe Chief of Staff General Walther Wever had pushed for construction of a strategic 'Ural' or 'America' bomber and two four-engine Dornier Do 19 and Junkers Ju 89 prototypes were nearly ready at the time of Wever's death in a plane crash in June 1936. But Wever's successor, General Albert Kesselring, concluded that what Germany required for the Blitzkrieg was a large number of two-engine medium bombers behind a spearhead of dive-bombers. The strategic bomber project was effectively dropped. The *Luftwaffe* was not ready for strategic bombing in 1940. It was essentially flying artillery, developed for a close ground support role.[14]

The strain on personnel on both sides in the battle was immense. Air crews flew as many as a half dozen sorties daily, but the Germans knew that if they bailed out over the operations area, they would be captured. They also had the chronic worry of having sufficient fuel to make it home. Finally, there was the German concentration on London. On the night of August 24–25, 10 German bombers were sent to attack an oil storage depot at Thames Haven, 25 miles downriver from central London. Somehow they got lost and dropped their bombs on London. The German bombers had hardly departed early on August 25 when Churchill gave the order to retaliate. Until this point Bomber Command had been raiding the Ruhr, which was of little help in the Battle of Britain. Flying with reduced bomb loads, its aircraft could reach Berlin 500 miles distant, but clouds and poor navigation equipment meant that only about a third of the 81 British aircraft departing that night actually reached the German capital. The next day German newspaper headlines, conveniently forgetting Warsaw and Rotterdam, proclaimed, 'Cowardly British Attack. Air Pirates over Berlin.' Berliners were stunned; Göring had boasted that British bombers would never reach Berlin, and Berliners did not think this could happen to them.[15]

The Bomber Command raid on Berlin was by any standards not a tactical success, but it had an immense impact in that it led Hitler into a fatal mistake. He now ordered the *Luftwaffe* to concentrate on London, rather than the vastly more important RAF airfields and production facilities. Even Göring saw this as a serious error, while Air Marshal Dowding heralded the shift to bombing London on September 7 as a 'supernatural intervention.' He recalled, 'I could hardly believe the Germans would have made such a mistake.' The switch to the bombing of cities ended any remaining chance of the *Luftwaffe* obtaining air superiority over southern England.[16]

The Germans hoped their concentration on London would bring up the remaining British fighters to be destroyed. The German Naval Staff noted on September 10: 'The Führer thinks the major attack on London may be decisive, and as a systematic and prolonged bombing of London may result in the enemy's adoption of an attitude which will render Sea Lion superfluous.' But Dowding refused to be drawn into a fight for the city or other forward areas. Instead, he concentrated his aircraft over vital sectors, particularly the airfields. This decision by Dowding was probably not a planned strategy as usually thought, but was forced by the scarcity of fighter assets.[17]

Dowding's decision was unpopular, but it proved decisive in the long run. Some 14,000 people died in London alone but the city absorbed punishment and diverted much more crippling attacks against the air defense system. London's productive activity continued and, far from breaking civilian morale as the air power theorists had predicted, the bombings strengthened British resolve to resist. The Battle of Britain provided the first proof that bombers, at least when used against civilians, had been overestimated. Dowding's policy of going after the bombers while as much as possible avoiding the German fighters paid handsome dividends.[18]

Pilot replacement, rather than planes, was key in the Battle of Britain and a greater source of anxiety to Dowding than any other. In retrospect this was not as threatening as thought at the time. The British had suffered greater casualties in the Battle for France in May and June. Fighter Command managed to keep replacements ahead of casualties and increases in aircraft. Foreign pilots were very important; they came from such nations as South Africa, Australia, New Zealand, and Rhodesia. There was a Canadian squadron by October, and there were pilots from France, Belgium, The Netherlands, and even volunteers from neutral America. Most importantly, there were two Polish squadrons (302 and 303) and two Czech squadrons (310 and 312).

Mussolini insisted that Italian aircraft participate in the battle, against the advice of his own air staff and the Germans, who believed, correctly, that the Italian planes would be better employed in North Africa or against Malta. But *Il Duce* thought Britain would soon be defeated, and that Italian participation would allow him to lay claim to part of the British Empire at the peace conference. The 300 Italian planes sent to

Belgium in October 1940 to take part in the battle were hopelessly obso-lescent and, within a few weeks, the surviving aircraft returned to Italy.[19]

Finally, on November 1, with the *Luftwaffe* taking prohibitive losses, the Germans shifted to night bombing, what Londoners called 'the Blitz.' On the night of November 14–15 the Germans dropped a million pounds of bombs on Coventry. This totally indiscriminate attack flat-tened the center of the city, destroyed a dozen armaments factories and the fourteenth-century cathedral and destroyed or damaged 60,000 buildings. It also killed 554 people. One enduring myth of the war is that Ultra provided Churchill with knowledge of the destination of the raid in advance and that he refused to reveal this for fear of compromising the source. In fact the Air Staff knew on November 11 only that a large German attack was in the offing by both Air Fleets (*Luftflotten* 2 and 3), but not the actual target. The best Bomber Command could do was a series of preventive strikes on German airfields. Bletchley Park did not identify the code word for Coventry, and so Churchill never had to make that difficult decision.[20]

During the height of the Blitz an average of 200 German planes came over London for 57 days in a row. Heavy bombing continued into May 1941. The last big raid was also the worst. On May 10, 1941, more than 700 German bombers hit the old medieval center of the city, much of it of wood. The German attack began at 10:00 p.m. The Germans targeted the water system with high-explosives and, with the Thames at low tide, this denied water to the fire fighters. The Germans then dropped tens of thousands of two-pound magnesium and fire bombs. By midnight some 2000 fires were raging. The House of Commons was destroyed, and Westminster Abbey and St. Paul's Cathedral were among the buildings damaged. In all 3000 people were killed or injured and 700 acres of the city were burned out. In the morning hundreds of fires were still raging, and all but one of the railway stations were out of service for weeks.[21]

The lack of an effective British night fighter permitted the Germans to bomb at night from high altitude almost at will. But although it was savage and relentless, night area bombing could have no strategic result. The German air offensive had failed. The Battle of Britain was the first serious German military setback of the war. On October 12, 1940, Operation SEALION was officially shelved until the spring, when it was put off indefinitely.[22]

For years afterward it was held that the Battle of Britain was a very close-run thing, but historian Roger Parkinson believes that the Germans had 'no real chance of success' in the summer of 1940, whatever they might have done:

Given the RAF casualty replacement achievement, the growing skill of the fighter pilots, and their advantage of shorter operational range, Fighter Command would still have survived. As it was, in early September Fighter Command had more machines and more men than three months before, and even without decisive measures by the Royal Navy was in a far better position to prevent invasion. The Battle of Britain never came near to being lost by Fighter Command; the post-war belief that the 'few' battling for Britain's very survival, came to within days of defeat, is totally false.[23]

German army and navy chiefs, never happy about the prospect of crossing the Channel in numerous small vessels over several days, were glad of the excuse provided by the *Luftwaffe* failure to suspend SEALION.[24] More surprising is Hitler's support of the decision. In another far-reaching military blunder he failed to recognize the need to continue the pressure on Britain. He could have intensified aircraft and submarine attacks against shipping to the British Isles. These might have brought starvation and eventual British collapse; but Hitler's attention was increasingly drawn eastward, to the Soviet Union, and he came to believe that the way to defeat Britain ran through it.

Italy's invasion of Greece

Other events also intruded as Italy, seeking to take advantage of the defeat of France and Britain's weakness, opened new fronts in Africa and in Greece. On October 28 Mussolini sent Italian forces into Greece from Albania without informing Hitler ahead of time. Mussolini told his son-in-law Ciano, 'Hitler always faces me with a *fait accompli*. This time I am going to pay him back in his own coin. He will find out from the papers that I have occupied Greece. In this way, the equilibrium will be re-established.'[25]

Hitler most certainly knew of the Italian plans ahead of time, even the exact date, but he did not act to restrain his ally. He did not reproach Mussolini and even offered to assist him by taking Crete before the British could land there. Mussolini's decision, which was taken on short notice and against the advice of his military leaders, had immense repercussions. Not only did the Greeks, who outnumbered the invaders by more than two to one, contain the Italians; they drove them back and began their own counter-invasion of Albania. That winter the campaign settled down to deadlock. This caused Hitler to consider sending in German troops to rescue the Italians.[26]

In the summer of 1940 both German Chief of Staff Admiral Erich Raeder and Göring had encouraged Hitler to continue the war against Britain by pursuing a Mediterranean option. Raeder talked with Hitler on both September 6 and 26 and 'tried to turn his thoughts to the Mediterranean,' which he thought could have 'decisive results.' Raeder pointed out the importance to Britain of Gibraltar, the Suez Canal, Malta, and the Near East. He urged that Germany, in cooperation with Italy and France, seek to control the Mediterranean and establish bases in North Africa, cutting Britain's lifeline to India and the East. He strongly opposed an attack on the Soviet Union.[27]

Göring's plan was much the same. More precise than Raeder's, it envisaged the employment of three army corps. Göring would send one through Spain to seize Gibraltar, then move across the Mediterranean to North Africa where it would head east along the coast to Tunis. The second would go from Italy to Tripolitania, while the third would thrust through the Balkans and Greece to secure the Dardanelles, take Turkey and then Syria, and push to Egypt and the Suez Canal. These operations completed, the Germans would control the Mediterranean and the British would have to accept German peace terms.[28]

In April 1941 the pro-German Rashid Ali and some army officers seized power in Iraq. Hitler and Mussolini immediately offered arms to the new government and demanded and received approval from Vichy France for German and Italian planes to land in Syria to refuel on their way to Baghdad. The next month London dispatched troops from India and Transjordan to overthrow the new Iraqi government. Fearful that Hitler might send forces to Syria and Lebanon, in June British troops also occupied these two French mandates. The Vichy government ordered its troops to resist, leading to five weeks of fighting. The French there surrendered on July 14. Britain now controlled the entire eastern Mediterranean. In August, following Germany's invasion of the Soviet Union, British and Soviet troops occupied Iran, the Soviet Union from the north and the British from the south, in order to secure this important oil source and strategic supply corridor.

Had Hitler been willing, a modest German investment in the Mediterranean Theater of war probably would have been successful. Even in the summer of 1942 an additional two panzer divisions might have secured the defeat of Britain in the Middle East, and in late 1940 the British were far weaker and fighting in the Soviet Union was not yet consuming 90 percent of German resources. General Walter Warlimont recognized the need for Germany to take Gibraltar, Malta, Cyprus, and the Suez Canal. Guderian, too, saw the critical importance of driving Britain from the war: 'the end of the war with Great Britain was the most important, indeed the only important thing.'[29]

Raeder and Göring both believed that the defeat of Britain would leave Germany in a much stronger position *vis-à-vis* the Soviet Union. Hitler failed to see this. He argued that the Soviet Union was preparing to attack Germany and that Britain was holding out only because its leaders held out the hope that Germany and the Soviet Union would go to war. If he could eliminate the Soviet Union, then surely Britain would give up. This was no doubt true but it rested on the 'if' of the defeat of the Soviet Union.

Beyond this Hitler lacked patience. He also did not understand the limitations of the Blitzkrieg in terms of distance and resupply of attacking forces; nor did he appreciate interdiction or an indirect approach. He understood only seizure of territory. Finally, in the case of the Soviet Union, Hitler was driven by ideological and political factors that ran counter to sound strategic imperatives; he sought *Lebensraum* for the *Herrenvolk* (master race). Hitler's underestimation of Soviet strength affected all aspects of German planning for the Russian campaign. Even before the invasion of the USSR he ordered a shift in armaments production from the army into aircraft and submarines for a renewed offensive against Britain on the defeat of the Soviet Union. Hitler predicted a quick victory, 'in three months at the latest.'[30]

As early as the end of July 1940 Hitler had decided to invade the Soviet Union. Chief of the General Staff Halder noted in his diary:

> Britain's hope lies in Russia and America. If that hope in Russia is destroyed then it will be destroyed for America too because elimination of Russia will enormously increase Japan's power in the Far East . . . . But if Russia is smashed, Britain's last hope will be shattered. Then Germany would be the master of Europe and the Balkans. Decision: In view of these considerations Russia must be liquidated. Spring 1941.[31]

In ordering planning to begin for the invasion of the Soviet Union, code-named Operation BARBAROSSA, Hitler made the same miscalculation as that other would-be conqueror of Europe, Napoleon Bonaparte.

The alliance between Nazi Germany and the Soviet Union resembled that between Napoleon and Tsar Alexander I in that both were based on convenience. Stalin had entered into the alliance to gain time to rebuild the Red Army, which he himself had devastated in the Great Purges. Hitler gained the protection of Germany's eastern flank, allowing it to strike west with the bulk of its resources and defeat France, but Germany had also secured great economic advantage from the pact, enabling it to nullify the effects of the British naval blockade. The Soviet Union supplied the Reich with vast quantities of raw materials, in return for which the Soviet Union had secured only certain industrial machinery and a few weapons of war, including an uncompleted cruiser. The Soviets had also acted as a purchasing agent for Germany abroad, freighting strategic essentials that it was unable to provide, such as rubber and copper. German officials involved in this trade were stunned by the news of the invasion; they were well aware of the importance of these materials to the German war machine. Hitler, of course, expected to soon secure these assets for himself.

Stalin directed that the Soviet Union live up to the letter of its agreements with Germany and allow Hitler no pretext for an invasion. Soviet trains laden with goods continued to roll into Germany right up to and during the invasion. It is impossible to explain why Stalin, one of the most paranoid leaders in history, accorded greater trust to Hitler than he ever extended to Churchill or Roosevelt. But he was shocked at the speed with which Hitler's legions had defeated France. Given the punishment that little Finland had inflicted on the Soviet Union, it is no wonder that Stalin worried about the ability of the Red Army to withstand the German juggernaut. He counted on a repeat of the stalemate of the Western Front of 1914–18 or at least a campaign of a year or two. Soviet leaders also reckoned that any war between the USSR and Germany would last a minimum of three years. Critical to ensuring a protracted war would be denial of the eastern Ukraine to the Germans, which is why so much Soviet armor was in forward positions in June 1941.

With the collapse of France, Stalin moved swiftly to secure the gains promised under the Nazi-Soviet pact. On June 15 the Red Army occupied Lithuania, and a few days later Soviet troops moved into Latvia and Estonia. In July Soviet-style elections occurred in all three states, with the new parliaments requesting incorporation as member republics of the Soviet Union, to which the Kremlin speedily agreed in early August. This was expected, although Hitler professed himself surprised by the outright Soviet annexation. Stalin also ordered the annexation, in late June 1940, of the Romanian provinces of Bessarabia and northern Bukovina. Bessarabia had been assigned to the Soviet sphere under the non-aggression pact, but northern Bukovina had not. Also, unlike

Bessarabia, Bukovina had never been part of Imperial Russia. It was also the gateway to the Romanian oil fields at Ploesti, vital to the German war machine.[32]

At the same time Stalin sought frantically to improve both the quality and quantity of his armed forces. The success of the German panzer divisions in France led Stalin to reverse his decision of Fall 1939 doing away with the five Soviet tank corps. A decree of July 6, 1940, ordered the creation of nine new mechanized corps and, in February and March, other decrees called for the establishment of an additional 20.[33]

On November 12, 1940, Soviet Foreign Minister Molotov arrived in Berlin for talks. Both Foreign Minister Ribbentrop and Hitler urged the Soviet Union to join hands with Germany, Italy, and Japan in dividing the world into spheres of influence. Having established their 'new order' in Europe, Germany and Italy would expand into Africa. Japan was interested in Southeast Asia, and the Soviet Union should expand south 'to the sea.' Molotov demanded to know specifics and also brought up the fact that Germany had sent troops into Romania. Hitler was shaken by Molotov's brazenness and the discussion soon became heated. Molotov left Berlin on November 14, and after his departure Hitler informed his confidants that he had not expected the talks to succeed. He also ordered an acceleration in invasion plans.[34]

On November 26 Molotov informed German Ambassador to Moscow Friedrich Werner von der Schulenburg that the Soviet Union was willing to join a four-power pact with Germany, Italy, and Japan, but it would have to be allowed to expand into the Persian Gulf and to annex Finland, establish a 'protectorate' over Bulgaria, secure bases in Turkey, and regain South Sakhalin Island from Japan. Hitler declared Stalin 'a cold-blooded blackmailer' and ordered Ribbentrop not to reply.[35]

Meanwhile, on 29 October 1940, British forces had landed in Crete. Then, early in March 1941, honoring the pledge to defend Greece, Churchill sent troops there from North Africa under General Sir Henry Maitland Wilson: the British 1st Armored Brigade, New Zealand Division, and the 6th Australian Division. Churchill hoped thereby to forestall a German invasion, but this step also forced British Middle East commander General Sir Archibald Wavell to halt his successful offensive against the Italians in North Africa.

By early 1941 Hitler had moved aggressively in the Balkans to counter Soviet moves and shore up his southern flank before the invasion of the Soviet Union. In November 1940 he forced Hungary and Romania to join the Axis and accept German troops. Bulgaria followed suit at the beginning of March 1941. Hitler took advantage of irredentist sentiment but also used hard-ball tactics to secure their support. Hitler also pressured Yugoslavia and, under German threats, in late March Prince Regent Paul reluctantly agreed to join the Axis.

German invasion of Yugoslavia

On March 27 elements in the Yugoslavian Army carried out a *coup* in Belgrade that overthrew Paul and repudiated the German alliance. This was motivated, above all, by popular sentiment among the Serbs against the alliance. Furious at the turn of events, Hitler ordered German forces to invade Yugoslavia. Marshal Wilhelm List's Twelfth Army and General Paul Ludwig Ewald von Kleist's First Panzer Group, positioned in Hungary and Romania for the forthcoming invasion of the Soviet Union, now shifted to southwestern Romania and Bulgaria.[36]

The invasion of Yugoslavia began on April 6, 1941. Early that morning *Luftwaffe* bombers arrived over Belgrade. A few hours later they left behind them a flattened city and 17,000 dead. On the ground German columns invaded from the north, east, and southeast. Other Axis troops took part, but Hungarian Premier Pál Teleki committed suicide rather than dishonor himself. The invasion was conducted so swiftly that the million-man Yugoslav Army was never completely mobilized. Yugoslavia surrendered unconditionally on April 17. Perhaps 100,000 Yugoslavs were killed or wounded in the invasion; another 300,000 were taken prisoner. Total German casualties were only 558 men, 151 of them killed in action.[37]

Resistance to the Germans did not cease with the formal Yugoslav surrender, however. The lead was taken by army elements known as 'Chetniks' and headed by former Defense Minister Draža Mihailović. Soon there was a rival resistance group, known as the Partisans, headed by Josip Broz (who took the *nom de guerre* of Tito). The two groups came to be bitter enemies, even to the point of fighting one another. The Chetniks were reluctant to embark on activities against the Germans that might bring civilian reprisals. The Partisans had no such inhibitions, and ultimately the British, who oversaw Allied aid to the Yugoslav resistance, decided to back only the Partisans, a decision that helped bring Tito to power in Yugoslavia after the war.[38]

Simultaneously with their move into Yugoslavia, the Germans came to the aid of the hard-pressed Italians by invading Greece. This caught the Greeks with 15 divisions in Albania and only three divisions and border forces in Macedonia, where the Germans attacked. Also, the scratch British Expeditionary Force in Greece was woefully unprepared to deal with German armor and the *Luftwaffe*, and between April 26 and 30 it precipitously evacuated Greece. Many of the 43,000 troops taken off were then landed on Crete. During the evacuation of Greece, British naval units were savaged by the *Luftwaffe*, the Royal Navy losing two destroyers and 24 other vessels to German air attack; many other vessels were badly damaged. Meanwhile, the Germans had decided to reinforce the Italians in North Africa with the *Afrika Korps*, This opened a further drain on Germany's overextended resources, particularly air transport and helped insure that the ultimate Axis defeat in North Africa would be much more costly.

German capture of Crete

In May 1941 the Germans continued their push south by occupying the island of Crete in the eastern Mediterranean in the first airborne invasion in history. Conceived and planned by General Student, it turned out to be the graveyard of German paratroop forces. Student saw the operation against Crete as the forerunner of other more ambitious airborne operations, against Malta or even Suez. Hitler saw it only as a cover for his planned invasion of the Soviet Union, securing the German southern flank against British air assault and helping to protect the vital oil fields of Ploesti. The German invasion would be conducted by parachutists and mountain troops brought in by transport aircraft. MERKUR (Mercury), as the Germans called it, began on May 20. Churchill's decision to try to hold Crete, unprepared and bereft of RAF fighter support, ignored reality. With no British fighters available, the *Luftwaffe* was able to hit Crete and the Royal Navy offshore with impunity.

A British corps, commanded by Major General Bernard Freyberg and centered on the 2nd New Zealand Division, defended Crete. Ultra intercepts provided Freyberg with advance knowledge of German intentions and identified the German drop zones and targeted airfields. They also hampered Freyberg's dispositions because they revealed that the Germans were sending a seaborne force as well. This latter turned out to be only a small-scale operation, which was turned back at sea, but the threat led Freyberg to divert some of his scant resources from the three airfields to the coast, which probably cost him the battle. Freyberg also made a major blunder in not releasing stocks of weapons and forming a Cretan home guard before the invasion.

The Germans barely managed to secure one airfield. That was suffi-cient, however, as they were then able to bring in mountain troops by transport aircraft and expand the perimeter. In little more than a week the British were forced into another evacuation. In the battle British and Empire forces sustained 3479 casualties (1742 dead) and 11,835 prison-ers. The Cretans also paid a heavy price. They fought the Germans with what little means they had and suffered savage reprisals in the battle and during the subsequent occupation. The Germans sustained 6700 casual-ties (3300 dead) and 200 transport aircraft destroyed. Although there were concerns in the *Luftwaffe* that codes might have been broken, noth-ing was done about it.[39]

Hitler was furious at the casualties and removed Student from command during the battle. Never again did Hitler employ paratroops in airborne assault in significant number. From that point on Student's men were used mainly as elite infantry. Ironically, the Allies now embraced paratroop operations.

The Battle for Crete also demonstrated that warships without fighter support were defenseless against attacking aircraft. Admiral Andrew Cunningham's Mediterranean Command smashed the German amphibi-ous operation of May 21–23 sent to reinforce the airborne troops on Crete, sinking a number of the small craft shuttling troops and killing several hundred Germans; but the *Luftwaffe* then mauled the Royal Navy, which lost three cruisers and six destroyers; six others ships, including two battleships and an aircraft carrier, were heavily damaged. More than 1800 British sailors died. Churchill ignored the lesson, cost-ing the Royal Navy two capital ships in the South China Sea in December 1941.[40]

Hitler, by his aggressive Balkan moves, barred Soviet expansion there and secured protection against possible British air attack from the south. These goals accomplished, he was ready to move against the Soviet Union. Victory here would end the threat from the East, secure *Lebensraum* and with it the wheat of the Ukraine and the oil of the Caucasus, and force Britain to the bargaining table. Hitler was so confi-dent that the Soviet Union could be defeated in a single short campaign before the onset of winter that he did not put Germany on a full wartime footing. Some German troops were actually being demobilized to return to industrial labor.

The German military attaché in Moscow, General Ernst Köstring, had sent numerous reports home on Soviet military strength and industrial capacity, but Hitler rejected these estimates, as he also discounted the strength of the Soviet political system. Optimism permeated both OKH

(*Oberkommando des Heeres*, Army Supreme Command) and OKW (*Oberkommando der Wehrmacht*, Armed Forces Supreme Command or Hitler's personal staff). The army had winter uniforms for only about 20 percent of the force; not until the end of August did OKH become seriously concerned about supplying German troops in the Soviet Union with winter clothing.[41]

Hitler also did not consider it necessary to coordinate his plans with Japan. On April 23, 1941, meanwhile, in Moscow Japanese Foreign Minister Matsuoka Yosuke signed a non-aggression treaty with the Soviet Union. The pact 'guaranteed the preservation of peaceful and free relations' between the two powers, which 'promised not to violate each other's territory even though the other nation became involved in a war.' Stalin welcomed the pact as greatly reducing concern over a possible joint attack against the Soviet Union by Germany and Japan.

German invasion of the Soviet Union (Operation BARBAROSSA)

Stalin received many warnings of an impending German attack before the actual invasion. In January 1941 Washington received from its commercial attaché in Berlin, Sam E. Woods, via anti-Nazi Hans H. H. von Bittenfeld, a copy of Hitler's December 18 directive for Operation BARBAROSSA. After weighing the options, Roosevelt decided that the Soviets should be warned. Under-Secretary of State Sumner Welles then met with Soviet Ambassador to Washington Konstantin Oumansky and passed the information to him to convey to Moscow.[42]

Other confirming data, much of it coming from Japanese Ambassador to Germany General Ōshima Hiroshi, continued to be sent into the spring.[43] On June 10 the head of the British Foreign Office, Sir Alexander Cadogan, called in Soviet Ambassador to Britain Ivan Maisky and gave him a detailed report, including names, numbers, and locations, of German military preparations that signaled intention to attack the USSR. On June 14 Admiral A. A. Kuznetsov reported that German ships were leaving Soviet ports with their loading not complete, and that all of them would be gone by June 21. Molotov's response was, 'Only a fool would attack us.'[44]

In all, Moscow received more than 100 reports of impending German invasion. The Germans located new landing strips close to the Soviet border and, in an effort to gain intelligence information, the *Luftwaffe* conducted frequent overflights of Soviet territory in some 500 violations of Soviet air space before the invasion. Stalin bears responsibility for the failure to take the Western warnings seriously. Former Foreign Minister Litvinov, named Soviet ambassador to the United States in November, acknowledged that the Kremlin received all these reports, but shrugged them off as attempts by the West to drive a wedge between the Soviet Union and Germany. Litvinov said that the reports were disregarded by the Kremlin 'because it considered it would have been madness on Hitler's part to undertake a war in the East . . . before finishing off his war in the West.'[45]

Stalin trusted Hitler much more than he ever did Western leaders, especially Churchill, who had long opposed Communism and, following World War I, had advocated Western military intervention to overthrow it. Stalin professed to see in the growing number of warnings from the West an elaborate British plot designed to bring about war between Germany and the Soviet Union. Even Soviet master spy in Tokyo Richard Sorge's reports were disbelieved.[46]

Soon it was no longer possible to explain away the growing German troop build-up on the western Soviet borders and, in the course of a private lunch at the German Embassy, German Ambassador to the Soviet Union Schulenberg informed an astonished Soviet Ambassador to Germany Vladimir Dekanozev that Germany would invade. Schulenberg said that he was telling him this because he agreed with Bismarck, always an opponent of war with Russia. Dekanozev duly reported the information, but Stalin's reaction was to inform the Politburo that, 'Disinformation has now reached ambassadorial level.'[47]

Stalin also seems to have believed that the German military was to a degree independent of Hitler and pursuing its own goals, and that German military intelligence was fabricating evidence and mounting provocations in order to precipitate a war with the Soviet Union. That would, for example, explain German overflights of Soviet airspace. Thus Stalin was anxious that there be no Soviet military deployments that might justify a German attack. This did not mean that Stalin disbelieved in an inevitable war between Germany and the Soviet Union. He was reported as predicting that such a war would occur in 1942 or perhaps 1944, and that he was keeping his options open for a pre-emptive attack on Germany at the appropriate time.[48]

Hitler had ordered that preparations for the invasion of the Soviet Union be complete by May 15, but the invasion did not occur until June 22, almost the very day that Napoleon Bonaparte had begun his invasion of Russia in 1812. Heavy spring rains were the most important factor as the panzers needed dry, hard ground for an advance across a country with few roads. Also it took more time than anticipated to bring together an invasion force of more than three million men, the largest in history. Motor transport had to be allocated, and the *Luftwaffe* was also slow to build forward airfields. And units taking part in the Balkans campaign had to be relocated and refitted.[49]

As with Napoleon before him, Hitler was unfazed. He, and many of his generals, expected a short, victorious campaign concluded well before the onset of winter. The delay, however, may have been the final blow preventing a German victory in 1941.[50]

On June 22 the German Army deployed 205 divisions, but the Red Army had 303. In the campaign in the Soviet Union Hitler's strategic overreach finally caught up with him. In garrison or fighting elsewhere the Germans had 60 divisions: 38 in France, 12 in Norway, 1 in Denmark, 7 in the Balkans, and 2 in North Africa. This left just 145 divisions available for operations in the east. The Germans invaded the Soviet Union with 102 infantry divisions, 14 motorized divisions, 1 cavalry division, and 19 armored divisions. In addition they deployed nine divisions to maintain lines of communication as the invasion progressed. There was virtually no strategic reserve. Finland, Romania, and Hungary supplied perhaps 705,000 men in 37 divisions.[51]

The disparity in military hardware was even more striking. The *Luftwaffe*, still waging operations against Britain and also supporting the *Afrika Korps* in North Africa, was forced to keep 1150 combat aircraft in these theaters. Only 2770 combat aircraft were available against the Soviet Union. These faced 18,570 Soviet aircraft, 8154 of which were initially in the west. The bulk of these were tactical aircraft. Although the Soviet Union had experimented with long-range strategic bombers, the Spanish Civil War had convinced its military leadership of the need to concentrate on tactical aviation.[52]

The Soviets also concentrated on mass production of sturdy basic designs, including the Ilyushin Il 2 Shturmovik ground attack aircraft. Entering service in May 1941 just before the German invasion, it continued in production until 1955 and had one of the largest production runs – 36,000 aircraft – in history. Its most distinguishing feature was a highly armored 'tub' that included the engine, pilot, and fuel supply, and was largely impervious to ground fire. When many of these tank-busting aircraft were lost for the lack of a tail gunner, a two-seat version was introduced in 1942 with even heavier weaponry, including the world's first air-to-ground rockets.[53]

Germany had some 6000 tanks, the Soviets 23,140 (10,394 in the west). Even in 1941 the Soviets possessed some of the best tanks of the war. Their BT-series fast tanks and T-26 were superior in armor, firepower, and maneuverability to the German light PzKpfw I and II and could destroy any German tank. Similarly, the Soviet T-34 medium tank and KV-1 heavy tank were superior to the PzKpfw III and IV, and indeed any German tank in June 1941. The Soviets had purchased several tanks developed by American John Walter Christie, who had come up with a revolutionary new suspension system of large weight-bearing wheels on torsion bars as well as sloped armor to help increase resistance to armor-piercing shot.

The Soviet T-34, mounting a 76mm gun and employing the Christie suspension system, was probably the best all-round fighting vehicle of the entire war. Easily produced and maintained, it was the top tank in the world in 1941. The T-34 had a relatively lightweight diesel engine, which was safer for the crews than the gasoline engines on the German tanks. It also had a wide track, which translated into lower ground pressure and therefore it was less likely to get bogged down than its German counterparts. Its sloped armor was a major advance, and its frontal armor could be penetrated only by 50mm anti-tank rounds at under a range of 500 meters. The 45mm guns on Soviet light tanks could penetrate all German tanks except for the PzKpfw IV.[54]

The German invasion plan called for three axes of advance. Rundstedt's Army Group South of four armies (one Romanian) and one panzer group would drive on Kiev and the Dnieper in order to destroy Soviet armies between the Pripet Marshes and the Black Sea. Bock's Army Group Center of two armies and two panzer groups were to strike east, taking Smolensk and Moscow. Field Marshal Werner Ritter von Leeb's Army Group North of two armies and one panzer group would thrust north, capture Leningrad, and pin the Soviet forces there against the Baltic Sea. Finland would act in concert with the Germans, re-entering the war to reoccupy the Karelian Isthmus and threatening Leningrad from the north. Farther north German General Nikolaus von Falkenhorst's Norway Army was to carry out an offensive against Murmansk in order to sever its supply route to Leningrad.

The invasion began at 3:00 a.m. on June 22, the longest day of the year with only two hours of total darkness. The Germans and their allies moved into the Soviet Union along a 2000-mile front and achieved complete surprise. The bulk of the Red Army's western forces were in forward positions where they were cut off and surrounded. On the first day alone, 1200 Soviet aircraft were destroyed, most of them on the ground. Within two days 2000 Soviet aircraft had been lost. Within five days the Germans had captured or destroyed 2500 Soviet tanks. Within three weeks the Soviets had lost 3500 tanks, 6000 aircraft, and 2 million men, including a significant percentage of the officer corps.[55]

The day before the invasion, Soviet Generals Gregori Zhukov and Semon Timoshenko, worried about signs of an attack, had requested that border troops be put on alert. Stalin refused, not wishing to provoke the Germans. Even when informed that German troops were invading and firing on Soviet positions, Stalin refused for hours to allow an order to be issued to return fire; Stalin claimed Hitler must not be aware of what was going on. Only when the Soviet Foreign Ministry confirmed the war was on did Stalin at 7:15 a.m. authorize return fire; and Stalin left it to Molotov to make the radio declaration to the Soviet people, late on the day of the invasion.

Stalin in fact disappeared completely and for over a week he was virtually incommunicado in his *dacha*, stunned by his failure and hiding from his people. This too had its effect on the fighting. Members of the Politburo finally met with him and brought him back to his senses; later he would confess that he thought they had come to demand his resignation. Not until July 3 did Stalin himself address the nation.[56]

Colonel General Dimitri Pavlov, commanding the sector of the front that bore the brunt of the German attack, had pleaded with Stalin a week before the invasion to establish rearward defensive positions. He now became the scapegoat for the military fiasco. Accused of collaboration with the Germans, Pavlov and eight other senior generals and political officials were tried and shot. Stalin also issued orders to be read to all troops of the army that anyone who surrendered was 'a traitor to the Motherland.' Their families were to be deprived of all state allowances and assistance and, if recovered, such individuals were to be shot.[57]

In the early months of the German invasion Stalin consistently ignored sound military advice from his generals, often with disastrous result. His orders that the army stand and fight merely meant that larger chunks of it were cut off and destroyed. German armored pincers took Minsk in mid-July, along with 290,000 prisoners, 2500 tanks, and 1400 guns. Smolensk followed a week later with 100,000 prisoners, 2000 tanks, and 1900 guns. During August and September, instead of letting his armies escape a German panzer pincer on Kiev carried out by Kleist from the south and Guderian from the north, Stalin ordered it held. German infantry then sealed off Kiev. It fell on September 19 and with it most of five Soviet armies: 665,000 prisoners and vast quantities of weapons. Hitler called Kiev 'the greatest battle of world history.' Halder, however, referred to Kiev as the greatest German strategic mistake of the campaign. He believed that the army should have concentrated on the center of the front, against Moscow.[58]

German forces seemed unstoppable. By the autumn of 1941 they had overrun Byelorussia and most of Ukraine. By the end of November the Red Army had sustained about three million casualties, half of them prisoners.

In the north, Leningrad was encircled by land. The siege of the city, which began in September 1941, was the longest in history since Biblical times and the most costly in terms of loss of human life. Hitler did not intend to take Leningrad by storm, but rather to starve it into submission. He said he was 'indifferent' to the plight of the civilians there. Leningrad depended on food and supplies brought in across Lake Ladoga, a tenuous route at best. By December 1941 rations were reduced to 900 calories per person per day, as the inhabitants tried to survive by eating dogs, cats, rats, and even the glue from wallpaper. The temperature dropped to 30 degrees below zero. There was no heat, no light, no transport, and little food. Starvation, disease, and the fighting reduced the city population from 4 million to only 2.5 million, most of the deaths occurring in the period from late October 1941 through mid-April 1942. Leningrad held out for 900 days until it was relieved by the Red Army in early 1944.[59]

In the south the Germans entered the Crimean peninsula and laid siege to Sevastopol. In the center of the front the Germans stood three-quarters of the way to Moscow. This great advance had not come without cost. By mid-July the German drive was slowing, and by the end of August the Germans had lost 400,000 men. By the end of November German casualties had reached 743,000 men, nearly a quarter of the average army strength of 3.5 million.[60]

Despite spectacular successes, the Germans failed to achieve overall victory against the Soviet Union in 1941. Russia, it is said, has two generals – space and winter. The Blitzkrieg had enjoyed success in Poland and France, but this was in large measure a function of the relatively short distances involved and because France had a developed road network. Neither condition was present in the Soviet Union, where the bulk of roads were unpaved. Roads marked on maps often did not exist in fact, those that did often turned into quagmires under the autumnal rains, causing the panzers to become hopelessly bogged down. The *Wehrmacht* is often falsely seen as a thoroughly modern panzer-centered force, but the bulk of the German infantry moved on foot. For the invasion of the Soviet Union the German Army assembled 625,000 horses, 180,000 of which were lost in the first winter. The horses moved guns, ambulances, and ration wagons. Simply securing feed for so many horses was in itself a tremendous logistical problem. Supplies and the bulk of the forces simply could not keep pace with the panzers. In the vast expanse of the Soviet Union, German logistical shortcomings became glaringly apparent for the first time. The number of German trains was barely sufficient to supply the front; the creation of new bases could not keep up with the pace of the advance, and the poor state of the Russian roads precluded the use of trailers.[61]

Winter was a cruel problem. The short, six-week campaign anticipated by Hitler had failed to materialize, and by November 13 temperatures were down to −5 degrees Fahrenheit. Ultimately temperatures plunged to −60 degree, and this for troops largely clad in summer uniforms and manning unclimatized equipment. Oil in the crankcases of German vehicles acquired a tar-like viscosity; to start their tanks and truck engines, the Germans had first to build a fire under them.[62]

There was also the extraordinary endurance of the USSR's soldiers and Russian people, who were defending the Motherland. More fundamental was Hitler's miscalculation of Soviet resources and the reserves that Stalin could mobilize. In 1941 some 22 million Soviet citizens had had some degree of military training.

Before the invasion the Germans had estimated Soviet strength in the west at about 155 divisions: 100 infantry, 25 cavalry, and the equivalent of 30 mechanized. This was not far off the mark; actual Soviet strength facing them was 177 divisional equivalents, but this included air force and border troops and Soviet divisions were smaller than their German counterparts. By mid-August the Germans had met and defeated the Soviet force they had expected, but by then another 160 Soviet divisions had appeared.[63]

Hitler's decisions also played a role. While the German advance in the center of the Soviet front went well, those on both Leningrad and the Crimea slowed. This was in part the result of command decisions and in part because of the greater distances involved. In July and August, despite vigorous protests from his commanders in the field, Hitler decided that large-scale envelopments were not justified, and he detached both panzer groups and one army from Army Group Center. He sent Guderian's panzer group and Maximilian von Weichs's army south, while General Hermann Hoth's panzer group went north. Guderian was convinced that if the panzer forces had driven right on for Moscow in the summer, the Soviet capital would have fallen and the campaign 'brought to a speedy and successful conclusion.' Not until early September did Hitler agree to Operation TYPHOON, the drive on Moscow.[64]

Still the situation appeared desperate for the Soviets. Having lost the border battles, Stalin reorganized the Red Army, in the process creating the *Stavka*, a military high command to oversee operations under his personal direction. By the end of September the Germans had reduced the Kiev Pocket, and on their southern flank they reached the Crimean Peninsula. In October Manstein's new Eleventh Army opened a drive on Sevastopol.

In these circumstances Richard Sorge in Tokyo provided Moscow with vital information. Sorge, sometimes heralded as the greatest spy in history, on September 14 sent word that the Japanese were not going to take advantage of the Soviet Union's weakness by striking north against Siberia. This information provided confirmation for Stalin to shift resources from the Far East to the west, a decision he would have had to make eventually in any case. By late November half of the Soviet Far Eastern armies had been sent west: 22 divisions – 15 infantry, 3 cavalry, and 4 air (1500 planes) – as well as 8 tank brigades (1700 tanks). Sorge did not know of Japanese plans to strike Pearl Harbor, let alone the timing of the attack, but he did inform Moscow that Japan intended to hit the United States before moving farther south. Stalin did not share any of this information with Washington.[65]

Meanwhile, the German advance continued. On October 15 Rundstedt reached the Don River, threatening both Rostov and Kharkov. Early that same month von Leeb's forces had invested Leningrad. The Finns, however, refused to advance beyond their former border and to the north Falkenhorst's advance against Murmansk bogged down. Hitler then changed plans again. He reinforced von Bock's Army Group Center with the panzer and aircraft units taken from it earlier and ordered it to drive on Moscow. At Vyazma in early October the Germans took more than 650,000 prisoners. By then, however, the weather had become a factor. 'General Mud' arrived as a consequence of the autumn rains, slowing the advance. Soon 'General Winter' also weighed in. By October 20 the Germans were only 40 miles from Moscow; but Soviet resistance was stiffening, while German units, down to 50 percent of their strength, were at the end of their tether.

As the inhabitants of Moscow were digging anti-tank ditches and other defenses in front of the city, Stalin brought General Zhukov from Leningrad to command the forces defending the capital. Zhukov, who had survived the Great Purges probably because he was in the Far East, now had at his disposal the crack Siberian divisions trained in winter warfare. A ruthless commander, Zhukov understood the new techniques of mobile war, for at Nomonham/Khalkin Gol in August 1939 he had employed tanks and motorized infantry to make deep penetrations of the Japanese positions. Zhukov played a key role in the war, coming to be known as 'Stalin's Fireman.' Other capable Soviet officers were released from prison and given commands. Konstantin K. Rokossovsky, who had lost all his teeth under torture during the Great Purges, received a new stainless steel set and command of a division. Later he became a Soviet marshal.[66]

The momentum was shifting. In mid-November a Soviet counterattack pushed Rundstedt's forces out of Rostov. Rundstedt resigned just as Hitler relieved him, replaced by Reichenau. Meanwhile, Kluge, commanding Army Group Center, continued the advance on Moscow and got to within 25 miles of the city. Some light German units actually reached the last tram stop in the city proper and could see the spires of the Kremlin in the distance.

Russian winter had now arrived, hitting German forces largely unprepared for winter conditions. On December 6 Zhukov, reinforced by 100 fresh Soviet divisions, launched a counter-offensive that surprised the Germans and drove them back from Moscow. Hitler refused to sanction a withdrawal. Disgusted with the progress of the campaign, he dismissed a number of his senior generals, including Walter von Brauchitsch, Bock, Leeb, Rundstedt, and Guderian, and took over personal direction of the army. By early January Zhukov had driven back the flanks of Army Group Center, but German forces dug in and slowly recovered. The Red Army, suffering from the appalling casualties of the previous six months, was unable to maintain its momentum. By the spring thaws in mid-March 1942, the fighting had died down as both sides regrouped for a resumption of heavy combat in the summer.

Hitler's 'no retreat' order may indeed have saved the German Army from complete collapse and enabled it to survive and renew the offensive. It also might be argued that the Germans lost the campaign in the Soviet Union, as well as the war, in the 1941 battle for Moscow. Beyond that, heavy German casualties in the campaign to that date reduced the number of men available for resumption of offensive action in the spring of 1942, whereas the Soviets were able to replenish their manpower losses.

The campaigns in North Africa

The strain on the German armed forces was all the worse because, as noted, in 1940 the war had been extended to the Mediterranean. The desert campaigns had begun in Africa in late summer of 1940 when Mussolini sought to take advantage of the defeat of France and the weakness of Britain. The stakes here were high: control of the Mediterranean, the Suez Canal, and access to Middle East oil. On August 6 Italian forces invaded British Somaliland from Italian East Africa; it fell to the Italians in two weeks. Then on September 13, 1940, Field Marshal Rudolfo Graziani invaded Egypt from Tripoli at the head of five divisions (two others were in reserve), a tank brigade, and 300 aircraft. This began a critical campaign for the British. If the Italians reached Suez, they could control the canal and cut Britain's imperial lifeline to Asia. The Italians would also perhaps be able to secure the oil assets of the Persian Gulf. At the height of the Battle of Britain, Churchill had to divert vitally needed military resources to the Near East.

Fortunately for the British, Graziani moved at a snail's pace on a narrow front along the coast. This allowed British outpost forces to fall back and General Wavell to reinforce. Within three days Graziani's men had reached Sidi Barrani, where they established a number of fortified camps. Meanwhile, Wavell gathered two divisions at Mersa Matruh, while General Sir Henry M. Wilson, commander of British forces in Egypt, prepared for a counter-attack.

Wavell's North African offensive, delayed by the need to dispatch forces to Greece, finally began on December, 9 1940, when Major General Richard N. O'Connor hurled his Western Desert Force against the Italians. Largely drawn from the Indian Army, the Western Desert Force was only a quarter of the Italian in numbers. They consisted of 2 divisions (1 infantry and 1 armored), 2 brigades, and 1 battalion of new Matilda tanks: in all, 31,000 men, 120 guns, and 273 tanks. Despite its smaller size, the Western Desert Force proceeded to roll up one Italian strongpoint after another.

The Matilda played an important role in the success of the Western Desert Force. The best tank in the fighting in North Africa in 1940, the Matilda's armor rendered it impregnable to any Italian tank or anti-tank gun until mid-1941 when the Germans began employing their 88mm anti-aircraft gun in an anti-tank role. British land forces were also well supported by air assets and naval gunfire. Within a week the British had not only ejected the Italians entirely from Egypt, but secured 38,000 prisoners and great quantities of war *matériel*.

After a two-week pause to resupply, on January 1 O'Connor's Western Desert Force assaulted the remnants of Graziani's force, at Bardia. On January 5, supported by naval bombardment, he took the Italian positions. The 7th Armored Division ('The Desert Rats') cut off the Italian garrison at Tobruk on the coast, assaulted it from the south, and on January 22 forced it to surrender. The Desert Rats then drove due west across Cyrenaica cutting off remaining Italian troops, while the main British forces proceeded along the coastal road. On February 5 at Beda Fomm on the Gulf of Sirte, remaining Italian forces surrendered. In just two months Western Desert Force had advanced 500 miles, destroyed 9 Italian divisions, and taken more that 130,000 Italian and Libyan prisoners, 380 tanks, and 845 guns. British losses were 500 killed, 1373 wounded, and 55 missing. It was a brilliant campaign in which O'Connor's men had defeated a numerically superior enemy. O'Connor never utilized more than three divisions of 35,000 men; 7th Armored Division was in action throughout, supported by not more than two infantry divisions. O'Connor also enjoyed excellent naval and air support.[67]

In January 1941 Wavell sent some 70,000 men against 110,000 Italian troops in East Africa. Lieutenant General William Platt commanded two Indian divisions and supporting Sudanese forces thrusting east from Khartoum, while Lieutenant General Sir Alan A. Cunningham took one South African division, two African divisions, and supporting Commonwealth and Free French forces northeast from Kenya. Commander of Italian East Africa, the Duke of Aosta was largely cut off from resupply and two-thirds of his troops were unreliable native levies. He thus ceded most of East Africa as indefensible. Addis Ababa fell on April 5 and a month later Emperor Haile Selassie returned to power. Cunningham's advance on Addis Ababa had covered 35 miles a day, and he captured 50,000 prisoners at a cost to his own forces of 135 killed, 310 wounded, 52 missing and 5 captured. Aosta surrendered East Africa on May 16, although the last Italian forces fought on until November 27.[68]

The Western Desert Force could have driven on to Tripoli and cleared the Axis out of Africa completely, but, as previously noted, Wavell was forced to halt O'Connor's offensive in order to shift assets to Greece. In January 1941 the first German reinforcements arrived in North Africa in the form of air assets: X Air Corps of 500 planes from Norway to Sicily. Its bombers soon neutralized Benghazi as a base for Western Desert Force. O'Connor was now down to only 2nd Armored Division, part of an infantry division, and a motorized brigade.

In March Hitler sent Major General Erwin Rommel and his *Afrika Korps* to Tripolitania. Rommel, a charismatic commander who led from the front, began an offensive against O'Connor's weakened force. Striking with 21st Panzer Division and two Italian divisions (one armored and one motorized), he drove back the British at El Aghella on

March 24, 1941. He then sent *Afrika Korps* in a reprise of O'Connor's advance, only in reverse. The Italian forces followed the coastal road to Derna, while 21st Panzer sliced across the desert of Cyenaica for the port of Tobruk. O'Connor's 2nd Armored Division, endeavoring to delay the Axis drive, was split. One brigade, short of fuel, was cut off at Derna and forced to surrender on April 6. The remainder of the division was captured the next day. The 9th Australian Division reached Tobruk. Unfortunately for the Allied cause, on April 17 O'Connor was captured by a German patrol while on reconnaissance.

Wavell was determined to hold Tobruk in order to deny it to the Axis as a supply port, but also to provide a threat to Rommel and the *Afrika Korps* from the flank. Wavell reinforced Tobruk by sea, inserting the 7th Australian Division along with some tanks. On April 10 Rommel launched a determined attack on the port, but was thrown back after three days of savage fighting. He then encircled Tobruk from the land and besieged it. Rommel's supply situation was by now difficult, especially given the fact that the Allies, thanks to Ultra and their possession of Malta, were extracting a steady toll of Italian shipping across the Mediterranean.

Under pressure from Churchill, on June 15 Wavell prematurely launched Operation BATTLEAXE, a two-division effort (one armored and one infantry) in an effort to relieve Tobruk. The battle played out over three days, but the attackers, split into six small semi-independent task forces and committed piecemeal, failed in their effort. On July 1 Churchill replaced Wavell with General Sir Claude Auchinleck. In effect, Wavell became the scapegoat for Churchill's own decision to expand the already stretched-thin theater to include Greece and Crete.[69]

During July–October both sides built up their strength to renew the offensive. Western Desert Force, now renamed Eighth Army and with General Alan Cunningham in command, was built up to 7 divisions and 700 tanks, supported by 1000 aircraft. Rommel also reorganized the Italian-German *Panzerarmee Afrika* of 10 divisions: 15th and 21st Panzer and the understrength 90th and 164th Light Infantry Divisions, and 6 weak Italian divisions, along with 260 German and 154 Italian tanks, supported by 120 German and 200 Italian aircraft.

Auchinleck attacked first, on November 18. Cunningham's Eighth Army, utilizing new US 'Stuart' light tanks, struck west from its base at Mersa Matruh. Rommel checked the British thrust in a series of uncoordinated battles around Sidi-Rezegh, and Axis forces also halted a sortie from Tobruk. Rommel then took the offensive, slashing into the British rear areas. Cunningham considered withdrawal, but Auchinleck insisted on a stand and Rommel was halted. The *Afrika Korps* then withdrew to the west and south of Tobruk. Auchinleck, displeased with Cunningham's performance, replaced him with Major General Neil M. Ritchie.

At the end of December, under British pressure, Rommel withdrew to his original position at El Agheila in Cyrenaica, 459 miles from the main Axis base of Tripoli. Axis personnel losses were 8900 killed and wounded and 28,500 missing or prisoners; Commonwealth casualties totalled 17,700.

Undaunted, in January 1942 Rommel launched a second offensive. Striking on a narrow front, he drove the widely dispersed British forces back beyond Benghazi, where Auchinleck dug in. Having outrun their supply lines, Axis forces halted. Over the next four months both sides rested and resupplied. The Eighth Army, built up to 125,000 men with 740 tanks and 700 aircraft, now confronted an Axis force of 113,000 men, with 570 tanks and 500 aircraft. Eighth Army established a heavily mined and fortified line extending from Gazala on the coast 40 miles south to Bir Hacheim, held by Major General Marie Pierre Koening's Free French Brigade Group. Auchinleck concentrated his armor behind the French to protect the Eighth Army's open left flank.

Rommel struck on May 28, concentrating his resources to the south. Italian forces failed to take Bir Hacheim, but Rommel's panzers swept south of the British, then turned north inside their line. But the British held and Rommel's tanks were running out of fuel. On May 31, however, Italian infantry managed to penetrate the British minefield belt between Bir Hacheim and Gazala and open a supply route to Rommel. This forced the French to evacuate Bir Hacheim, and on June 13 Ritchie ordered a general retirement.

During the next two weeks the British withdrew in disorder back into Egypt. Tobruk fell on June 21 to a well-planned air and ground attack, the Germans taking 33,000 prisoners. Auchinleck then took personal command of the Eighth Army and briefly held Rommel at Mersa Matruh, before falling back on Alam Halfa ridge between El Alamein on the Mediterranean and the Qattara Depression 40 miles south. Following several German probing attacks in early July, the two lines stabilized only 70 miles from Alexandria. Rommel's offensive had cost the British 75,000 casualties and the Axis only 40,000, but his forces were now stretched thin and his logistical situation had worsened, thanks to a British naval and air build-up in the theater.

The Allies had superior equipment and numbers. Their basic problem was that they did not understand the use of combined arms as well as the Germans did, especially tanks and anti-tank guns working in concert.

Major General Eric Dorman-Smith, Auchinleck's chief of staff, summed up early British generalship in North Africa in these words:

> In the Middle East Command, during the autumn of 1941, there arose the tactical heresy which propounded that armour alone counted in the Desert battle, therefore British armour should discover and destroy the enemy's equivalent armour, after which decision the unarmoured infantry divisions would enter the arena to clear up what remained and hold the ground gained.[70]

Eighth Army learned through bitter experience how to conduct mobile warfare effectively. Rommel employed anti-tank guns in an offensive role ahead of tanks, which waited in cover, rarely firing on the move. Highly trained infantry worked in close concert to reduce enemy anti-tank defenses. Later, General Bernard L. Montgomery summed up: 'I cannot emphasize too strongly that victory in battle depends not on armoured action alone, but on the intimate cooperation of all arms; the tank by itself can achieve little.'[71] The Americans would have to learn the same lesson in 1943.

The British retreat led Churchill again to shake up Middle Eastern Command. On August 13 he relieved both Auchinleck and Ritchie. General Harold R. L. G. Alexander took over Middle Eastern Command and the then Lieutenant General Montgomery assumed command of Eighth Army.

With British strength increasing faster than his own, Rommel mounted a pre-emptive strike on August 31, initiating the week-long Battle of Alam Halfa. As at Gazala, he attempted to outflank the left of the British line in the desert, then slice north. Rommel enjoyed initial success, but was halted by a British tank brigade on Alam Halfa ridge. Short of fuel and under relentless British air attack, the 'Desert Fox' then withdrew. He had no hope of resuming the offensive and could only await the inevitable British attack. The Axis drive in North Africa had been halted.

4

Japanese Successes

December 1941 saw two very different and separate conflicts joined together when the Japanese attacked Pearl Harbor and the United States came into the war. For some time the new nations had been at logger-heads. The basic reason Washington was negotiating with Japan was its unreadiness for war, let alone one that might see the United States fight-ing on two fronts simultaneously. In 1939 the United States was spend-ing just 2 percent of GNP on the military while Japan was spending 71.7 percent of its national budget. When the war began in Europe the US Army ranked nineteenth in the world; its 190,000 men placed it just after Portugal. Its navy was incapable of fighting a struggle in one ocean, let alone a two-ocean war.[1]

In June 1940 Congress had voted to expand the navy but it would be years before that could be translated into ships at sea. In September Congress approved the Selective Training and Service Act (the Burke-Wadsworth Act), creating the first peacetime draft in the nation's history. It provided for the registration of all males between the ages of 21 and 35 and the induction into the armed forces of 800,000 draftees. It was designed to raise and train for one year 1,200,000 troops and 800,000 reserves.

That same month saw the Destroyers for Bases Deal with Britain and on March 8, 1941, the US Congress passed Lend-Lease legislation. This landmark act provided arms, raw materials, and food to powers at war with the Axis. Roosevelt likened it to a man loaning a neighbor his garden hose when the neighbor's house is on fire. This act would protect the lender's own house from fire and, after the fire was out in his own house, the neighbor would return the hose. The amount of Lend-Lease was staggering. One scholar has estimated that the United States ulti-mately provided its allies with industrial production and food to a value equivalent to that of 2000 infantry divisions or 555 armored divisions.[2]

In all the United States distributed some $50 billion in aid to 38 coun-tries. Britain would receive nearly half the total, including 2107 vessels of all types. The Soviet Union, which was extended Lend-Lease aid beginning in November 1941, was the next largest recipient. China and Australia also benefitted enormously from Lend-Lease assistance. In a speech to Parliament Winston Churchill characterized the legislation as the 'most unsordid act in the history of any nation.'[3]

The United States gave much more than it received, but Washington also extracted major concessions from London in trade with the British Commonwealth, the acquisition of British assets abroad, and limitations on British exports. The United States also received an estimated $8 billion in reverse Lend-Lease, most of this from Britain and including facilities and other assistance to US troops in Britain and advanced technology such as radar (in which Britain led the world). In 1940 the Tizard Mission to the United States, headed by Sir Henry Tizard, began the close technological cooperation between the two nations that provided the United States with important British technology, including radar and a prototype cavity-magnetron, vital in development of short-wave radio. Indeed, the war saw close cooperation between the scientists of all the Western nations.[4]

Gearing up US military production took time. A single medium tank, for example, contained 4500 separate parts. The prime contractor might provide 3500 of these, but hundreds of subcontractors would have to supply the remainder. It would be years before production could come fully on line, and much of what was being produced was going to Britain. While this aid kept that nation in the war, it also hindered the US military. Army Chief of Staff General George C. Marshall's draftees were training with broomsticks for rifles and logs representing artillery pieces. The army's Tank Corps had been disbanded in 1919 and the two-division Armored Force was created only in July 1940, after the fall of France. In maneuvers trucks bore signs with the word 'tank.' The Japanese militarists took note of the US military weakness.[5]

President Franklin Roosevelt was especially anxious to expand US air power. In early 1939 Congress approved his request to more than double the size of the Air Corps from 2320 aircraft to 5500. Manpower would increase apace. This plan was rendered obsolete by the outbreak of war in Europe. By July 1941 the United States was producing 1374 aircraft per month, but 349 of these were going to Britain. In July 1941 the United States had only 2366 front-line fighters and bombers; the British Empire had 3100, Germany had 3451, and Japan 2950. As of June 1, 1941, tanks were being turned out at the rate of only 300 a month.[6]

On September 1, 1939, Roosevelt had appointed Brigadier General George C. Marshall as army chief of staff, jumping 60 more senior general officers. A brilliant appointment, Marshall came to be known as the 'Organizer of Victory.' Marshall stressed firepower and maneuver, which meant not only tanks but the entire army would be mechanized and motorized to a degree beyond any other military in the world. It would also enable the army to make effective use of the 'triangular' concept, conceived while Marshall was deputy commander of the Infantry School at Fort Benning, Georgia, during 1927–32, taking the US Army from large, foot-bound 'square' divisions of 28,000 men (two brigades of two regiments each) to highly mobile three-regiment, 15,000-man divisions. The triangular concept extended to the lowest level of combat formations. One maneuver unit would fix an enemy formation in place, while another turned its flank and the third maneuver unit remained in reserve.[7]

In July 1941 Roosevelt called for an estimate of the forces required to defeat 'our potential enemies.' Marshall selected Major Albert C. Wedemeyer of the general staff for the task. Wedemeyer estimated that by the end of 1943, Germany and its allies might field 400 divisions. Conventional wisdom held that attacking forces needed a 2:1 ratio to overcome defenders, and Wedemeyer hypothesized a requirement at 800 divisions. He omitted the Soviet Union, which he believed might not be able to withstand the German onslaught, but he calculated that other allies could provide 100 divisions. This left the United States to raise 700. Counting support troops, this would mean a total US military of 28 million men. But the US population was only 135 million, and industrial production requirements, which experts believed would limit any military to a maximum of 10 percent, meant that the US armed forces could be no more than 13.5 million men, of which the army would get 8.8 million: 2.05 million in the air forces and 6.75 in the ground forces. The latter were to be formed into five armies, three purely offensive task forces and two defensive. Wedemeyer postulated 215 maneuver divisions, of which 61 were to be armored, 61 mechanized, 54 infantry, 4 cavalry, 10 mountain, and 7 airborne. He thought that with overwhelming air superiority, firepower, heavy armored components, and a high degree of mechanization and motorization, such a figure would be sufficient. Transporting such a force to Europe would require 1000 ships of 7000 tons each, and building these alone would take two years, as would raising, equipping, and training the troops.[8]

As it was the United States raised only 91 army divisions in the war, the so-called '90 division gamble' (two of which were deactivated before the end of the war) of 66 infantry, 1 cavalry, 16 armor, 5 airborne, and 1 mountain. There were also 6 marine divisions. During the war the US Army was top-heavy with officers. In 1944 officers were only 2.86 percent of the *Wehrmacht*, whereas they were 7 percent of the US Army, but many of the best officers were not in the infantry. The Army Air Forces and specialist branches, such as rangers and paratroops, and the service staffs were permitted to cream off too high a proportion of the best-educated and fittest recruits. The infantry rifle companies called upon to fight the highly skilled German Army, consisted of men who were in all too many cases the least impressive material America had called to the colors.[9]

The army also worked to develop new high-firepower weapons, including remodeled Browning automatic rifles, the Browning air-cooled lightweight .30 machine gun, the M-2 ('Mod Deuce') .50 caliber machine gun (which remains in use today), and the superb M-1 Garand infantry rifle with an 8-round clip. The M-1, designed by John C. Garand, fired 40 rounds a minute in the hands of the average rifleman, had 40 percent less recoil than the Springfield '03 it replaced, and only 72 parts. The Garand could be entirely broken down using only one tool: a .30-caliber round. The artillery also developed new techniques to minimize the time necessary for all guns in a battery to be firing on a target, and US fire control systems became the best in the world.[10]

The army was not so efficient in other areas. Congress had abolished the Tank Corps in 1920 and relegated tanks to the infantry. Not until 1931 did the cavalry, which still employed horses, receive light 'tankettes,' known as 'combat cars.' The US Armored Force came into being only in July 1940, after the defeat of France. Its M3 Grant, designed hurriedly in 1940, was obsolete before it was built.[11]

Its weapons would provide the US Army with greater firepower than any other army in the world. It was not merely the quality and quantity of military equipment and supplies the United States produced, but the speed with which new weapons came on line. The bazooka anti-tank weapon, for example, went from development to production of 5000 units in only 30 days.[12]

The US Army would not only be the best-armed in the world, it was also the best-supplied, and it had superior communications and unparalleled mobility. In early 1943 Marshall reorganized the army into three major components: the Army Ground Forces; Army Service Forces; and Army Air Forces. In personnel the army grew by April 1945 to 8,157,386 men and women, of whom 1,831,091 were in the 16 Army Air Forces.[13]

The navy, marines, and army air force all grew apace. The navy during the war incorporated the US Coast Guard, their 327' Campbell-class cutters proving invaluable for hunting submarines. The marines, which came under the navy, expanded to six divisions and more than 485,000 men and women.[14]

Until 1943 the navy accepted only volunteers, but Marshall protested to Roosevelt that the navy and the army air forces were skimming off the best personnel, leaving only the dregs for the infantry, and that year the navy began taking draftees. Total navy personnel strength grew to 3,408,347 men and women by August 1945. The US Navy had 1099 vessels of all types in June 1940. By 1944, in numbers of ships alone, it would be larger than all the rest of the world's navies combined. By August 1945 the US Navy had in commission 10 battleships, 27 aircraft carriers (CV and CVL), 111 escort carriers (CVE), 47 cruisers, 370 destroyers, 504 destroyer escorts, 217 submarines, 975 minecraft, 1915 patrol ships and craft, 1612 auxiliary ships, 66,055 landing craft, and 3053 district craft (yard craft).[15]

The longer Roosevelt could delay actual US participation in the war, the better prepared the American military would be to fight it. Time was essential to this effort, and the gains registered were phenomenal. In 1940 the United States produced 12,804 aircraft, but this figure jumped to 26,277 in 1941 and 47,836 in 1942. Tank production registered even greater increases, from about 400 in 1940 to 4052 in 1941, and 24,997 in 1942.[16]

To protect shipping to Great Britain, the United States also secured bases in Greenland and Iceland. It convoyed as far as Iceland US ships and those of other nations as wished to be included, most notably British vessels. On September 4, 1941, a German submarine attacked the convoy-escorting US destroyer *Greer*, firing two torpedoes at her without effect. A British aircraft sighted the sub, and the *Greer* pursued the U-boat and helped locate it for the aircraft. The American destroyer was unmarked and the German U-boat commander had in any case fired in self-defense, but the incident led President Roosevelt on September 11 to issue a 'shoot on sight' order against German submarines. Then, on October 31, 1941, a U-boat sank an American destroyer, the *Reuben James*, which was escorting a convoy about 600 miles west of Iceland in the Atlantic. The first US Navy combat ship sunk in the war, she went down with 115 of her 160-man crew. Within days, Roosevelt transferred the US Coast Guard to navy control, and the next week Congress authorized the arming of US merchantmen and removed restrictions that denied European waters to US merchant ships. As in 1917, German submarine sinkings probably would have provoked war with the United States had it had not come from another quarter.[17]

The United States military had developed color-coded plans for war with potential enemies. The war plan for its most likely enemy, Japan, was codenamed ORANGE. Washington recognized that, although it had a smaller fleet than that of the United States overall, Japan would, by reason of concentration, have naval predominance in the western Pacific, while US and British naval strength would have to be split between the Atlantic and the Pacific.

American military planners saw the war beginning with a Japanese assault on distant US Pacific garrisons, most notably in the Philippines, as the US battle fleet fought its way westward across the Pacific to relieve them. Plans for the Philippines called for its garrison to withdraw into the Bataan Peninsula and the fortified island of Corregidor until the US fleet arrived with reinforcements. Washington never held out much hope of relieving the garrison before it would have to surrender, but this plan contained more merit than General Douglas MacArthur's ill-advised attempt to hold all of the Philippine Islands. He also believed he could prevent any Japanese landing, a claim that was manifestly outrageous.

The problems for the United States in fighting in the Far East were considerable, and the distances were vast. It is 2416 miles from San Francisco to Honolulu and 3904 miles from Honolulu to Yokohama. Forward bases would have to be (re)taken and Japan economically strangled by surface and submarine blockade. The US Navy recognized the distances at which it would have to operate and began work on 'fleet train' planning and underway refueling and replenishment. This logistical effort was critical to the Allied Pacific victory and is often overlooked. The Marine Corps had also worked on amphibious operations, which became its *raison d'être*. Planning was, however, handicapped by a shortage of landing craft. This and a shortage of shipping in general plagued Allied planners in both theaters throughout the war.

Another factor figuring prominently in the war against Japan was the unjustified and racially tinged contempt in which many British and Americans held the Japanese. Early Allied disasters against Japan were not all the result of paucity of resources; local commanders, British and American alike, did little in the fall of 1941 to prepare for war because they did not take their enemy seriously. This was evident in the Philippines and in Malaya. The Japanese, it should be noted, were equally contemptuous of their 'soft' Western adversaries.

Japan had begun its march of conquest in 1931 by annexing Manchuria. Then, in 1937, Japanese forces invaded China proper and soon occupied the coastal areas, driving the Nationalist government of Jiang Jieshi into the interior; but China appeared too vast for Japan to conquer and hold. The outbreak of war in Europe in September 1939 presented Japan with a dramatically changed situation. As during World War I, the preoccupation of the world with European events allowed Japanese leaders an opportunity to expand their nation's power in the Far East.[18]

Japan is a collection of islands approximating the state of California in size. Highly mountainous, Japan is largely bereft of natural resources. This fact, coupled with an expanding population, the traditions of the *samurai* and *bushido* (the way of the warrior), and prior military victories over major powers, China in 1894–1995 and Russia in 1904–05, made it almost inevitable that Japan would seek to fill the power void in Southeast Asia created by the war in Europe.

Both Germany and Japan had relied on the other's victories to divide American attention and resources. In July 1940 an army-dominated government took power in Tokyo. Its goal, as US Ambassador Joseph Grew put it, was to seize the 'golden opportunity' presented by German successes in Europe to build a 'new order' in East Asia. The term 'new order' and the subsequent 'Greater East-Asian Co-Prosperity Sphere' were euphemisms to mask the expulsion of American, British, French, and Dutch interests from Asia and total domination of East Asia by, and for the benefit of, the Japanese. The United States was the major obstacle in that path. Convinced of the inevitability of war, Grew wrote to Roosevelt in December 1940, 'The principal question is whether it is to our advantage to have that showdown sooner or have it later.'[19]

While Roosevelt sought to aid those powers actively fighting the Axis, he also had to contend with public opinion polls that indicated a majority of Americans opposed direct involvement. He had to weigh the lack of US preparedness for war and political factors at home and abroad. A presidential election was looming in November 1940, and Roosevelt, deciding that his leadership was critical, broke with precedent to run for a third four-year term. As the United States built up its own military strength – a process slowed by the substantial production going to Britain – Roosevelt adopted the 'Short of War' policy. This was designed to keep Britain in the war until such time as the United States was ready to fight. In the meantime the president sought to restrain Japan through diplomacy, economic pressure, and naval deterrence.

Japan's leaders saw the defeat of France and the Low Countries as the ideal opportunity for a strike south. Their principal goal was to secure the Dutch East Indies, one of the richest concentrations of natural wealth in the world. Japan desperately needed oil, having very little of its own, and the United States was the chief obstacle in the path of Japanese expansion, with relations between the two countries badly strained. Tokyo had long objected to restrictive US immigration policies against Japanese. Its leaders also saw the vast US naval expansion program underway as aimed primarily at them. The Naval Expansion Act of June 1940, whereby Congress appropriated $4 billion to build a two-ocean navy and more than double the fleet's 1.2 million tons of combat shipping, in effect presented the Japanese with a go-now-or-never dilemma, as in a few years their navy would lose any chance of victory.

There was also the matter of China. The United States, long a friend of that nation, was applying pressure on Japan to quit China and actively assisting the Nationalist government to resist. Tokyo had not declared war on China, which allowed Japan to purchase needed *matériel* in the United States but also permitted Roosevelt to extend aid to China without triggering neutrality legislation. Roosevelt and his advisors were in disagreement as to how to persuade Japan to abandon China without bringing on a war before the United States was rearmed. Chief of Naval Operations Admiral Harold Stark was among those urging restraint in confronting Japan. He argued that the navy was not ready and might, in any case, soon be needed in the Atlantic.

At the same time Tokyo sought policies that would achieve its ends while avoiding a shooting war with the United States. What Washington failed to understand was the depth of Japanese resolve. Tokyo was committed to expansion. If Washington would stand aside, well and good; if not, there would be war. Even a moderate such as Premier Prince Konoye Fumimaro declared, 'I am convinced that the firm establishment of a Mutual Prosperity Sphere in Greater East Asia is absolutely necessary for the continued existence of this country.'[20]

By late July 1940 Roosevelt embraced the views of administration hardliners toward Japan, and he forbade the sale to Japan of petroleum, petroleum products, and scrap iron. Then, in early August, Roosevelt restricted the export of aviation gasoline to nations of the Western Hemisphere. Japan had been importing significant amounts of scrap iron from the United States, but even more serious from the Japanese perspective was the embargo on oil, of which Japan had only a maximum two years' supply. Without oil, Japan would have to evacuate China, an intolerable situation for the Japanese militarists. Tokyo immediately characterized the US actions as an 'unfriendly act.'

On September 26 the Roosevelt administration embargoed all iron and steel scrap, save to Western Hemisphere nations. This and the

September Destroyers for Bases Deal between the United States and Britain made the Japanese more amenable to Hitler's overtures. On September 27, 1940, in Berlin Japan signed an alliance with Germany and Italy, the Tripartite Pact, which recognized Japanese leadership in 'Greater East Asia' and German-Italian leadership in establishing 'a new order' in Europe. Aimed directly at the United States, the pact pledged mutual assistance if any of the signatories was attacked 'by a power at present not involved in the European war or the Sino-Japanese conflict.' German Foreign Minister Ribbentrop predicted to Mussolini and Ciano a week before its signing that the pact would deter both the Americans and the Russians from entering the war.[21]

Meanwhile, the Japanese moved to fill the vacuum left in the Pacific by the defeat of France and the Netherlands. Tokyo brought heavy pressure to bear on the Vichy government for bases in Indo-China, ostensibly to cut off supply routes to the Nationalist government of China from that direction. With the French in no position to resist, in September 1940 Tokyo sent 25,000 troops into northern Indo-China. Then in July 1941, after Germany's invasion of the Soviet Union, Japanese forces moved into southern Indo-China. Although the Japanese left the French administration in place, it was clear that Tokyo was in control.

Japan then had one of the finest air forces in the world with modern aircraft flown by highly skilled air crews who had been trained in fighting in China. The Japanese presence in southern Indo-China brought this air force within striking range of Thailand (then under Tokyo's influence), Malaya, the Dutch East Indies, and the Philippines. Little wonder then that Japan's move into southern Indo-China brought joint retaliation by the United States, Britain, and the Netherlands. On July 26 Roosevelt endorsed the views of the hardline advisors by freezing Japanese assets in the United States. The British and the Dutch followed suit. Simultaneously, Roosevelt incorporated the armed forces of the Philippine Commonwealth into the US Army. He also recalled to active US military service Field Marshal and Commander of the Philippine military General Douglas MacArthur and gave him control of all US Army forces in the Far East.[22]

The Soviet Union was a threat to Japanese expansion. As noted, in 1938 and 1939 there had been battles between Japan and the USSR in the Manchuko–Siberia–Korea border area, during which the Russians had fought well. Given this fact and the stalemate in China that had already claimed the lives of 185,000 Japanese soldiers, it is little wonder that the Japanese military preferred the vacuum of Southeast Asia. But could Japan strike south while the Soviet Union maintained substantial military forces in the Far East? On April 13, 1941, Japan and the Soviet Union had concluded a neutrality pact, although this treaty did not prevent Tokyo from contemplating an attack on the Soviet Far East after the German invasion of that country in June.[23]

Japan's decision not to take advantage of the Soviet Union's weakness by acting in concert with Germany was certainly one of the major strategic blunders of the war. Had Japan and Germany cooperated, the Soviet Union probably would have been defeated, and the Axis powers might well have won the war. Tokyo reached its momentous decision as a consequence of the earlier fighting with the Soviets, because of the severe Siberian weather, and because that region lacked petroleum and rubber, Japan's two principal raw materials strategic needs at the time. The resources of Southeast Asia were simply too tempting, even if this meant war with the United States.

Negotiations proceeded between Washington and Tokyo, but it was the case of an irresistible force meeting an immovable object. Washington insisted that Japan not only withdraw its forces from Indo-China but also China, and the army-dominated government in Tokyo refused to do either. The only way for the United States to avoid war was to give way to Japan's demands. Japan was bent on securing her resource base.

Japanese Premier Konoye sought a conference with Roosevelt in an attempt to avoid war but, with the Japanese Army flatly refusing to withdraw from China, Secretary of State Hull opposed a meeting. Such a conference would not have resolved differences between the two countries, but in retrospect it should have been attempted simply to have delayed the final collision, which would have been to US advantage. Diplomatic negotiations between Japan and the United States continued up until the eve of the Japanese attack on Pearl Harbor, but to the end Washington insisted on Japan's withdrawal from China and Indo-China as a precondition for American trade. Tokyo held this as equivalent to defeat and thus unacceptable.

On September 5, 1941, Emperor Hirohito personally questioned the Japanese Army and Navy chiefs prior to an imperial conference. Here the military gave Premier Konoye a deadline of six weeks to secure an agreement with Roosevelt, during which Japan would prepare for war. At the private meeting Hirohito asked Army Chief of Staff Colonel General Sugiyama Hajime about the probable length of hostilities in case of a Japanese–American war. Sugiyama replied that he believed operations in the South Pacific 'could be disposed of in about three months.' The emperor noted that in 1937 Sugiyama had informed the throne that the China 'incident' would be disposed of in a short time. 'But has it yet ended after more than four years? Are you trying to tell me the same thing again?' An embarrassed Sugiyama explained that China's vast hinterland had made it difficult to bring operations there to a conclusion. At this, the emperor 'raised his voice and said that if the Chinese hinterland was extensive, the Pacific was boundless.'[24]

With no agreement forthcoming between Washington and Tokyo, on October 14 the Japanese Army demanded that negotiations be broken off and that Konoye resign. On October 17 General Tōjō Hideki succeeded him as premier. The strike against the United States would proceed.

In December 1941 the Imperial Japanese Army (IJA) fielded 58 divisions. Stationed in Japan, Manchukuo, Formosa, Korea, China, and Southeast Asia, these divisions varied widely in size from 13,500 to 29,000 men each. Many Japanese formations were basically light infantry. The IJA leadership regarded tanks as little more than armored personnel carriers or infantry support vehicles. Not until the summer of 1942 did the Japanese activate their first two tank divisions, but production and shipping difficulties forced abandonment of the armored force the next year. The army was also sadly deficient in numbers and types of artillery. The failure of the Japanese to develop a satisfactory machine gun between the wars is more surprising, given their reliance during the war on infantry charges. The principal Japanese rifle, the Arisaka M-38, was 35 years old and a clumsy weapon, particularly in the jungle. Actually too big for the average Japanese soldier, it had been adopted as a good example of a Western weapon.

Japanese soldiers were highly motivated and taught to die to the last man, as they often did. They were also poorly equipped and supplied. One source has estimated that every American field soldier in the Pacific fighting was supported by four tons of equipment, every Japanese soldier by two pounds.[25]

Despite its efficiency and high motivation, the Japanese military remained seriously handicapped throughout the war by a lack of cooperation between the services. The army and navy worked at cross purposes, often failing to coordinate plans and efforts. This rivalry had hardened into what one study has styled as 'implacable hostility and mistrust.' The Japanese had no joint chiefs of staff along the lines of the US or British models. The only central directorate was the Imperial Conference presided over by the emperor, and it met but rarely. As a consequence the Japanese often handicapped their own efforts. For example, the army and navy failed to share research on radar technology. By 1943 the United States had a dependable radar; the Japanese counterpart was primitive and employed only on the largest Japanese vessels. American destroyers and even the TBF Avenger aircraft had radar.

Each Japanese service hoarded resources, even those desperately needed by the other; they never did agree on a common machine gun, forcing different types of ammunition; army and navy aircraft employed different electrical systems; and, when the Japanese did develop an IFF (Identification Friend or Foe) capability, army operators on Iwo Jima in 1944 could not identify Japanese Navy aircraft as friendly. Aircraft factories were divided between those areas that made army planes and those producing naval aircraft and each kept design developments secret from the other. Each service also concealed its weaknesses from the other; thus it was 1945 before army leaders discovered how catastrophic the 1942 Battle of Midway had been for the Japanese naval air arm.[26]

Navy leaders were never so doctrinaire as those of the army. A number had studied overseas, and many highly placed officers were well aware of the difficulties Japan would face in a war with the United States. Japanese Navy leaders took their cue from their last great triumph, the defeat of Russia in 1904–05. There they had relied on a pre-emptive naval attack, prior to a formal declaration of war, in order to secure control of the seas and allow the transport of sizable land forces to Korea and Manchuria. The Russian Baltic Fleet had then undertaken a long desperate voyage around the world, only to meet defeat in Japanese home waters at Tsushima.

Both sides, in fact, saw the same scenario for a Pacific War. The Japanese would secure the islands of the western Pacific, including the Philippines. Then the US Pacific Fleet would fight its way westward, culminating in a great Tsushima/Jutland-type fleet engagement.

All major naval powers saw the battleship playing the dominant role at sea, and in this Japan and the United States were no exception. In the 1920s the Japanese were thinking of fighting the war in the western Pacific and therefore stressed speed, armor, and extra guns as crucial, all of which could be secured at the expense of range. In the 1930s both navies devoted much attention to longer-range gunfire, and the US Navy converted a number of older battleships to greater range (30,000–40,000 yards) gun platforms. The Japanese also worked on new battleships and massed torpedo attacks in order to whittle down the American battle strength before a decisive fleet encounter.

The Japanese placed great reliance on the Yamato-class battleships, the largest ever built. In 1936 Tokyo denounced the 1922 Washington and 1930 London naval limitation agreements that had only allowed

Japan nine battleships (vs. 15 each for the USA and Britain), and renewed construction of battleships. Built in great secrecy, the Yamato-class ships weighed 72,000 tons at full load versus 35,000 tons for existing US battleships. The Japanese took advantage of the innovation of small tube boilers, which meant smaller engines and greater speed. The Yamato-class would have a speeed of 27-knots versus 21 knots for the existing US battleships. New US battleships would have the same higher speed.

The Yamato-class mounted 9 x 18.1-inch guns and had 25-inch face armor on their turrets. Their 18.1-inch guns were in fact the largest ever to go to sea. They hurled a 3200-pound projectile, versus 2700 pounds for those fired by the 16-inch guns on the US Navy Iowa-class battleships. The Japanese planned four of these but finished just three, and only two as battleships: *Yamato* (completed just after Pearl Harbor) and *Musashi* (1942). *Shinano* was completed as an aircraft carrier. *Yamato* and *Musashi* were built in great secrecy and remained unknown outside of Japan until they were commissioned, but because of their great cost and national prestige they did not see combat until late in the war.[27]

Although Washington was in the dark as to the construction of the Yamato-class ships, in response to the Japanese withdrawal from the treaty strictures, in 1937 the US Congress reluctantly authorized additional US battleships, the first in 15 years. Over the next three years Congress voted construction of ten new fast battleships to go with the 15 already in commission. The four Iowa-class ships (the *Iowa*, *New Jersey*, *Wisconsin*, and the *Missouri*), of six authorized in 1938-40, were, at 33 knots, the fastest battleships ever built. They mounted 9 x 16-inch guns and weighed 57,540 tons at full load, but they were close to the Yamato-class in gun power and protection.[28]

The great fleet action between battleships to decide the Pacific War anticipated by both sides never occurred. Carrier aviation bested the battleship at Pearl Harbor, yet so deep-seated was the traditional view of the battleship that it still had not faded after Pearl Harbor. In fact, after Pearl Harbor the US Navy lost no more battleships throughout the Pacific War. Battleships joining the fleet served as shore bombardment ships, anti-aircraft platforms, and high-speed tankers to accompany the aircraft carriers.[29]

Japan also had the 'Long Lance' torpedo. The apex of Japanese naval technology, this 24-inch diameter torpedo carried a 60 percent greater warhead and had four times the range of the comparable US weapon. Oxygen driven, it left no wake, as opposed to the US torpedo. The Long Lance was carried on destroyers and, unlike the US Navy, on cruisers.

The Japanese counted on the Long Lance as a means by which they could savage the US battlefleet as it worked its way across the Pacific toward the climactic fleet battle. The Long Lance also appeared in an 18-inch version to be carried by naval aircraft. These were the type employed at Pearl Harbor. In contrast, the US Mark XIV 21-inch torpedo was unreliable. It ran too deep and there were also problems with its magnetic exploder, which caused many to be duds.[30]

The longer range guns on battleships by the late 1930s added to problems of spotting, particularly over the horizon. Partly for this reason both the Americans and the Japanese embraced carrier aviation. Naval aircraft would be used for reconnaissance, spotting, and securing air superiority. Both navies built large, efficient fleet carriers. In December 1941 the US Navy had seven of these, along with 15 battleships.

The Japanese embarked on an effort qualitatively to have the top navy in the world. Japanese sailors were superbly trained and the navy drilled repeatedly at and excelled in night fighting. The US Navy had given little attention to this, as such training was bound to result in casualties that would cost admirals their jobs. Japanese commanders did not have to worry about such pressure. The IJN's skill in night fighting was apparent in the early naval battles off Guadalcanal, especially at Savo Island.

Both the IJN and the US Navy also stressed development of long-range submarines. In fact, however, the Japanese never employed their submarines effectively and they largely ignored the substantially defensive anti-submarine warfare. The IJN employed its long-range submarines as an adjunct to the fleet and later as supply ships rather than as commerce raiders. The Japanese also emphasized aerial reconnaissance aircraft, which enjoyed early superiority over those of the United States. As a result, the Japanese usually located American ships first.

The Japanese initially possessed some superb aircraft, most notably the Mitsubishi A6M Reisen Type O fighter, known as the *Reisen* ('Zero'). The best-known Japanese aircraft of the war, and produced in greater quantity (10,449) than any other Japanese aircraft and in service throughout the war in the Pacific, the highly maneuverable Zero was the first carrier-based aircraft to outperform its land equivalents. It had a top speed of 332 (later 356) mph and armaments of 2 x 20mm cannon and 2 x 7.7mm machine guns. The Nakajima Ki 43 Hayabusa (known as 'Oscar' in the Allied code) was another fine fighter. Numerically, it was the most significant fighter in the IJA's air force (5919 built). Fast (top speed of 308 mph) and agile, it enjoyed supremacy over Allied fighters early in the Pacific War.

The Japanese also had excellent medium bombers in the twin-engined Mitsubishi G3M (known as 'Nell' by the Allies) and G4M ('Betty).' More Bettys were produced (2446) than any other Japanese bomber of the war, and Japan had 160 in service at the time of Pearl Harbor. An excellent aircraft capable of carrying a ton of bombs or torpedoes up to 2694 miles, it and other Japanese aircraft sacrificed armor for speed. Early Japanese planes lacked self-sealing tanks, and they came to be called 'flying cigarette lighters.'[31]

The rivalry between army and navy led to parallel development of aircraft, and the Japanese tended to over-engineer small assemblies. They also failed to adopt modern mass-production techniques, which meant that parts for one plane would often not fit another. As a result many Japanese aircraft could not be repaired locally and had to be written off. Most important, the success of their air force against the Chinese led Japanese leaders to assume that a small number of aircraft, flown by well-trained crews, would suffice for victory.[32]

In a war between the United States and Japan the IJN would enjoy the advantages of interior lines and concentration of force, whereas US naval units would be divided between the Atlantic and Pacific and spread out over both. In the Pacific and Indian Oceans in December 1941, the naval balance was as follows: 10 Japanese battleships to 12 Allied (9 US and 3 British); 10 aircraft carriers to 4; 18 heavy cruisers to 15 (13 US and 2 British Empire); 20 light cruisers to 25 (11 US, 10 British Empire, and 4 Netherlands); 112 destroyers to 90 (68 US, 14 British Empire, 7 Netherlands, and 1 Free French); and 71 submarines to 73 (57 US, 1 British, and 15 Netherlands).[33]

Japan had concentrated its limited industrial capacity on construction of warships and it remained sadly deficient in merchant shipping capacity, an appalling weakness given its reliance on imports, especially oil. In December 1941 Japan possessed only 49 tankers totalling 587,000 tons. By way of contrast, in 1939 Britain, which was also dependent on foreign oil, had 425 tankers of 2,997,000 tons; the United States had 389 tankers of 2,836,000 tons.[34]

In August 1939 Admiral Yamamoto Isoroku had taken command of the IJN fleet. Yamamoto opposed war with the United States, but he lost this issue as well as a struggle against battleships as the mainstay of the fleet. Believing that aircraft carriers would be the key in any Pacific encounter, he was able, however, to see to it that Japan entered the war with more than any other power. On December 7, 1941, Japan had 10 carriers, the US only 7, of which 4 were in the Atlantic. Throughout the late 1930s Japan built up the largest and best-trained naval air arm in the world; fighting in China provided battle experience. In 1941 first-line Japanese pilots had 500–800 flying hours and 50 percent of army pilots and 10 percent of navy pilots had combat experience against China and/or the Soviet Union. By 1941 the IJN was fully prepared to strike anywhere in the Pacific in a new form of battle at sea.[35]

Despite his fine personal qualities and leadership traits, Yamamoto proved wanting as a strategist. It was he who persuaded Tokyo to abandon its earlier plan to carry out the southern conquests while the battle fleet and the carriers awaited the US fleet. Yamamoto reversed this strategy in favor of a pre-emptive strike on the US base at Pearl Harbor. He predicted that the US Pacific Fleet would take two to three years to recover from such an attack, and in the meantime Japan would have secured the oil and other resources of the Dutch East Indies. Yamamoto also expressed the hope that destruction of the Pacific Fleet at Pearl Harbor would induce the United States to lose heart and negotiate with Japan. This proved a strange misreading of American psychology by a man who had studied in the United States and claimed to know that country well. Unlike IJA leaders, however, Yamamoto understood the limitations of Japanese strength. It was this realism that had led him to urge the Premier, Prince Konoye, to resolve the dispute with the United States without war.[36]

The Pearl Harbor attack

As part of his program to confront Japan, in the summer of 1940 President Roosevelt ordered the Pacific Fleet to relocate from San Diego to Pearl Harbor on the Hawaiian Island of Oahu. Japanese naval intelligence officers posted to the consulate in Honolulu immediately gathered information on the base and ship movements there. Meanwhile, Yamamoto bent every effort to make certain that his men, ships, and aircraft were ready. Ship and aircraft crewmen went through intensive training, including at least 50 practice flights by bomber crews. The successful November 1940 British strike at Taranto in Italy by torpedo-bombers provided confirmation that the Japanese plan, already well underway, could work.[37]

The Japanese were also concerned about the need to penetrate the heavy deck armor of the US battleships. Thus, in addition to utilizing 18-inch torpedoes dropped from torpedo bombers, the Japanese fitted 16-inch armor-piercing shells with fins. Experiments showed that, dropped vertically as bombs from as low as 3000 meters, these could penetrate the heavy deck armor of the US ships.[38]

To avoid detection, the Japanese planned to approach Pearl Harbor from the northwest via the Kurile Islands. They also planned to launch their strike aircraft close to Pearl Harbor, then recover them at a distance. This 'unequal leg' tactic would mean that any US planes retaliating against the Japanese ships would have to fly two long legs, out and back. The US Navy, meanwhile, sought to counter the danger of a Taranto-type torpedo attack by fitting its larger ships with anti-torpedo nets. But Pearl Harbor has a narrow mouth and Commander of the Pacific Fleet Admiral Huband E. Kimmel wanted to be able to sortie his ships as quickly as possible in the event of attack. The cumbersome nets would be a hindrance, and so they were not deployed on December 7 of 1940, a decision that added to the subsequent destruction.

Many factors determined timing of the attack. The Japanese knew that the US ships were usually at Pearl Harbor on weekends, when they were not fully manned. Sunday was thus a natural choice for the day of the attack, but after mid-December monsoons would hinder task force refueling at sea and also adversely affect amphibious landings in Malaya and the Philippines. Finally, on Sunday December 7 there would be a waning moon, aiding chances of the Japanese carriers reaching Pearl Harbor undetected. The Japanese priorities were first battleships, then aircraft carriers, then cruisers. There is no mention in Japanese records of targeting shore installations.[39]

Vice-Admiral Nagumo Chuichi had command of the attacking task force, centered on 6 carriers with 411 aircraft, of which 350 were employed in two attacking waves: 129 high-level bombers, 103 dive-bombers, 40 torpedo-bombers, and 78 fighters. Accompanying the carriers were 2 battleships, 3 cruisers, 9 destroyers, 3 submarines, and 8 tankers. Early on the morning of December 7 about 275 miles from Pearl Harbor, after a brief delay by bad weather, Nagumo ordered his aircraft to launch. In only 15 minutes the Japanese had gotten off 183 of 185 aircraft scheduled in the first attack wave. At 6:20 a.m. the planes set course for Pearl Harbor.

Fortune favored the Japanese. A series of lapses on the part of the defenders conspired to give the attackers complete surprise. The first warning was in the form of submarine sightings. The Japanese employed five midget submarines. Virtually suicide craft, these were released by mother submarines near the harbor entrance. They were then to make their way into the harbor before dawn, settle on the bottom, and await the air strike. As it worked out, only one of the midgets may actually have fulfilled its mission. In any case, at 3:42 a.m. on December 7 a US minesweeper spotted a periscope indicating a submarine moving toward the harbor entrance. With no US submarines supposed to be in the area, it reported the sighting to the destroyer *Ward*, which then looked for but failed to locate it. At 6:40 a.m. the *Ward* encountered a midget submarine on the surface outside the harbor entrance and promptly sank it. This was an hour before the Japanese aircraft arrived, but previous bogus submarine sightings led officers in the Operations Center on Ford Island to discount the event, pending further verification.[40]

Another warning came in the form of a radar report. At 7:00 a.m. a US mobile radar station near Kahuku Point on the northern tip of Oahu detected the approach of a large number of aircraft about 130 miles out. However, personnel at the Information Center at Fort Shafter interpreted this as a flight of B-17s scheduled to arrive from California. The radar operator failed to report the key point that it was probably more than 50 aircraft; there were only 12 B-17s, which were in any case approaching from the east rather than the north.[41]

Finally, US decoding of a Japanese message ordering the destruction of documents and breaking-off of discussions at 1:00 p.m. Washington time clearly indicated a Japanese attack at about that time against a US installation. Warnings went out from the War Department to all US Pacific installations, but Hawaii received its warning via Western Union telegram because atmospheric conditions would not allow radio transmission. The message did not mention the timing of the attack as it might relate to Hawaii time (7:30 a.m.) and, in any case, it reached Pearl Harbor only after the attack was in progress.[42]

The Japanese aircraft thus arrived over Pearl Harbor unannounced. In their attack the Japanese sank four battleships: the *Arizona*, *California*, *Oklahoma*, and the *West Virginia*. The *Nevada* was extensively damaged, and the *Maryland*, *Pennsylvania*, and the *Tennessee* were lightly damaged. Japanese aircraft also sank five smaller ships, including three destroyers; three light cruisers and a seaplane tender were damaged.

Army commander at Pearl Harbor Lieutenant General Walter C. Short, fearful of sabotage by the many Japanese living in the Hawaiian Islands, had packed his aircraft closely together. This, of course, made them perfect targets for aerial attack. Ammunition was also stored separately from the planes and would not be immediately available. All of this assured that most US Army aircraft could not take to the air for several hours.[43]

In the attack, the Americans lost 188 aircraft destroyed and 63 badly damaged. The Japanese lost only 29 planes destroyed and 111 damaged, apart from the five midget submarines sunk. The disparity in casualties was even more telling. The Americans suffered 2280 dead and 1109 wounded; Japanese losses were under 100 dead.[44]

Historian Gordon Prange, who wrote the exhaustive history of the Pearl Harbor attack, has Commander Fuchida Mitsuo, who commanded the Japanese strike aircraft, reporting to Admiral Nagumo that his planes had sunk four US battleships and badly damaged four others but urging that a second attack be launched that afternoon against the oil tank farms, repair and maintenance facilities, and remaining ships. Prange claimed that Commander Genda Minoru, chief air officer of First Air Fleet, who had helped develop the attack plan, joined Fuchida in pointing out to Nagumo that the Japanese controlled the air over Oahu and the sea. But with the US carriers undetected and now certainly alerted as to events, Nagumo refused. Genda is said to have wanted Nagumo to remain in the area for several days and try to finish off the US carriers.[45]

Historian H. P. Willmott has noted, however, that Genda, who was indeed on the bridge of flagship *Akagi* during the operation, claimed that no proposal for a second strike was ever made. Prange's statement was evidently based solely on his postwar interview with Fuchida. Genda did, however, note that he had told Nagumo before the attack that a second strike might indeed be necessary. No attacks on port facilities were ever mentioned, but had the Japanese mounted an additional strike and destroyed the oil tanks and facilities, the Pacific Fleet would have been forced to relocate to San Diego. But Nagumo did not want to risk his own ships. He had achieved his objectives at virtually no cost, and the fleet would now return home.[46]

The Pearl Harbor attack brought great advantages to Japan. First, the US Pacific Fleet was virtually put out of action, allowing the Japanese to carry out their aim of amphibious operations in the west and southwest Pacific without serious US naval interference. The Japanese also won time to extend and build up their defensive ring.

There were, of course, negatives. The Japanese had missed the carriers, which were then at sea on ferrying duties. Furthermore, all US battleships were refloated save *Arizona*, and all of these save *Oklahoma* saw subsequent service. The loss of US life in the attack, while tragic, was not catastrophic to the subsequent US war effort and certainly was far less than what it would have been had the fleet been caught at sea. But the primary negative for Japan was psychological. Coming without declaration of war, the attack aroused such anger in the United States as to sweep away any isolationist sentiment and mobilize the entire nation behind the war effort.

The Japanese had intended to keep just within the bounds of legality. Their declaration breaking off talks with the United States was to have been delivered to the US government just prior to the attack and thus the attack would fall within the constraints of international law. But the extreme length of the Japanese note (5000 words) and delays in decoding it at the embassy meant that it could not be delivered until 2:20 p.m. Washington time, 35 minutes *after* the start of the Pearl Harbor attack. The failure of the carefully scripted Japanese scenario secured the moral high ground for Washington.

The Germans did not know of the attack in advance. Neither did Japanese Ambassador to Berlin General Ōshima, who received only 'limited indications of the impending hostilities.' This fact did not prevent Germany and Italy from declaring war on the United States on December 11, however. Undoubtedly Hitler believed that the United States was already working hard for the Allied cause and that eventual US involvement in the war was a virtual certainty. He completely underestimated the power of the United States, and he believed that, if Germany failed to support Japan, it would damage relations with that country and preclude future Japanese assistance against the Soviet Union. Also, Hitler hated Roosevelt; here was a chance to show what he really thought of him. The Tripartite Pact did not cover acts of aggression, and so he might have continued his policy of postponing the showdown with the United States. Had Germany not declared war on the United Stares, Roosevelt would have been obliged to concentrate the US military effort solely against Japan. The decision was another one of Hitler's major mistakes.[47]

For Americans, the attack against Pearl Harbor produced widespread criticism of the authorities. Kimmel and Short, the two US commanders involved, were subsequently relieved of command. On November 27 Marshall had issued a message to Pacific army commanders warning of 'hostile action possible at any moment' and the Navy Department had sent an even stronger 'war warning' to Kimmel that read in part, 'an aggressive move by Japan is expected within the next few days.'[48]

Despite this many Americans believed then, and some continue to believe today, that Roosevelt had somehow set up the Pacific Fleet at Pearl Harbor in order to bring the United States into the war. It is true that Roosevelt was indeed hoping to bring America's weight into the war against Hitler, but there is sufficient evidence of army and navy inefficiency and miscalculation to outweigh the arguments of 'revisionist' historians. There is simply no truth to the charge that Roosevelt knew about in advance, or set up, the Pearl Harbor attack. He loved the navy and it is inconceivable that he would have done anything to harm it. Aside from that, any conspiracy would have had to involve a number of key people, including his service chiefs and intelligence personnel, all of whom would have to have gone to their graves without revealing the secret. The case against Roosevelt is entirely circumstantial.[49]

The Japanese now went on a far-flung offensive. Free from interference by the Pacific Fleet, they took Guam, Hong Kong, Singora, Kota Bharu, and Wake Island. They also attacked the Philippines. Plan ORANGE had held out little hope for the immediate relief of the American Pacific outposts: US planners estimated more than two months would elapse before the navy could reinforce the Philippines. This compares to only eight days for the Imperial Navy steaming from Japan or two days if from Formosa.[50]

The fall of the Philippines

Much of the blame for the subsequent US disaster in the Philippines rests with MacArthur. Remote, aloof, uninterested in logistics, he was convinced of the superiority of his own forces. Brigadier General Lewis H. Brereton, commander of his air force, observed regarding the US military leadership in the islands, 'The idea of imminent war seemed far removed from the minds of most.'[51]

MacArthur was serenely confident that he could defend from the beaches the big island of Luzon against invasion. He had 22,400 US regulars (including the excellent 12,000-man strong Philippine Scouts), 3000 Philippine Constabulary, and 107,000 poorly trained and equipped Philippine Army troops. He also had B-17 bombers, which he planned to utilize to attack any invading Japanese fleet, and submarines. But there were a plethora of potential landing points and a lot would depend on where the Japanese came ashore. Also MacArthur scrapped the original plan to pre-position depots on the Bataan Peninsula and Corregidor sufficient for 43,000 men on Bataan and 7000 on Corregidor for 180 days. As one historian has noted, 'It is in the nature of warrior generals to prefer combat and combat support troops to logisticians.'[52]

MacArthur kept most of the regulars back near Manila. The extensive coastline was covered only by low-grade Philippine Army troops, meaning that the Japanese would encounter little resistance in getting ashore. Much of Admiral Thomas C. Hart's US Asiatic Fleet, already weak, was withdrawn. Only four destroyers, 28 submarines, and some torpedo boats remained. US air assets in the islands were also woefully inadequate.[53]

News of the attack at Pearl Harbor reached Manila at 2:30 on the morning of December 8. The Japanese were forced by ground fog to postpone a strike by 500 Formosa-based aircraft against targets in the Philippines. But this turned to Japan's advantage. Meanwhile, Brereton put his aircraft on standby and reported to MacArthur's headquarters at 5:00 a.m. He had 35 B-17s at two fields, and he also had 90 fighter aircraft. Most were modern P-40s, along with a few obsolete P-35s. The Philippine Army had an additional 12 P-26s.

Brereton wanted an immediate strike on Takao Harbor, Formosa, against Japanese warships and shipping gathering there for the invasion of the Philippines. MacArthur refused permission and his aide, Brigadier General Richard K. Sutherland, would not even let Brereton see his superior, who by all reports appeared shaken by events, even catatonic. MacArthur never gave Brereton an explanation for his refusal to allow the strike but later held that his task was to defend the Philippines rather than initiate an attack. Some US bombers and fighters ordered into the air as a precaution now returned to base, and with few exceptions all US aircraft in the Philippines were on the ground when, around 11:30 a.m. the first wave of Japanese aircraft arrived over Clark Field.

There was no advance warning. One Zero pilot described 'sixty enemy bombers and fighters neatly parked along the airfield runways . . . the Americans had made no attempt to disperse their planes to increase their safety.' The Japanese fighters, followed by the bombers, went to work. An hour later Japanese aircraft also struck Iba Field, destroying most of its aircraft and the only operational radar station in the islands. By that evening, MacArthur's air arm was in ruins. Seventeen of the 35 B-17s had been destroyed, along with 55 of the 72 P-40s and many of the older fighters. Only seven Japanese planes were shot down. Although Short and Kimmel had been sacked for their command shortcomings at Pearl Harbor, MacArthur escaped any censure and, indeed, on December 22 was promoted to temporary full general.[54]

The first Japanese troops came ashore on Bataan Island on December 8 and at Aparri on the big island of Luzon on the 10th. The Aparri landing was unopposed. Major General Jonathan Wainwright, commander of the North Luzon Force, assumed the main Japanese landings would take place in the Lingayen Gulf and had the bulk of his forces there. The main body of 43,000 men of Lieutenant General Homma Masaharu's Fourteenth Army went ashore from 85 transports in the southern Lingayen Gulf on the 22nd. Many of the poorly trained Philippine infantry broke on the first appearance of the Japanese.

MacArthur now reverted to the original plan of withdrawing all his forces into the Bataan Peninsula. Unfortunately for the defenders, the movement of supplies into the peninsula was mishandled. Many supply dumps, relocated when MacArthur altered his plans, were simply lost in the hasty retreat into Bataan, with the result that the defenders went immediately on half-rations. Helped by the fact that Japanese strength was half their own, MacArthur's troops withdrew into the peninsula by the beginning of January 1942.[55]

The peninsula is only about 20 by 25 miles and MacArthur now had to feed 110,000 people on Bataan and the island of Corregidor, as well as civilians, rather than the 43,000 in the original plan. The peninsula was also extremely malarious. Many of the defenders soon fell sick, and barely a quarter were able to fight.

Washington decided not to attempt a relief of the Philippines, which was deemed impossible. Rather than yield a tremendous propaganda advantage to the Japanese with the capture of the US commander in the Far East, Roosevelt ordered MacArthur out to Australia on March 10. MacArthur, derisively referred to by many of the defenders as 'Dugout Doug' for his failure to leave Malinta Tunnel on Corregidor (he visited Bataan but once), later received the Medal of Honor. Wainwright took up the command, but Filipino morale was shattered by MacArthur's departure. On April 9 the Americans surrendered the peninsula.[56]

The Japanese forced the weakened survivors of Bataan to march 55 or 60 miles to prisoner-of-war camps. Most of the prisoners were sick and hungry and there was little food. In fairness to the Japanese, they were unprepared for the large influx of prisoners, but it also true that they behaved with a shocking disregard of the norms of warfare and even denied the prisoners water. Up to 650 Americans and 5000–10,000 Filipinos died in the 'Bataan Death March' to Camp O'Donnell, and another 1600 Americans and 16,000 prisoners died in the camp in the first six to seven weeks of imprisonment.[57]

The fight then shifted to Corregidor, separated from the Bataan Peninsula by only two miles. This enabled the Japanese to bombard it by artillery and attack it from the air. On May 5 the Japanese staged a successful amphibious assault accompanied by tanks. The next day, his resources exhausted and with less than three days of water remaining, Wainwright ordered US forces throughout the Philippines to surrender to avoid unnecessary casualties. Formal resistance ended on June 9.

What is remarkable about the Philippine campaign is not its conclusion but the skill and determination of the defenders, who held out for six months. Tokyo had expected the conquest to take only two months, and General Homma was called home to Japan in disgrace. Perhaps the greatest surprise was the loyalty of the Filipinos to the United States. The Japanese expected only the Americans to fight and the Filipinos to rally to them. But after its first hasty retreats, the poorly trained and inadequately equipped Philippine Army settled down and fought well. It and the vast majority of the Filipino people also remained loyal to the United States during the campaign and the long Japanese occupation that followed.

The capture of Malaya and Singapore

Japan now ran riot in southeast Asia. Simultaneously with Pearl Harbor, on December 8 the Japanese struck Malaya from the air, and Lieutenant General Yamashita Tomoyuki's Twenty-Fifth Army landed at Kota Bharu and at Singora and Patani in the north of the country. Again the Japanese invasion force arrived undetected. Yamashita's 60,000 men, supported by artillery and tanks, moved south, easily brushing aside the few British defenders in the north. Throughout the campaign for Malaya and Singapore, Yamashita kept up the pressure and held the initiative. British commander Lieutenant General Arthur E. Percival had about 100,000 men, but he anticipated the Japanese attack farther south and had the bulk of his defenders deployed there.

Despite its recommendations and largely because of pressure by Churchill for a show of strength, at the end of October the British Admiralty ordered out to the Far East the new King George V-class battleship *Prince of Wales* and old battle cruiser *Repulse*, the new aircraft carrier *Indomitable*, and four destroyers. The *Indomitable* had run aground near Jamaica while undergoing trials, forcing her repair. The remaining ships, which arrived at Singapore on December 2, were thus dependent for air cover on the few British land aircraft available.

On learning of the Japanese invasion of Malaya, new British Eastern Fleet commander, Admiral Tom Phillips, immediately departed Singapore with Force Z, the two capital ships and four destroyers, to attack Japanese ships supporting the landings. But lacking reconnaissance aircraft, Phillips was unable to find the Japanese. Force Z was returning to Singapore when it was attacked on December 10 by at least 80 Japanese aircraft based in southern Indo-China. Despite evasive tactics and anti-aircraft fire, both ships were sunk by Japanese torpedo bombers. The Japanese lost only three aircraft in the attack. British loss of life was heavy; some 900 men died, including Phillips. Destroyers rescued the remainder. Churchill later blamed Phillips for the disaster, claiming he should not have attempted to intercept the Japanese invasion force. In fact, Churchill, Phillips, and the Admiralty had previously rejected the notion that battleships underway and firing anti-aircraft guns could be sunk by air attack. The engagement demonstrated that battleships would have to have air cover if they were to survive.[58]

With the loss of the *Prince of Wales* and *Repulse*, the Allies had no capital ships in the Pacific save the three US aircraft carriers. The event also sealed the fate of Malaya and Singapore. The great British naval base of Singapore, 20 years in the building and long touted for its supposed impregnability, fell on February 15, 1942, a victim of British complacency and the failure to anticipate an overland attack. The 'Gibraltar of Asia' had been built to withstand an attack from the sea rather than the land. It had coastal defense guns of up to 15-inches and, contrary to popular misconception after its fall, these did not just point toward the sea; most of the defending batteries were capable of 360-degree traverse. The problem lay in their ammunition. Large quantities of armor-piercing shell for use against ships were available, but there was little in the way of high-explosive shell for employment against troops.

In early 1942 British Empire forces were stretched thin, defending not only the British Isles but the Mediterranean. There was a limit to what the British could do, but London expected Singapore to hold out until it could be relieved by naval units sent out from Europe. Once the Japanese invasion was underway, the British did send some reinforcements, but these only assured that the ultimate defeat was more costly. With few British aircraft on hand, the Japanese dominated the skies. The defenders of Singapore, many of them Australian and Indian units, were also poorly trained and lacked anti-aircraft and anti-tank guns.

In their assault on Singapore Japanese forces were actually outnumbered 30,000 to 85,000 men, their ammunition was low, and they had no reserves; but Percival's defensive dispositions were faulty. British forces were all put in forward defensive positions, and the Japanese cut the water supply to Singapore Island. Many of his troops deserted, including the engineers who were to destroy the naval dockyard, and Percival also had the welfare of civilians to consider when he surrendered unconditionally on February 15. The Japanese took 70,000 prisoners. Malaya and Singapore had fallen in only 70 days, and in the entire campaign the British sustained 138,700 casualties, mostly captured; Japanese loses were only 9824. British prestige in Asia never quite recovered from the shock. The fall of Singapore signalled the end of the colonial era in Asia and is rightly considered Britain's greatest military defeat in its modern history.[59]

The Japanese had only contempt for their captives who, they believed, had not shown proper martial spirit. Some of the British, including those already sick and wounded in Singapore's Alexandra Hospital, were simply massacred, along with the medical staff. Others were imprisoned and still others were shipped to various points in the Japanese Empire as slave labor on military projects. General Itagaki Seishiro explained the shipping of British prisoners to Korea as necessary 'to stamp out the respect and admiration of the Korean people for Britain and America and establish a strong faith in Japanese victory.'[60]

The Japanese also captured Hong Kong. The garrison there numbered only 10,000 men, supported by five aircraft and three old destroyers and some smaller craft. In a needless tragedy, London dispatched nearly 2000 poorly trained and ill-equipped Canadian soldiers to help defend the outpost, when it had already been written off. The Japanese committed 60,000 troops to the capture of Hong Kong and, striking from Kowloon across the narrow strait, they hit the city from behind. Hong Kong surrendered on December 25 after 17 days of fighting (more than the ten days the Japanese had allocated to the operation). The Japanese then went on a two-week rampage, attacking and killing patients in a hospital, and raping hundreds of women and looting the possessions of the inhabitants.[61]

As other Japanese forces took Malaya, the Fifteenth Army occupied Thailand. Part of the Japanese force captured the British air base at Victoria Point, severing British communications between Malaya and India. The remainder prepared to invade Burma.

Fighting in Burma

The Japanese invaded Burma with two divisions on January 12, 1942. In their advance the Japanese had control of the skies and also made effective use of Burmese nationalists, who had been promised independence from British rule. Headed by Aung San, the nationalists led minor uprisings against the British and conducted sabotage operations. British commander Lieutenant General Thomas Hutton's rag-tag force approximating two divisions of British, Burmese, and Indian troops was soon driven across the Salween River. In February they were forced across the Sittang. Hutton got out most of his men, but was forced to abandon his heavy equipment.

In early March Lieutenant General Alexander arrived in Rangoon to replace Hutton. Although the British brought up some reinforcements from India, they were still outnumbered and their forces were widely scattered and demoralized. In consequence Alexander abandoned Rangoon on 7 March. Nationalist Chinese leader Jiang Jieshi then offered assistance, sending his chief of staff, US Army Lieutenant General Joseph Stilwell, with the undermanned and indifferently equipped Nationalist Fifth and Sixth Armies. Stilwell and the Chinese advanced down the Burma Road and linked up with Alexander and the British at Maymayo, where the Allies set up defensive positions. In mid-March Major General William Slim arrived from the Middle East to take command of the Burma Corps.

Fighting resumed, both sides reinforcing in early April, with the Japanese renewing their offensive later that month. A series of hard-fought battles saw the Japanese victorious. Mandalay fell on May 1. Most of the Chinese retreated back on Yunan, while Slim got his Burma Corps across the Chindwin River and withdrew to Imphal. In this First Burma Campaign the British suffered 30,000 casualties of 42,000 men in their force. About half the casualties were 'missing,' and many of these were Burmese. Of 95,000 Chinese, only Major General Sun Li-jen's 38th Division withdrew as a fighting unit. Sun Li-jen, later known to the Chinese as 'the ever-victorious general,' turned out to be one of the better Chinese generals of the war. Chinese losses are unavailable, but the Japanese sustained only about 7000 casualties. During the next six months, while the Japanese consolidated their hold on Burma, the British prepared to defend India. China was now cut off from its allies, forcing the Chinese to rely on resupply by air over the world's highest mountains, the eastern Himalayas (dubbed the 'Hump' by American pilots).[62]

Operations against the Dutch East Indies

In January Japanese heavy cruisers and destroyers escorted transports carrying elements of the Japanese Sixteenth Army to the northern Netherlands East Indies. Japanese land-based aircraft and Admiral Nagumo's First Air Fleet supported the operation. Japanese surface ships easily swept aside the outgunned naval units of the ABDA (American-British-Dutch-Australian) Command under US Navy Admiral Thomas Hart. A series of sea battles followed.

On January 22, four American destroyers intercepted a Japanese invasion force approaching Balikpapan and, in the Battle of Macassar

Strait, sank a small Japanese warship and four troopships. The Japanese rushed in reinforcements, and on January 30 they took the main Dutch base of Amboina.

On February 4 Japanese airplanes attacked Dutch and American ships in Madoera Strait, damaging the cruisers *Houston* and *Marblehead*. The *Marblehead* steamed for the United States and repair, leaving the *Houston* as the only major US surface combatant in the area. On February 19 Nagumo's First Air Fleet carried out an air strike on Darwin, Australia, inflicting major damage on shipping in the port and shore installations.

On February 27 Dutch Rear Admiral Karel Doorman initiated the Battle of the Java Sea when he led 5 cruisers and 9 destroyers to intercept a Java-bound Japanese invasion force of 41 transports, escorted by Rear Admiral Takagi Takeo's 4 cruisers and 14 destroyers. In a seven-hour running battle, Doorman's force was crushed. Doorman went down with his flagship, RNNS *De Ruyter*. Only cruisers *Houston*, HMAS *Perth*, and HMS *Exeter* and five destroyers (four American) survived the battle. During February 28–29, in Sundra Strait, the *Houston*, *Perth*, and several destroyers ran into a Japanese landing force. Although they were badly outgunned, the Allied ships attacked and were sunk. On March 1 the *Exeter* and two Allied destroyers were sunk off Surabaya. Only four American destroyers of the ABDA force escaped to Australia.

With 85,000 Dutch Army defenders scattered about the islands and supported only by a few obsolete aircraft, the Japanese took Batavia, capital of Java, on March 8. The next day the entire Netherlands East Indies surrendered. Thus, within only six months of its attack on Pearl Harbor, Japan had achieved its offensive aims in the Pacific. The Japanese had conquered states totalling 100 million people and captured 250,000 enemy soldiers at a cost to themselves of only some 15,000 casualties (including wounded), fewer than 2600 aircraft (including those lost to accidents), 1 small carrier, 5 destroyers, and 8 submarines. It was an amazing string of victories without modern historical precedent.[63]

The original Japanese plan was to halt at this point and fortify their defensive perimeter, forcing the United States into a protracted struggle that would culminate in negotiations and the recognition of Japanese hegemony in East Asia. The Japanese touted themselves as the liberators of Asia from European colonialism. 'Asia for the Asians' was their call, and almost everywhere the Japanese found native collaborators. But Tokyo's proclamation of a Greater East Asian Co-Prosperity Sphere under Japanese leadership was in fact a cover for its own brutal exploitation of the resources of Asia. Japan's very conquests proved its undoing, for it had insufficient manpower to garrison these holdings and lacked sufficient time fully to exploit the economic resources they contained.

The British and Americans pooled their resources in a manner unprecedented for two sovereign states. They established a Combined Chiefs of Staff Committee and a command structure closely integrated at every level. A British commander would have an American deputy and vice versa. For the most part this worked very well indeed. The Combined Chiefs of Staff directed a vast, worldwide effort which, in sharp contrast to World War I, had an overall strategy in place from the onset. British and US leaders agreed that Germany was the more formidable military opponent and that its defeat should be the chief object of Allied resources. As it worked out, however, manpower could not be employed in the European theater quickly enough, so the Pacific build-up went forward faster than anticipated.

Close Allied military cooperation stood in sharp contrast to that of the Axis powers. Germany, Japan, and Italy never could agree on common military objectives, did not act in concert, and for the most part never informed the other of their military operations. Given this, it is understandable that the Axis leaders would fail to establish a unified command structure. Their disunity was an important factor in the ultimate Axis defeat.

5

Japan Checked

At the beginning of April 1942 the United States and Britain delineated areas of responsibility for the war against Japan. The Americans assumed control of the entire Pacific area, except Sumatra; the British took responsibility for Sumatra and the Indian Ocean area, and they had oversight over India and Burma. China remained a separate theater under US oversight.

There was no unified US command in the Pacific Theater, largely because of MacArthur. Navy leaders did not want to serve under him, and the general refused to serve under the navy. There was some thought of bringing MacArthur to Washington as commander of US armed forces, a project anathema to both the Chiefs of Staff and to President Roosevelt, who already saw him as a possible political rival. MacArthur had to remain in the Pacific. The solution hit upon was to divide the Pacific between MacArthur and Admiral Chester Nimitz. With head-quarters in Melbourne, Australia, MacArthur assumed command of the southwest Pacific, while Nimitz had charge of the central Pacific. Guadalcanal was the meeting point between the two, requiring close cooperation between their respective ground and naval forces.

On January 23, 1942, the Japanese took Rabaul, and only Australia and New Zealand barred their further advance in the southwest Pacific. Both nations had made a major military commitment to the Middle East, the New Zealand Division there representing in terms of population the equivalent of 25 British divisions. Three of four divisions of the all-volunteer Australian Imperial Forces were also in the Middle East, while the fourth was lost in the Singapore débâcle. The Australian Navy was relatively weak and much of the air force was in the Middle East. There remained only the 250,000-man Australian Military Forces, a poorly trained reserve.

There was anger in Australia over their country's assistance to defend Britain against Germany and the perceived failure of Britain in turn to honor its pledge to hold Singapore and protect Australia's long and vulnerable coastline against the Japanese.[1] In these circumstances Prime Minister John Curtin of Australia demanded the return of Australian military units from the Middle East. While some did indeed return home, Churchill was reluctant to see such battle-hardened desert fighters lost.

Churchill called on the United States to take up the slack, and in April 1942 the US 41st Infantry Division shipped out to Australia, followed by the 32nd Division. Ultimately half a million US forces arrived there. US forces were also sent to southwest Pacific islands, including New Caledonia and Fuji. In New Caledonia Major General Alexander Patch took command of the 23rd Infantry Division. Made up of a majority of US troops, it also included New Caledonians and was known as the Americal Division (*Ameri*ca and *Cal*edonia). The US troop build-up allowed MacArthur to take the offensive himself. His immediate fixation was to recapture Rabaul, held by a large Japanese garrison.[2]

Meanwhile, Tokyo also weighed its options. Following their easy military triumphs, Japanese leaders were understandably reluctant to continue with their original strategy of shifting to a defensive posture. They feared the adverse impact this might exert on Japanese fighting spirit and believed that it would work to Japanese disadvantage to allow the Western powers time to collect and regain their strength. Spurring them on was the United Nations Declaration of January 1, 1942, by which 26 states agreed to make common cause against the Axis and promised not to conclude a separate armistice or peace.

Japanese naval leaders in particular were anxious to occupy the Hawaiian Islands and Australia, the two chief points from which US forces might mount offensive operations. US carriers were operating out of Pearl Harbor, still the headquarters of the US Pacific Fleet. If Japanese forces could occupy the Hawaiian Islands, it would be virtually impossible for the US Navy to conduct long-range Pacific naval operations. Also, securing the islands to the north and east of Australia – the Solomons, New Caledonia, and Samoa – would enable the Japanese to establish bases to cut the Allied lifeline from the United States to Australia. Japanese long-range bombers would then be able to strike targets in Australia itself, preparatory to an invasion and occupation of that continent.

The Japanese Army was not enthusiastic about either proposal. Most of its assets were tied down in China and the Kwantung Army continued to garrison Manchuria. Japanese forces controlled the coastline and much of the eastern interior of China but, given their wide-ranging commitments elsewhere, they lacked the manpower to conquer and occupy all of it. Invading Australia and occupying even the populated areas would require significant military resources that the army could not spare. The Army Ministry and General Staff in Tokyo therefore advocated holding the gains already achieved in the southern advance and shifting resources to China. The army formally vetoed the navy plan on April 7, 1942, but in effect it was dead by the end of January. Japanese Navy leaders hoped, however, that a success either eastward toward Pearl Harbor or southwest toward Australia might overcome army opposition.[3]

Admiral Yamamoto and the Combined Fleet Staff favored taking Midway Island, 1100 miles west of Pearl Harbor, as a preliminary to invading Hawaii. Once secured, Midway (actually a number of islands more properly known as Midway Islands) would provide a staging area for the Hawaii invasion. Until that could be mounted, it would serve as a base for long-range Japanese reconnaissance aircraft and submarines. Yamamoto expected this to provoke a strong US naval reaction, enabling him to set a trap for, and destroy, the US aircraft carriers. The Japanese Naval Staff, however, preferred the southeasterly drive to isolate Australia. By the end of March the Japanese had already advanced from Rabaul into the Solomon Islands and along the northern coast of New Guinea.

Debate over the two different plans was interrupted and ultimately influenced by a half dozen US carrier raids conducted over February to May 1942. At the end of December 1941 there had been major US Navy command changes; Admiral Nimitz replaced Admiral Kimmel as commander of the Pacific Fleet and Admiral Ernest J. King replaced Admiral Stark as chief of naval operations. Nimitz and King both realized that for the indefinite future the US Navy would have to remain on the defensive, but they were also determined to hold Midway and to maintain the lines of communication from Hawaii to Australia.

In late January Nimitz ordered Vice-Admiral William F. Halsey to take the offensive. On February 1 aircraft from the carriers *Enterprise* and *Yorktown* and cruisers and destroyers struck the Marshalls and also Makin Island in the Gilberts. Halsey's force inflicted only minimal damage on the Japanese.

Yamamoto then sent 4 carriers, 2 fast battleships, 3 cruisers, and 9 destroyers against Darwin in Australia, the logical staging point for any Allied invasion of Java. On February 19 a total of 188 Japanese aircraft struck Darwin city and port and sank a destroyer and a number of transports, shooting down 11 Allied aircraft and killing 200 civilians.

Simultaneously, the Japanese ran riot in the Indian Ocean south of Java. On March 23 they secured the Andaman Islands to safeguard their sea route from Singapore to Rangoon. Several days later Nagumo's First Air Fleet of 5 carriers, 4 battleships, and accompanying cruisers and destroyers moved into the Indian Ocean to reduce British bases on Ceylon and destroy warships and merchant shipping in the Indian Ocean and Bay of Bengal.

British Admiral Sir James Somerville's Far Eastern Force, consisting of 4 battleships, 3 carriers, 8 cruisers, and 15 destroyers, moved to intercept Nagumo, disregarding instructions to adopt a fleet-in-being role. His force was sharply inferior to that of Nagumo; four of the five British battleships were both old and slow, and his carriers were small. Somerville concluded he would lose his entire force in a major confrontation with Nagumo, so he sent the older battleships back to the coast of Africa and attempted to harass Nagumo with his remaining forces. In the first week of April Nagumo's aircraft attacked and damaged several bases on Ceylon. They also engaged Somerville's remaining ships, sinking a carrier, two cruisers, and a destroyer. The Japanese ships came under attack by British land-based aviation and Nagumo was fortunate not to have lost any of his carriers.

In order to forestall Japanese control of the Indian Ocean, in early May British forces took Diégo-Suarez on the northern tip of Vichy-administered Madagascar. After a Japanese midget submarine damaged the British battleship *Ramillies* in late May, the British decided to take all of Madagascar, which they did during September–November.

In early 1942 Nimitz did not dare send US carriers into the Indian Ocean, but the Marshall Islands raid in February demonstrated the feasibility of utilizing the big ships elsewhere. Thus while the Japanese were hitting Darwin, Vice-Admiral Wilson Brown led a carrier task force centered on the *Lexington* against the principal Japanese base of Rabaul in the Solomon Sea. Nimitz hoped this raid would divert the Japanese from attacking Port Moresby on the south coast of New Guinea, revealed by radio intercepts as a Japanese objective.

On February 20 the *Lexington* was about 400 miles from Rabaul when she was spotted by a Japanese flying boat. Soon thereafter she came under attack from Betty bombers. The Americans shot down 16 of the attackers for the loss of only two F4F Wildcat fighters. Although the Japanese pilots had saved Rabaul from attack, the abortive US raid paid an important dividend by convincing the Japanese command on Truk that landings scheduled for Port Moresby and Tulagi that March were too risky and should await the arrival of additional carriers sent by

Yamamoto. This delayed the Japanese invasion attempt until the end of April, which culminated in the Battle of the Coral Sea.

Another US carrier strike occurred on February 24 with aircraft from the *Enterprise* attacking Wake Island. Then, on March 4 her planes hit Marcus Island, halfway between Wake and Iwo Jima near the Japanese Bonin Islands and only 1000 miles from Tokyo. Again, there was little damage. On March 10 the United States conducted a further carrier raid in the Huon Gulf, against Lae and Salamaua on the north coast of Papua/New Guinea where Japanese forces had just gone ashore. The strike, the heaviest by the United States thus far, involved 104 aircraft from two carriers. The attackers sank four Japanese transports and damaged a number of other vessels at a cost of only one US plane lost.

A month later the Americans carried out their most ambitious raid to date. Although the least successful in military terms, it was spectacular in its propaganda value. The Tokyo raid of April 18, 1942, usually known as the Doolittle raid for its commander, Army Lieutenant Colonel James H. Doolittle, was the first US bombing raid of the war on the Japanese home islands. Largely a fillip to morale rather than a meaningful military strike, it nonetheless had a decisive impact on Japanese policy. The raid originated with Captain Francis S. Low, an operations officer on the staff of Chief of Naval Operations King. Low suggested the possibility of such a raid utilizing army bombers flying off carriers. King approved the scheme, which was embraced by Army Air Forces commander Lieutenant General Henry W. 'Hap' Arnold, who picked his staff officer Doolittle as the army coordinator and later as mission commander.

With Japanese picket ships stationed 500 miles off the home islands, any attacking aircraft would have to launch at 550 miles. The B-25 Mitchell was the only army bomber that could probably fly off a carrier, but it could never land on one. Thus the planners decided that, after striking Japan, the B-25s would fly on to China and land there, a flight of 2000 miles. The B-25Bs in the raid were modified accordingly. To save weight and space for collapsible fuel tanks, the lower turret was removed and a fake .50 caliber machine gun fashioned from a broomstick was planted in each plane's tail. Each plane would carry only four 500-lb bombs, one an incendiary cluster.

Following extensive training on land, 16 B-25s were loaded on board carrier *Hornet*. Commanded by Captain Marc Mitscher, *Hornet* sailed from San Francisco on April 2. On the 13th the carrier *Enterprise*, with Task Force commander Admiral Halsey aboard, and escorts rendezvoused with the *Hornet*. The *Enterprise* was along to provide air cover. Task Force 16 (TF 16) thus consisted of the 2 carriers, 4 cruisers, 8 destroyers, and 2 oilers. Two US Navy submarines also operated near the Japanese coast to report on enemy ship movements and weather conditions. TF 16 followed the approximate route taken by the Japanese in the Pearl Harbor attack. The Japanese were aware from radio traffic that something was in the offing, perhaps an attack on Japan itself. Combined Fleet Headquarters ordered naval aircraft concentrated in the Tokyo area and alerted picket boats off shore beyond the range of carrier aircraft.

Early on April 18 Japanese picket vessels detected the US ships at about 600 miles out. Although the US cruisers sank one of the Japanese vessels, she was able to get off a radio message reporting the presence of American carriers. Halsey now jettisoned the plan to fly the B-25s off on the afternoon of April 19 and bomb Tokyo at night. At 8:00 a.m. Halsey flashed this message to the *Hornet*: 'Launch planes. To Colonel Doolittle and his gallant command Good Luck and God bless you.'[4] Doolittle's B-25 was the first launched, at 8:20; all the planes were away within an hour. TF 16 then turned about and departed the area at flank speed. Bad weather hid the task force from Japanese search planes and it escaped unscathed.

Despite the warning, the B-25s achieved surprise because the Japanese assumed an attack by carrier aircraft with a range of 200 miles and hence a later launch. At 12:30 Tokyo time Doolittle's plane dropped the first bombs. No B-25s were shot down and only one was hit by anti-aircraft fire. All, however, were subsequently lost. The air fields in China were not ready to receive Doolittle's force and the crews had to bail out or crash land. One plane landed at Vladivostok and was promptly interned. Three crewmen died of injuries and eight were subsequently captured by the Japanese, interrogated, and tortured. In August 1942, at Shanghai, all those captured were tried by a military court on charges of bombing and strafing civilian targets. Found guilty, three were executed. Of the remaining five, one died in prison; the other four survived the war. The raid inflicted little material damage on Tokyo, and Doolittle later said he expected to be court-martialed for his failure. Instead, he found himself a hero. Presented the Medal of Honor, he was also advanced two ranks to brigadier general.

The Doolittle raid and the other US carrier attacks had far-reaching effects. They greatly boosted American morale and were the first US 'payback' for Pearl Harbor. They also provided valuable experience and revealed equipment and tactical shortcomings, such as the need for delayed action fuses to allow bombs to penetrate below decks before exploding. The raids were a great embarrassment to the Japanese and caused them to shift four fighter groups to the defense of Tokyo and other cities. The Doolittle raid also produced a Japanese Army punitive expedition in China in which 53 battalions killed perhaps 250,000 Chinese in a massive campaign of retribution. (Nationalist leader Jiang Jieshi had opposed the raid for this very reason.[5])

The Doolittle raid also formalized decisions already taken in Tokyo to expand the Japanese outer defensive ring. It also silenced critics of Yamamoto's plan to draw out the US fleet and destroy it. On May 5 Imperial Headquarters directed Yamamoto 'to carry out the occupation of Midway Island and key points in the western Aleutians in cooperation with the Army.'[6]

The Japanese intended to prevent further US raids both by mounting the Midway operation and by cutting off Australia. They first planned to seize Tulagi as a seaplane base and then take Port Moresby on the south coast of New Guinea, bringing Queensland, Australia, within bomber range. Once that had been accomplished, Yamamoto's Combined Fleet would occupy Midway. Following destruction of the US Pacific Fleet reacting to the Midway attack, the Japanese planned to resume their southeastern advance to interdict the sea routes from the United States to Australia.

The Battle of the Coral Sea

The Japanese now initiated their first move, the invasions of Tulagi and Port Moresby. Vice-Admiral Innoye Shigeyoshi at Rabaul in New Britain Island had overall command. He planned to seize Tulagi on May 3 and Port Moresby a week later. To prevent any US interference with the landings, Innoye deployed two covering forces: a Close Covering Group centered on the light carrier *Shoho* (30 aircraft), four heavy cruisers, and a destroyer, all under Rear-Admiral Goto Aritomo; and Vice-Admiral Hara Chuichi's Carrier Division 5 of fleet carriers *Zuikaku* and *Shokaku* (124 aircraft). They were escorted by Vice-Admiral Takagi Takeo's two heavy cruisers, and six destroyers. An additional 150 Japanese aircraft were available if needed at Rabaul. The two naval covering forces sortied from Truk in the Carolines, 1000 miles north of Rabaul, on April 30 and May 1 respectively.[7]

US codebreaking uncovered the outline of the Japanese plan. To intercept the Japanese, Nimitz sent from Pearl Harbor a task force under Rear-Admiral Frank Fletcher centered on carriers *Yorktown* and

Lexington and 141 aircraft. Royal Navy Rear-Admiral J. G. Crace's small force of US and Australian cruisers and destroyers joined him. Nimitz also ordered carriers *Enterprise* and *Hornet*, returning from the Tokyo raid, to the Coral Sea, but they arrived too late to participate in the action.

The first Japanese move went well, with troops going ashore at Tulagi on May 3. Warned of their approach, the small Australian garrison on the island was hastily extracted. The *Shoho* then steamed north to join the larger Japanese force at Rabaul bound for Port Moresby. On May 4 aircraft from the *Yorktown* struck Tulagi, sinking a Japanese destroyer. The carrier then joined other Allied ships in the central Coral Sea. Meanwhile, the Japanese carrier group passed east of the Solomons, entering the Coral Sea from that direction to take the American carriers from the rear as they moved to intercept the Port Moresby invasion force. The latter was entering the Coral Sea from the Solomons to the north *en route* to the Louisiade Islands and thence to Port Moresby. On the 5th and 6th the two carrier groups searched for one another without success, although at one stage they were only 70 miles apart.

On May 7 Japanese reconnaissance aircraft reported sighting a carrier and a cruiser, whereupon Japanese aircraft carried out an all-out bombing attack. They sank both ships, which turned out to be a tanker and escorting destroyer. Hara then gambled on a night strike by 27 aircraft. The Japanese attackers encountered F4F Wildcats. Some of the Japanese pilots located the American carriers, but in the dark they assumed them to be friendly and tried to land on them. Only six Japanese planes returned to their carriers.   On the same day Fletcher's aircraft were also led astray by a false report and expended their effort on the covering force for the Port Moresby invasion. They sank the light carrier *Shoho*, however; she went down in only ten minutes. The loss of his air cover led Admiral Inouye to order the invasion force to turn back.

On the morning of the 8th the two carrier forces at last came to blows. They were evenly matched. The Japanese had 121 aircraft, the United States 122. The Japanese had 4 heavy cruisers and six destroyers, the United States 5 heavy cruisers and 7 destroyers. But the US vessels were under a clear sky, whereas the Japanese ships had the advantage of cloud cover. As a result *Zuikaku* escaped detection. US aircraft located and badly damaged *Shokaku*, however. Seventy Japanese aircraft attacked the American carriers; *Lexington* was struck by two torpedoes and three bombs. Subsequent internal explosions forced her abandonment, and the US destroyer *Phelps* later sank her with torpedoes. The *Yorktown* was damaged. Both sides then departed the Coral Sea, the Japanese in the mistaken belief that both US carriers had been sunk.

Losses in the Battle of the Coral Sea were almost even. The Americans lost 74 planes, the Japanese more than 80. But the Americans lost a fleet carrier and the Japanese only a light carrier. Even so, the Americans had prevented the Japanese from realizing their principal objective of capturing Port Moresby. The Americans were also able to ready the *Yorktown* sufficiently to allow her to fight in the next battle at Midway, whereas *Shokaku* could not be readied in time for that second and decisive fight. Carrier *Zuikaku*, which could have participated, was not able to take part in that battle simply because of the lack of trained pilots. Thus, while the Battle of the Coral Sea may have been a tactical Japanese victory, strategically it went to the Americans. The Battle of the Coral Sea also inaugurated a new era in naval warfare. It was the first battle in naval history between fleets that never came in sight of one another. A greater repetition soon followed at Midway.[8]

Amazingly the Japanese continued their mistaken naval aviator policy, the shortcomings of which had been revealed in the Coral Sea fight. The Japanese retained their most senior pilots on line until they were killed, whereas the Americans rotated their pilots, allowing seasoned aviators to help train new pilots coming on line. As a result of this policy, the Japanese had no reserve of trained pilots available after the Coral Sea and Midway. Captain Fuchida later called this an important factor in Japan's ultimate defeat.[9]

The Battle of Midway

The Midway plan, demanded by Yamamoto and produced by the Combined Fleet Staff, was extraordinarily comprehensive and complex; indeed, it was too elaborate and too polycentric. It also lacked strategic flexibility. Yamamoto and his planners, drawing on Japanese naval successes to that point in the war, were confident and tended to denigrate US capabilities. The plan had a two-fold purpose. Tokyo sought the capture of Midway and several islands in the Aleutian chain to expand its defense perimeter. The most important part, however, was luring out the US fleet, especially the carriers, providing the Japanese an opportunity to destroy it. As noted, Yamamoto hoped then to use Midway as a stepping-stone for an invasion of Hawaii if the US fleet were destroyed. If not, Midway would at least provide Japan an important airstrip for surveillance of the US fleet.

For the operation Yamamoto assembled the largest task force in the 70-year history of the Japanese Navy and the greatest armada to date in the Pacific Ocean. The plan utilized almost the entire Japanese Navy, including 8 aircraft carriers, 11 battleships, 22 cruisers, 65 destroyers, and 21 submarines. Yamamoto had in all some 600 aircraft, including land-based planes at Tinian, Kwajalein, Aur, Jaluit, and Wotje. Nimitz, on the other hand, possessed but 76 ships, and a third of these were in the north Pacific force that never came into the battle.

Yamamoto's plan for the Midway operation was extraordinarily complex. Close to Pearl Harbor, the presumed location of the US fleet, the Japanese positioned a line of ten submarines supported by a light cruiser and submarine tender. This Advance Force, commanded by Vice-Admiral Komatsu Teruhisa, was to provide intelligence on US ship movements and await the US surface ship reaction to the Midway attack. Hopefully, it would sink or damage a number of US ships before they could close with the Japanese main body.

The first Japanese blow was to fall on the US Aleutian Island chain off Alaska, the shortest route to Japanese home waters. Vice-Admiral Hosogaya Moshiro's Northern Force would carry out this attack. It consisted of Second Air Fleet and invasion forces. In addition to light carrier *Ryujo* and carrier *Junyo* (82 aircraft total), Hosogaya had 3 heavy cruisers, 3 light cruisers, 1 auxiliary cruiser, 12 destroyers, 1 minelayer, 3 minesweepers, and 3 transports lifting 2500 troops. After hitting US bases, Hosogaya's troops would occupy islands in the US western island chain. Yamamoto hoped that this action, designed to prevent a US invasion of Japan from Alaska, would also draw north any US Navy assets in the vicinity of Midway as well as the reacting US Pacific Fleet, which Yamamoto expected to sortie from Pearl Harbor. The Japanese would then be in position to crush the Americans between the Northern Force in the Aleutians and the more powerful southern forces at Midway.

The remaining Japanese ships steamed toward Midway in three main groups. First there was Nagumo's First Air Fleet of four carriers: *Hiryu*, *Soryu*, *Kaga*, and *Akagi* (261 aircraft total). Two battleships and 2 heavy cruisers supported the carriers, and Nagumo had a screening force of one light cruiser and 11 destroyers. Once Nagumo's planes had reduced the island's defenses, the second Japanese element would advance: Vice-Admiral Kondo Nobutake's Midway Invasion Force of shore bombardment vessels and transports. Centered on Kondo's powerful Second Fleet, it consisted of 2 battleships, 1 light carrier *Zuiho* (24 aircraft), 2 seaplane carriers (32 aircraft) 8 heavy cruisers, 2 light cruisers, and 21 destroyers, along with 3 destroyer-transports and 12 transports lifting the landing force of 5000 troops, and 4 minesweepers, 3 submarine chasers, and 3 supply/cargo ships. The final element, trailing the others, was the Main Force, with which Yamamoto expected to engage and destroy the reacting Americans. It consisted of 7 battleships (including the giant *Yamato*, the Combined Fleet flagship), light carrier *Hosho* (8 bombers), 3 light cruisers, 21 destroyers, and 2 seaplane carriers carrying midget submarines. In the Battle of Midway no Japanese battleship fired a shot in anger.[10]

Yamamoto believed that the Coral Sea fight had sunk two US carriers. He thus expected to meet only one and at the most two US carriers at Midway. Before these could come into the battle, Yamamoto expected to savage them with his submarines. No matter the US moves, Yamamoto was confident that his superior fleet would bring victory.

The Japanese plan called for the Aleutian strike to begin on June 3, followed by landings there on the 6th. Meanwhile, on June 4 Nagumo's carrier planes would strike Midway, and the next day troops would land at an atoll 60 miles to the west to be utilized as a seaplane base. On the 6th cruisers would bombard Midway and troops would land, covered by Kondo's battleships. Yamamoto miscalculated by not expecting any US ships in the Midway area until after the landings. His hope was that the Americans would move in the direction of the Aleutians when they learned of Japanese attacks there. His plan, although carefully worked out, lacked flexibility. Also, by dispersing his ships, Yamamoto sacrificed his chief advantage of superiority of force.

Admiral Nimitz's chief concern was his vast inferiority in ships. Thanks to the Japanese attack on Pearl Harbor he had no battleships available and, after the Battle of the Coral Sea, only two carriers fit for action – *Enterprise* and *Hornet*. However, by astonishing efforts the *Yorktown* was rendered battle-worthy in only two days. But the United States had one great advantage: thanks to communications intelligence, the US side had an astonishingly accurate picture of the Japanese order of battle and plans. The Japanese, on the other hand, possessed virtually no intelligence regarding the US fleet. One key command change occurred on the eve of the battle. Halsey was hospitalized with a skin allergy, and on his recommendation Nimitz named Rear-Admiral Raymond Spruance as his replacement. Although Spruance lacked carrier experience, he proved an excellent choice indeed.

The Japanese pilots, fresh from earlier triumphs at Pearl Harbor and off Ceylon, were bursting with confidence. Captain Fuchida, who took part in the operation, later noted that all the Japanese involved, from commanders to junior officers, pilots, and sailors, were infected with the 'victory disease.' Nagumo himself was not so certain. He had no idea of the whereabouts of the American carriers.[11]

Nimitz knew Midway to be the Japanese destination thanks to code-breaking. In their radio traffic the Japanese repeatedly referred to the objective as 'AF.' To confirm 'AF' as Midway, the commander there was ordered to broadcast that his distillation plant had broken down; the Japanese then promptly reported by radio that 'AF' was short of water. Nimitz now deployed B-26 and B-17 bombers to Midway. As it worked out, the army aircraft proved quite ineffective against ships. Nimitz also laid on an ambush position for the three US carriers (233 planes) approx-imately 300 miles northeast of Midway. He hoped that the carriers could avoid Japanese reconnaissance aircraft, while they secured early word of Japanese movements from long-range Catalina aircraft based on Midway. Nimitz wanted to catch the Japanese carriers by surprise with their planes on their decks while avoiding the same scenario himself.

In the actual battle there were 86 Japanese ships against 27 US. The Japanese had 354 aircraft of all types against 348 US (including the 115 land-based aircraft on Midway). Carrier strength was six (two fleet carriers and two light carriers) for Japan and three for the United States. Ironically, the bulk of the Japanese reconnaissance aircraft were in the rear element, while the carrier element in the van had only a limited reconnaissance capability.

On June 3, the day after the US carriers were positioned, air recon-naissance detected the slow-moving Japanese transports approaching some 600 miles west of Midway. Gaps in search patterns flown by Japanese aircraft, on the other hand, allowed the American carriers to remain undetected. Yamamoto was not unduly concerned; he did not expect the Pacific Fleet to be at sea.

Early on June 4 Nagumo launched a strike by 108 aircraft against Midway; a second wave of similar size was then prepared to attack any warships that might be sighted. The first wave of attackers inflicted seri-ous damage on Midway's installations at little cost to itself, but the pilots reported to Nagumo that there was need for a second attack. Since his own carriers were being bombed by the land-based planes from Midway, Nagumo concurred in the need to neutralize the island's airfields and ordered the second wave to change from torpedoes to bombs for that purpose. There was still no evidence of US carriers. Shortly afterwards a patrol plane, delayed in taking flight by mechanical problems, reported US ships about 200 miles away, but these were first thought to be only cruisers and destroyers. Then, at 8:20 a.m. came a more precise report identifying a carrier.

Nagumo now faced a difficult decision, as most of his torpedo-bombers were now equipped with bombs and most of his fighters were on patrol. He also had to recover the first wave of aircraft returning from Midway. Nagumo ordered a change of course to the northeast. This shift in position helped his carriers avoid the first wave of US dive-bombers sent against them; in any case, US torpedo-bomber and dive-bomber attacks that followed were hopelessly uncoordinated. When three successive waves of slow-moving torpedo-bombers attacked the Japanese carriers between 9:30 and 10:24 a.m., Japanese fighters or anti-aircraft guns shot down 47 of 51 of them. The Japanese believed with some justification that they had won the battle.

But at 10:26 a.m. 37 American dive-bombers from the *Enterprise* suddenly swooped down on the Japanese carriers from 19,000 feet, so unexpectedly that they met no opposition. The Japanese fighters that had shot down the third wave of US torpedo-bombers had no chance to climb and meet them. Bombs striking Nagumo's carrier flagship *Akagi* exploded many of the torpedoes on deck, forcing the crew to abandon ship. The *Kaga* suffered bomb-hits that caused her to sink that evening. The *Soryu* sustained three hits from 1000-lb bombs from *Yorktown*'s dive-bombers that had just arrived on the scene. She was abandoned within 20 minutes. Thus the outcome of the battle was largely a matter of luck on the American side – the uncoordinated concentration of the dive bombers hitting the three Japanese carriers at just the correct time. Save for those few minutes, the Japanese would have won.

Hiryu, the only Japanese fleet carrier still intact, struck back at the Americans. Her aircraft damaged the weakened *Yorktown* so badly that she had to be abandoned. Later taken under tow, she was torpedoed and sunk by Japanese submarine *I-168*, which penetrated the destroyer screen. But 24 US dive-bombers, including ten from *Yorktown*, caught *Hiryu* in the late afternoon and hit her so badly that she was abandoned early the next day.

Yamamoto's first action on learning of the loss of *Akagi*, *Kaga*, and *Soryu* was to bring up his battleships and recall the two light carriers from the Aleutians in hopes of fighting a more conventional sea battle. But the loss of *Hiryu* and Nagumo's gloomy reports caused him to call off the attack on Midway. Yamamoto still hoped to trap the Americans by drawing them westward into his heavy ships, but Spruance refused to play his game and reported to Nimitz, 'I did not feel justified in risking a night encounter with possibly superior enemy forces . . . .'[12]

In contrast to their operations off Midway, the Japanese attack on the Aleutians went more or less according to plan. The air assault of June 3 did little damage, thanks to clouds obscuring the ground at Dutch Harbor, but a follow-on strike the next day had more success. On June 5 the carriers were called southward, but two days later the Japanese invasion forces landed on Kiska and Attu. Japanese propaganda made much of this accomplishment, but in fact the two islands were entirely unsuited as air or naval bases, even had the terrible Aleutian weather of almost perpetual mist and snow not been a factor.

A year later US forces retook Attu and Kiska. In May 1943, violating the military principal of economy of force, the United States committed 100,000 men to the task. The Japanese fought for Attu, and it took the US Army 7th Infantry Division three weeks rather than the planned three days to secure the island. Japanese resistance, miserable weather, rough terrain, and inadequate clothing that resulted in numerous cases of frostbite all took a toll. In late July, before Kiska could be assaulted, the Japanese secretly evacuated the island. Despite arguments in some quarters that the Aleutians be used as a stepping-stone to Japan – it was clearly the shortest route there by air – the region's inhospitable weather and the substantial logistical requirements such an effort would entail made it a non-starter.

Taken in sum, the Battle of Midway was a crushing blow to Japan. In the battle itself it had lost four fleet carriers and 332 aircraft, most of which went down with the carriers. The Japanese also lost heavy cruiser *Mikuma* sunk and heavy cruiser *Mogami* severely damaged. Battleship *Haruna*, three destroyers, and a fleet oiler were slightly damaged. Despite their numbers, Japanese aircraft, warships, and submarines attacked just one US warship, the *Yorktown*. They sank only that ship and a destroyer, the latter going down to a torpedo aimed at the *Yorktown* that missed. The Americans lost 147 aircraft (38 of these shore-based).[13]

The Japanese performance had been rife with errors. These included an overly complicated plan with no capacity to redeem the situation once it had gone awry; over-confidence that ignored American capabilities; Yamamoto's location, far removed from the battle; the failure to fly sufficient search planes to locate US ships; the lack of high-altitude fighter cover; inadequate fire precautions aboard ship; and striking Midway simultaneously with planes from all four carriers, meaning that they would have to rearm and refit at the same time when they would all be vulnerable.

The Imperial Japanese Navy was still a formidable fighting force, but it never regained the ascendancy of earlier days. Once the Japanese had lost the four fleet carriers and their well-trained air crews, their continued preponderance in battleships and cruisers counted for little. These ships could only venture out in areas covered by Japanese land-based aircraft, and the subsequent Japanese defeat in the long struggle for

Guadalcanal was owing in part to lack of air assets. The Battle of Midway provided the Americans an invaluable breathing space until, early in 1943, the new Essex-class fleet carriers became available.

The Solomons

Meanwhile, in January 1942 Japanese amphibious forces had landed in the Bismarck Archipelago between New Guinea and the Solomons. They quickly wrested Kavieng on New Ireland Island and Rabaul on New Britain from the Australians. The Japanese consolidated their hold and turned Rabaul into their principal southwest Pacific base. By early March the Japanese had landed at Salamaua and Lae in Papua and on Bougainville.

During the period from May to July the Japanese expanded their ring further in the central and lower Solomons. These operations were carried out by the Japanese Eighth Army, commanded by Lieutenant General Imamura Hitoshi from Rabaul. The Japanese landed on Guadalcanal with the intention of establishing a base there, and on July 6 began construction of an airfield. Despite their rebuff in the Battle of the Coral Sea, the Japanese landed forces on the northwest coast of Papua at Buna on July 21. They then turned that village and nearby Sanananda and Gona into a base area for an advance south over the Owen Stanley Mountains to Port Moresby.

Following the US victory in the Battle of Midway, MacArthur and Chief of Naval Operations King both urged that the United States take the offensive, hitting the Japanese and keeping them off-balance before they could recover from the reverse of Midway. MacArthur and King disagreed on the best approach, however. King wanted to use the navy in an island-hopping approach to Rabaul; MacArthur favored a more direct army-controlled assault on Rabaul itself. These plans were reconciled by the Joint Chiefs of Staff decision of July 2. Vice-Admiral Robert L. Ghormley, commanding the South Pacific under Nimitz, would have charge of operations to take the southern Solomons, while MacArthur secured the remainder and the northwest coast of New Guinea with the final objective being Rabaul.

Papua/New Guinea

From July 1942 to January 1943 Australia and the United States were locked in combat with the Japanese on Papua/New Guinea. On July 21

Major General Horii Tomitoro, personally commanding the Japanese South Seas Detachment on Papua, pushed a force inland from Gona, drove back local Allied troops, and moved up the rugged and treacherous track known as the Kokoda Trail that ran south to Port Morseby. By mid-August the Japanese had seized the passes over the Owen Stanley Mountains that ran across the island. The Japanese then pushed south, coming within 30 miles of Port Moresby. Here Australian and US forces under Major General Edmond F. Hering, benefitting from Allied air superiority, halted their advance.

On August 25 the Japanese landed 1900 men at Milne Bay at the eastern tip of Papua. This force was to make its way west and support Horii's drive on Port Moresby. Australian forces, not greatly superior to the Japanese in size but benefitting from air support, contained the landing and then mounted a counter-attack. On the nights of September 5 and 6 the Japanese evacuated 1300 survivors, half of them wounded. By contrast the Australians suffered only 373 battle casualties, 160 of whom were killed and missing. The Australian victory in the Battle of Milne Bay was extremely important. Both a humiliation for the Japanese and a lift for the Allies, it proved the Allies could defeat the Japanese in jungle warfare. And its outcome isolated the Japanese coming off the Kokoda Trail.[14]

Fighting on Guadalcanal deprived the Japanese of resources for Papua, and during October Allied pressure and orders from Imamura caused Horii to remove his men back over the Owen Stanley Mountains. The Australian 7th Division followed. Instead of withdrawing to the coast at Buna, Horii decided to make a stand near the Kokoda Trail between the settlements of Oivi and Gorari, a few miles east of Kokoda. He was confident of victory, but by early November the Allies had learned much about jungle warfare and, in the November 5 Battle of Oivi-Gorari, the Australians flanked the Japanese position, driving Horii's men off the trail and into a river. Taking advantage of the dense jungle, many Japanese managed to make it the coast. Horii was not among them; he drowned a week later while crossing the Kumusi River.[15]

The Japanese brought engineers with them when they landed at Buna in the hopes of constructing a small road along the Kokoda Trail. When this proved impossible, the engineers fortified an area about ten miles long and several miles deep between Gona and Buna on the Solomon Sea. There 7000 Japanese, half of them survivors of the Kokoda Trail march, awaited an Allied attack. In November Tokyo activated the new Eighteenth Army and sent it to New Guinea; Seventeenth Army had charge of the defense of the Solomons. In 1943 the Japanese committed an additional 200,000 men to New Guinea and the Solomons, as well as army air force units operating primarily out of a new base at Wewak in New Guinea.

In late November 1942 the Australians approached Buna from the Kokoda Trail. Meanwhile, the US 32nd Division moved up the Papuan coast. This latter operation was undertaken before the arrival of specialized shallow-draft landing craft, and US forces advanced in a strange collection of fishing boats and coastal vessels. Because the coast was poorly charted and there were numerous reefs and concerns over Japanese aircraft, the US Navy did not support the operation with transports or warships, which adversely affected its progress. The Kokoda Trail was far too rugged to bring artillery and significant quantities of supplies by that route; nor could artillery be brought in on the small US Army vessels. Thus the 32nd Division, unprepared for the jungle conditions in any case, had to go into battle without artillery support against well-dug-in Japanese machine gun nests concealed in the dense jungle. The Australian/US advance against the Buna-Gona fortified zone began on 18 November. Progress in the jungle and swamps was slow and many of the troops were incapacitated by disease. Fortunately for the Allies, fighting on Guadalcanal meant that the Japanese on Papua received few supplies; they had to deal not only with disease but also with malnutrition.

MacArthur, unaware of conditions at the front and making no effort to understand them, now intervened. He had previously drawn Australian Army displeasure by criticizing the withdrawal down the Kokoda Trail. His attack had forced a reorganization of the Australian command and ruined some careers. In June MacArthur brought in US Army Lieutenant General Robert A. Eichelberger to command I Corps. A resourceful commander committed to the welfare of his men, Eichelberger led from the front and came to be regarded as one of the best Allied commanders in the Pacific. Certainly, he had to tread warily as far as MacArthur was concerned. Press coverage of his successes later got him into trouble because MacArthur always insisted that he, rather than his subordinates who had done the work, receive the credit.

Eichelberger restored Allied morale and improved the logistical situation. In early December US engineers were able to open an airfield near Buna, significantly improving the Allied supply situation. The Australians brought in some artillery by air, and they also managed to bring in light tanks by coastal barges. The latter, although few in number, proved invaluable. The fighting was bitter but on December 9 the Australians took Gona. The more heavily fortified Buna resisted US pressure. Finally, on January 23 a concerted attack by Australian and US forces secured it as well.

Casualties in the fighting for Papua during July 1942 to January 1943 had been heavy, worse in terms of percentage of force engaged than in the more widely known fighting for Guadalcanal. Counting naval and air personnel, the Japanese sustained approximately 13,000 killed on Papua, along with 350 wounded prisoners. An unknown number were evacuated. Australian casualties were 2165 killed, 3500 wounded, and 15,575 treated for disease. Losses in the US 32nd Division came to 930 killed, 1918 wounded, and 8700 disease-related casualties.[16]

The struggle for Guadalcanal

Meanwhile, the Allies learned that the Japanese were building an airfield on Guadalcanal. From it they would be able to bomb the advanced Allied base at Espiritu Santo. US plans to take the offensive were now stepped up and a task force hurriedly assembled. From Nouméa Admiral Ghormley dispatched an amphibious force under Rear-Admiral Richmond K. Turner lifting Major General Alexander A. Vandegrift's 19,000-man reinforced 1st Marine Division. A three-carrier task force under Vice-Admiral Frank J. Fletcher provided air support. In all, this operation involved some 70 ships.

On August 7, 1942, the Marines went ashore at Tulagi and Guadalcanal, surprised the small Japanese garrisons (2200 on Guadalcanal and 1500 on Tulagi), and that same day seized the harbor at Tulagi and the airfield on Guadalcanal. Supplies began coming ashore from transports in the sound between Guadalcanal and Florida Islands, but this activity soon came under attack by Japanese aircraft based at Rabaul. Vandegrift told Fletcher he would need four days to unload the transports, but Fletcher replied that he could not risk keeping his carriers in position off Guadalcanal for more than 48 hours.

The struggle on Guadalcanal turned out to be protracted, and the period from August 1942 to February 1943 saw some of the most bitterly contested fighting of the entire war. In all there were some 50 actions involving warships or aircraft, seven major naval battles and ten land engagements. Stakes were high for both sides. The Japanese could not afford to let the United States establish a major base on Guadalcanal while the Americans could not afford to let it go. The fiercest fighting occurred for the airfield, renamed Henderson Field for a marine aviator killed in the Battle of Midway.

Henderson field was critical to the Americans. Vandegrift recognized its importance and immediately established a perimeter defense around it. Eating captured rations and utilizing Japanese heavy construction equipment, US engineers rushed to complete the field and as early as August 21, the day the Japanese mounted a major attack on the field, the first US aircraft landed there. From this point on the Japanese could not keep their ships in waters covered by the land-based US aircraft, and they could not conduct an air campaign over the lower Solomons from as far away as Rabaul.[17]

The lack of a harbor compounded supply problems, as did Japanese aircraft attacks. 'Coast watchers' on islands provided early warning to US forces of Japanese air and water movements down the so-called 'Slot' of the Solomons. The battle went on for months in a complex campaign of attrition. The Japanese did not send their main fleet, but rather sent vessels in driblets. American land-based air power controlled the 'Slot' during the day but the Japanese initially controlled it at night. The Imperial Japanese Navy excelled at night fighting, for which the crews had been intensively trained. The Battle of Savo Island provided an excellent example of this. Savo guarded the western entrance to Ironbottom Sound, as US sailors came to call the waters between Guadalcanal and Florida Islands because of all the ships lost there. Vice-Admiral Mikawa Gunichi at Rabaul learned of the landings at Guadalcanal the same day they occurred. He immediately made plans to reinforce the Japanese garrison on Guadalcanal and to attack the vulnerable ships at the landing site. Mikawa's troop reinforcement was negligible. It consisted of 200 men on the transport *Meiyo Maru*, which was sunk off Cape George on August 8 by US submarine *S-38*.

The Japanese effort to destroy the assault shipping was another matter. On the evening of August 7 Mikawa assembled a force of five heavy cruisers, two light cruisers, and a destroyer, and made for Guadalcanal. His plan, communicated under radio silence by hooded blinker, was to enter the sound in the early morning hours of August 9, attack the protecting Allied warships, destroy the ships at the landing site, and then retire, all before dawn. Mikawa had the advantage of concentration of force. Rear-Admiral Victor Crutchley, a British Navy officer serving in the Australian Navy, commanded the screening force, which he divided into three elements to protect all the approaches to Ironbottom Sound. One force was to the east, and the western force was split into two groups, one north and one south on either side of Savo

Island. Defense of the western approach fell to six heavy cruisers and four destroyers.

Meanwhile, on the evening of August 8 Fletcher began withdrawing his three-carrier task force protecting Guadalcanal and Tulagi with the explanation that his aircraft strength had been diminished by 21 percent and that he was short of fuel. The real reason was that Fletcher, who had lost both *Lexington* and *Yorktown*, did not intend to lose another flat-top. Believing that no attack would occur that night, Crutchley departed the area in his flagship, heavy cruiser *Australia*, to confer with Turner.

Mikawa's force entered the Sound on schedule, undetected by the American picket destroyers. At 1:33 a.m. Mikawa ordered all ships to attack, and within five minutes his cruisers had fired off torpedoes. In slightly more than a half-hour the Japanese had administered the worst defeat ever suffered by the US Navy. For only moderate ship damage and personnel losses of 35 killed and 57 wounded, the Japanese sank four Allied cruisers (three US and one Australian) and a destroyer. Three other ships sustained heavy damage. Allied personnel losses were heavy: 1270 dead and 709 wounded. The Japanese victory resulted from the poor disposition of the Allied ships, superior night fighting techniques, excellent gunnery, the Long Lance torpedo, and superb ship handling.

Mikawa did lose one of his heavy cruisers on the return trip to Rabaul, however, when the *Kako* was torpedoed by a US submarine. Although Mikawa had achieved a brilliant tactical victory, he broke off the attack before reaching the amphibious force, thus missing an opportunity to retrieve the initiative. Turner now withdrew these ships as well, to Nouméa. The marines on Guadalcanal were cut off without adequate supplies. The battle taught the United States important lessons on how not to fight a battle, and the US Navy immediately took steps to rectify the situation, including new command procedures and improved night-fighting and fire-fighting techniques.[18]

Both sides reinforced Guadalcanal, and the result was a protracted and bloody struggle. The Japanese sent aircraft from Rabaul, while US land-based aircraft flying at long range from the New Hebrides provided air cover for the marines and fast destroyer transports brought in some supplies. American possession of Henderson Field tipped the balance. Rushed to completion, its strength gradually increased to about 100 planes.

At night the so-called 'Tokyo Express' of Japanese destroyers and light cruisers steamed down the 'Slot' and into the sound to shell marine positions and to deliver supplies. The latter effort was never sufficient and only haphazard. It often took the form of drums filled with supplies pushed off the ships to drift to shore. One of the great 'what ifs' of the Pacific War was the failure of the Japanese to exploit the temporary departure of the US Navy by rushing substantial reinforcements to Guadalcanal.

The next major naval action after Savo Island was the Battle of the Eastern Solomons on August 24–25. Rear-Admiral Tanaka Raizo dispatched to Guadalcanal a small convoy of destroyers and transports carrying 1500 troop reinforcements. To provide air cover, Admiral Kondo Nobutake steamed from Truk toward the Solomons with a task force centered on fleet carriers *Shokaku* and *Zuikaku* and light carrier *Ryujo*. Although the Japanese changed their codes after Midway, the increase in their radio traffic alerted the United States that something was in the offing. Ghormley then ordered Fletcher to intercept the Japanese. On the mistaken assumption that the Japanese ships were farther off, Fletcher allowed the carrier *Wasp* to refuel. This decision reduced his force for the ensuing battle to only two carriers. He also had the new battleship *North Carolina*, nine cruisers, and 17 destroyers.

On the 24th Fletcher's planes located the *Ryujo*, whose aircraft were attacking Henderson Field, and sank her, but this alerted the Japanese. The two US carriers were operating independently, and the Japanese planes first located *Enterprise*, which they attacked and badly damaged. *Saratoga* escaped attack, in part thanks to highly effective anti-aircraft fire provided by *North Carolina*. Fletcher's planes were unable to locate the two Japanese carriers, but they badly damaged a Japanese seaplane carrier. Fletcher's ships then withdrew, followed by Kondo's force. Rear-Admiral Tanaka's destroyers, meanwhile, delivered their reinforcements and shelled Henderson Field. The next day marine aircraft damaged Tanaka's flagship and a B-17 sank one of the destroyers. The battle was a draw but the Japanese had lost a light carrier and 90 aircraft; on the US side the *Enterprise* was damaged and three-dozen aircraft were lost.

On August 31 Japanese submarine *I-26* torpedoed and severely damaged the *Saratoga*, which was then out of action for three months. This reduced US carrier strength in the South Pacific to only the *Wasp*. Two weeks later Admiral Ghormley sent Admiral Turner with six transports carrying marine reinforcements from the New Hebrides to Guadalcanal. Their escort included the *Wasp* and battleship *North Carolina*. On the afternoon of September 15 Japanese submarines *I-15* and *I-19* intercepted the US ships. The *I-19* hit the *Wasp* with three torpedoes, setting her on fire and forcing her crew to abandon ship.

Some of the same spread of torpedoes fired by *I-19* went beyond the *Wasp* and damaged the *North Carolina* and the destroyer *O'Brien*. The latter sank on her way home for repairs. With fires aboard the *Wasp* out of control, Captain Forrest Sherman reluctantly directed the destroyer *Lansdowne* to sink her with torpedoes to keep her from falling into Japanese hands. Turner brazenly continued on with the transports, safely landing the marines.

Actions ashore were marked by clashes between patrols from both sides. From September 12–14 strong Japanese forces attempted to seize US marine positions on Lunga Ridge overlooking Henderson Field from the south. The Japanese left 600 dead on the battlefield, while American casualties were 143 dead and wounded.

Both sides continued building up their ground strength while naval and air battles raged over and off Guadalcanal. From October 11–13 Japanese and US covering forces collided in the Battle of Cape Esperance. On the 9th Admiral Turner had departed Nouméa for Guadalcanal with 8 destroyers and 2 transports carrying the army's 164th Infantry Regiment. Rear Admiral Norman Scott's 2 heavy cruisers, 2 light cruisers, and 5 destroyers covered the operation. At the same time the Japanese sent 2 seaplane carriers and 6 destroyers down the 'Slot' to Guadalcanal with supplies and elements of Lieutenant General Hyakutake Hurukichi's Seventeenth Army. Rear-Admiral Goto's 3 heavy cruisers and 2 destroyers protected them.

On October 11 Goto's ships bombarded American positions ashore. Near midnight, as both sides were landing reinforcements, the US covering-ships detected Goto's force on radar, between Savo and Guadalcanal Islands. The first indication the Japanese had of the US naval presence was when US ships opened fire. In the ensuing battle the Japanese lost two ships, a cruiser and a destroyer, and they had a cruiser heavily damaged. Goto was among the Japanese dead. The United States lost a destroyer sunk and two cruisers damaged. The next day the Americans upped their tally when US aircraft from Henderson Field sank two Japanese destroyers searching for survivors. Although the Battle of Cape Esperance was not decisive, it was the first US night victory against the Japanese and it substantially lifted US morale. During the nights of October 13–15 Japanese battleships *Kongo* and *Haruna*, supported by cruisers and destroyers, shelled the American positions at Henderson Field while covering the arrival of additional Japanese reinforcements. By mid-October Vandegrift had more than 23,000 men on the island, while General Hyakutake commanded 23,000 men of the Seventeenth Army.

October also witnessed important US Navy command changes. In mid-month Vice-Admiral Halsey replaced Ghormley as commander of the South Pacific Area, and Rear-Admiral Thomas C. Kinkaid took over command of the carriers *Hornet* and *Enterprise* from Fletcher. Yamamoto, meanwhile, had given Kondo command of two fleet and two light carriers to use them to secure control of the southern Solomons. Kondo shifted many of his naval assets south from Truk but he was reluctant to employ his carriers without control of Henderson Field. In Japanese hands the base would both deny the Americans a location from which they could attack Japanese ships and planes and provide an emergency landing site for Japanese aircraft, especially should a carrier be lost. Between October 23 and 25 the Japanese launched strong land attacks against Henderson Field. Fortunately for the marines, these attacks were dispersed and uncoordinated. The Japanese suffered 2000 dead, while US casualties were fewer than 300. Immediately after halting the Japanese offensive, Vandegrift began a six-week effort to expand the defensive perimeter beyond which the Japanese could not bring Henderson under artillery fire.

Meanwhile, Kondo's repositioning of vessels and Halsey's instructions to Kinkaid to seek out the Japanese fleet brought on a fourth naval battle for control of the Solomons, the October 26 Battle of the Santa Cruz Islands. In it each side launched simultaneous strikes against the other. US dive-bombers from the *Enterprise* passed the Japanese planes, and the escorting Zeros shot up the Americans. Worse for the Americans, the *Hornet*'s combat air patrol (CAP) was vectored to the wrong location and the US carrier was hit hard. Meanwhile, US strike aircraft badly damaged the light carrier *Zuiho* and fleet carrier *Shokaku*. The *Enterprise* then came under Japanese attack and was also damaged. Heavy anti-aircraft fire from battleship *South Dakota* provided tremendous assistance against the attackers, but Kinkaid had to withdraw. *Hornet* was placed under tow, but with Kondo closing in, she was abandoned to be sunk by Japanese destroyers. Kondo then retired.

The Battle of the Santa Cruz Islands was a Japanese victory leaving the United States with only one carrier in the South Pacific, but the Japanese took such losses that they were unable to exploit the situation. Kondo erred; had he continued the pursuit, he might have sunk the *Enterprise* along with other combatants that Halsey would undoubtedly have detached to protect her. But the Japanese had also lost 100 aircraft, about half as many again as the Americans, who in 1942 produced more than five times as many aircraft as Japan and had a far-superior pilot replacement system.[19]

From November 12–15 a series of intense sea fights took place off Guadalcanal. The first, on November 12–13, saw US ships and land aircraft blocking reinforcement of the island by 13,000 Japanese troops in 11 transports, protected by destroyers, all commanded by Admiral Tanaka. At the same time Vice-Admiral Abe Hiroaki led a powerful force of 2 battleships, a light cruiser, and 6 destroyers to shell Henderson Field. Rear-Admiral Daniel J. Callaghan, commanding 5 cruisers and 8 destroyers that had escorted reinforcements to Guadalcanal, moved to intercept. In the night action that followed east of Savo Island, both sides suffered heavily. Abe lost battleship *Hiei* (badly damaged in the fight, it fell prey to US aircraft the next morning) and 2 destroyers; all other Japanese ships sustained damage. The United States lost 2 cruisers and 4 destroyers. Another cruiser and a destroyer were close to sinking, and all other ships save one were damaged. Among those killed were Rear-Admirals Callaghan and Norman Scott. But Tanaka was forced to turn back and the planned Japanese bombardment of Henderson Field was cancelled.

On November 13–14 Tanaka returned with his reinforcement convoy and his cruisers shelled Henderson Field, but the Americans sank six Japanese transports and a heavy cruiser; another cruiser was damaged. In the third phase of the Naval Battle of Guadalcanal, between November 14 and 15, Rear-Admiral Willis A. Lee with battleships *Washington* and *South Dakota* and four destroyers met and defeated yet another Japanese force under Admiral Kondo near Savo Island. The Americans lost two destroyers, but Kondo lost the battleship *Kirishima* and a destroyer to the *Washington*'s radar-directed guns. The net effect of this three-day battle was that Tanaka landed only some 4000 troops. He rescued another 5000 on his return to Rabaul. The Japanese had lost six transports sunk, but they had to beach another four, representing some 70,000 tons of scarce shipping. Most important from the American standpoint, US forces now had round-the-clock control of the waters around the island.[20]

On November 30 US and Japanese naval forces again clashed in the Battle of Tassafaronga. Rear-Admiral Carlton H. Wright moved with five cruisers and seven destroyers to intercept Tanaka's 'Tokyo Express' of eight destroyers carrying supplies to Guadalcanal. As the Japanese entered Ironbottom Sound, the Americans sank the leading destroyer, but Tanaka managed to position his remaining destroyers to fire torpedoes and escape without further loss. The Americans had one cruiser sunk and three others badly damaged.

On December 8 Vandegrift turned command of the island over to Army Major General Patch, who organized all forces on Guadalcanal into the XIV Corps, including the 2nd Marine Division, replacing the veteran 1st Marine Division which was withdrawn, and the 25th Infantry Division. At the beginning of January 1943 Patch commanded 58,000 men, while Japanese strength was less than 20,000. Ultimately, the Americans won the battle for Guadalcanal thanks to superior supply capabilities and the failure of the Japanese to throw sufficient resources into the battle. The Americans were now well fed and supplied, while the Japanese were desperate, losing many men to sickness and starvation. At the end of December Tokyo decided to abandon Guadalcanal.

Meanwhile, on January 10 Patch began an offensive to clear the island of Japanese forces, mixing army and marine units as the situation dictated. In a two-week long battle the Americans drove the Japanese from a heavily fortified line west of Henderson Field. At the end of January the Japanese were forced from Tassafaronga toward Cape Esperance, where a small US force landed to prevent them from escaping by sea. Dogged Japanese perseverance and naval support, however, enabled some defenders to escape. The Japanese invested in the struggle 24,600 men (20,800 troops and 3800 naval personnel). In daring night operations between February 1 and 7, 1943, Japanese destroyers brought off 10,630 of them (9800 army and 830 navy). The United States committed 60,000 men to the fight for the island; of these the marines lost 1207, while army casualties came to 562. US casualties were far greater in the naval contests for the island, where the navy and marines lost 4911 and the Japanese at least 3200. Counting land, sea, and air casualties, the struggle for Guadalcanal had claimed 7100 US dead and permanently missing.[21]

The Japanese advance had now been halted, and MacArthur could begin the long and bloody return to the Philippine Islands. The Japanese had lost in the Guadalcanal effort an aircraft carrier, 2 battleships, 3 heavy cruisers, 1 light cruiser, 14 destroyers, and 8 submarines. In the previous six months Japan had also lost 140 transports. Twenty-nine destroyers were damaged or in need of repair; their absence contributed to the later destruction of Japanese aircraft carriers. Particularly serious from the Japanese point of view was the loss of 2076 aircraft (1094 to combat) and so many trained pilots.[22]

US control of the air rendered Japanese ships vulnerable to attack and allowed the United States to neutralize Japanese bases without their actual capture. It also allowed Allied forces to determine the timing and location of offensive operations without Japanese foreknowledge.

6

The Tide Turns in Europe

The tide of war turned in 1942, although this was not so obvious at the time. In the Pacific theater of operations Japan met rebuff on the seas in the Battle of Midway and was defeated on land at Guadalcanal. In the European theater the Soviet Union checked Germany's advance in the titanic struggle at Stalingrad, while in northwestern Africa US and British forces landed in Morocco and Algeria. Further east, British Empire forces defeated the Germans and Italians at El Alamein in Egypt and drove the Axis forces from Egypt. The next year the Allies caught Axis forces in a gigantic vice in Tunisia.

As US military strength developed and the Soviet Union rebuilt its own forces, the defeat of the Axis powers became inevitable, barring some kind of miracle weapon or separate peace. The combined military potential of the Allied powers was much greater than that of Germany, Italy, and Japan. The best the aggressor states, now largely on the defensive, could hope for was to prolong the war to secure better peace terms or that there would be a break in the Allied coalition, most probably between the Soviet Union and its Western partners.

The best hope for the Axis powers in prolonging the war was to consolidate their fighting fronts. Smaller fronts could be held more effectively by fewer men and less equipment; but none of the Axis leaders could bear to lose face by voluntary withdrawal, which would in any case have been difficult to carry out. Hitler, Mussolini, and Japan's leaders chose to cling to all the territory they acquired, thereby insuring that their defeats, when they came, would be more costly.

In Europe, throughout early 1942, the Germans appeared to retain the advantage. German troops were poised to move into the Caucasus and the *Afrika Korps* was advancing in North Africa. German U-boats, meanwhile, wreaked havoc on Allied shipping off the eastern seaboard of the United States. In the Mediterranean there was virtually no Allied shipping. The United States was redirecting its vast industrial base from civilian to military production, but in 1942 Stalin was calling for an immediate invasion of western Europe by British and US ground forces. Distrustful of his allies as ever, Stalin chose to regard the failure of the Western forces to open a 'second' front on the ground as fresh evidence of anti-Soviet sentiment and the desire of the West to fight 'to the last Russian.' But America's armies were as yet unready, the ships that would bring them to Europe and supply them were still unbuilt. The German submarine menace in the Atlantic had yet to be tamed. If the United States was going to make a contribution to the war in Europe in 1942, it would have to be in the form of strategic bombing.

The Americans wanted the earliest possible cross-Channel invasion of northern France. Army Chief of Staff General Marshall was a strong supporter of Operation SLEDGEHAMMER, an invasion of north-western Europe in the fall of 1942. The British – Churchill but also Chief of the Imperial General Staff General Alan Brooke – were rightly leery of this plan, fearful that it would lead to a repeat of the catastrophic casualties in northeastern France in World War I.

The Dieppe raid

Proof that the Western Allies were not ready to undertake a cross-Channel invasion was provided in one of the war's most debated and controversial actions on August 19, 1942. Operation JUBILEE, which began as Operation RUTTER, was undertaken at the instigation of Chief of Combined Operations Lord Louis Mountbatten against Dieppe, on the Normandy coast of France between Le Havre and Boulogne. Ironically, Dieppe was the same location from which William the Conqueror had set out to conquer England in 1066.

The stated idea behind the raid was to demonstrate to Stalin that the Western Allies intended and were able to launch a cross-Channel operation. Mountbatten was under pressure from Churchill for some action; he was also eager to test Britain's capabilities, and he said later that he hoped to prove that such operations could succeed. The Dieppe raid may have been the largest operation of its type and, with 800 RAF aircraft, the biggest air battle to that point in history. Unfortunately, heavy ship-to-shore bombardment and bomber participation planned for Operation RUTTER vanished when it was postponed in early July. Throughout, JUBILEE was marked by poor planning, for which Mountbatten must take the blame.

Just before dawn on August 19, 6000 soldiers and marines, including a few US rangers, went ashore at Dieppe against strong German defensive positions. The plan was to be in and out in one day. The nine-hour foray accomplished this but at heavy cost: over 1000 Allied participants dead and 106 aircraft shot down. The overall Allied personnel casualty rate was more than 40 percent, the highest of the war for any major offensive involving all three services. The Canadians suffered the worst; with 4963 men, they made up 80 percent of the attackers, and 3367 were casualties (907 killed). Some Canadians have called it the worst military disaster in their history. The British claimed 150 German planes downed, but the actual figure was 48. German losses in personnel were 311 dead and 280 wounded.

The Dieppe raid led to bitter recriminations between Britain and Canada, and with the United States and the Soviet Union. It also produced its share of historical controversies and myths, including the mistaken belief that the Germans must have known of it in advance. One of the chief mysteries is why the raid was even attempted. The British government and Chiefs of Staff were aware that such an operation made little sense. Evidence that it had virtually no hope of success was subsequently concealed under the patent lie that the raid had been undertaken to provide vital future lessons. It did reveal that equipment, organization, and command structure were all sadly deficient.

Hitler expected the Allies to undertake some such operation as a demonstration to Stalin. Earlier, the Soviet dictator had dropped a not-so-subtle hint that the Soviet Union might leave the war, and Hitler was certain the British would try to bolster Stalin's resolve by attempting a raid against the northern coast of France. Hitler even predicted its location; there was nothing difficult in this as the likely point of attack was determined by the range of covering fighter aircraft from England.

Many Canadians remain bitter about the raid. Historian Brian Villa has gone so far as to charge that Dieppe was set up to fail. In any case, the raid did bury the myth that SLEDGEHAMMER would have been feasible in 1942, and it cast grave doubts on Operation ROUNDUP, the Allied plan for a cross-Channel invasion in 1943. It neither intimidated the Germans nor caused Hitler to transfer forces from the Soviet front. Quite the contrary, it starkly demonstrated the pathetic state of Allied preparations to open a second front. The Dieppe raid was more than a political setback. Its most telling consequence was to dissuade Churchill and the British Chiefs of Staff from any commitment to cross-Channel operations. This view, correct in 1942, was certainly not the case by 1944.[1]

The Allied invasion of French North Africa

Roosevelt promised Stalin that the Western Allies would undertake an invasion by the end of 1942, and he was determined to honor that pledge. But if it was not waged across the English Channel, then where might it be mounted? Churchill argued for attacks against what he termed the 'soft underbelly of Europe,' in the Mediterranean. The Americans reluctantly conceded that the failure of JUBILEE had demonstrated that a cross-Channel invasion was months, if not years, in the future.

Even before JUBILEE, Roosevelt and Churchill had settled on an invasion of North Africa. Control of Vichy-administered Morocco, Algeria, and Tunisia would provide bases from which the Allies could mount air operations to help secure their Mediterranean shipping. It would also provide a location from which to invade islands such as Sicily, Sardinia, or Crete, or even Italy or Greece. In North Africa the Allies could establish bomber bases and use these to mount operations against Axis-occupied southern Europe. The North African foray would also provide badly needed combat experience for green US troops against a military that would be substantially inferior to the *Wehrmacht*. Roosevelt was its chief proponent, and insisted on it over objections by many of his own service chiefs. The invasion, codenamed Operation TORCH, was timed to coincide with the planned break-out of British Empire forces at El Alamein in Egypt. The Allies hoped to be able to crush Axis troops in a pincer movement between their two forces.

The Battle of El Alamein

Eighth Army commander General Montgomery initiated the final contest for control of North Africa. Carefully gathering the resources he thought necessary for success, he held off Churchill's demands for an earlier offensive. When Operation LIGHTFOOT began, Montgomery had an overwhelming advantage of 195,000 men, 1029 tanks (including 300 US-built M-4s), 2311 artillery pieces, and 750 aircraft. Opposing these were 104,000 men (50,000 Germans and 54,000 Italians), 489 tanks, 1219 guns (80 of them 88mm), and 675 aircraft. The restricted front from the sea to the depression could not be turned and was heavily fortified in depth, the defenders relying on an estimated 450,000 mines.

Afrika Korps commander Erwin Rommel had no confidence he could hold against the anticipated British offensive. Montgomery hoped to catch the Axis defenders off guard with a feint to the south while the main thrust was delivered in the north against the strength of the Axis line by Lieutenant General Sir Oliver Leese's XXX Corps; indeed, elaborate British deceptions led the Germans to expect the major offensive to come in the south.

The Battle of El Alamein began under a full moon, October 23, at 9:40 p.m., when 1000 British guns bombarded a six-mile sector of the German left flank near the Mediterranean. Twenty minutes later XXX Corps moved out, while Lieutenant General Sir Brian Horrocks' XIII Corps began the southern diversionary attack near the Qattara Depression to fix Axis forces there. XXX Corps infantry managed to clear two corridors in the German mine-fields and Lieutenant General Herbert Lumsden's X Armored Corps then moved through them. The Italians, who held this sector, fought well, and a counter-attack by the 15th Panzer Division nearly halted the British advance. Rommel, in Germany on sick leave when the attack began, hurried back to North Africa and resumed command on the 25th.

Montgomery soon halted the southern diversion and concentrated his effort along the coast. Over the next week both sides flung armored units into the main battle sector south of the coastal road and railroad. The Eighth Army enjoyed air superiority, and the German tanks, which came into the battle piecemeal, were steadily reduced in number. Rommel's lack of armor reserves and his chronic shortages of fuel and ammunition proved influential in the battle's outcome. He managed to extricate his 164th Division, which had been pinned against the coast by the Australian 9th Division, and on November 1 withdrew to new positions three miles to the west. The next day the 2nd New Zealand Division managed to clear a path through the mine-fields for the British tanks. Rommel then mounted a panzer counter-attack, but by the end of the day he had only 35 tanks remaining. British tactical air and artillery fire neutralized the German 88mm anti-tank guns. Hitler held up the general withdrawal west of *Afrika Korps* for two days with an inane order that Rommel hold in place. British forces now broke cleanly through the German lines, and Rommel disregarded Hitler's command, disengaged, and withdrew westerly. The ever-cautious Montgomery delayed his pursuit for 24 hours.

The Battle of El Alamein was one of the decisive engagements of the war. As Churchill wrote of it, 'Before Alamein we never had a victory. After Alamein we never had a defeat.'[2] Casualty figures for the battle vary. The British claimed to have inflicted 55,000 casualties, but the *Afrika Korps* probably sustained something on the order of 2300 killed,

5500 wounded, and 27,900 captured. Rommel also lost almost all his tanks and many of his artillery pieces. Eighth Army casualties were far less: 4600 killed and 9300 wounded. Montgomery had 432 tanks destroyed or disabled.

Despite the outcome of the battle, military historians have criticized Montgomery for his attacking the strength of the German line and the high cost of the victory. Montgomery's assertion that everything went according to plan is simply not true. But the chief negative for the Allies was in Eighth Army's leisurely pursuit of the *Afrika Korps* after the battle. Despite Montgomery's plans to keep constant pressure on the Germans, during the period November 5 to December 11 Rommel made good his escape. Again and again, *Afrika Korps* eluded Montgomery's lethargic encirclement attempts.

Operation TORCH

On November 8 in Operation TORCH Anglo-American forces carried out surprise landings in Morocco and Algeria. The British had favored landings in central North Africa, at Tunis and Bizerte in Tunisia, or at least at nearby Bône in eastern Algeria, but the Americans were more cautious and won the point. The landings occurred at Casablanca in Morocco; and Oran and Algiers in Algeria in what was to that point the largest amphibious operation in history. US Army Lieutenant General Dwight D. Eisenhower, commanding US troops in Britain, had overall command. His staff was entirely integrated with US and British officers and British Fleet Admiral Andrew B. Cunningham directed all naval forces.

The most westerly landing, at Casablanca on the Atlantic, assured the Allies a lodgement in North Africa even if the other two landings inside the Mediterranean went awry. Major General George S. Patton commanded this Western Task Force of 38,000 men, escorted by warships commanded by US Rear-Admiral Henry K. Hewitt. It had steamed all the way from Norfolk, Virginia, one of the longest expeditionary efforts in history.

The other two invasions had been mounted from England. They came ashore in Algeria. Central Task Force under US Army Major General Lloyd Fredendall numbered nearly 41,000 men (37,100 Americans and 3600 British), supported by British Commodore Thomas H. Troubridge's covering warships. The 55,000-man Eastern Task Force headed for Algiers was largely British in composition (45,000 British troops and only 10,000 Americans) but to give the illusion that it was largely American, US Major General Charles Ryder had command. Once Algiers was secured, British Lieutenant General Kenneth A. N. Anderson took charge. British Vice-Admiral Sir Harold M. Burrough commanded its covering warships.

During the landings the Allies made every effort to play up the US role and downplay British participation. Allied leaders assumed correctly that Americans would receive a far friendlier reception from the French than would the British, and efforts were made, quite literally, to show the American flag wherever possible. No one knew the extent to which French troops would resist the invasion. Preliminary contacts with Vichy French officials in North Africa conducted by US diplomat Robert Murphy also involved a secret mission to North Africa by US Army Major General Mark Clark, but did not bring the desired agreement. For the most part, the French troops resisted.

The landings began early on the morning of November 8. The Casablanca operation was widely dispersed, at Safi, Fedala, Mehdia, and Port Lyautey. Although taken by surprise, the French troops fought well. The unfinished French battleship *Jean Bart* lay at Casablanca. Incapable of movement, her 15-inch guns soon began a duel with US battleship *Massachusetts*. French naval units, including the cruiser *Primauguet*, attempted a sortie, but superior US naval strength beat them back. The battle cost the French Navy 4 destroyers and 8 submarines sunk or missing, and 490 killed and 969 wounded. The *Jean Bart* was beached. The French at Casablanca surrendered on 11 November.

The two Allied landings east and west of Oran encountered heavy French resistance. An attempt by two US Coastguard cutters to run into the port was unsuccessful and a US airborne battalion, flying all the way from Britain, was only partially successful in securing nearby airfields. At Algiers the frontal naval assault failed, but the city was soon ringed by Allied troops on the land side. Within several days the Allies had secured their objectives. Casualties were light and the landings provided excellent training for the Allies and their subsequent invasion of Europe. Although the British were correct in that they could easily have landed farther east, Hitler now decided to reinforce North Africa. Had these resources been sent to Rommel earlier, the Axis powers might have secured the Suez Canal. Hitler's belated decision only delayed the inevitable and insured that the ultimate Axis defeat there would be more costly.

Despite misgivings, the Allies negotiated with the commander of Vichy France armed forces and former premier, Admiral Jean Darlan, who was in Algiers on a visit at the time of the landings. On November 11 Darlan agreed to assist the Allies by ordering a cease-fire in return for heading the administration of French North Africa. Darlan was subsequently assassinated on December 24, allegedly by a monarchist acting alone, a deed that removed a potential embarrassment for the Western governments. The British and French then installed General Giraud, who had escaped from France, as commander of French forces in North Africa, ignoring De Gaulle. The latter, understandably furious, had not even been informed of the landings beforehand.[3]

On November 9 Marshal Pétain's Vichy French government had responded to the Allied North African invasions by breaking relations with the United States. Nonetheless, Hitler ordered German troops into 'unoccupied' France. Operation ATTILA had been drawn up by the Germans in 1940. Its main objective was to capture the main French naval units at Toulon. On November 27, however, French crews frustrated the German attempt and sent to the bottom 77 ships, including 3 battleships (the *Strasbourg*, *Dunkerque*, and *Provence*), 7 cruisers, a seaplane tender, 32 destroyers, 16 submarines and 18 smaller craft. Five submarines were able to avoid mines and German bombs and escape to the open sea; three made it to North Africa and another to Spain; the fifth was lost at sea. The Germans and Italians subsequently raised and repaired 4 destroyers, 2 torpedo boats, and 2 submarines.[4]

Once the Allied forces that had landed in North Africa secured their initial objectives ashore, they proceeded on to two key objectives: to secure ports in Tunisia in order to block resupply of Axis forces there and in Libya, and to build up a force in Morocco to occupy Spanish Morocco if Spain, or the Germans acting through Spain, should attempt taking Gibraltar. As it turned out the latter was unnecessary, the landings alone caused Franco to bring Spain into a more neutral stance.

Allied forces were unprepared for immediate overland operations, but nonetheless were forced into them by Hitler's prompt reinforcement of North Africa. As early as November 9 he had dispatched troops to Tunisia to occupy the important airfield at El Aouina. German and Italian units began arriving in North Africa at about 1000 men a day.

Patton's force at Casablanca linked up with units moving west from Oran to threaten Spanish Morocco, and the British moved east to secure airfields in eastern Algeria, necessary for providing air support for ground operations beyond the range of Gibraltar. On November 12 two British parachute companies dropped on Bône, supported by commandos from the sea. Souk-el-Arba airfield fell on the 16th. The next day General Anderson's I Corps drove from Oran and Algiers into Tunisia with the objective of the principal port of Bizerte. Although I Corps had moved from Bône into the mountains only 20 miles southwest of Bizerte, the drive stalled after several weeks. It fell victim to insufficiently aggressive Allied leadership, rainy weather delaying reinforcements from Algiers 500 some miles to the west, the rapid Axis reinforcement, and aggressive defensive actions by Lieutenant General Walther Nehring, whose counter-attacks ended the Allied 'race for Tunis.' But Nehring, who was pessimistic about Axis chances, soon found himself replaced by General Jürgen von Arnim. Thus 1942 ended in a temporary stalemate once Rommel's *Afrika Korps* successfully linked up with von Arnim's Tunisian defenders.

By February von Arnim's Fifth Panzer Army of 100,000 men faced the bulk of the Allied forces centered on Bizerte and Tunis. The British First Army, a provisional French corps, and some US troops were positioned in the north, while General Fredendall's II Corps held the southern front. To the east, Rommel's *Afrika Korps* of 70,000 men occupied the old French Mareth fortified zone against Montgomery's Eighth Army. Montgomery now concentrated his resource at Mareth for an assault there. The *Luftwaffe* dominated the skies as Arnim kept Anderson's forces off balance by launching a series of spoiling attacks.

On February 9 Marshal Kesselring arrived in Tunisia to plan a coordinated strike west of the Eastern Dorsal. In the north Arnim was to push beyond Faid toward Sbeitla. Rommel, to the south, would head for Gafsa. The chief problem with the plan was that there was no overall commander and the two generals operated independently of each other. Arnim struck first. Without coordinating with Rommel, on February 14 he attacked and destroyed American and French forces, pushing the survivors back to Sbeitla. Learning the next day that the Americans and French had abandoned Gafsa, Rommel sent troops there, then ordered them on to Feriana and to the airfields at Thelepte, which they secured on the 17th.

Rommel wanted to capture Tebessa, an important Allied supply point just across the border in Algeria, and sought a wide envelopment of the Allies forces. He received permission for a more limited thrust toward Sbiba and the Kasserine passes in the Western Dorsal. If he could get through the mountain passes he could threaten the entire Allied position in Tunisia. The blow fell on February 19, 1943. Three days of attacks against Sbiba came to nought, but in a battle at Faid Pass east of Kasserine, usually known as the Battle of Kasserine Pass, Rommel won a tactical victory. On that day German panzers, supported by dive-bombers and fighters, caught the US 1st Infantry Division by surprise and rolled through it. Nightfall found American survivors scattered over a ten-mile area and the Americans driven back 15 miles.

Eisenhower immediately rushed up reinforcements, and the next day US forces attempted a counter-attack, which the Germans beat back. By the 22nd, his thrust having been halted by US infantry and concentrated artillery fire, Rommel retired back to the Mareth Line. Rommel had sustained only 1000 casualties (200 killed) and lost 20 tanks. The Allies (chiefly Americans) sustained nearly 4000 casualties and lost 400 tanks and 200 pieces of artillery.[5]

Poor American communication, inept leadership, lack of cooperation, and command rivalries all contributed to the defeat. Eisenhower must also share blame for being too involved in the North African political turmoil and not enough in the military situation. In fairness to the United States, the outcome of the battle should have been expected given that seasoned *Afrika Korps* veterans with air superiority were pitted against inexperienced US troops. As it was, the Americans rallied and redeemed themselves; while Rommel's tactical victory proved indecisive. Arnim had failed to support him in time. Too late, on February 23 Rommel received command of Army Group *Afrika*, with authority over both Arnim's Fifth Panzer Army and Italian General Giovanni Messe's First Italian Army that included remnants of the Afrika Korps among its 50,000 German and 35,000 Italian troops. Had he secured overall command in Tunisia earlier he might have been able to deal a crushing defeat on the Allies.

The Americans spent the next weeks regrouping and reshuffling their command structure. On February 20 Allied ground forces in Tunisia were formed into the 18th Army Group under British General Sir Harold Alexander. On March 6 Patton replaced Fredendall in command of II Corps. Another consequence of the battle was that the Americans adopted the more flexible British system of air support. Indeed, Tunisia turned into a giant trap for the Axis. The British contained Arnim's February 26 attack against their positions and a British counter-attack on March 26 restored the Allied line. On March 6 Messe conducted a probing attack against the Mareth Line but was repulsed. Three days later Rommel flew to Rome to confer with Mussolini and Kesselring. He told them the Axis position in North Africa was irretrievably lost and that to stay there would be 'plain suicide.' They urged that he confer with Hitler, but Hitler would have none of Rommel's pleas to evacuate Axis forces from North Africa. Hitler decorated Rommel and ordered him on extended sick leave. Arnim now assumed overall command of Axis North African forces.[6]

The Allies now held the initiative, and at last Montgomery launched his offensive against the German and Italian lines. The Battle of Mareth from March 20 to 26 forced the Axis defenders to withdraw. By now their supply situation was desperate. Allied control of Malta, 'the unsinkable aircraft carrier,' proved crucial. Thanks to Ultra and to ships and planes from Malta, the Allies intercepted and sank most supply ships bound for North Africa. The badly stretched German airlift capacity was insufficient to take up the slack. In any case, many of these transport aircraft were shot down by Allied fighters.

First and Eighth Armies now closed in for the kill, which occurred in the May 3–13 Battle of Tunis ('Tunisgrad'), in which the Allies took 275,000 prisoners. Since the beginning of the war, Axis forces in North Africa had lost upwards of 620,000 men, a third of them German. On the Allied side, British Empire losses amounted to 220,000 men; the French had lost 20,000; and the Americans had suffered 18,500 casualties. But Africa was now at last clear of Axis forces and the threat to Egypt and Suez was over.[7]

The Eastern Front

At the same time it became clear that in the winter of 1942–43 the Germans suffered a catastrophic reversal in the great Battle of Stalingrad. On the Eastern Front the winter belonged to the Soviets, the summer to the Germans. The Soviet counter-attack of December 1941 had sent German forces reeling. Hitler had initially agreed to withdrawals, but on December 16 he changed his mind and ordered the army to stand fast. On the 20th he issued firm orders to that effect. He also forbad construction of second-line defenses, which he believed would only encourage the tendency to retire. His orders to the *Wehrmacht* to stand fast, to hold or die, in effect saved the army, but at a high price. Three dozen generals who disobeyed, including Rundstedt, were cashiered. Tens of thousands of German soldiers died, but the front gradually stabilized, and Hitler had most probably avoided complete disintegration of his army and a repetition of Napoleon Bonaparte's 1812 disaster. This achievement, however, convinced Hitler that only he could master the military situation.

On December 19, General von Brauchitsch resigned. He had been nominal commander of the army, but in reality was a mere fig leaf for the *Führer*. Henceforth Hitler, as supreme commander of the armed forces and commander-in-chief of the army, personally commanded all

German military operations, insisting on prior consultation before even a battalion could be committed. As Manstein noted later, Hitler lacked 'military victory based on experience [emphasis in original] – something for which his "intuition" was no substitute.'[8]

Conditions on the Eastern Front were horrible. The winter of 1941–42 was the coldest in 100 years; temperatures reached –50 degrees celsius and worse. Still, German all-around defenses, known as 'hedge-hogs' and located along major communication nodes, held and prevented major breakthroughs. The Soviet counter-offensive slowly ground to a halt; but by the time the front had stabilized in February 1942, the Soviets had made deep penetrations almost everywhere; only in Finland had they met rebuff. From March to May there was a stale-mate. The Soviets had outrun their supply line, and the Germans were not ready to resume the offensive. In fact, Germany increasingly was hard-pressed for manpower and Hitler had to call on his allies to provide armies to launch his summer 1942 offensive. In all, he secured 51 allied Axis divisions (Italian, Hungarian, Romanian, Slovakian, and the Spanish Blue Division). Hitler's immediate goal was to eliminate the salients created by the previous Soviet offensive.

Before Germany could launch its offensive the Soviets struck. Noting German offensive preparations, Stalin insisted on a spoiling attack against Army Group South's logistics base at Kharkov. The Soviet offensive, which began on May 12, broke through into the German rear areas and for a time appeared as if it might succeed in reaching Kharkov, but then the Germans counter-attacked. Stalin refused appeals from his generals and insisted that the offensive continue, with the result that the Germans took 240,000 prisoners and destroyed some 1200 Soviet tanks. To the south the Soviets suffered a second major reverse in June when Manstein's Eleventh Army swept the Kerch Peninsula, inflicting 150,000 casualties, and then broke through the Soviet defenses at Sevastopol, where the Soviets lost another 100,000 men by early July.

The great German summer offensive opened on June 28. General Manstein had wanted mobile operations in the center of the front that would prevent Soviets forces from taking the initiative. Believing that Stalin would pour in all available resources to save Moscow, Manstein thought this approach offered the best chance of smashing the Red Army once and for all. It would also leave the Germans defending a more compact front.[9]

Hitler rejected this sound approach and divided his resources. In the north he would push to take Leningrad, still under siege, and link up with the Finns. But the main effort would be Operation *BLAU* (Blue) to the south. He sent Bock's Army Group South east from around Kursk to take Voronezh, which fell to the Germans on July 6. Hitler then reorganized his southern forces into Army Groups A and B. Army Group A, the southern formation, was commanded by General List; General Weichs had charge of the northern formation, Army Group B.

Hitler's original plan was for Army Groups A and B to cooperate in a great effort to secure the Don and Donets valleys and capture the cities of Rostov and Stalingrad. The two could then move southeast to take the oil fields so important to the Red Army. On July 13, however, Hitler ordered a change of plans, now demanding the capture of both Stalingrad, a major industrial center and key crossing point on the Volga River, and the Caucasus simultaneously. Dividing the effort placed further strains on already inadequate German resources, especially logistical support. The twin objectives also meant that a gap would inevitably appear between the two German army groups, enabling most Soviet troops caught in the Don River bend to escape eastward. Meanwhile, on July 23 Army Group A captured Rostov. It then crossed the Don River, advanced deep into the Caucasus, getting to within 70 miles of the Caspian Sea.

Hitler now intervened again, slowing the advance of General Friedrich Paulus's Sixth Army of Army Group B toward Stalingrad when he detached General Hermann Hoth's Fourth Panzer Army to join Army Group A in order to assist in securing the Caucasus oil fields. Nonetheless, Sixth Army reached the Volga north of Stalingrad on August 23. The great city of Stalingrad curved for some 20 miles along the high western bank of the Volga River. Hitler's original intent was merely to control the Volga River by gunfire and destroy the city's arms factories, notably the Tractor, Red October, and Barricades works, but now he demanded a full occupation of the Soviet dictator's namesake city. Stalin, meanwhile, poured men and equipment into the city. Ruthless young General Vasily Chuikov, a Zhukov protege, commanded Sixty-Second Army, holding on the west bank of the Volga.

The Germans now had a new tank. Guderian had earlier suggested that the Germans merely replicate the Soviet T-34, but Hitler rejected this. The PzKpfn VI Tiger with a long 88mm gun entered production in August 1942. Guderian had urged the Tigers be held back until sufficient numbers were available to enable them to effect a major victory, but Hitler insisted on trying them out on the Leningrad sector that September in a situation where they fell prey to well-sited Soviet anti-tank guns. The Soviets learned that in tank-on-tank combat they could nullify the longer-range gun of the new German tanks by closing the distance before firing. And, in the close quarters of the Stalingrad fighting, distances hardly mattered.[10]

Angry over the slow progress of Sixth Army into Stalingrad, Hitler on August 11 ordered Hoth's Fourth Army there, north from the Caucasus and leaving a badly depleted Army Group A holding a 500-mile front, thus stalling the southernmost drive. Hitler also ordered his sole strategic reserve in the area, Manstein's Eleventh Army, all the way north to Leningrad.

Such wide-ranging shifts of scant German resources took a terrible toll on men but especially on equipment. They also used up precious fuel and stretched the German lines far beyond what was reasonable or safe. OKH Chief of Staff General Halder and other generals grew more and more alarmed. They pointed out to Hitler that the German Army in Russia now had to maintain a front of more than 2000 miles. Between the two armies of Army Group B a sole division held a 240-mile gap. North of Stalingrad, Romanian troops protected the single railroad bringing supplies to the Sixth Army. The possibilities open to the Soviets were enormous, providing they had the resources available. Hitler claimed they did not. Halder continued warning Hitler and tried to get him to break off the battle for Stalingrad. This time Hitler sacked Halder. He also relieved List, taking personal command from a distance of 1200 miles of Army Group A, nominally under Kleist. The irony is that the Germans might have taken Stalingrad in July had Hoth not been diverted south by Hitler to assist Kleist.

The Battle of Stalingrad

From August 24 a costly battle of attrition raged over Stalingrad. *Luftwaffe* carpet-bombing at the end of August killed some 40,000 people and turned the city into defensive bastions of ruined buildings and rubble. Stalin refused to allow the evacuation of the civilian population, believing that this would force the defenders, especially local militia forces, to fight more tenaciously.[11]

The ruined city posed a formidable obstacle. Germany's strength lay in maneuver warfare, but Hitler now threw this away by compelling Sixth Army to engage the Soviet strength of static defense. Stalin ordered the city held at all costs, and Soviet forces resisted doggedly. Chuikov ordered his troops to keep within 50 yards of the Germans, in order to make it as difficult as possible for German artillery and aviation. Zhukov, who had just been appointed deputy supreme commander, second in authority only to Stalin, arrived at Stalingrad on August 29 to take overall charge of operations there.

Meanwhile, Hitler became obsessed with Stalingrad and wore down his army in repeated attempts to capture that symbol of defiance. Taking Stalingrad was unnecessary from a military point of view; the 16th Panzer Division at Rynok already controlled the Volga with its guns, closing it to north–south shipping. But Hitler insisted the city itself be physically taken. For a month Sixth Army did its best. The German troops pressed slowly forward, but casualties in the meat-grinder battle were enormous on both sides, with advances measured in yards. The battle disintegrated into a block-by-block, house-by-house, even room-by-room struggle for sheer survival.

General Paulus has been much blamed for refusing to disobey Hitler's order to stand firm and extracting his army before it was too late, but his and Hitler's greatest failing lay in not anticipating the Soviet encirclement. While feeding the cauldron of Stalingrad with only sufficient troops absolutely necessary to hold the city, Zhukov patiently assembled a million men in four fronts (army groups) for a great double envelopment. This deep movement, Operation URANUS, began on November 19 and was timed to coincide with the frosts that would make Soviet cross-country tank maneuvers possible against Axis infantry. For the northern pincer the Soviets assembled 3500 guns and heavy mortars to blast a hole for three tank and two cavalry corps, and a dozen infantry divisions. They encountered Romanian infantry divisions, which fought bravely, but their 37mm guns and light Skoda tanks were no match for the Soviet T-34s. The southern Soviet prong of two corps, one mechanized and the other cavalry, broke through on the 20th, against two Romanian infantry divisions.

By November 23 URANUS had sealed off Sixth Army, driving some units of Fourth Army into the pocket. Hitler now ordered Manstein from the Leningrad Front and gave him a new formation, Army Group Don drawn from Army Group A, with instructions to rectify the situation.

Hitler forbade any withdrawal, convinced that Sixth Army could be resupplied from the air. Göring is usually blamed for assuring Hitler that this could be done, but responsibility is more properly shared between Göring, Chief of the General Staff of the *Luftwaffe* General Hans Jeschonneck, and Hitler. The *Führer* was no doubt misled by *Luftwaffe* success the previous winter in supplying by parachute drops 5000 German troops cut off at Kholm near Moscow and 100,000 men at Demyansk. The latter had held out for 72 days, thanks to 100 *Luftwaffe* flights a day bringing in 60,000 tons of supplies and evacuating 35,000 wounded, until it was relieved at the end of April.

The belief that Stalingrad could be supplied by air was taken at a time when the Soviets enjoyed air superiority. By November 20, the second day of URANUS, the Soviets committed between 1350 and 1414 combat aircraft (depending on the source) to Stalingrad, while General Wolfram Frieherr von Richthofen's *Luftflotte 4*, flying in support of Sixth Army, had 732 combat aircraft, of which only 402 were operational. The Soviets used their air superiority to attack German Army positions but also for bombing raids on the main Ju 52 base at Zverevo, where they destroyed a substantial number of German transport aircraft. Worsening weather also made flying a severe test, and much of the *Luftwaffe* airlift capability was redeployed to resupply Axis troops in North Africa following the Allied landings there.

A fair appraisal for air transport available, even in the best weather conditions, was that the *Luftwaffe* could only bring in one-tenth of Sixth Army's requirements. By the last week in December it delivered only an average 129 tons a day, condemning the German forces in the pocket to slow starvation and death. Then, on January 16, the Soviets took Pitomnik, the principal airfield within the Stalingrad pocket. Its loss dealt a death blow to the airlift operation. The last days saw only supplies dropped by parachute and many of these fell into Soviet hands.[12]

Hitler would not authorize any attempt by Sixth Army to break out, only a link-up of forces. None of the hard-won land was to be surrendered. But it was simply impossible for Sixth Army to accomplish both. Paulus favored a break-out, but he was not prepared to gamble either his army or his career. Manstein's scratch force of three understrength panzer divisions managed to get to within 35 miles of Sixth Army positions, and he urged a *fait accompli* to force Hitler's hand, but Paulus replied with a pessimistic assessment of his army's ability to close the short distance to reach Manstein's relief force. There was insufficient fuel, the horses had mostly been eaten, and it would take weeks to prepare. The relieving forces would have to come closer. A link-up could succeed only if Sixth Army pushed from the other side against the Soviets, but this could not be done without shrinking the Stalingrad pocket, which Hitler had expressly forbidden.

In mid-December the Volga froze, allowing the Soviets to cross vehicles over the ice. In the next seven weeks they sent 35,000 vehicles over the river, along with 122mm howitzers. By then seven Soviet armies surrounded Sixth Army, and break-out was impossible. Even with the situation hopeless, Paulus refused to disobey Hitler and order a surrender. He himself surrendered on January 31 (he claimed he had been 'taken by surprise') but refused to order his men to do the same. The last German units surrendered the next day.

There may have been 294,000 men trapped at Stalingrad, including Hiwis (Soviet auxiliaries working with the Germans) and Romanians. Of only 91,000 taken prisoner (22 generals) by the Soviets, fewer than 5000 survived the war and Soviet captivity. The last Germans taken prisoner at Stalingrad were not released until 1955. Counting casualties in allied units and the rescue attempts, Axis forces lost upwards of a half-million men. The Stalingrad campaign may have cost the Soviets 1.1 million casualties, more than 485,000 of them dead. But in the entire war the Soviet Union sustained 9 million military and 18 million civilian deaths.[13]

The effect of Stalingrad on the German war effort has been hotly debated. More than El Alamein, Stalingrad is frequently seen as the turning-point in the European theater of war, the decisive defeat from which the *Wehrmacht* could never recover. The battle was both focused and dramatic, and it was the first encirclement and defeat of a large German army in the war, but militarily Stalingrad was not irredeemable. The German front lines had been largely rebuilt by the end of the battle, and this was not the last time the Soviets would be tested by the *Wehrmacht*. No, Stalingrad was more important for its psychological than its military value. It did not deny the Germans victory; the Battles of Britain, Moscow, and the Atlantic had already accomplished that. Neither did it mean that a German defeat was inevitable. If any single battle could make that claim, it would be Kursk, six months and a number of German successes in the future.

Hitler finally authorized Army Group A to withdraw from the Caucasus, although the Red Army isolated part of it on the Kuban peninsula. Then, in late January the Soviets mounted a new series of attacks against Army Group B, virtually wiping out the Hungarian Second Army. The Soviets were able to push the Germans back in the 200-mile stretch from Voronezh to Voroshilovgrad. Manstein assured Hitler that the Germans could reestablish their position only by temporarily giving up Kharkov, which the Soviets took on February 15. Manstein correctly held that the objective should be not the occupation of cities, but the defeat, and if possible the destruction of Red Army units.[14]

German forces, reformed into Army Group South (the former Army Group Don and part of Army Group B), soon again took the offensive. Supported by Richtofen's aircraft, Manstein struck only four days after the fall of Kharkov. Caught unawares by the speed of the German recovery, the Soviets were driven back out of Kharkov and to the Donets River, a gain of about 100 miles. Both sides now regrouped. As Manstein wrote later:

> By the end of the winter campaign [of 1942–43] the initiative was back in German hands, and the Russians had suffered two defeats. Though not decisive in character, these did lead to a stabilization of the front and offer the German Command a prospect of fighting the war in the east to a draw. Nevertheless, we could clearly bury any hope of changing the course of the war by an offensive in the summer of 1943. Our loss of fighting power had already been too great for anything of that order.[15]

Guderian remained implacably opposed to further large-scale offensives in the East. Manstein was more ambivalent. What he sought was to wear down the Soviet Union 'to such an extent that it would tire of its already excessive sacrifice and be ready to accept a stalemate. At the time in question this was far from being wishful thinking. On the other hand, such an aim could not be realized by going over to purely defensive, static warfare.'[16]

There is a tendency to assume that from late 1942 Soviet forces had reached a high level of organizational skill and military sophistication that led to a constant stream of victories. That myth was carefully nurtured by Soviet historians, who downplayed the major military reversal of Operation MARS, Zhukov's offensive against Army Group Center during November–December 1942. Soviet historians treated it as a diversionary effort in support of URANUS at Stalingrad, but in his excellent study of the battle, historian David Glantz argues that Zhukov and Stalin planned MARS to be decisive. MARS, however, was both poorly planned and indifferently executed. Its chief failure was in securing too small a bridgehead. The Soviets also committed their tanks prematurely without having brought forward sufficient artillery support. The cost for the Soviets was about 100,000 dead and 235,000 wounded. Indeed, despite their preponderance of resources – with the exception of Stalingrad where Hitler had provided the opportunity – the Red Army was never able to replicate battles of encirclement on the scale of German successes in 1941.[17]

7

Home Fronts and Axis Occupation Policies

World War II was total war, with the entire strength of warring societies mobilized. Victory was contingent upon not only armed forces, but also industry, technology, and entirely mobilized populations. Not only leadership and military strength but natural resources, population size, and industrial might were key elements in victory or defeat for a nation at war. Germany, Italy, and Japan all went to war in large part to secure the natural resources that they lacked. The quest for land and resources – what Hitler called *Lebensraum* (living space) – drew the Axis in particular directions. Italy sought control of the Mediterranean and East Africa, Japan to dominate South Asia for the oil and other resources of the Netherlands Indies, and Germany to acquire the grain of Ukraine and the oil of Baku. Such decisions had a decided impact on the course of events. But the conquest of these territories stretched thin Axis manpower. This, coupled with the inability of the Axis states to exploit promptly their new territorial acquisitions, ultimately led to their undoing.

The three Axis powers all exploited the peoples they conquered. Their occupation policies, which reflected the nature of their regimes, alienated the indigenous populations and stimulated the growth of resistance movements that forced the occupiers to divert larger numbers of fighting men away from the fighting fronts and into rear-area security. The resistance in Yugoslavia in early 1944, for example, required Germany, Italy, and Bulgaria to maintain there combined forces in excess of 300,000 men. Germany also had 365,000 men garrisoning Norway. Such a drain on manpower seriously impeded success at the front. The Allies by comparison had little to worry about in that regard and could concentrate their own military resources more effectively on the task of defeating Axis field forces.

Leadership, often overlooked in a rush to explain events in statistical terms, was critical in the war, and it would be hard to dispute that Churchill, Stalin, and Roosevelt were extraordinarily effective war leaders. Their military chiefs ranged from brilliant to competent. The same cannot be said of the Axis states. Hitler, Mussolini, and Tōjō all proved incompetent as military leaders and failed to heed the sound advice proffered by many capable subordinates.

The Allies were much more successful in utilizing human resources, especially the employment of women in the military and in industry. A review of the home fronts and economic policies of the opposing powers underscores the important role these factors played in the war's outcome.

Germany

The popularly held assumption of Nazi Germany as a well-organized war machine is patently false, but it is true that no time was likely to be as favorable for Hitler joining war with the Western powers as September 1939. Britain and France were only then rearming and Germany had a population of 80 million people, a strong industrial base, and the world's most powerful army and air force. The economy was out of balance, with imports running well in excess of exports, but Hitler planned to redress this imbalance by seizing in war all that the Reich required.

The National Socialist state controlled all the media, and Minister of Propaganda Joseph Goebbels adroitly manipulated the press, radio, film, and party rallies. Informers on every block and the *Gestapo* (Secret State Police) kept a close watch, but most Germans supported the *Führer*'s policies. Sullen acceptance of the war in September 1939 turned to euphoria after Germany's victories over France and the Low Countries. When the military situation began deteriorating on the plains of Russia in the winter of 1941, Germans settled into a sort of stoic determination that lasted until near the end. Most Germans were aware of the price their nation was exacting from the rest of Europe, and they could thus believe the Allies would repay them in kind, but to ensure the loyalty of the Reich's citizens Hitler ordered that judges ignore established law and procedure and dispense only 'National Socialist justice.' Hitler expressly approved of the Gestapo's use of torture. The complete subversion of the German legal system to Nazi rule came with the appointment in August 1942 of Roland Freisler as president of the *Volksgerichthof* (People's Court).

Hitler was a disaster as a strategist. His initial risky military decisions worked out to his advantage, but this left him with a false impression of his own abilities. In the winter of 1941, Hitler took over personal direction of the war, ignored glaring evidence of German weakness and enemy strength, and proceeded to made mistake after mistake, ranging from military strategy to weapons procurement and occupation policies. Hitler had little interest in technology and did not understand the strengths and limitations of particular weapons systems. And unlike practices in the Soviet Union and United States, Hitler placed inordinate emphasis on size, such as bigger tanks, rather than developing simple weapons more easily mass produced and maintained. He was constantly shifting programs and priorities, much to Minister of Armaments and Production Albert Speer's dismay. Most important, he consistently ignored realistic appraisals of his opponents' industrial capacity.[1]

While Germany was a major industrial power, with substantial coal and iron deposits, it lacked key natural resources to wage prolonged war. Much of this had been offset by Germany's alliance with the Soviet Union, as Churchill reminded Stalin. Certainly, the German economy was inefficient, the direct result of Hitler's system of divide-and-rule governance. Nazi Germany was a maze of overlapping satrapies and administrative practices. The navy hoarded stocks of scarce aluminum required by the air force, the SS ran its own arms factories, and the *Luftwaffe* insisted on controlling everything associated with the air, including anti-aircraft artillery, naval aviation, and airborne forces.

Germany sought to offset its economic weaknesses by ruthlessly exploiting the territories it captured. Curiously, Germany did not go fully to a war footing in September 1939; it continued producing both guns and butter into 1942 and beyond. This was because Hitler feared the negative effect of the war on the population and because he believed his own charges of a collapse of the German home front in 1918. Even in 1942 consumer expenditures were maintained at about the 1937 level and few new economic restrictions were imposed. Raw materials were in short supply but these were deliberately depleted in the expectation of a quick victory over the Soviet Union. This optimistic outlook changed with the German reverses in the winter of 1941, and in February 1942, when Minister of Armaments and Production Fritz Todt died in a plane crash, Hitler named Speer as his replacement. An organizing genius with a keen interest in efficiency rather than ideology, Speer created a centralized machinery of control in the Central Planning Board. By 1943 Speer had complete control of the national economy and was able substantially to boost production. In March 1944 German aircraft plants went on double-shifts with a seven-day working week. Thus Germany attained its highest level of aircraft, tanks, and munitions production in late 1944 while bearing the full brunt of Allied bombing. But by then it was too late. When the Allies shifted their bombing emphasis to lines of communication and petroleum production, the transportation system collapsed and there was no fuel to operate the tanks and new jet aircraft.[2]

Speer might have accomplished even more had he not been handicapped by jealous rivals, such as Göring and *Reichsführer* (leader) of the SS Heinrich Himmler. Himmler was a major hindrance. Constantly scheming to build the power of the SS within the Reich, he actually undermined the economy. The SS came to be a state-within-a-state, and Hitler even approved Himmler's proposal to build an SS-owned industrial concern to make it independent of the state budget.[3]

A major factor behind Speer's success, of course, was the substantial territory and resources Germany had acquired by 1942. Germany could exploit the resources of this new empire, such as the skilled labor, industry, and metallurgical resources of France and Belgium; and foodstuffs and other resources of Denmark, Norway, and the Balkans. There were also substantial resources in the vast stretches of Russia occupied from June 1941 onwards, although much of these were simply those Germany had depended on in the past. Thus Germany had been the largest prewar purchaser of oil from Estonia's oil-shale fields.[4]

Spain was also a friendly neutral while Sweden, Portugal, and Switzerland continued to trade with the Reich and conduct its business. In addition, there were ruthless German financial exactions that helped finance the war. Thus France was forced to pay 'administrative costs' to the Germans at the absurdly high sum of 20 million Reichsmarks a day, calculated at a greatly inflated rate of exchange of 20 francs per Reichsmark, and amounting to some 60 percent of French national income.[5]

The Nazi state failed to make use of two ready sources of labor, however. The National Socialist regime had done everything it could to reverse the emancipation of women during the Weimar Republic. Restricting women to the 'three Ks' of *Kinder*, *Kirche*, and *Küche* (children, church, and kitchen) meant that during the Great Depression jobs were secured for men, but the system carried forward into the war with serious implications for the war economy. Speer claimed that mobilizing the five million women capable of war service would have released three million German males for military service. Such a step would undoubtedly have altered the outcome of battles and campaigns, although the influx probably would not have won the war for Germany.[6]

As early as 1942 Speer recommended that women be recruited for industry, but Hitler rejected this advice. Not until 1943 were women between 17 and 45 years of age required to register for compulsory work. Later, the age for women was raised to 50 and that of men set at 16 to 65. By 1944, at 51.6 percent, German women actually outnumbered men in the civilian labor force.[7]

Another available source of skilled labor that had served the Fatherland well during World War I was the Jews. Numbering about 600,000 when Hitler came to power, many German Jews had escaped abroad, while virtually all who remained and were identified perished in the 'Final Solution.' The systematic extermination of European Jewry also took its toll on the war effort as considerable manpower was occupied simply in rounding up and transporting European Jewry to the death camps.

The Third Reich tried to compensate for labor shortages by utilizing foreign workers. The Germans did what they could to attract them with financial incentives but, when these failed, the Germans simply rounded up those they thought necessary and shipped them to the Reich to work in appalling conditions. At the end of the war there were upwards of ten million foreign workers in the Reich. Such labor was not efficient. Speer noted that in October 1943 some 30,000 prisoners working in armaments production produced over a seven-month period only 40,000 carbines, while 14,000 US workers turned out 1,050,000 carbines in the same time frame.[8]

Nazi ideology mandated that Germany wage a 'race war' on the Eastern Front. This had a profound impact on the outcome of the war. The German Army was involved in these excesses to a considerable degree. Of 5,754,000 Soviet miliary personnel taken prisoner by the Germans, only 1,150,000 survived the war. It was the army rather than the SS that was responsible for most of these prisoners.[9]

Motivated in large part by the desire to survive, many captured Soviet soldiers worked as auxiliaries – drivers, cooks, and orderlies – for the German Army. In 1942 the Germans captured Soviet Lieutenant General and Hero of the Soviet Union Andrei Vlasov. Intelligence officers tried to get Hitler to accept Vlasov as head of a volunteer armed Russian force to fight on the German side against the Red Army. Vlasov was willing, providing he received in return recognition by the Germans of an independent Russia. Hitler refused. Not until 1944, when it was too late, were a tiny portion of the Russian auxiliaries organized into the 'Vlasov Army.' At the end of the war, in accordance with agreements reached at Yalta, Vlasov and his men – who had surrendered to the British and

Americans – were all handed over to the Soviet Union to be shot or condemned to death in the Siberian labor camps. Ultimately, the Western Allies repatriated to the Soviet government some two million people, many of them non-Russians and some of whom had fled Russia 30 years before.[10]

Eastern Europeans were ground down under the Nazi boot. Ultimately, the Nazis intended to push Germany's racial frontier some 300 miles east and build a new 'greater Reich' of 120 million people. The Germans garrisoned virtually the whole of their empire with their own soldiers, creating what they called '*Festung Europa*' (Fortress Europe). In every country the Germans counted on collaborators, 'Quislings' as they came to be known after the Norwegian Nazi Vidkun Quisling. Although Hitler's empire at its height approximated that of Napoleon, the new German 'Continental System' brought only repression and exploitation. The Germans looted and ransacked much of the art treasures of Europe. What they did not want themselves, they often destroyed. Millions of priceless artifacts were lost as a result. Hitler never enjoyed Napoleon's following, and he never realized the French emperor's success at raising an international army to fight his battles. Apart from Mussolini's Italy, there were only the Hungarians and Romanians, and scattered support from elsewhere. Spain was at best a casual ally and Finland sided with the Germans only to recover territory it had lost to the Soviet Union in 1940.

German occupation policies proved so brutal that they were a major factor in the German defeat. Early in the German invasion of the Soviet Union Hitler announced that the rules of war would not apply on the Eastern Front. In his Commissar Order he called for the execution out of hand of any communist commissar captured. *Einsatzgruppen* (special deployment groups) of 3000 men each followed in the wake of each German Army group, rounding up and executing partisans, political leaders, and Jews. The German Army was fully aware of these activities and indeed took an active role in them. German barbarities against the Slavs, Jews, gypsies, and gays eclipsed even those of Japan in China and South Asia.

Alfred Rosenberg, the Nazi Party theoretician on racial matters, urged Hitler to delay implementing his policies until victory over the Soviet Union was achieved. But the *Führer*, always the ideologue, would have none of it. Certainly, a major factor in the success of the German armies in the Soviet Union in the summer of 1941 was that many inhabitants of Ukraine and other western portions of the Soviet Union had welcomed the Germans as liberators. They soon discovered to their dismay that German rule was even worse than that of the Soviet Union. German policies certainly greatly aided the European resistance movements, if they did not create them. Ultimately, the Germans were forced to keep half of their combat strength in the east behind the front, protecting lines of communication stretching back to Germany. The Reich's occupation policies may thus have cost it the war.

In 1941 Hitler decreed the death penalty for any offense endangering German occupation forces. Undesirables and enemies of the Reich were simply to 'disappear' under General Wilhelm Keitel's decrees of December 7 and 12 ('*bei Nacht und Nebel*,' under cover of night and fog). In July 1944 the Terror-and-Sabotage decree treated as treason and sabotage all acts of violence by non-Germans in occupied territory, with any offense there falling under its provisions. The Germans took large numbers of hostages throughout the territories they occupied, and many were executed in reprisal for attacks on German soldiers, often at the ratio of 20:1 or more.

Whole villages were razed and their inhabitants killed or deported. Following the assassination at Prague at the end of May 1942 of the 'Blond Beast,' Reichsprotektor of Bohemia and Moravia Reinhard Heydrich, by Czech commandos parachuted in to do the deed at British insistence, Hitler ordered Himmler to execute 30,000 politically active Czechs. Ultimately, two villages, Lidice and Ležáky, were wiped out – the adult inhabitants shot and only those children with Aryan features spared, to be raised by Nazi families in Germany. In all some 5000 Czechs died in the reprisals.[11]

The Nazis viewed Slavs simply as '*Untermenschen*' (sub-humans). Nazi overseers, such as Erich Koch in Ukraine, were determined to take everything by force. As the true nature of Nazi rule revealed itself, the Germans were forced to deal with increasingly larger resistance movements. Where there was open combat, the Germans were able to defeat the more poorly armed partisans, as on the Vercours Plateau in southeastern France and in the Warsaw Ghetto in Poland. But despite their shortcomings in open combat, the resistance movements accomplished much. They tied down large numbers of German troops; they provided crucial intelligence information, as in the case of the French Resistance and preparations for the Normandy Invasion and the Polish Resistance in recovering the German V-weapons; they rescued downed Allied pilots and spirited a number of them to Spain and then on to Portugal and to Britain; they conducted sabotage operations against German installations; and they provided information in the form of leaflets and pamphlets, exposing Nazi atrocities and keeping hope alive throughout occupied Europe.

The Final Solution

The German attack on the Soviet Union accelerated Hitler's policies toward the Jews. As the German armies moved into the Soviet Union they were followed by four *Einsatzgruppen*. Between June and December 1941 they and other support units murdered some 500,000 Jews in eastern Poland, the Baltic states, and western Russia. Another combing of this territory from fall 1941 into 1942, annihilated close to 900,000 more. Most of the executions took the form of mass shootings at large grave sites. In September 1941 after the Germans had taken Kiev and an explosion set by Soviet sappers ripped through the German headquarters in the city, over a two-day span the Germans shot some 30,000 Jews at a nearby ravine named Babi Yar. In October Romanian military headquarters in Odessa was also rocked by an explosion that claimed 60 lives. In reprisal Romanian forces went on a rampage, massacring some 35,000 Jews. These two were the single greatest massacres of World War II.[12]

In late July 1941, most certainly on Hitler's order, Göring instructed Heydrich, then chief of the Reich Security Main Office, to organize 'a complete solution of the Jewish question in the German sphere of influence in Europe.' Heydrich, who had charge of the mobile killing operations in the Soviet Union, began preparations to collect the Jews in the rest of Nazi-controlled Europe. From October 1941 Jews were forbidden exit from German-held territory. Planning for the extermination of the Jews took place at the Wannsee villa in Berlin on January 20, 1942. Here Heydrich outlined the program to officials whose agencies would collaborate in carrying out what the conference minutes called 'the final solution (*Endlösung*) of the Jewish question.'

In 1977 controversial British historian David Irving created a storm of protest in his book *Hitler's War* by maintaining there is no evidence directly linking Hitler to the Final Solution and that this had been the work of Himmler and his SS without the *Führer*'s knowledge. Other historians, such as Gerald Fleming, have conclusively shown that Hitler had full knowledge of plans to exterminate the Jews, that it was done at his express order, and that he went to considerable lengths to conceal his direct role in it. Irving claimed that there is no written order with Hitler's signature ordering the killing of the Jews. While this is true, it is inconceivable that his aides would have acted without his direct command. When queried by his subordinates, Himmler repeatedly referred to a 'very hard' *Führer* Order, which conveyed the force of law, as the justification for the extermination of the Jews. Himmler said that Hitler had ordered 'without exception' the elimination of 'whatever Jews we can reach' during the war. Fleming further demonstrated that Hitler was kept well informed of all the work of the *Einsatzgruppen*. There is also conclusive proof that he was given totals of Jews executed in the winter of 1941 in Russia.[13]

Hitler's orders were, in any case, issued to his comrades in casual conversations. Martin Bormann, secretary to the *Führer* and chief of the party chancellory, and Hitler's 'Brown Eminence,' would then see that they were carried out. Indeed, the only real issue to be resolved by historians regarding this matter is whether Hitler intended the extermination of the Jews from the beginning or whether it evolved as other options closed. Since Hitler deliberately concealed his true plans, even from his close associates, we will never know for certain. German army commanders were well aware of the Final Solution, and many field commanders gave the SS units every assistance. They were undoubtedly relieved that Hitler had not assigned the task of extermination of civilians to front-line soldiers. Probably, most Germans were aware of what was going on. There were, of course, millions of perfectly decent German citizens who were appalled by what went on around them. The vast majority chose to keep silent.[14]

Special SS units were formed to carry out this task. Some of the individuals had been involved in Hitler's program of euthanasia for the incurably ill and the mentally and physically handicapped. By 1941 more than 70,000 people had been killed before it was halted under church protests, although mentally defective and Jewish children continued to be murdered after that date.

The SS established a vast network of camps in Poland. Some of these camps – Sobibor, Treblinka, Belzec, Chelmno – were purely for extermination; others – Majdanek and Auschwitz – were combination concentration and extermination camps. Other camps were simply concentration camps or work camps. Auschwitz was the largest. Its former commandant, Rudolf Hoess, told British officers in 1946 that he had personally arranged for the gassing of two million people. Not only did the largest German firms, such as I. G. Farben, set up factories at the camps to work the slave labor to death, but German doctors also used the inmates for ghoulish medical experiments into the effects of decompression and cold, as well as various diseases.[15]

The first of these death camps, Chelmno, began its work in late 1941, utilizing gassing vans. The victims, packed into the enclosed trucks, were suffocated by carbon monoxide piped in from the vehicles' exhaust systems. By the spring and summer of 1942, gas chambers and crematoria were in use in various locations. Gassing was by carbon monoxide fumes or, in the case of Auschwitz, by the crystalline Zyklon B (hydrogen cyanide, or prussic acid).

Country by country, the Jews of Europe were crowded into freight cars and shipped to these assembly lines of death throughout 1942, 1943, and 1944. Nearly three million Jews were murdered in the six killing centers. Another million and a half were massacred in the mobile killing operations. Most of the remainder died in other mass shootings or in the deportation trains, or from the lethal conditions in the ghettos, of starvation, cold, disease, and overcrowding. Of an estimated 5,933,900 Jews who perished in the Holocaust, the largest number by far (3,000,000) came from Poland, followed by the USSR (1,252,000). The prewar Jewish population of Poland went from 3.3 million in 1939 to only 6000 in 1946. It was said after the war that other peoples could count their losses; the Jews could count only their survivors. Genocide, the attempted destruction of whole ethnic groups or peoples, was the greatest Nazi crime against mankind.[16]

In order to kill the Jews, the Nazis were willing to weaken their capacity to fight the war. The Final Solution had top priority. Moving millions of Jews to Poland overloaded the transportation system and often priority military trains were diverted to sidings so that a train transporting Jews could pass. But while Hitler was willing to go to any lengths to kill Jews, the United States and its allies were willing to attempt almost nothing to save them.

Much has been made of the fact that hundreds of thousands of Jews went to their deaths with scant resistance, but tens of millions of other citizens of occupied states refused to do anything to oppose Nazi policies. There are reasonable explanations for the lack of general Jewish resistance. Many simply refused to believe what was to be their fate, despite mounting evidence of it. Many were worn down, starving, sick, and/or in a state of shock. Dissension within Jewish communities also undermined resistance, and there was little international support. But perhaps the question should not be why there was so little resistance, rather it should be why there was so much. In April 1943, aware that they were being deported to Treblinka to be gassed, the Jews of the Warsaw Ghetto staged an uprising. It took 2000 well-armed German soldiers a month to subdue about 750 poorly armed Jews, and there were in fact nearly 60 such risings in Jewish ghettos.[17]

German resistance to Hitler included a number of prominent individuals and had existed before the war, when its leaders had tried to persuade Britain to stand firm against Hitler's expansionary policies.

The resistance had been discredited by Hitler's success at Munich, but it revived with the war. Those who actively opposed Hitler were diffuse. The civilian wing included both the political left and the right. Former mayor of Leipzig Carl Goerdler was the liaison between the civilian factions and those military officers who believed that Hitler's strategies doomed Germany. There were a variety of plots to assassinate Hitler, even before the war. All failed. The most spectacular and extensive attempt occurred in July 1944 and centered on Colonel Klaus von Stauffenberg, a *Wehrmacht* officer disillusioned by Hitler and his policies. In North Africa Stauffenberg had lost his left eye, right hand, and two fingers on his left hand. These liabilities did not prevent him from taking the lead role in a conspiracy to assassinate Hitler.[18]

As chief of staff to Reserve Army commander General Friedrich Fromm, Stauffenberg had access to Hitler's conferences, and on July 20 at 'Fortress Wolf' in Rastenburg, East Prussia, Stauffenberg placed a bomb in the meeting room and left the building. When it detonated Stauffenberg believed Hitler had been killed, but the briefcase containing the bomb had been moved, and Hitler escaped death. The conspirators had, in any case, come out in the open. Their actions were hesitant and ineffective and most were quickly rounded up. Stauffenberg was shot. Hitler now used this as an excuse for a thorough purge of his opponents. The Gestapo arrested 7000 individuals. Most were tortured, given cursory trials, and executed in barbaric fashion, the latter being filmed for subsequent Nazi entertainment.[19]

Among other noteworthy opponents of the regime were leaders of the German Confessional Church, including ex-World War I submarine captain Martin Niemöller, a protestant pastor imprisoned for standing up to the Nazis. Another was the theologian Dietrich Bonhoeffer, who was executed in the last days of the war. There was also the White Rose at Munich University led by young Hans and Sophie Scholl. They too suffered martyrdom but were not forgotten.

Japan

Although Japan had a population in 1939 of 73 million people and was a major world industrial power, its industrial capacity was slight next to that of the United States. In 1941, for example, Japan produced 6.7 million tons of steel, while the United States produced 73.9 million tons. Japan had virtually no natural resources and was not even self-sufficient in food. Oil was essential to machine-age armies, navies, and air forces;

the lack of this essential commodity was a major problem for all three Axis states but especially for Japan. Virtually all of Japan's raw materials had to come by sea, whereas Germany and Italy could at least draw most of what they required by land.[20]

Japan's economy, as with that of Germany, was overly concentrated on war. In 1939 it was spending about 36 percent of GNP on the military, as opposed to 23 percent in Germany, and 8 percent each for Italy and Britain. Japan's leaders discounted their nation's material weaknesses. They would make these up from the territories they conquered, and they believed they could overcome Western advantages in technology and numbers through sheer will power. It is not an understatement to say that most Japanese leaders and especially those of the army, including general and premier HidekiTōjō, were sadly out of touch with reality.[21]

The Japanese people were solidly behind the war effort. They saw the war as a conflict forced on their nation by the United States. This view was reinforced by the heavily controlled media, which gave a distorted view of events, extolling Japan's early victories and hiding its defeats. The government so feared the effect of the Battle of Midway on public morale that it placed the returning seamen incommunicado. The media continued to tell the people that Japan was winning the war, although this became impossible by late 1944 with the destruction of Japanese cities by B-29 bombers.[22]

The bureaucratic inefficiency and lack of coordination that troubled German and Soviet war efforts was even more pronounced in Japan. Although army general Tōjō was premier (1941–44), he lacked the power enjoyed by Hitler and Stalin, or even Roosevelt and Churchill. A collective army-navy leadership, in which the army had clear advantage, dominated the government; but there was also intense inter-service rivalry between army and navy leaders over allocation of resources and strategy, a problem never resolved. Indeed, army and navy representatives dealt directly with industry without consulting each other and without regard for the overall national war interest. Civilian agencies created to control production had no success in this regard; neither did a new munitions ministry headed by Tōjō himself.

Such problems may be seen in the failure of the army and navy to agree on either common caliber for machine guns or on aircraft designs. The aviation industry produced only 58,882 planes throughout the entire war, despite its capacity to manufacture many more. The army controlled 85 percent of oil from the Netherlands East Indies, leaving the navy short of fuel for its ships. The army built ships, including tankers and transports for aircraft complete with flight decks. It also had submarines under construction, which it planned to use to supply its distant garrisons.[23]

Japan did have some success increasing industrial output, which rose 25 percent between 1940 and 1944. The government accomplished this by consolidating industrial production in the bigger firms at the expense of small- and medium-sized industry. Nonetheless, Japan's results were negligible when compared to US accomplishments, and neither did the Japanese government make efficient use of labor. The army insisted on drafting industrial workers, especially those supporting the navy, and the national leadership initially refused to employ women in war industries, sneering at US practices in this regard as a sign of weakness. Not until 1943 did Tokyo make women liable for such service. By 1944, however, women made up 41.9 percent of Japan's civilian work force, as opposed to 35.7 percent in the United States.[24]

Women and children made up the loss of male workers in rice production, so there was no fall-off in this until 1945. The fishing industry was harder hit, especially at the end of the war with the increasing US naval and air presence off the Japanese coasts. Imports of food, as well as raw materials, fell dramatically as US submarines torpedoed Japanese merchant vessels. Mining of the coast and air attacks also took their toll and, despite efforts to utilize all available land for food production, most Japanese were on a starvation diet by war's end.

Japanese treatment of prisoners of war was especially hellish. This stemmed in part from the Japanese warrior code, *bushido*, which held that the honorable course for a soldier was to die fighting, and the Japanese military consistently violated international conventions regarding the treatment of prisoners. Many US and other Allied prisoners also perished in unmarked Japanese 'Hell Ships,' torpedoed by US submarines and bombed and strafed all unknowingly by US aircraft as they steamed for Japan at the end of the war.

The Japanese ruthlessly exploited their empire. Their call of 'Asia for the Asians' was simply a euphemism for Japanese dominance, and they worked that part of Asia under their control to their selfish advantage. Much of South Asia suffered intensely under Japanese rule, as the Japanese forced the conquered nations to produce what the government in Tokyo judged its chief needs. In Vietnam, for example, the Japanese insisted that extensive areas previously growing rice be given over to jute instead. Everywhere, the occupiers expropriated resources at the expense of the local population. In 1945 enforced shortages in planting and Japanese requisitions of rice led to widespread starvation in which hundreds of thousands of Vietnamese died. Resentment still simmers in South Asia, especially in the People's Republic of China and the Republic of Korea, over Japan's role in the war and the failure of the Tokyo government to admit responsibility for it.[25]

Great Britain

In contrast to the Axis powers, the Allies were much better situated economically. Britain, with a population of nearly 48 million people, was a major industrial state, which nonetheless had to import the majority of its food and raw materials. It could utilize its large merchant marine to tap the resources of the British Empire and the rest of the world. Maintaining control of the seas, and particularly the lifeline between Britain and the United States, was critical.

The chief problem facing the Allies in September 1939 was not resources, but time; redressing the military imbalance would take years, especially building up air forces and navies. It was thus essential that Germany not win the war in one quick campaign. The best hope of Britain and France in September 1939 was to protract the conflict in order to be able to build up their armed forces. It was largely for this reason that they had been willing to sacrifice Czechoslovakia in September 1938. The two Allies could also hope that the Soviet Union and the United States, the best-placed of the Great Powers in terms of natural resources, would ultimately enter the war on their side.

Although France was defeated early, Britain survived, thanks to the English Channel and the Royal Navy. Despite depredations by Axis submarines, Britain continued to access the world resources, and the Soviet Union and United States did enter the war on its side. Although difficult to foresee in 1940, 1941, or even 1942, barring some sort of Axis miracle weapon or serious strategic mistake on the part of the Allied leaders, the preponderance of population, resources, and industrial strength of the Allies would eventually bring them victory.

Conservative Neville Chamberlain, who headed a coalition government on the outbreak of war, was forced from office in May 1940 and replaced by Winston Churchill, who was completely committed to total victory. Perhaps more at home in the nineteenth century, as far as his attitude toward colonialism was concerned ('I have not become the King's First Minister in order to preside over the liquidation of the British Empire'[26]), he was an eloquent and effective war leader and rallied the British people behind the war effort. Flashing his famous 'V for victory' sign, he took it upon himself to visit the bombed-out areas of London, unlike Hitler who never mingled with the German people. To the rest of the world, Churchill was the embodiment of British pluck and resolve. Despite the efforts of his service chiefs to keep him at arm's length, he insisted on a hands-on approach to the war, often intervening in military matters. The one sin for Churchill was inaction, but his decisions often had deleterious effects. Churchill also took a lively interest in scientific developments and a wide range of schemes and gadgets that might be employed against the Axis.[27]

Early on Churchill worked out a close relationship with President Roosevelt of the United States, but the British leader's vision of the world, in which Britain was a major imperial power, was fading. Churchill's influence over strategy also waned as the military strength of the United States grew dramatically *vis-à-vis* Britain's own. Churchill wanted to concentrate efforts in Italy and the eastern Mediterranean and he saw the Balkans as the 'soft underbelly' of Europe that might be exploited in order to 'shake hands with the Russians as far east as possible.' He also opposed a cross-Channel invasion of France until the last possible moment.[28]

Although Parliament passed an Emergency Powers Act in September 1939 granting the government control of the economy, Prime Minister Chamberlain sought a more limited effort than was essential to bring victory. Aerial attack was a great concern and the government made efforts to relocate families, especially those in London, to rural areas of the country. But Britain was slow to mobilize its assets for the war, especially its land forces. In the spring of 1940 Britain was still producing civilian automobiles and unemployment was at a million people. Not until the German invasion of France and the Low Countries in May 1940 did the government and the people discover the true seriousness of the situation.

With the fall of France and a new prime minister, Britain at last committed itself to total war. Economist John Maynard Keynes headed a survey of British resources which, when completed in 1941, greatly aided the government in assuming direction of the entire economy. The government introduced strict price controls and rationing and more fully mobilized its civilian population for the war effort than any other major combatant. Parliament passed the National Services Act, authorizing conscription of all males ages 18 to 50 for the military, industry, or other national service. Women also came to be included, and by 1944 women comprised 37.9 percent of the civilian labor force.[29]

The British government enjoyed great success increasing its production of armaments. In 1940, for example, Britain produced more aircraft than Germany (15,049 to 10,249). Labourite Ernest Bevin served as minister of labor. There was little unrest among British workers, especially as burdens were seen to be shared and the standard of living was not seriously depressed.[30]

About half of the national resources were going into the war effort, as exports dropped off and imports, especially of food, rose. The government sharply raised taxes to avoid as much borrowing as possible. The basic tax rate was 50 percent, while excess business profits were taxed at 100 percent. Without Lend-Lease from the United States and assistance from Commonwealth nations, however, it would have been very difficult for Britain to survive.

Britain suffered far less material damage than most other warring states. She sustained in the war 244,723 military and 60,595 civilian deaths. But Britain's massive wartime effort, the expenditure of capital at home and its recall of overseas investment, the disruption of trade, and deficit spending all hastened a national economic decline already in progress. The hardships of war that imparted a sense of a shared national effort also heightened interest in reform at the end of the war. As early as 1942 the Beveridge Report called for establishment after the war of a minimum income level, medical insurance, and 'cradle to grave' security for all citizens. Even during the war, Parliament extended to the entire population the right to a secondary school education. Popular interest in wide-sweeping reform was not understood by Churchill, who was focusing almost exclusively on winning the war, but led the Labour Party after the defeat of Germany to demand elections. Held in July 1945, while the war against Japan was still in progress, the elections produced a surprising Labour upset. In a near seamless transition, Labour leader Clement Attlee replaced Churchill as prime minister in the midst of the Potsdam Conference.

The Soviet Union

The Soviet Union was an immense state of vast area and resources. In 1941 its 15 member republics numbered 193 million people and extended over 11 time zones, but it suffered from vast inefficiency and, at the beginning of the German invasion, appallingly poor leadership. Josef Stalin's refusal to prepare adequately for a German invasion and to believe it was even a possibility was followed by orders that Red Army units stand fast rather than retreat, leading to the cutting off and surrender of vast numbers of Soviet soldiers. Stalin was largely responsible for the disastrous Red Army encirclements at Kiev and Vyazma in 1941 and Kharkov in 1942. Decisions such as these almost drove the Soviet Union from the war. But while Hitler unlearned the art of war, Stalin proved he was capable of learning it, absorbing specialist knowledge and technical information, and paying attention to knowledgeable subordinates. He continued to make the major decisions, shifting about units and commanders. Front commanders reported to him at the end of each day and received their instructions directly from him.

During the war Stalin deliberately downplayed Communism, touting Russian patriotism instead. He even enlisted the services of the Russian Orthodox Church. Indeed, World War II is known in Russian history as 'The Great Patriotic War.' Soviet citizens were more used to deprivation and suffering than most peoples, but the war took a huge toll on the population as German and Soviet forces fought back and forth across the Russian heartland and practiced 'scorched earth' policies. These left a legacy of burned villages and hatred reflected in the brutal Soviet treatment of its zone of Germany at the end of the war.

At the time of the German invasion some 11 million Soviet citizens had undergone some military training over the previous 15 years, and a like number had received some military instruction. Stalin had done what he could in the Third Five-Year Plan (1938–42) to increase armaments production and capacity; to develop new industry in the east; and to relocate existing production east of the Ural Mountains, where it would be safe from the *Luftwaffe*. After the German invasion, whole factories were disassembled, loaded on flatcars, and then shipped east, where they were reassembled and resumed production of tanks, planes, and guns. Unfortunately for the USSR much of the industrial effort was inefficient, the product of an inept bureaucracy and confusion. On the plus side, much of the conversion from peacetime to wartime production was carried out by local initiative, without central intervention. Not even a majority of production could be relocated so quickly, and in the second half of 1941 the Soviet Union lost 68 percent of its iron production, 63 percent of its coal, 58 percent of its steel, and 40 percent of its farmland. The loss of the Ukraine was a particularly heavy blow, for it boasted the USSR's most fertile farmland.[31]

Unlike Germany, the Soviet Union tended to concentrate on production of simple yet durable weapons. The Russian Ilyushin IL 2 Shturmavik ground attack aircraft and the T-34 tank were also easy to produce and maintain. The significant Soviet weapons production should also be noted. During 1940–45 the Soivet Union manufactured 146,929 aircraft, 102,301 tanks, and 14,631,000 rifles and carbines.[32]

The vast casualties sustained by the Red Army in fighting the Germans, the manpower requirements of the armed forces, and the demands of war industries all led to a severe labor shortage. This was taken up in part by women, who had long been in the industrial work force in the Soviet Union, by men who were too old for the army, and by teenage boys. Women were the major labor source in the agricultural sector, and by the end of the war they were a majority of the workers in the industrial sector as well. The Soviet standard of living, already low, plummeted during the war. The war exacted a frightful human toll on the Soviet Union. Immediate postwar calculations set this at 20 million people dead, an estimate now raised to as many as 27 million or more.[33]

The death toll swelled in part because of Stalin's own policies. During the war the Soviet authorities executed an astonishing 157,000 of their own soldiers. Stalin wrote off Soviet POWs held by the Germans, for to surrender was regarded as treason. When Hitler offered to exchange Stalin's only son, Yakov, for his nephew Leo Raubal, Stalin refused, and Yakov died in captivity. Even those Soviet prisoners who managed to escape from the Germans were severely punished, sometimes with death. To add insult to injury, Red Army POWs captured by the Germans who managed to survive the cruel circumstances of imprisonment were treated as traitors at the end of the war. Many were executed out of hand; others were shipped off to the gulags.[34]

The United States

With a population of about 140 million people, the United States possessed the world's largest industrial base and was one of the best-placed nations on earth as far as the location of key natural resources within its borders. But in September 1939 the nation was almost totally unprepared for war. In that year the United States was spending just 1.5 percent of GNP on its military. In 1940 Congress appropriated some $10 billion for a military build-up, including a two-ocean navy. Substantial strides had been made by December 1941. President Franklin D. Roosevelt (FDR) understood the stakes in the war, and in 1939 he had created the War Resources Board to plan conversion of US industry to war production. The War Production Board followed just after Pearl Harbor, answering directly to the president. In this, as in its military operations, the United States demonstrated adaptability, ingenuity, and flexibility.

Roosevelt was a superb war leader, perhaps the finest in the nation's history. Through his 'fireside chats' Roosevelt became the first president to speak directly to the American people on an informal basis, and when war came he used his considerable communications skills to mobilize public opinion behind the war effort. As commander-in-chief of the armed forces, Roosevelt chose capable military leaders such as General Marshall as chief of staff of the army and Admiral King as chief of naval operations. He also saw to it that Rear-Admiral John Towers headed the Bureau of Aeronautics. Towers completely reorganized US naval aviation, preparing it for the war. FDR recognized what the fascist dictators did not – that a national leader is best served by strong, forceful individuals with independent views.

Roosevelt developed a close friendship with British Prime Minister Churchill, despite their sharp differences over strategy, the status of European colonies following the war, and approaches toward the Soviet Union. Roosevelt pushed for aggressive US military action, and it was on his insistence that US forces raided Tokyo in April 1942 and landed in North Africa in November 1942. Believing that his leadership was essential to the nation at war, Roosevelt stood for the presidency again in 1944, becoming the only US president to be elected to four terms.

The December 1941 Japanese attack on Pearl Harbor united the country behind the war as nothing else could; even isolationists supported the war as just. The United States became the great 'arsenal of democracy,' supplying immense quantities of weapons to allies fighting the Axis. For that reason alone, it was important to keep as many workers in industry as possible. That the United States was able to both fight and to produce so many weapons was a major achievement, unmatched by any other state in history before or since.

During the 1930s American industry had become much more efficient. A good deal of its capacity also lay unused; ten million Americans were out of work as late as 1939. Thus the United States was well placed to expand production of war materials rapidly, although the lead time required, especially in warship production, meant that it would be 1942 and 1943 before the new manufacturing would have major impact. Of course, the United States and the Soviet Union benefitted immensely from having virtually all of the strategic raw materials necessary for modern war within their borders, a far cry from the situation in Britain, Germany, and Japan.

In 1940 US steel production was 67 million tons, or 82 percent of capacity. By 1944 it was full blast at 89 million tons, about half of the world's total. All this translated into vast numbers of weapons. Roosevelt announced plans to build 50,000 aircraft in 1943 and Hitler scoffed. In fact, the United States built more than 85,898 planes in 1943 and 96,318 in 1944. During the period from May 1940 to July 1945, the United States produced 297,299 aircraft, including 99,742 fighters and 97,592 bombers. Of this number, some 185,000 went to the Army Air Forces, 60,000 to the navy, 33,000 to Britain and Commonwealth nations, 18,000 to the USSR, and 4000 to China. The United States also manufactured 86,333 tanks, 650,000 Willys 'jeeps,' and 12,573,000 rifles and carbines. The army had so many vehicles that it could place every man and woman in the service in them at the same time and still have room left over. American shipyards launched 14 million tons of warships, including 88,000 landing craft and 8812 major naval vessels (147 aircraft carriers). During the war the Ford Motor Company alone produced a greater value of durable goods than did the entire nation of Italy. America's wartime industrial capacity provided the nation with tremendous strategic flexibility and allowed it to conduct warfare world-wide while also supplying the British Empire, the Soviet Union, and China through Lend-Lease.

By way of contrast, during 1940–45 Germany manufactured 109,586 aircraft, 56,000 tanks, and 1255 submarines of all types. Japan made a major effort but built only 74,656 aircraft, 4571 tanks, and 568 major naval vessels. In other words, the United States outproduced Germany and Japan combined, 3:2 in aircraft and 4:3 in tanks. The imbalance in warship tonnage was far greater.[35]

As with those of the Soviet Union, US weapons systems tended to be durable and easy to maintain, such as the rugged jeep and magnificent 2.5-ton ('deuce-and-a-half') truck. The controls of US Army vehicles were also made almost identical, allowing a driver to move easily from one to the other.[36]

The great industrial effort by the United States imposed severe constraints on the number of men (and women) the nation could put into the armed forces. Only 89 army and 6 marine divisions of all types were fielded in the war. This may be compared to the Germany Army's final tally of 414 divisions and the Soviet Union's 625 albeit smaller formations. By 1945 Britain had raised 34 divisions and 16 armored brigades, Japan 191 divisions, and Italy 94.[37]

Older factories were converted to the production of war materials, while new plants sprang up across the nation. Some of these were quite large. At Willow Run, Michigan, west of Detroit, Henry Ford established a plant to make the B-24 Liberator bomber. The largest aircraft assembly plant in the world, the Willow Run Plant at one time employed 42,000 workers. By August 1944 it churned out 500 B-24s a month, and over its 43 months of operation it produced 8685 planes, one every 103 minutes.[38]

Henry Kaiser built large shipyards on the west coast to construct Liberty ships to carry supplies on the Atlantic run. Many Liberties were prefabricated. Based on a simple, late nineteenth-century design, these could be built in sections, some of the work being done in the interior of the country. The sections would then be shipped to the coasts to be welded together. Larger and faster Victory ships appeared later. Smaller ships, including some large landing craft, were launched at Memphis, Tennessee, to travel down the Mississippi to the sea.

Science too played an important role in the war. The Axis powers did enjoy successes in rocketry and torpedo technology, but the Allies certainly won this war of scientists, in which close cooperation between Britain and the United States was vital. Scientists of the two nations worked to develop microwave radar, while US chemists produced 100-octane aviation fuel, which allowed aircraft higher speeds, faster rates of climb, and greater maneuverability. US Navy researchers also perfected the proximity fuse, which made aircraft 50 times easier to hit. In the MANHATTAN Project, Allied scientists produced the atomic bomb. Another major accomplishment, the fruits of which were evident later, was the first programmable electronic computer, developed at the University of Pennsylvania in 1945 to calculate artillery tables.[39]

The United States financed its vast war effort in part through deficit spending. The budget deficit went from $49 billion in 1941 to $259 billion in 1945. The government borrowed huge sums, it sold War Bonds, and it sharply raised taxes. The goal for the average tax bill was 10 percent, but in 1944 the top tax bracket was 94 percent. High taxes on the rich also held down war profiteering. Inflation was kept in check through wage and price controls set by the Office of Economic Stabilization, headed by James Byrnes. In May 1943 Roosevelt appointed Byrnes to head the new Office of War Mobilization, which had considerable authority over the entire domestic industrial effort. The Truman Committee, named for Missouri Senator Harry S Truman, kept a watch on wartime profiteering, and offenders went to jail. Truman's resulting high national popularity led FDR to select him as his vice-presidential running mate in 1944.

Americans supported their men in the field by collecting scrap metal, waste fat, toothpaste tubes, and nylon and silk stockings. Most items were rationed by a point system. The normal gasoline ration was five gallons per car per week. The national speed limit was reduced to 35 mph to save both gasoline and tires, and between 1942 and 1946 no new automobiles were made for civilian consumption. These plants quickly converted to manufacturing jeeps, trucks, tanks, and other military vehicles. Indeed, the government practically shut down the production of non-war related goods, and virtually all industrial efforts were focused on the war. Fully 90 percent of government spending was directed to the war effort.

Unemployment all but disappeared. Real incomes increased, in part because of deficit spending. There were also great advances in health care. Despite military deaths of 292,131 during the war (only 6000 civilians died), life expectancy jumped by three years, the consequence of penicillin (a British development); advances in heart surgery; blood banks; blood plasma; and better diets, especially for those in the armed forces. Selective Service rejected one-third of those it called for military service, and as a consequence the average draftee was better educated and healthier than the average American. The US Army was the best educated army in history; nearly half of all white draftees were high school graduates, and one in ten had some college education. At the end of 13 weeks of basic training the average soldier had also gained six or seven pounds of muscle, an indication of how poorly many were eating before induction.[40]

Many people had money to spend on medical care for the first time; there were new health insurance programs, such as Blue Cross, the Kaiser Permenente Foundation, and free medical care for those in the services and their dependents. After the war, the GI Bill of Rights (officially the Servicemen's Readjustment Act of 1944) provided educational assistance to veterans.[41]

The South benefitted especially from the war effort, with the establishment there of new factories and military bases. Of 43 new large military bases built to train the millions of men in the armed forces, all but one – Fort Lewis, Washington – were constructed in the South, the consequence of less expensive land and labor costs and favorable climate. The West Coast states of California, Oregon, and Washington also benefitted from their location, with a boom in new war industries, especially shipping and aircraft production, and substantial population growth.

The war produced great changes for American women. Many joined the armed forces, and nearly 400,000 served in the four branches of the US military. The numbers of women in the navy alone – 86,000 – freed men sufficient to man 10 battleships and 10 aircraft carriers, 28 cruisers, and 50 destroyers. Women also left home to take up jobs in previously male-dominated professions, such as banking and industry. Women as a percentage of the total labor force rose from 22.5 in 1940 to 30.3 percent in 1945, and they performed virtually all jobs previously held by men, including welding. The social implications were immense. Many women, enjoying their new-found independence, refused to return to their previous status of housewife after the war.[42]

The war brought great shifts in the US population, beginning the mobile home industry. It profoundly impacted African-Americans, who moved from the South in large numbers to take well-paying jobs in northern factories. Posters proclaiming 'United We Win' showed blacks and whites working together. A Fair Practices Committee, created by Roosevelt, managed to eliminate some discrimination in the work place, at least as far as government employment was concerned. Segregation remained, but the ranks of the National Association for the Advancement of Colored People (NAACP) swelled and its leaders told African-Americans to think in terms of a double V – victory in the war and victory at home. The army formed two black divisions during the war – the 92nd and the 93rd – with many white officers. The two were kept out of combat until near the end, but Colonel Benjamin O. Davis, Jr's 332nd Fighter Group served with distinction in North Africa, Italy, and the Balkans. Davis went on to become the first US Air Force African-American general officer. African-Americans believed with justification that their role in the war entitled them to full freedoms at home. In a very real sense World War II became the genesis of the 1960s Civil Rights movement.

One group of Americans especially suffered in the war – Japanese-Americans. Security concerns led the government to round up West Coast Japanese and those having at least one grandparent who had emigrated from Japan. Some 112,000 Japanese-Americans were interned in camps, although ultimately the government allowed 35,000 to leave in return for loyalty oaths and pledges not to settle on the West Coast. Strangely, given the government logic for this decision, Japanese living on the Hawaiian Islands were untouched because interning them would have destroyed the local economy. Despite its action, the government recruited these 'Niesi' for the armed forces, and their 442nd Regimental Combat Team became one of the most highly decorated units in US military history. Not until a half-century later did the US government admit its mistake regarding the Japanese-Americans and make partial restitution.

In many ways the war helped knit the nation together more closely. New pipelines, including one from Texas to the northeast, lessened reliance upon coastal shipping. Inland waterways were improved, and the Alcan Highway, a major engineering feat, connected Alaska to the lower 48 states. Americans purchased large numbers of Liberty Bonds to demonstrate their patriotism. For those with modest incomes there were War Stamps, a set number of which could purchase a bond. Such patriotic purchases helped absorb the money not being spent on non-available consumer goods, and at the end of the war these savings and pent-up demand fueled a great US economic expansion. Unlike the case for most of the major warring powers, the United States enjoyed both prosperity and victory.

8

The War at Sea

Naval technology at the beginning of World War II was little changed from that of World War I. Warships of the 1920s and 1930s were larger and faster than in World War I, and surface ships boasted improved gunnery control; but, with the exception of radar, there were few technological breakthroughs. The aircraft carrier, which had appeared at the end of World War I, while regarded as an important ship type, was not yet seen as the new dreadnought. The world's admirals still gave the battleship primary place.

The naval balance of forces

Unlike the fighting on land, the sea struggle proceeded more nearly according to expectations. In September 1939 Allied superiority at sea was even more marked than in World War I. With 12 battleships and three battle cruisers in commission in September 1939, Britain had one of the world's two most powerful navies. Most British capital ships were old, however; ten of the battleships had entered service during World War I and the remaining two (*Nelson* and *Rodney*) were commissioned in 1927. Others were being built; both *Prince of Wales* and *King George V* were commissioned in 1941. Two of Britain's three battle cruisers were World War I vintage, and the newest, *Hood*, had joined the fleet in 1920. In addition to its 12 battleships and 3 battle cruisers, the Royal Navy had a respectable air component of 7 aircraft carriers, with another 7 under construction.[1]

Only one of the completed British carriers, *Ark Royal*, was modern. Commissioned in 1938, she was the first large British carrier designed from the keel up. Concern over operating their carriers in narrow seas such as the North Sea or Mediterranean, subjecting them to attack from land-based aircraft, led the British to introduce an armored flight deck.

The subsequent four-ship Illustrious-class, which entered service in 1940 and 1941, carried heavier anti-aircraft protection and an armored flight deck and armored 'box' protecting the aircraft storage area, designed to withstand hits from 500-lb bombs and 6-inch shells. Their armored decks provided greater protection but also limited British carriers to a smaller number of aircraft than their US and Japanese counterparts.[2]

Because the Royal Navy had only secured control of its aircraft from the RAF in 1937, it commenced the war with markedly inferior aircraft. In addition to its battleships and aircraft carriers, the Royal Navy also fielded 15 heavy cruisers (8-inch guns), 50 light cruisers (6-inch guns or smaller), 181 destroyers, and 60 submarines. There was little appreciation of the threat posed to ships by aircraft. The Admiralty still regarded the battleship as the queen of the seas and also discounted the threat of submarines.[3]

British naval resources were stretched thin at the start of hostilities and, although duties and scope of operations roughly corresponded to those of World War I, ships were far fewer. Thus, instead of major surface actions, the majority of the fighting at sea in the European theater centered on the destruction and protection of seaborne trade, especially in the Atlantic Ocean, which was the critical area of operations. The Royal Navy's chief responsibility was maintaining Britain's seaborne lines of communication, upon which the very survival of the nation depended. It transported the British Expeditionary Force (BEF) to France and then to Greece, and it reinforced and supplied garrisons in North Africa among other places. It also rendered invaluable service by extracting the BEF from France in 1940 and from Greece and Crete in 1941. Had the Royal Navy not been able to carry out these operations, Britain could have been forced from the war.

The United States, with 15 battleships in commission in September 1939, had perhaps the world's most powerful navy. It also operated 5 fleet carriers, 1 light carrier (*Langley*), 18 heavy cruisers, 19 light cruisers, 149 destroyers, and 71 submarines. Japan, the only major naval power at war in the Far East in September 1939, had in commission 10 battleships, all of which were of World War I-era construction (super battleships *Yamato* and *Musashi* entered service in December 1941 and July 1942 respectively), 6 aircraft carriers, 18 heavy cruisers, 25 light cruisers, 116 destroyers, and 64 submarines.

France, with the world's fourth largest navy, counted 7 older battleships and 2 new battle cruisers, *Dunkerque* and *Strasbourg* (1934 and 1938 respectively) along with an old aircraft carrier (*Béarn*), 7 heavy cruisers, 12 light cruisers, 64 destroyers, and 77 submarines. Many of the French ships were modern, the result of a major building program undertaken in the years immediately before the war, draining sizeable resources from the army. French naval strategy at the beginning of the war centered on cooperation with the Royal Navy. The French North Atlantic Fleet had two principal missions: to work with the British in protecting merchant shipping and escorting convoys; and to utilize its most powerful assets, built around the battle cruisers and organized in the *Force de Raid*, against German Navy surface raiders.

For the German Navy, war came a half-decade early. When Adolf Hitler took power in 1933, the *Kriegsmarine* was basically a coastal defense force. Hitler wanted a powerful navy that might one day challenge Britain, or even Britain and the United States, for Atlantic mastery; but he assured German Navy chief Grand Admiral Erich Raeder that he had no intention of waging war with Britain, Italy, or Japan. In November 1937 Hitler had stated that a war to bring about *Anschluss* and deal with Czechoslovakia would not occur before 1943 or 1945. Raeder thus set out, in the Z Plan of January 1939, to construct a balanced fleet of six battleships and three battle cruisers, along with aircraft carriers, cruisers, destroyers, and a force of 249 submarines. He fixed 1948 as the date for its completion, but Hitler gave him a deadline of six years (i.e. 1945). Strangely, given his later preference for land operations, Hitler initially assigned priority to the navy over the army and air force.[4]

With the lead time on capital ship construction as much as three to four years, the outbreak of the war caught the navy with the wrong mix of vessels. In September 1939 Germany had only 7 capital ships: 2 battle cruisers (*Scharnhorst* and *Gneisenau*), 2 obsolete 1908 battleships, and 3 pocket battleships. The latter were, in effect, small battle cruisers built under Treaty of Versailles restraints: the *Deutschland* (renamed *Lützow* on Hitler's orders), *Admiral Graf Spee*, and *Admiral Scheer*. Battleships *Bismarck* and *Tirpitz* were as yet under construction, as was a carrier, the *Graf Zeppelin*, never completed. Germany's naval air arm never developed during the war because *Luftwaffe* commander Hermann Göring insisted on *Luftwaffe* control of all naval aircraft, which Hitler supported. Germany also had in commission at the start of the war 2 heavy cruisers, 6 light cruisers, 22 destroyers, and 56 submarines (U-boats). The number of submarines represented only a slight improvement over 1914.[5]

The Soviet Union's third five-year plan, which gave priority to armaments production, projected by 1943 a powerful blue-water fleet of

19 battleships, 20 cruisers, 18 flotilla leaders, 145 destroyers (all new construction), 341 submarines, 44 river monitors, and 514 torpedo boats. In 1939, however, the Soviets had in service only 3 battleships (all of World War I-vintage), 5 cruisers, 3 flotilla leaders, 26 destroyers, and 164 submarines, the world's largest such force. It also possessed 14 river monitors and several hundred patrol craft. By the time of the German invasion in 1941, the Soviets had added 74 surface warships, the largest of which were four Kirov-class cruisers. The Soviet naval minister in Moscow was subordinate to the army and ships were under the control of front commanders; thus the navy played little role in World War II.[6]

Italy, neutral until 1940, had an impressive medium-sized navy of 6 battleships (only two of which were ready for service in June 1940), 7 heavy cruisers, 12 light cruisers, 90 destroyers and large (600–1000-ton) torpedo boats, and 113 submarines. Poland had only 4 destroyers, 5 submarines, and some smaller units. Canada possessed but 6 destroyers and 5 minesweepers.

Naval war in the European theater of operations

When the war began, crushing Allied naval superiority (Raeder characterized it as 'tenfold') promptly drove German shipping into neutral or home ports. Except in the Baltic, the German flag disappeared from the seas. The Allies seemed in no hurry to take the offensive on either land or sea, however. The British were content to institute a naval blockade of Germany with the aims of both preventing the escape into the Atlantic of powerful German naval ships such as *Scharnhorst* and *Gneisenau*, allowing them to ravage Britain's imperial lifeline, and denying Germany imports. Such a blockade in 1914–18 had been a key factor in the German defeat, but the British-initiated blockade of the German North Sea coast in 1939 had little effect on Germany, given its economic arrangements with the Soviet Union and Italy. After Germany's victories of 1940 and 1941 in Denmark, Norway, the Low Countries, France, Yugoslavia, and Greece, moreover, it could tap the agricultural and industrial production of most of Europe.

Admiral Raeder sought to pursue a commerce-raiding strategy, and he struck back with surface raiders, land-based aviation, mines, and, above all, submarines. His goal was to disrupt Britain's seaborne trade and starve Britain into submission. Germany had a submarine commander of genius in Karl Dönitz, who had assumed control of the U-boat program in 1935. On September 1, 1939, Dönitz submitted a memorandum to

Raeder stating that the paucity of U-boats made it impossible for him to wage any meaningful campaign against Allied shipping. He pointed out that the only way that Germany could pressure Britain was through interdicting its Atlantic shipping lanes and estimated that 90 submarines on station would ensure success. As some submarines would be taking up or returning from station and others would be undergoing routine maintenance and repair, this would entail a total force of about 300 submarines. Dönitz had advocated this number for some time, but at the start of hostilities Germany possessed but 56 submarines in commission, of which 46 were ready for action with only 26 suitable for Atlantic operations. This meant that the German Navy could have on station at any one time only eight or nine submarines. Once the war began, though, Raeder accepted Dönitz's position that the Z Plan should be suspended and priority should go to submarine construction and a commerce-raiding strategy, but much valuable time had been lost.[7]

Hitler began the war with a strategic mistake similar to that of 1914. To Dönitz's great dismay, he directed that German submarines attack not merchant ships supplying Britain and France, but rather British warships. Such attacks were bound to extract a far greater cost in U-boats, but Hitler did not want to antagonize the United States at this stage of the war. He reasoned that sparing Britain's merchant marine would make it easier to negotiate peace with that country. Thus Hitler was displeased when, on September 4, 1939, the *U-30* torpedoed and sank the British liner *Athenia*. She went down with the loss of 112 lives, including 28 Americans. Hitler publicly claimed that the liner had been sunk by the British as a provocation, a fiction Raeder maintained even after talking to her captain. Hitler stipulated, 'until further orders no hostile action will be taken against passenger liners even when sailing under escort.'[8]

Despite Hitler's prohibition, German U-boats registered some spectacular successes early in the war. On September 19 *U-29* (Lieutenant Commander Schuhart) attacked and sank the British aircraft carrier *Courageous* in the Atlantic. Then on October 14 Günther Prien succeeded in getting his *U-47* into the British fleet anchorage at Scapa Flow and there sank the British battleship *Royal Oak*. She went down in only two minutes with 786 officers and men. *U-47* escaped and Prien found himself an instant celebrity in Germany. (He was lost at sea in March 1941, with his U-boat.) German U-boats were also employed in mine-laying operations in British territorial waters. From the start of the war to March 1, 1940, the British lost to mines 115 ships totalling 394,533 tons.[9]

The Battle of the River Plate

The British scored a considerable propaganda success of their own in the first major surface action of the war, the Battle of the River Plate. At the outbreak of the war the German pocket battleship *Admiral Graf Spee* was already at sea, having departed Germany on August 21. Her captain, Hans Langsdorff, was ordered to cruise the South Atlantic and destroy shipping and had some success, sending to the bottom ten merchant ships totalling some 50,000 tons by December. Meanwhile, Commodore Henry Harwood's Force G of cruisers *Ajax, Achilles, Cumberland*, and *Exeter* searched for the German ship. Harwood placed the heavy cruiser *Exeter* and light cruisers *Ajax* and *Achilles* in position about 150 miles off the River Plate estuary between Uruguay and Argentina, hoping that the pocket battleship would pass that way.

On the early morning of December 13, 1939 the British ships sighted the *Admiral Graf Spee* and immediately attacked. The British ships were heavily outgunned: the *Admiral Graf Spee* mounted 6 x 11-inch guns while *Exeter* had only 6 x 8-inch guns and the two light cruisers only 8 x 6-inch guns. Harwood tried to close the range as much as possible in order to nullify the German advantage and had his ships attack from different directions. Langsdorff, however, concentrated his heavy guns on the largest British ship, the *Exeter*, while only secondary batteries engaged the two light cruisers. The Battle of the River Plate lasted an hour and a half until the British hauled off. The *Exeter* had suffered heavy damage and 71 dead. The British, however, had hit the *Admiral Graf Spee* about 20 times and heavily damaged her superstructure and killed 36 men. Although the *Admiral Graf Spee*'s ordnance was not damaged, Langsdorff put into the port of Montevideo, Uruguay, to effect repairs. At the same time the *Cumberland* arrived to join the remainder of Force G. Believing a ruse broadcast by the BBC that the battle cruiser *Renown* and aircraft carrier *Ark Royal* had arrived off Montevideo and, knowing that international law would allow a combatant vessel only 72 hours in a neutral port, on December 17 Langsdorff took his ship out to the mouth of the River Plate and scuttled her. Three days later he committed suicide, wrapped in his ship's ensign.[10]

The North Atlantic

The April 1940 Norwegian Campaign saw major naval engagements. While it ended as a brilliant strategic success for Hitler, it also ruined the German surface navy. The *Kriegsmarine* lost three cruisers and ten destroyers, half the German total, as well as having a number of other ships damaged. On the plus side, the many Norwegian fjords provided additional bases for German surface raiders and submarines, but the great gain for Germany in this regard came in the defeat of France in June 1940.

The acquisition of the French Atlantic coastline was of immense benefit for the U-boat war in the Atlantic, and by early August 1940 German submarines were operating from Lorient on the Bay of Biscay. This provided easier access for the U-boats to the Atlantic shipping lanes and French repair facilities were superior to the overburdened shipyards in Germany. This translated into faster turnaround time for the U-boats and more of them at sea.[11]

The Mediterranean theater

After the defeat of France and the loss of its powerful navy, Britain found itself in desperate naval straits, though the British did gain part of the French fleet in Operation CATAPULT. Churchill also secured 50 aged US Navy destroyers in the Destroyers for Bases deal with the United States. But a new naval threat now arose in the form of a belligerent Italy, which joined the war with the defeat of France, opening the Mediterranean Sea as a major theater of war. It also posed a severe strategic threat to the key British lines of communication through the Mediterranean. The Italians had some excellent ships and their navy, although far weaker in total strength than that of Britain, was concentrated, giving them what appeared to be local naval superiority.

Oil from the Persian Gulf and other resources vital to the British war effort passed through the Suez Canal into the Mediterranean, then through the Straits of Gibraltar into the Atlantic and to Britain. Without this route, British shipping would have to go all the way around the Horn of Africa. Italian dictator Mussolini had as one of his goals seizing the Suez Canal by means of a land offensive from Ethiopia and Italian Somaliland in the east and from Libya in the west. Churchill recognized the danger and during the height of the Battle of Britain diverted scarce military and naval resources, including Britain's sole remaining armored division, to this theater.

Admiral Sir Andrew B. Cunningham commanded the British Mediterranean Fleet of 1 small aircraft carrier, 3 battleships, 3 heavy and 5 light cruisers, and a number of destroyers. On paper the Italian Navy appeared larger, but the latter lacked radar until 1942 and was deficient in night-fighting equipment, anti-aircraft protection, and anti-submarine capabilities. The Italians also did not have a naval air arm, which Mussolini and Italian admirals had opposed, claiming that Italy was itself an aircraft carrier. There was no doctrine, however, for employment of land-based aviation in concert with naval units.

In many ways, the island of Malta, what Churchill called 'the unsinkable aircraft carrier,' was the key to the Mediterranean campaign. The struggle centered on Britain's attempts to keep its line of communication open and defend the island, which lay astride the main east–west and north–south shipping routes. Malta was also a key Ultra listening post. The Italians well understood the importance of Malta and, immediately on declaring war on June 11, 1940, Mussolini sent land-based bombers against it in the first of many such raids. Over the next two and a half years, until the end of 1942, Malta was under Axis siege. Despite constant attacks against it, the British were able to utilize Malta to harry Axis reinforcement and to resupply North Africa.[12]

Italian deficiencies at sea were revealed on July 9 in the Battle of Calabria, fought off the southern Italian coast near Cape Spartivento. Flying his flag on the battleship *Warspite*, Cunningham aggressively took the naval war into Italian waters off the Straits of Messina in order to cover the evacuation of non-combatants from Malta. Cunningham had virtually his entire naval force with him: the small aircraft carrier *Eagle* with 19 aircraft, 3 battleships, 5 light cruisers, and destroyer escorts.

At the same time, Italian Admiral Angelo Campioni was at sea with a powerful force returning from a convoy to Libya. Campioni had battleships *Giulio Cesare* and *Conte di Cavour*, six heavy and 12 light cruisers, and destroyers. Alerted by aircraft from Malta and from the *Eagle*, Cunningham maneuvered to cut them off from their Taranto base. Although aircraft from the *Eagle* failed to locate the Italian ships, on the afternoon of July 9 Cunningham's light cruisers engaged the Italian cruisers. The *Warspite* then arrived on the scene, followed by the two Italian battleships, and the opposing capital ships opened up at long range. The Italians registered no hits, but a British shell struck the *Giulio Cesare* and damaged her, causing Campioni to break off the battle. He ordered his destroyers to mount a torpedo attack and then lay smoke to cover his withdrawal; superior speed allowed the Italian ships to escape.

The Italians did launch land-based aircraft against the British fleet; but these attacks, which occurred after the naval battle had ended, were poorly coordinated and were by mistake directed partly against Campioni's own ships. No Italian ships were struck by friendly aircraft though, and the planes registered only one hit on a British cruiser, struck on the approach to the battle. The Battle of Calabria had damaged one Italian battleship and a cruiser, but produced little damage to the British side. Ten days later the Australian light cruiser *Syndey* and four destroyers encountered two light Italian cruisers off Crete, sinking one of them. London now reinforced Malta, sending Cunningham two cruisers, and the new fleet carrier *Illustrious*, the latter making possible an audacious naval air strike against Taranto.

The British attack on Taranto

In order to reduce the Mediterranean odds, Cunningham prepared a preemptive strike against the principal Italian naval base of Taranto. Cunningham and Rear-Admiral A. L. St G. Lyster planned the operation, codenamed JUDGMENT and centered on aircraft carriers *Illustrious* and *Eagle*. It was to take place on October 27, 1940, the anniversary of the Battle of Trafalgar and a night with a full moon, with 30 vintage Fairey Swordfish torpedo-bombers. The Swordfish, a 10-year-old biplane, was nonetheless a reliable, sturdy torpedo platform, especially effective in night operations. However, a fire on the *Illustrious* destroyed several aircraft and forced a delay. Then the *Eagle*, which had sustained near misses from Italian bombs, was found to have been more seriously damaged than originally estimated – Cunningham now postponed the attack to the next full moon.

The *Illustrious* would conduct the raid alone. Twenty-one Swordfish fitted with extra fuel tanks took part, 11 armed with torpedoes and the remainder carrying bombs and flares. The torpedoes had been modified to negate the effects of 'porpoising' in Taranto's shallow harbor. On November 11 at 10:30 p.m. *Illustrious* began launching her aircraft some 170 miles from Taranto. All six of Italy's battleships were in the harbor, protected by barrage balloons, more than 200 anti-aircraft guns, and torpedo nets – defenses far short of what the Italian Navy thought necessary. The planes launched in two waves an hour apart. The first wave achieved complete surprise when it arrived at Taranto at 11:00. The pilots cut their engines and glided in to only a few hundred yards before releasing the torpedoes against the battleships, illuminated by the flares and Italian anti-aircraft tracers. The *Conte di Cavour* was the first battleship struck, followed by *Littorio*. In the second British attack at 11:50, *Littorio* was struck again, and *Duilio* was damaged.

The *Conte di Cavour* was the only battleship sunk, and she went down in shallow water. Tugs towed the other two damaged ships to shore. *Conte di Cavour* later underwent repair, but this work was never completed, and she remained out of commission. Repairs to the other two ships took up to six months. The cruiser *Trento* and a destroyer were also hit, but the bombs did not explode. Fifty-one Italian sailors died in the attack. The British lost two planes, with the crew of one being rescued by the Italians. This single raid deprived Italy of its naval advantage and at least temporarily altered the Mediterranean balance of power. It also underscored the effectiveness of naval aircraft, although Italian land-based aircraft flying from bases on Sicily, Sardinia, and in North Africa continued mounting attacks on British Mediterranean shipping and Malta. The *Regia Marina* was largely occupied with supporting Italy's efforts in North Africa, which led to a number of major naval engagements with the Royal Navy.

The Germans, meanwhile, built up their air strength in Sicily and established air control of the central Mediterranean. Axis air forces, spearheaded by the Germans, struck hard at Malta. On January 10 German dive-bombers and Italian high-level and torpedo-bombers badly damaged the carrier *Illustrious* 60 miles west of Malta. Saved from destruction only by her armored flight deck, she was nonetheless put completely out of action and sustained 200 casualties. The next day German bombers from Sicily also caught the cruiser *Southhampton* and set her on fire, forcing her scuttling.

In February 1941 Vice-Admiral Somerville steamed from Gibraltar with two battleships, a carrier, and a cruiser to bombard the northwest Italian coast, including Genoa. In late March Italian Admiral Angelo Iachino put to sea with a battleship, 8 cruisers, and 13 destroyers and other craft supported by Axis aircraft, to attack British convoys of troops and equipment from Egypt to Greece. Admiral Cunningham learned through radio intercepts of the Italian foray and ordered the convoys back to Egypt. He then steamed north to intercept the Italians with a force of 3 battleships, 1 carrier, 4 cruisers, and 13 destroyers.

In the resulting March 28–29, 1941, Battle of Cape Matapan, Iachino sought to withdraw, but Cunningham made good use of his radar advantage to inflict serious damage upon the Italians. On March 28 British carrier aircraft with torpedoes succeeded in damaging the Italian battleship *Vittorio Veneto*, slowing her sufficiently to enable Cunningham's slower battleships to close. Cruiser *Pola* was also damaged by an aerial torpedo and dead in the water. After dark Iachino dispatched the remainder of the 1st Division, 2 heavy cruisers and 4 destroyers, to tow the *Pola*. Cunningham's pursuing battleships caught these Italian ships, sinking the 3 cruisers and 2 of the destroyers. The Italians sustained 2300 dead and 1400 prisoners. The British suffered only light damage to one cruiser and one aircraft shot down. Cunningham failed to locate the

Vittorio Veneto in the darkness, however, and she returned to base with the remaining Italian warships. The near-total lack of Axis air reconnaissance and support had transformed this offensive sortie into a defensive retreat. The Italians now knew the British had ship-borne radar. From this point forward, the bulk of Italian Navy operations were aimed largely at running convoys to North Africa or intercepting British convoys to Malta.

During late April to early June Cunningham's force was stretched thin, tasked with carrying out hasty evacuations of the BEF first from Greece and then from Crete. In these operations British ships came under incessant *Luftwaffe* attack from bases in both Italy and Greece. During the evacuation of Greece Cunningham had two destroyers and 24 other ships sunk and a number of other warships badly damaged. Cunningham then learned through Ultra intercepts of a German seaborne assault on Crete. Cunningham's ships intercepted the small Axis ships shuttling German troops from Greece to Crete, sinking a number of them. But German aircraft pounded British naval units around Crete. Cunningham lost 2 cruisers and a destroyer sunk and 2 battleships and 2 cruisers damaged. Although he was able to rescue most of the BEF from Crete in the last days of May, Cunningham lost 4 cruisers and 6 destroyers sunk, and a carrier and 3 battleships badly damaged and out of action for some time. Operations off Crete cost the Royal Navy more warships than any other major operation of the war.

For the British in the Mediterranean the year ended disastrously. The Germans sent two dozen U-boats into that sea and intensified air attacks on Malta, from which the British were then punishing Axis supply runs from Italy to North Africa. On November 13, only 30 miles from Gibraltar, *U-81* torpedoed and sank the *Ark Royal*, Somerville's one surviving aircraft carrier. On November 25 *U-331* torpedoed Cunningham's sole remaining capital ship, battleship *Barham*, sinking her with heavy loss of life. On the night of December 18 British Navy Force K of three cruisers and two destroyers ran into a freshly laid Italian mine-field off Tripoli. One cruiser went down; the other two, while damaged, reached Malta safely. One of the destroyers was so badly damaged that she had to be scuttled. The next day, December 19, three Italian SLCs (slow torpedoes, guided by two men each) entered Alexandria harbor and damaged British battleships *Queen Elizabeth* and *Valiant*, putting them out of action. Cunningham's strength was now reduced to three cruisers and a few destroyers. The British managed to conceal news of the extent of their losses and Cunningham employed his few remaining ships aggressively. Units of the Italian Navy remained largely quiescent, endeavoring to remain within effective range of land-based aviation support. Italian convoys to North Africa protected by battleships in the winter of 1941/2 did prove successful, allowing the build-up of Axis resources for an Axis land offensive there in the summer of 1942.

The *Luftwaffe* pounded Malta throughout 1942. Although British naval units at Gibraltar and Alexandria did what they could to protect convoys bound for the island, Britain's hold remained tenuous until September. In turn, however, British aircraft from Malta continued to intercept Axis convoys bound for North Africa, especially after the siege of the island was lifted. By the end of the year British aircraft were sinking three-quarters of the Axis ships involved in the effort, with profound impact on the North African campaign.

German surface raiders

In the Atlantic, in late September 1940 the British Navy and Free French forces attempted to seize control of Dakar, West Africa. It was loyal to the Vichy government, and the Allies feared the Axis might use it as a submarine base. The Dakar government rejected an Allied ultimatum and repulsed the landing that followed it. Meanwhile, the struggle for control of the North Atlantic shipping lanes continued with mounting convoy losses from Dönitz's U-boats. The Germans used long-range bombers based in Norway and France to good effect, keeping them beyond the range of British fighters, and they employed surface raiders.

In late October 1940 Captain Theodor Krancke slipped the pocket battleship *Admiral Scheer* through the British blockade and into the North Atlantic to raid commerce. On November 5 she came upon 37-ship eastward-bound British Convoy HX 64 escorted by Captain E. F. S. Fegen's auxiliary cruiser *Jervis Bay*. Despite hopeless odds – the *Jervis Bay* had only 6-inch guns against 11-inch guns for the *Admiral Scheer* – Fegen ordered the convoy to scatter and immediately attacked, his ship firing quickly and accurately. Although torn apart by German shells, the *Jervis Bay* diverted the *Admiral Scheer* until almost nightfall, allowing most of the convoy to escape in the darkness. Only five of its ships were lost. Fegen, who went down with his ship, posthumously received the Victoria Cross. The *Admiral Scheer*, meanwhile, continued her foray, taking 16 ships in the south Atlantic and Indian Oceans before returning to Germany in April.

In November 1940 the German heavy cruiser *Hipper* also got out but soon developed engine trouble that forced her into the French port of

Brest. The threat posed by the *Admiral Scheer* and *Hipper* consequently led the British to strengthen their convoy escorts. In January 1941 Vice-Admiral Günther Lütjens took the battle cruisers *Gneisenau* and *Scharnhorst* into the North Atlantic, where they sank five unescorted merchant ships. Not until March 18, however, did the German raiders locate a British convoy unprotected by battleships. On that date their quarry had just scattered from a submarine attack and they sank 16 ships before retiring to Brest ahead of British battleships. A subsequent RAF bombing attack on Brest damaged both of the raiders severely and put them out of action for several months. From February to April 1941 the *Hipper* also cruised the North Atlantic before returning to Germany.

The sinking of the Bismarck

The most spectacular surface battle in the Atlantic occurred in May 1941 in the course of another such German raid, when the British hunted down the German battleship *Bismarck*. Laid down in 1936, the *Bismarck* did not undergo her trials until March and April 1940. The largest warship Germany ever built, she displaced about 50,000 tons and mounted 8 x 15-inch guns with a secondary armament of 12 x 5.9-inch guns. Shortly after the *Bismarck* had completed her trials, Raeder ordered Admiral Lütjens to take the ship to sea on a commerce-raiding mission. Lütjens tried unsuccessfully to talk Raeder into delaying her sailing until the *Tirpitz* or *Scharnhorst* could join. Only the cruiser *Prinz Eugen* was available. On May 18 the *Bismarck* and *Prinz Eugen* departed Gdynia, Poland for Bergen, Norway. Supply ships, tankers, and a half-dozen submarines had sortied earlier. The British were soon aware that the *Bismarck* was at sea, and on May 21 RAF reconnaissance aircraft located her. Whitehall immediately ordered British ships to intercept.

On May 23 the *Bismarck* briefly encountered British cruisers *Suffolk* and *Norfolk* then, near dawn on the 24th, Rear-Admiral Lancelot E. Holland's battle cruiser *Hood* and battleship *Prince of Wales* arrived. At about 5:55 a.m. the Battle of the Denmark Strait, between Iceland and Greenland, began. It lasted only a quarter of an hour. The *Bismarck*'s fourth salvo struck the *Hood*'s magazines, starting a fire that blew up the British battle cruiser. Only three of the 1419 crew members survived. The *Prince of Wales*, hit seven times (four from the *Bismarck*), made smoke and retired. The *Bismarck* had been hit only three times but was leaking oil. The *Prinz Eugen* departed the scene at around 4:00 p.m. to draw off the British pursuit, but just before midnight 15 British aircraft from the carrier *Victorious* attacked the German battleship. They scored one torpedo hit, which resulted in little damage, and on May 25 the *Bismarck* eluded its pursuers.

Early on May 26 a Catalina flying boat spotted the *Bismarck* steaming for France, and the cruiser *Sheffield* gave chase. In a desperate effort to stop the *Bismarck* from reaching port and safety, 15 Swordfish torpedo aircraft from the carrier *Ark Royal* attacked at 9:00 p.m. Two torpedoes struck the German battleship, jamming her rudder at 12 degrees to port. Unable to escape, the *Bismarck* awaited her pursuers. On the morning of the 27th British battleships *King George V* and *Rodney* arrived on the scene, and at 8:45 a.m. they opened fire. By 10:00 the *Bismarck* had been struck repeatedly and was largely *hors de combat*. As heavy cruiser *Dorsetshire* prepared to fire torpedoes into the German ship, the *Bismarck*'s crew detonated internal scuttling charges. Three torpedoes then struck and the *Bismarck* sank at 10:39 p.m. Only 115 crew members survived of 2300 aboard; 500–600 men were in the water, but efforts to rescue them were cut short by reports of German submarines in the area.[13]

The Baltic and Black Seas

In June 1941 the Soviet Union entered the war, but this had slight impact on the war at sea. The combined Soviet fleet at the time of the German invasion numbered 3 old battleships, 7 cruisers, 54 destroyers, and as many as 240 submarines. Fleet units were divided between the Baltic, Black Sea, Arctic, and Pacific; but the bulk of these resources – 2 battleships, 2 cruisers, 41 destroyers, and some 70 submarines – were in the Baltic. The Soviet Navy's lack of balance, the absence of an air component, and poor training were all reflected in its performance in the war. The Navy, like the army, was caught unprepared for the German invasion and the Baltic Fleet had no submarines at sea. The Baltic Fleet sustained heavy losses early in the invasion from German mine-laying activities that sealed the Gulf of Finland and the Gulf of Riga. A makeshift Lake Ladoga flotilla did perform useful service in helping to keep open lines of communication from Leningrad to the east.

Although Russian submarines of the Baltic Fleet, assisted by minesweepers, succeeded in penetrating the German mine-fields in 1942, they accomplished little against German Baltic shipping, and in 1943 a German submarine net completely prevented Soviet access to the Baltic. At the end of the war the Soviets did register a few spectacular successes with submarines and naval aviation.

In the Black Sea the Soviets had an old battleship, 4 cruisers, 16 destroyers, and nearly 50 submarines. The Germans, who had only some old Romanian destroyers, were largely restricted to air operations. In the Black Sea Soviet ships provided gunfire support to beleaguered Red Army units on land, and they helped bring in supplies and assisted with evacuations of such seaports as Odessa and Sevastopol. Thereafter, the Black Sea Fleet was largely inactive, partly because of losses to German aircraft, although it occasionally conducted submarine operations with limited success. As the Red Army pushed the Germans back, Black Sea naval units provided gunfire support and helped speed the German collapse in Romania by conducting two amphibious assaults in late August 1944 involving 600 landing craft at the mouths of the Dniester and Danube Rivers.

The White Sea Fleet had little success, although at the very end of the war it greatly assisted the Soviet drive into Manchuria by conducting a series of amphibious operations. The Soviet Navy provided little in the way of support for the Arctic convoys, the burden of this protection being shouldered by the British Navy.[14]

Liberty ships

One of the persistent problems for both sides in the war was the lack of adequate merchant shipping. For Japan this proved fatal, but the Allies were able to prevail largely because of another US manufacturing triumph, the Liberty ship program. A standard design Liberty was developed, based on the Ocean-class ships ordered by Britain in the United States early in the war. Whole new yards came into being simply to produce it. Thirty-two states assembled the 30,000 components required for each Liberty; these were then sent by railroad or truck to the coasts for assembly, made possible by welding, which replaced riveting in construction and greatly speeded production. There were some problems, and a few of the ships did break apart on their welds before corrective measures could be put in place.

By October 1942 US shipbuilding capacity was more than 600 percent that of 1937, and the yards were launching Liberties at a rate of three each day. Henry J. Kaiser, 'Sir Launchalot,' was the major figure in the program. Although he had extensive experience in heavy construction, Kaiser had never built ships before. In 1942 his Oregon yard set a record that still stands, constructing the *Robert E. Peary* Liberty in only four days and 15.5 hours once the keel had been laid. By war's end the United States had launched 2610 Liberties, a number of which were fitted out as tankers and colliers, as well as the larger Victory ships. More than 200 Liberties were lost in the war. In all, the United States produced during the war a phenomenal 5200 merchant ships totalling 39 million tons.[15]

The Battle of the Atlantic

All this new Allied shipping would be necessary, for U-boats were taking a deadly toll in the contest for the North Atlantic. This campaign was certainly one of the key contests of the entire war, for without victory here Britain would have certainly been forced to sue for peace. It was a grim, no-holds-barred struggle, this war at sea. Vessels were torpedoed without warning and often at night. Chances of crew survival were slight, especially in the case of tankers, which were the primary U-boat targets. Death might come with the explosion of the torpedo striking the ship or from subsequent internal blasts. Crewmen might also be trapped below decks as the mortally wounded ship went down. Burning oil could extend hundreds of yards from a vessel, lengthening the odds against survival. If there was time to man the lifeboats, crew members might find themselves face to face with the U-boat that had sunk them as it surfaced to survey the destruction. Sometimes U-boat captains provided assistance, but there were also reports of the machine-gunning of lifeboats and floating survivors. Other ships in the convoy could not stop to pick up men in the water, lest they themselves become targets.[16]

On the outbreak of war, the Allies had promptly resorted to convoys. These were predicated on reducing the number of targets and the assumption that the more targets there were the more likely they were to be found. Large numbers of merchant ships would travel together, protected by escort vessels. The U-boats might still get their kills but the percentage of losses would be significantly less. Further, the submarines themselves ran the risk of being sunk by the convoy escorting destroyers and destroyer escorts. And, as we have seen early in the war Dönitz had few submarines. Despite the shift from surface ship construction to U-boats, only 37 new boats were commissioned in the first year of the war, when the earlier plan was to build 100 in that time frame. It was 1941 before the U-boat building program really got going. Although 230 new boats were under construction in April, only 32 were available for operations that month. Dönitz asserted that he would have won the Battle of the Atlantic in 1941 or 1942 had he possessed, at the beginning of the war, the 300 U-boats he deemed necessary. It is probably a false claim, as a higher rate of sinking of merchantmen would only have forced the Allies to shift assets earlier, including long-range aircraft to Coastal Command.[17]

Dönitz's submarines lacked an effective radar until near the end of the war and they struggled – at least in the first year – with defective torpedoes. Dönitz believed this cost at least two U-boats in premature explosions and that faulty magnetic torpedo detonators prevented the sinking of the *Ark Royal* and *Nelson*. This same problem of defective torpedoes plagued the Americans at the beginning of their submarine campaign against Japan.[18]

Dönitz developed new tactics for his submarines, the most important of which was the *Rudeltaktik* (Wolf Tactic, which the Allies referred to as the Wolf Pack). Here groups of up to 15–20 submarines would spread out along the Atlantic sea lanes. Merchantmen traveling alone would be immediately attacked, but if a convoy were sighted, the submarine would shadow it and radio for reinforcements. The closest U-boats would then converge for a night surface attack, which would maximize confusion for the defenders and minimize the possibility of submarine detection. The submarines would then submerge and reorganize for a second attack.

To enable his submarines to remain on station for longer periods, Dönitz sent out 'milk cow' supply submarines. The Germans also had success in codebreaking. The German Navy's *B-Dienst* intelligence service listened to Allied radio traffic and broke the British convoy codes, enabling Dönitz to direct his boats to where he believed enemy ships would be. The Germans also used aircraft, particularly the long-range Focke Wolfe Fw 200, with great effectiveness against Allied convoys in the eastern Atlantic when they came within range of German air bases. Yet Dönitz was handicapped because *Luftwaffe* commander Göring would not provide planes to reconnoiter at sea, and Hitler often ordered the U-boats to undertake missions for which they were not designed.

British defenses of the vital Atlantic trade routes were strengthened in May 1941 when the US Navy began escorting convoys between the United States and Iceland. Then, in June 1941 Canada created the Canadian Escort Force for the same purpose. The Royal Canadian Navy (RCN) played a key role in the Battle of the Atlantic. Comprising only 6 destroyers and 5 minesweepers at the beginning of the war, the RCN grew by war's end to 2 light carriers, 2 light cruisers, 15 destroyers, 60 frigates, 118 corvettes, and many other vessels. Virtually all these ships were committed to the Battle of the Atlantic.[19]

By June 1941, however, the Germans had sent to the bottom some 5.7 million tons of Allied shipping, with British shipyards able to launch only 800,000 replacement tons. Large Italian submarines, a number of them operating out of Bordeaux, were also effective and sank 500,000 tons of shipping in the course of the war. The large increase in U-boat strength enabled the Germans virtually to control the Atlantic for more than a year after America's entry into the war and, beginning in February 1942, Dönitz sent 19 U-boats to the US Atlantic coast in Operation DRUMBEAT. These found easy pickings, with tankers and other ships sailing alone and the US shoreline brightly illuminated at night. The U-boats sank 81 ships. Finally, the United States organized coastal convoys, and in May Dönitz redirected his submarines southward. He also dispatched some large boats into the South Atlantic and Indian Ocean, but supply problems and attacks by surface ships led to their recall. Dönitz was aided by the initiation of British and American convoys in the Arctic Ocean to Murmansk in the Soviet Union, which reduced the number of warships operating against U-boats in the Atlantic and Mediterranean.

By August 1942 Dönitz had 300 submarines at his disposal. The effect of this increase was augmented when, the month before, Germany changed its naval codes. The Allies had broken these early in the war and been able to monitor Germany's submarine deployments. This opened the critical period in the struggle for control of the Atlantic.

In January 1943 Hitler, displeased by the lack of results from his capital ships, sacked Raeder and appointed Dönitz to head the navy. Dönitz further intensified the U-boat war, and early in the year the toll of Allied shipping falling prey to submarines rose precipitously. By March Britain's food reserves were down to only three months; by May half of the world's 5600 merchant ships in 1939 had been lost. But large, fast unescorted converted luxury liners could outrun U-boats and make the trip safely, as could the heavily protected troop transports.

Although experts disagree, the Battle of the Atlantic probably turned with Royal Navy Commander Peter W. Gretton's ONS-1 convoy. From April 28 to May 6 of 1943 Gretton's 46 merchant ships steamed across the North Atlantic in a duel with 51 U-boats. Gretton lost 13 of his ships but 7 U-boats were sunk, 5 by the escorts and 2 by aircraft. The Allies went on the offensive thereafter. Coastal Command aircraft, equipped with lightweight 10cm radar and working with Royal Navy corvettes, attacked U-boats entering and leaving their French bases in the Bay of Biscay. In May 1943 Dönitz lost 38 U-boats, a dozen more than were built. At the same time only 41 merchantmen were lost. In June the US Navy Tenth Fleet began operating Hunter-Killer teams of escort carriers and destroyers in the Atlantic. And, in October the Allies acquired air bases in the Azores from Portugal, further closing the ring on the U-boats.[20]

Aircraft proved vital; they could deflect German bomber attacks and do battle with surfaced submarines before they could dive. One solution was to send fighter aircraft along with a convoy, and the British equipped a number of merchantmen with a forward catapult that held a modified Hurricane fighter. After launch and intercept, the fighter would try to make landfall or else land in the water. A more satisfactory solution was to fit a flight deck to a merchant-ship hull. The German cargo-passenger ship *Hannover*, taken in the West Indies in March 1940, became the first escort carrier. She underwent conversion into the flush-deck aircraft carrier *Audacity* and entered service in June 1941 carrying six fighters. Employed on convoy duty to and from Gibraltar, the *Audacity* gave effective service until she was sunk by *U-751* off Portugal in December 1941. Additional escort carriers soon appeared in the form of US-built conversions on C-3 hulls from the Maritime Commission: the *Archer* and the Avenger-class. Originally contracted for by the Royal Navy, they were transferred to Britain under Lend-Lease and entered service in the first half of 1942. Designed to carry 15 aircraft each, the escort carriers were slow (16.5 knots) but proved invaluable.

Unlike their British counterparts, US captains of escort carriers (CVEs, 'Jeep' carriers) had complete freedom of action to mount 'Hunt and Kill' missions. Teams composed of an escort carrier and a half-dozen destroyers or new destroyer escorts sank 53 U-boats and captured one; they may have been the single most important US contribution to the war against the U-boats.[21]

Long-range aircraft were essential in closing the mid-Atlantic gap, but the RAF's preoccupation with strategic bombing meant that Coastal Command possessed few such aircraft for such service as this. Bomber Command's Air Marshal Arthur Harris is said to have regarded Coastal Command with only slightly less animosity than that reserved for the *Luftwaffe*. Grudgingly, Harris finally made air assets available. The US Consolidated PBY Catalina and PB2Y Coronado and the British Short Sunderland flying boats proved invaluable, as did long-range B-24 Liberator and British Lancaster bombers.

Finally, in August 1944 RAF Bomber Command Squadron 617 (the 'Dam Busters') began attacks with Tallboy bombs against the concrete-reinforced U-boat pens of the Bay of Biscay. These raids were highly effective and U-boats in port were now vulnerable. In the last year of the war 57 U-boats were destroyed by bombing, compared with only five destroyed by bombers in the previous five years. This shows what might have been accomplished had the bombers been directed against the submarines earlier. Indeed, after March 1943 aircraft were probably the chief factor in the defeat of the U-boats. Between March 1943 and May 1945 a total of 590 U-boats were destroyed, compared to only 194 in the previous three-and-a-half years of war. Of the 590 destroyed, 290 were by air power, 174 by ships, and the remainder through a combination of the two or other causes.[22]

Even as it lost the Battle of the Atlantic, Germany increased its production of U-boats. The new Type XXI boats appearing in the last few months of the war had high underwater speed and greater endurance, and they might have been a factor if produced earlier. Few saw active service. Allied air attacks on their ports and aerial mine-laying in the Baltic Sea retarded their trials and the training of their crews.

A combination of factors brought the Allies victory in the Battle of the Atlantic. The convoy system was important but so too was technology, primarily 10cm radar sets that could be carried aloft in long-range aircraft, sonar, improved depth-charges, rockets fired from aircraft, and forward-thrown shipborne anti-submarine 'hedgehogs' or 'mousetraps' (small depth charges known to the British as Squids). The high-intensity Leigh Light on aircraft illuminated the sea at night. Radio detection equipment was vital, and long-range aviation helped close the so-called 'Black Hole' in the central Atlantic. Intelligence also played a role, chiefly Ultra intercepts of U-boat communications that guided aircraft to the submarines. The creation of Hunter-Killer groups operating independent of the convoys carried the war to the submarines. It is also true, however, that Allied and inter-service cooperation was far too long in coming.

The Battle of the Atlantic was a close-run thing, and it claimed vast resources. German submarines sank 2452 Allied and neutral ships totalling 12.8 million gross register tons. During the war the British merchant marine lost 40,248 men and the Royal Navy another 73,642. RAF Coastal Command sustained losses of 5866 men and 1777 aircraft. The Royal Canadian Navy lost 1965 men, while US Navy losses in the battle were 2443 men. The Germans also paid a high price. During the war Germany built 1162 submarines. Of 830 operational U-boats, 784 were lost (696 destroyed by enemy action). At war's end the crews of 220 surviving submarines scuttled their boats rather than surrender them, while 156 boats were surrendered. Two escaped to Argentina. Of 40,900 Germans who served in submarines, 25,870 perished and more than 5000 were taken prisoner. U-boat crew fatalities were thus 63 percent, and the overall loss rate was 76 percent, the highest for any service in the war.[23]

As the campaign against German U-boats in the Atlantic was being won, the Allies also had to contend with German long-range aircraft and surface ships attacking the Arctic convoys sailing for Murmansk. At the end of December 1943 the German battle cruiser *Scharnhorst* and five destroyers, operating out of Alta Fjord, Norway, steamed to attack a Murmansk convoy. Some 400 miles north of Trondheim the German ships blundered into two British task forces west of the North Cape. Hit at extreme range and slowed by gunfire from the British battleship *Duke of York*, the *Scharnhorst* was then subjected to a heavy pounding by naval gunfire. She finally succumbed to torpedo attack, with only 36 of the 1900-man crew surviving.

The *Bismarck*'s sister ship, battleship *Tirpitz*, proved more difficult to sink. Commissioned in February 1941, she too posed a significant threat to Allied shipping but saw her only real action on September 6, 1943, when, along with the *Scharnhorst*, and ten destroyers, she raided Spitsbergen and damaged Allied coal mining operations there. Beginning in January 1941 when she was still in drydock, the *Tirpitz* had been the target of numerous British efforts to destroy her. These included attacks by naval gunfire, midget submarines, and aircraft. Repeatedly damaged, she was each time repaired. Sir Barnes Wallis, who developed the 'skip' or 'bounce' bombs used in dam-busting oper-ations, then came up with a 12,000-lb 'Tallboy' armor-piercing bomb capable of penetrating the battleship's deck armor.

On September 15, 1944, 27 Lancaster bombers carrying 20 Tallboys attacked the *Tirpitz* at Kaa Fjord, Norway. The mountains screened their approach, and the bombers arrived undetected. This time the *Tirpitz* was damaged so badly that the Germans decided not to repair her but to relo-cate the ship at Tromso as a stationary battery. Another Tallboy bomber attack in October failed to register any hits but the third Tallboy attack, by 29 Lancasters on November 12, produced three hits. One of these exploded the *Tirpitz*'s magazines, causing her to roll over and sink; about 950 men of her crew perished. This action removed the last major surface threat to the Arctic convoys, although once the Allies had secured the Mediterranean most Lend-Lease shipments to the Soviet Union went by that route and thence through Iran.[24]

One last episode of the war at sea in the European theater needs to be told: the German Navy's evacuation of military personnel and civilians from the Baltic ahead of the advancing Red Army. This operation, the greatest German Navy success of the war, came not without cost. In

January 1945 a Russian submarine sank the German passenger liner *Wilhelm Gustloff*; she went down with 7100 people, most of them civilians. The next month the same Russian submarine sank another liner, the *General Steuben*, and 3700 people perished. And in April another Russian submarine sank a third liner, the *Goya*, killing nearly 6800 people. The sinking of these three German ships with the loss of nearly 15,000 people obscured the fact that the German Navy conducted the largest seaborne evacuation in history. Directed by Dönitz himself, the navy was able, despite fuel shortages, Russian mines, submarines, and air attacks, to evacuate nearly 2 million people from the Baltics with only a one percent loss rate.[25]

The naval war in the Pacific

In the vast Pacific theater sea power proved decisive. The fight here was largely a US Navy enterprise, and it ended in perhaps the most comprehensive victory in naval history. The naval strategies and most surface battles are covered in Chapters 4, 5, and 11, so this section will concentrate on submarine warfare.

In going to war with the United States, Japanese leaders completely miscalculated in a number of key areas. They assumed that they could cripple the US Navy, then carry out a series of conquests to secure desired natural resources and build a defensive ring that would hold the US Navy at bay until such time as it gave up and recognized the inevitability of a new Japanese empire. Yet the defeat of Japan was certain. The key to victory in the Pacific War lay in numbers of ships and planes, and Japan, with a vastly inferior industrial base, was bound to lose that race to the United States. Another important factor in the US Navy victory over Japan was the 'Fleet Train' concept enabling carrier task forces to operate for extended periods of time and at great distances from their bases. The Fleet Train was a vast enterprise that included supply ships, tankers, repair vessels, and tenders for seaplanes, destroyers, and submarines. As a result the US Navy enjoyed unparalleled mobility; its strategic reach in the war was unmatched by any other navy.

An essentially defensive policy forced the IJN to disperse its assets. In the course of the war the navy was never able to support individual isolated Japanese strongholds before the Americans overwhelmed them. Japan's leaders also miscalculated their vulnerability in a war against merchant shipping. Obsessed with carrying out fleet actions against the US Navy, the IJN gave scant consideration to the protection of their highly vulnerable merchant trade. Anti-submarine warfare was all but ignored. In December 1941 the IJN had but four purpose-built escort vessels, and it was not until the autumn of 1942 that any escorts were equipped with sonar. The United States led Japan by a wide margin in anti-submarine technology. During May 19–31, 1944, one destroyer, the *England*, sank six Japanese submarines, a record unequaled by any ASW warship in any navy in any war.[26]

Japan was highly dependent on imports and yet boasted only a marginal shipping capacity. Even with their early successes, the Japanese would not be able to capture, build, or salvage the necessary tonnage to replace even modest losses. As it turned out, US submarines devastated the Japanese merchant marine. The United States outbuilt Japan in submarines by 2:1. The US Navy entered the war with 114, while Japan had 64. During the war the United States built another 206 and Japan only 116; in the entire conflict the United States lost 52 submarines, Japan 128. During the Pacific war the US Navy became the most successful practitioner of the *guerre de course* (war against commerce) in history. One could argue that the submarine was in fact the most important factor in the Allied victory in the Pacific. In effect, the United States succeeded where Germany failed in both World War I and World War II.[27]

The United States built long-range submarines of 2000 tons with ten torpedo tubes each. Although the Japanese produced some fine boats and actually built the largest subs of the war (3500 tons and carrying three disassembled planes) with exceedingly long range (in 1942 a Japanese submarine shelled the Pacific US coast), their submarine strategy was flawed. They directed their subs against US warships. Although the Japanese had some successes, operating against enemy warships took a high toll. Later the Japanese employed their large submarines chiefly to supply isolated garrisons such as Rabaul. The obvious target for their submarines was the US supply vessels, but the Japanese never concentrated on the vulnerable US supply lines. The reason was probably psychological and found in the tradition of bushido and samurai.

US submarines had a deep-dive capability. The standard diving depth for subs was 300 feet, but US boats could reach 400 feet without stressing the hull and deeper if necessary. This was one of the best-kept secrets of the war, so enemy depth charges usually exploded above them. But for the first two years of the war, US submarines suffered from a poor torpedo. The magnetic pistol to explode the charge under the target ship often did not function correctly; the torpedoes also circled, and one US submarine, the *Tang*, was actually sunk by one of its own fish. In late 1943, however, new contact pistols were installed, and by 1944 the navy had a new magnetic pistol.

From the beginning of the war against Japan the United States waged unrestricted submarine warfare. In December 1941 Japan had 5.4 million tons of merchant shipping, only a marginal capacity. The Japanese constructed or acquired another 3.29 million tons during the war, but US submarines sank 6.9 million tons of merchant ships (1113 vessels).[28]

US submarines also exacted a heavy toll on Japanese warships, sinking 201 totaling 577,000 tons. These included the battleship *Kongo*, the aircraft carrier *Shinano* (a converted Yamato-class battleship and, at 64,000 tons, the largest aircraft carrier until the 1950s), and seven other carriers. The top priority targets for the US submarines were aircraft carriers and tankers. The Japanese were so short of aviation fuel by 1944 that they could scarcely train pilots; Japanese aviators had only about 120 hours of flying time before combat. In American submarine successes, codebreaking (Magic) played a major role. Although US submariners lost 3506 officers and men, a casualty rate of almost 22 percent and the highest for any branch of the US military, it was far less than the totals for Germany or Japan. Japan was brought to ruin by the triad of strategic bombing, carrier task forces, and submarine warfare well before the atomic bombs were employed against Hiroshima and Nagasaki.[29]

Japanese courage and tenacity had been overcome by American determination and numbers. In February 1945 the five carrier task groups operating against the Japanese home islands included 119 warships, yet only four of them had been in service before December 7, 1941. By 1945 the United States Navy counted 23 battleships, 19 fleet carriers, 1 light carrier, 108 jeep carriers, 351 destroyers, and 255 submarines. The US Navy was in fact larger than all the other navies of the world put together.[30]

9

The War in the Air: the Strategic Bombing of Germany and Japan

Strategic bombing in theory

At the beginning of World War II strategic air power proponents believed emphatically in the superiority of the bomber and that in sufficient numbers they might by themselves bring victory. These sentiments were particularly prevalent in Britain, Italy, and the United States. Germany, Japan, and the Soviet Union all developed air forces more geared to ground operations. Although they designed such aircraft, none placed long-range four-engine strategic bombers in service.

Strategic bombing originated in World War I when the Germans employed Zeppelin airships and then Gotha and Staaken long-range bombers to strike London. These raids, which continued into May 1918, inflicted fair amounts of damage with relatively little loss of life. They did divert some British fighter squadrons from the Western Front, but failed as a terror weapon. In 1917 Minister of Munitions Winston Churchill observed:

> It is improbable that any terrorization of the civil population which could be achieved by air attack would compel . . . surrender . . . we have seen the combative spirit of the people, roused, and not quelled, by the German air raids. Nothing that we have learned of the capacity of the German population to endure suffering justifies us in assuming that they could be cowed into submission by such methods, or . . . not be rendered more desperately resolved by them.[1]

Despite Churchill's statement, many influential individuals believed bombers could be decisive in a future conflict. The British, who created the RAF, the world's first independent air force, had their own Handley-Page

216

twin-engine bomber, which at the end of the war was dropping 1650-lb bombs (Britain's largest) on Rhineland factories. It was Italy that had the largest strategic bombing program of the war. They routinely attacked Austrian targets with their large Caprioni triplane bombers. But most World War I aircraft were utilized for reconnaissance, air superiority operations, and close air support missions. Strategic bombing did not come into its own until World War II.

During the inter-war years, in Britain and the United States at least, bomber advocates held sway. Air Marshal Hugh Trenchard, RAF Chief of Staff (1919–29), was an enthusiastic proponent of strategic bombardment. He believed emphatically that population centers were legitimate targets and that such bombing alone could bring victory. Influential writers in other nations held the same opinion. The Italian Guilio Douhet wrote in *The Command of the Air* (1920; revised 1927) that future wars would be decided from the air and there was no real defense against bombers. Douhet is best known for his belief that wars would be won by striking industrial centers and cities, shattering civilian morale. He advocated, in the interest of economy, that a nation concentrate on one type of aircraft, the self-defending bomber. Douhet held that navies could be destroyed from the air and that armies would be useful only to occupy countries defeated by air power. The way to defeat an enemy air force was to destroy its ground installations by bombing.

US Army Brigadier General William Mitchell was another enthusiastic bomber advocate. Mitchell, who had directed US air operations in France at the end of World War I, accepted most of Douhet's theories, although he proved not quite as doctrinaire as the Italian. Mitchell demonstrated, to his mind at least, that the day of the battleship was over when, off the Virginia Capes in June 1921, bombers under his direction sent the former German battleship *Ostfriedsland* to the bottom. It was the first time that a battleship had ever been sunk from the air. The admirals said this had proved nothing as the ship was stationary (it nonetheless proved difficult for the planes to sink) and in any case lacked anti-aircraft protection.

Mitchell further held that the United States would not be able to transport troops to Europe by sea in significant number without first securing the air. He stressed the importance of the polar air routes, advocated the development of specialized aircraft for reconnaissance and pursuit purposes, and urged the employment of paratroopers behind enemy lines. Mitchell also stressed that the enemy air force must be the primary target, for the first priority must be to gain command of the air; only then could a successful bombing campaign proceed.

US strategic bombing doctrine was hammered out between the wars at the Army Air Corps Tactical School. This doctrine held that the primary target should not be population centers but industry. The planners also believed that large numbers of self-defending bombers could defeat an industrial enemy state by destroying the most vulnerable sectors of what was known as its industrial web. Eliminating these 'choke points' would end an enemy state's ability to wage war. In the 1920s, at least, it was difficult to argue against the supremacy of the bomber, especially as fighter and bomber aircraft flew at nearly the same speeds.

Then, too, Douhet's conclusions seemed validated by events in the 1930s: the successes of Italy's Air Force in Ethiopia in 1935–36 and of Germany's *Kondor Legion* in the Spanish Civil War of 1936–39. German and Italian air strikes against Guernica, Madrid, and Barcelona pointed to the possible destruction of Paris and London. At Guernica the Germans experimented with a mix of high-explosive and incendiary bombs. Ignored by air power enthusiasts was the fact that German and Italian air fleets in Spain flew largely unopposed, with few and outclassed Republican aircraft present and only limited anti-aircraft artillery. Japan experienced similar success in China during 1937–41, drawing identical conclusions.

Many military analysts accepted the argument that bombing by itself might win a war. British tank enthusiast and military theorist Major General J. F. C. Fuller gloomily predicted that civilian morale would break under the strain of air attacks and 'frantic terror-stricken mobs . . . will surge through the city [London].'[2] There were advocates of this view in Germany. Major General Walter Wever, first chief of the German *Luftwaffe* air staff, was a vocal advocate of strategic bombing to cripple an enemy's industry and shatter civilian morale. Wever was able to secure development of two prototype four-engined '*Amerika*' or 'Ural' bombers: the Dornier Do 19 and Junkers Ju 89. Although suffering from weak engines, both were adequate for subsequent development, but Wever died in a plane crash in May 1936. His successor, Albert Kesselring, in April 1937 requested and obtained a halt from Göring in their development. This would mean a larger number of medium types to support the army. The *Luftwaffe*, the world's strongest air arm in 1939, was basically a tactical air force, geared for ground support. One might argue, though, that this was an effective use of limited resources.[3]

The Germans had learned during the Spanish Civil War the necessity of close air–ground coordination and support, and they formulated techniques to accomplish this with the dive-bomber as the chief element. The Ju 87 Stuka was essentially a flying artillery piece that could deliver its ordnance with devastating accuracy, providing there were no enemy fighters around. The *Luftwaffe* had performed brilliantly in support of ground operations in Poland in 1939 and in France and the Low Countries in 1940. That changed in the subsequent 1940 Battle of Britain. Hitler's first defeat, the battle proved that air power enthusiasts were mistaken in at least some of their assumptions. The reasons for the *Luftwaffe*'s failure to win control of British skies have already been discussed, but one factor was certainly the lack of a heavy bomber.

The Germans went on to enjoy great success in the air on the Eastern Front against the Soviet Union, until the winter of 1942–43, when the tide turned in the air as well as on land. In the early fighting in the east, modern Soviet aircraft were just entering production, and the *Luftwaffe* had some extraordinarily skilful and determined pilots. Eric Hartman flew more than 1400 sorties and scored an incredible 352 aerial victories (some of these on the Romanian Front) making him the leading ace of all time. Stuka pilot Hans Rudel flew 2530 combat missions and had 11 aerial victories, despite amputation of a leg. He also sank the Soviet battleship *Marat* at Kronstadt in the Baltic. In April 1943 Rudel fitted a pair of 37mm cannon underwing on his Ju 87G as a tank buster and went on to destroy 532 Russian tanks in the last year of the war. The most highly decorated German of the war, Rudel was the only one awarded the Golden Oakleaves, Swords and Diamonds to the Knight's Cross of the Iron Cross.[4]

Britain was slower than Germany to build up its air force and in the mid-1930s had only a mix of light bombers and obsolete fighters. In 1937, however, the government ordered prototypes of the Lancaster, Stirling, and Halifax heavy bombers. The growing strength of the *Luftwaffe* also led the government in 1939 to order the creation of 18 new fighter squadrons. These aircraft came into service just in time for the Battle of Britain. In 1940 Britain surpassed Germany in aircraft production.

Although the new British heavy bombers were not available when the war began, supporters of strategic bombing never faltered in their belief that they held the key to victory. The RAF consisted of Fighter Command, Coastal Command, and Bomber Command, but the greatest resources by far went to Bomber Command. The strategic bombing program was seductive; in 1940 it was the only way Britain could get at Germany militarily. The same was true for the United States when it entered the war. Bomber Command leaders believed they had the means to accomplish what the Germans did not: win the war through an offensive with long-range, heavy bombers.

The strategic bombing of Germany

Initial British air activity was largely limited to dropping leaflets and attacks on selected naval targets. In December 1939, in its first real raid, Bomber Command sent 22 twin-engined Wellingtons against German North Sea coastal shipping. The raid was ineffective and 12 of the planes were lost; three others made forced landings on return. A greater than 50 percent loss rate was hardly an auspicious beginning.[5]

The British and French governments had vetoed attacks on German cities and industrial targets for fear of retaliatory raids on London and Paris, but this policy changed in May 1940 with the invasion of France and the Low Countries. RAF exponents of strategic bombing believed that they could carry out accurate daylight bombing, and over the next ten months Bomber Command concentrated on attacking German industrial targets, oil plants, and transportation. Bomb assessment was and remains difficult, but the plain fact is that the bombing was accomplishing little.

Bomber Command was also paying a heavy price in men and aircraft. British bombers carried only the .303-caliber machine gun to defend themselves against German Bf 110 interceptor aircraft with 20mm cannon. The German aircraft were thus able to take stand-off positions and blast away at the bombers without fear of being hit by the shorter range .303 rounds. Strangely, this British practice continued to the end of the war. US heavy bombers were better armed, with heavy .50 caliber machine guns.

Bomber Command then switched to low-level attacks, which resulted in prohibitive losses. By mid-1941 it was obvious that the bomber was not 'always getting through,' and Bomber Command was forced to find another way to proceed. Later that year the British bombers were painted dark colors and shifted over to night bombing, a practice the British continued for the remainder of the war. Accuracy remained a serious problem; it was so poor that the Germans often did not know which targets were under attack. A scientific study of 100 raids on 28 different targets came up with the conclusion that only one in three aircraft dropped its bombs within five miles of the target and that bombs were being dropped anywhere within an area 75 miles of the target. Obviously such poor performance would not work against industrial targets, and the leaders of Bomber Command finally decided to employ what came to be euphemistically described as 'area bombing.'[6]

Although the decision to employ night area bombing was taken before he was appointed chief of Bomber Command in February 1942, Air Marshal Arthur 'Bomber' Harris is the individual most closely associated with it. Harris believed throughout the war that improved heavy bombers and new navigational aids would enable Bomber Command to succeed whereas the *Luftwaffe* had failed. The best means of accomplishing this, he believed, was the wholesale destruction of German cities. Prime Minister Churchill embraced the concept and, somewhat surprising given his intervention in virtually every area of the military, allowed Harris virtual free reign. On August 8, 1940, Churchill declared himself in favor of 'an absolutely devastating, exterminating attack by very heavy bombers from this country on the Nazi homeland. We must be able to overwhelm them by this means, without which I do not see a way through.' By September the 'Former Naval Person' conceded, 'The Navy can lose us the war, but only the Air Force can win it.'[7]

Dissenters included Chief of the Air Staff Air Marshal Sir Charles Portal, Harris's superior, who favored more selective targeting, and Air Marshal Sir Arthur Tedder, later deputy commander of the Normandy invasion, who sought to concentrate attacks on the German transportation system. Portal, however, rarely intervened with his subordinate and Harris usually carried the day with Churchill. Throughout, Harris resisted focusing on what he called 'panacea targets,' and the prime minister had to order him to cooperate with General Eisenhower in carrying out raids against transportation and communication targets in northern France to prepare for the Normandy invasion and to support the navy in eliminating the German U-boat pens.[8]

In late August 1940 German planes had bombed London and Churchill immediately ordered a retaliatory strike on Berlin, his 1917 comments about the ineffectiveness of strategic bombing not withstanding. Both sides then struck civilian centers at will, although, at least according to Harris, it was the May 5, 1943, raid on Essen that first demonstrated the so-called 'indirect effects' of raids on working-class urban areas. Incendiary attacks could have a devastating impact upon 'services, houses, and amenities.' Collateral damage, he reasoned, would be as important as that resulting from direct hits on factories and railroads.[9]

Hitler steadfastly refused to visit the bombed areas, despite repeated pleas by Albert Speer and Joseph Goebbels to do so. Goebbels claimed that such activities would have great propaganda value. Hitler's attitude was in sharp contrast to that of Churchill, who was often pictured in the press and in newsreels in such activities flashing his 'V for Victory' sign.[10]

In March 1942 Professor Frederick Lindemann, Lord Cherwell, Churchill's scientific advisor, sent the prime minister a memorandum on the possible impact of bombing the industrial centers of Germany. Cherwell used as the basis of his estimates the very measurable effects of German bombing on Britain. He concluded that one ton of bombs would destroy 20–40 houses and thus render 100–200 people homeless. Extrapolating that the RAF would have 10,000 bombers delivered in the next year and that each should be able to make 13 operational flights with three tons of bombs per flight before being shot down, Cherwell held that it would be possible to 'de-house' (as he put it) the civilian population of some 60 German industrial cities.[11]

Advocates of going after civilian centers believed that their destruction and 'de-housing' of the civilian population would lower morale both among civilians and the military alike and bring on a revolt. This ignored the realities of the totalitarian state, and it also assumed that the civilians would blame their government for the destruction. In practice the bombing of civilian centers strengthened the resolve of those under attack rather than diminishing it.

Bomber Command also worked to develop new navigational aids, among them *Gee*. This allowed a navigator to calculate his aircraft's position by noting the time it took to receive pulse systems from three different ground stations. The Germans did not learn the mysteries of *Gee* until May and did not jam it until November. On the night of March 8/9, 1942, Bomber Command employed *Gee* to attack Essen. Of 211 aircraft on the raid, 74 had *Gee*. The weather was good but only 168 aircraft even claimed to have attacked the target. On the night of March 28/29, 234 Wellingtons, Stirlings, and Manchesters struck the German port city of Lübeck; this time 191 crews claimed to have reached the target. Harris said 'the first German city went up in flames' and photographic reconnaissance indicated that 45–50 percent of Lübeck, which was largely of wood, was destroyed. But of a population of 120,000 only 312 German civilians were killed and fewer than 16,000 were rendered homeless. Damage to the German war economy was slight.[12]

Harris then scored his most impressive feat. Securing the approval of both Churchill and Portal, he assembled the first 1000-bomber raid. By temporarily stripping training groups and utilizing some planes from Coastal Command, Harris cobbled together 1086 aircraft, enough to allow for a shortfall on take-offs. Hamburg and Köln were the two possible targets, with Harris preferring the former. Weather would be the determining factor, for Harris wanted ideal conditions for maximum effectiveness. But then the Admiralty, apparently acting largely from pique, withdrew the 250 Coastal Command aircraft assigned to the operation, reducing the force to 836 bombers. Harris was determined to reach the 1000-plane figure, even though this meant using crews not yet fully trained for operations. The raid was planned for the night of May 30/31, 1942.

Predicted cloud cover over Hamburg meant that Köln became the target. Harris's goal was to pass the 1000 aircraft over Germany's fifth largest city within only 90 minutes, an unprecedented feat rendered easier by *Gee*. As it worked out Bomber Command got 1047 aircraft aloft (more than 600 of them Wellingtons). A total of 890 planes reached Köln and dropped 1455 tons of bombs, two-thirds of them incendiaries. Köln was a modern city and, unlike at Lübeck, there was no firestorm. Even so the damage was great. More than 15,000 buildings were destroyed or damaged. Only 469 people were killed but more than 45,000 were made homeless. Forty-one bombers were lost, or 3.9 percent (just within the acceptable range of 4 percent). The large number of aircraft involved simply overwhelmed the German defenses. To avoid mid-air collisions while flying at night and to overcome German defenses, the British bombers flew singly in great concentrated streams.[13]

The Köln raid also destroyed many illusions in Germany about who was winning the war, but by that time accuracy had all but ceased to be a concern in strategic bombing. This raid and others that followed caught the headlines and enabled Churchill, during a trip to Moscow that August, to at least partially answer Stalin's charges that the Western Allies were not doing enough to relieve German pressure in the east.[14]

The Germans responded to the British bomber challenge. At the beginning of the war they did not possess anything like the British air defense system, relying only on searchlights and anti-aircraft guns. In July 1940 the *Luftwaffe* established the 1st Night Fighter Division under *Generalmajor* Joseph Kammhuber. He went on to develop a complex air defense system that included searchlights, anti-aircraft guns, night fighters, radar, and vector stations. This defensive belt, which came to be known as the Kammhuber Line, inflicted heavy losses on Bomber Command.

As an interceptor against Allied bombers the Germans employed the twin-engine Bf 110 aircraft. A failure in its designed role as a long-range bomber escort, the Bf 110 found its niche as a night fighter. Armed with 20mm cannon, the Bf 110 proved highly effective as a bomber interceptor. More than 6000 were built by war's end, and it made up 60 percent of German night-fighters. The Bf 110's 20mm cannon allowed its pilots to stand off beyond the range of British bomber machine guns. Kammhuber also used the Bf 110 to carry out intruder missions into British air space in order to shoot down bombers as they were taking off.[15]

The Germans lagged behind the British in radar development; but their early Lichtenstein airborne radar made possible 'Zahme Sau' ('Tame Boar') tactics against the bomber streams that exacted a high toll of Bomber Command aircraft. The Germans also steadily improved their early warning radar network of Wasseman, Freya, and Würzburg radars. The German radar net ran from Denmark to northern France and enabled Luftwaffe pilots to intercept British and US bomber formations as they approached the continent. In the autumn of 1942 the Germans also fitted some of their Bf 110s with 37mm anti-aircraft cannon, a single hit from which would disable even a Flying Fortress. The next year the Germans fitted some Bf 110s with rockets; others had two 30mm cannon pointing forward at an angle of 15 degrees off vertical; later some Ju 88s received 20mm guns mounted in the same fashion.[16]

By early 1943 the German combination of early warning, anti-aircraft fire, and interceptors was paying such handsome dividends that the entire strategic bombing campaign was in jeopardy. Beginning in March 1943 and utilizing Gee, Oboe (a precision positioning tool), and a new airborne radar scanner, H_2S, that provided accurate readings of the ground and facilitated bombing through clouds, Harris began a 3-month-long campaign against Germany's industrial heart, the Ruhr. In May 1943 Squadron 617 (the 'Dam Busters') employed a new 6000-lb round skip bomb (actually a mine) developed by Dr Barnes Wallis to destroy several key dams in the Ruhr River valley.[17]

Bomber Command also brought on line new aircraft, especially the four-engine Avro Lancaster, which entered service over Germany in March 1942. The premier British strategic bomber of the war, the Lancaster had a maximum speed of 287 mph, a ceiling of 24,500 feet, and a range of 660 miles. Relatively lightly defended (8 x .303 machine guns), it sacrificed defensive firepower for bomb load and could carry 18,000 lbs of bombs as opposed to 4000 lbs for the US B-17 (6000 for the B-17G). Within a year the Lancaster had largely supplanted the Handley Page Halifax and Short Stirling as the principal RAF bomber.[18]

Allied scientists also worked to defeat the German radar system. In July the British introduced a counter-radar measure known as 'Window' (the Americans called it 'Chaff' and the Germans '*Dupple*'). Window consisted of aluminum strips that gave off the same radar signature as a bomber. Thousands of these dropped from aircraft would hang in the air, blinding the German radars.[19]

Allied scientists also discovered that they could render radar useless by transmitting radio signals on the same frequency. Utilizing this 'jamming' technique, lead aircraft in Allied bomber formations began carrying in their bomb bays 'Carpet' or 'Mandrel' radio transmitters. The Carpet system was designed to operate against the German Freya system and the Mandrel against the Würzburg. Beginning in April 1943 specially equipped B-17s of the US Army Air Forces (USAAF) 16th Reconnaissance Squadron began flying missions to locate German radio radar sites so that they might be destroyed by other aircraft.[20]

In the summer of 1943 British and American bombers launched a devastating series of raids against German cities. On the night of July 24/25, 791 Bomber Command aircraft began Operation GOMORRAH against Hamburg, Germany's greatest port and second largest city, dropping 2290 tons of bombs. The weather was clear, the target area was well-identified by Pathfinder aircraft, and the British employed Window for the first time. Only 12 aircraft were lost. The next day, July 25, the Americans joined the attack with 127 B-17s of the Eighth Air Force and the specific objectives of shipyards and an aircraft engine factory. Smoke from the British raids obscured the target and bombardiers could not use their Norden bomb sight without visual contact. The Americans also paid a much heavier price. The *Luftwaffe* pounced on the planes as they exited the target area, shooting down 19 and damaging most of the remainder.

Nonetheless the attacks continued intermittently until August 3. A raid on the night of July 27/28 created a great firestorm. Bomb loads were a mix of high explosive (HE) and phosphorous bombs, the filler of which burned with intense heat. As many of the German cities were built largely of wood, the effects were devastating. Flames leapt thousands of feet into the air in great fire storms with winds of 300–400 miles an hour. The flames were visible to bomber crews more than 100 miles away. Temperatures reached 1000 degrees centigrade, and many people simply suffocated. Air raid shelters became giant ovens, baking their inhabitants alive. The RAF returned to Hamburg with 707 aircraft on the night of July 29/30 and with 740 on the night of August 2/3. In all the British lost 86 bombers and the Americans 43. Total Allied air crew casualties numbered about 1000 men. The number of Germans dying in the great raids on Hamburg is estimated at about 46,000 people, the majority of them women and children. Another 40,000 were injured. More than 60 percent of the city's housing was destroyed.[21]

Bomber Command continued its attacks on German cities during the remainder of 1943. Between the raid on Hamburg and the shift to Berlin in November, Bomber Command carried out 27 major attacks on targets throughout Germany, from Munich to Hanover, Nuremberg, Leipzig, and the Ruhr. Two of these were by more than 700 aircraft, seven by between 600 and 700 aircraft, and four by more than 500. During this period Bomber Command lost 609 aircraft destroyed and about 1000 damaged.[22]

Harris then turned his attention to Berlin, and from November 1943 to March 1944 Bomber Command waged a relentless campaign to destroy the German capital. Harris hated the idea of an Allied invasion of France and he was convinced of the need to drive Germany from the war before such an enterprise could take place. On November 3 he wrote to Churchill, 'We can wreck Berlin from end to end if the USAAF will come in on it. It will cost between 400–500 aircraft. It will cost Germany the war.'[23]

From November 18 to the end of March Bomber Command dueled with the German night fighters and flak over Berlin. (The term 'flak' became synonymous with anti-aircraft fire; it was derived from the German acronym for *Flugzeug* [aircraft] *Abwehr* [defense] *Kanone* [cannon]). This is not to say that other German targets were ignored during the aerial 'Battle of Berlin' – 19 out of a total of 35 operations were directed at other cities. But it was Berlin that mattered the most. It was the focus of Operation POINTBLANK, the biggest battle Bomber Command had yet fought. Berlin was battered by 9111 bomber sorties; the raids 'de-housed' 1.5 million Berliners. A total of 492 Bomber Command aircraft were shot down but 954 were damaged, and of these 95 were in fact destroyed. The US Eighth Air Force joined the effort in March.[24]

Poor weather frequently affected the raids and, more often than not, the bombers dropped their loads through clouds without any accuracy. The raids on Berlin, despite great destruction and loss of life, did not materially affect the course of the war. Berlin was similar to London in 1940, in that the city extended over a considerable area and could absorb great punishment. Indeed, Bomber Command was sustaining such heavy losses against the improved German defenses that Harris was forced to call off raids into central Germany. German defenses continued improving: more searchlights; improved SN2 radar; more and heavier anti-aircraft artillery, including 88mm as well as 105mm and 128mm pieces;

and new tactics for interceptors. Speer used his considerable organizational skills to expand fighter aircraft production both in Germany and in allied states such as Hungary, and by June 1943 Germany was producing 2316 fighters a month. Germany also concentrated production of fighter aircraft on the Bf 109 and Focke-Wulf FW 190. The new Heinkel He 219 *Uhu* (Owl), although produced only in small numbers, proved devastatingly effective at night.[25]

Speer and Fighter Commander General Alfred Galland had calculated that one German fighter would be lost for every bomber shot down but that the expenditure of *matériel* would be of the order of 1:6 and in attrition of pilots 1:2. Moreover, many German pilots would parachute to safety whereas Allied crews would be captured. Speer and Galland urged that Hitler shift aircraft production solely to fighters and use every available plane to combat the Allied bombers. Hitler was furious at their intrusion into 'operative measures' and ordered all fighter production halted and these workers shifted into anti-aircraft gun production. This was the first Hitler command that Speer refused to obey; he instead ordered fighter production be kept at the maximum possible, and later Hitler agreed that it should have the highest priority. Painful as this was for Allied bomber crews, the shift in German production to air defense had the indirect consequence of reducing assets available to Germany to fight the war on land. Every 88mm gun in anti-aircraft use, for example, meant one fewer tank or anti-tank gun.[26]

The USAAF, meanwhile, concentrated its bomber resources on broad-daylight attacks of German aircraft manufacturing plants or parts vital in their production. American bomber crews paid a heavy price for this, as was evident in the August 1943 Schweinfurt-Regensburg raid, when 60 bombers were downed. The USAAF concept of strategic bombing differed markedly from that of the British. In the period between the two world wars, leaders of the Army Air Corps believed that the long-range bomber offered the best chance to carve out an offensive role; it would also justify an independent air force, the goal of many senior officers. The plane chosen for that role was the new Boeing B-17 'Flying Fortress.' An excellent bombardment platform and very rugged, the B-17 was very much in keeping with Douhet's 'battle plane.' The B-17G of 1943, with a crew of ten men, had a maximum speed of 287 mph, a ceiling of 35,600 feet, range of 3400 miles, and armament of 13 x .50 caliber machine guns. Its bomb load of 6000 lbs was less than comparable British aircraft, which sacrificed defensive armament. The Air Corps had sold the B-17 to Congress in 1934 as a coastal defense weapon, and in 1937 three B-17s intercepted the Italian liner *Rex* 630 miles into the Atlantic.

Air Corps emphasis on the long-range bomber adversely affected development of fighter aircraft. Air Corps leaders believed that fighters could not intercept bombers and were in effect obsolete. Not everyone agreed. Major Claire Chennault, who developed an interest in fighter tactics and published a book on the subject in 1935, believed that fighters could intercept and destroy bombers. He had ample opportunity to demonstrate his theories flying against the Japanese in China from 1938, taking command of the American Volunteer Group in China in 1941. Using his hit and run 'guerrilla' tactics, this unit, the legendary 'Flying Tigers,' scored impressive victories against Japanese aviation. But early US fighters lagged far behind contemporary RAF and *Luftwaffe* designs.[27]

The Army Air Corps experienced tremendous expansion during the war. General Marshall, long an air power advocate, fully supported this growth. At the start of the war the Air Corps had fewer than 20,000 men, but by 1944 the Army Air Forces – as the Air Corps was renamed – had 2,400,000 personnel. During the war the USAAF put 194,000 men through pilot training and another 300,000 men through gunnery school. They were not rushed into combat. American airmen received 260 hours of flying time before combat. This contrasted with 110 for the *Luftwaffe* late in the war.[28]

When the United States joined the war in December 1941, if the army was to make a meaningful contribution in the European theater of operations in 1942 it would have to be in the form of strategic bombing, and yet Commanding General of Army Air Forces General Henry 'Hap' Arnold, the first commander of the Eighth Air Force Major General Carl 'Tooey' Spaatz, VIII Bomber Command commander Brigadier General Ira C. Eaker, and other USAAF generals opposed British terror bombing of civilian centers. They criticized the bombing campaign for moral reasons but primarily on practical grounds, because they believed it would fail. It would also hurt chances for an independent air force after the war. The Americans thought they had the answer in daylight precision bombing of key German industrial targets.[29]

General Arnold, who had learned to fly from the Wright brothers, and those around him came to be known as the 'Bomber Barons.' They were committed to the belief that vast bomber armadas could conduct pin-point raids against selected German targets in daylight without fighter escort. He based this optimism on the defensive firepower of the B-17 bomber as well as the Norden bombsight. The British iterated that pin-point bombing would not work against German defenses, and they pointed out that the Germans had failed in 1940 in their daylight precision bombing attempts against British defenses. If the Americans wanted to make a meaningful contribution to the war against Germany, it should be by joining them in bombing German cities at night. But the Americans thought they knew better.[30]

USAAF bomber crews were rightly skeptical about their chances, some referring to the B-17 as the 'Flying Target.' The USAAF bomber units began arriving in Britain in the summer of 1942, and on August 17 Major General Eaker led his 8th Bomber Command of 12 B-17s on the first US strategic bombing operation of the war, a strike against rail marshaling yards at Rouen, France. Initial US targets were within the range of accompanying fighter aircraft, but Eaker optimistically wrote his superiors that 'bombardment in force – a minimum of 300 bombers – can effectively attack any German target and return without excessive or uneconomical loss.'[31]

The bombing campaign was discussed by Roosevelt and Churchill at the Casablanca Conference in Morocco in January 1943. Eaker, who had succeeded Spaatz as commander of Eighth Air Force the month before, pressed for greater daylight B-17 raids on German-occupied Europe. Roosevelt and Churchill agreed to an 'around-the-clock' bombing campaign, known as the Combined Bomber Offensive. The resulting Casablanca Directive spelled out 'primary objectives' of submarine yards, the aircraft industry, transportation, oil refineries and storage tanks, and German industrial targets. But it also allowed those actually setting the targets – Harris, Eaker, and Spaatz – great latitude. Harris, for example, said that going off industry would allow him to 'attack pretty well any German industrial city with 100,000 inhabitants and above.' In effect, the British and Americans would go their separate ways. The Americans would carry out precision daytime raids on German industrial targets while the British conducted nighttime area bombing on civilian centers to break German morale.[32]

The USAAF Eighth Air Force flew from British bases to strike Germany while the Fifteenth Air Force operated from bases in North Africa and then in Italy. Allied planners thought that attacking the Reich from two directions would overextend its air defenses. It was a vast operation, with 158 US airfields constructed in Britain alone.[33]

The two aircraft carrying the brunt of the US strategic bombing campaign in Europe were the B-17 and the Consolidated B-24 Liberator. Eighth Air Force flew principally the B-17, while the Fifteenth flew the B-24. With a maximum speed of 300 mph, a ceiling of 28,000 feet, and range of 2100 miles, the B-24J of 1943 had a crew of 8–12 men, was armed with 10 x .50 caliber machine guns, and carried 8800 lbs of bombs. The B-24 was the most widely used US strategic bomber of the war; 18,188 were produced, more than any other bomber in US history. The B-24 was utilized in a variety of roles, including strategic bombing, naval reconnaissance, anti-submarine warfare, and transport. While the B-24 had longer range than the B-17, it was more difficult to fly, requiring considerable manual strength, and could not take the punishment of the B-17 because of its complex construction.[34]

Bombing missions were extraordinary tests of endurance for the crews involved. The planes were not pressurized and flew at 20,000 feet and above with temperature of 40 degrees below zero (Fahrenheit). Both the B-17 and B-24 had self-sealing gasoline tanks and armored seats for the pilot and co-pilot. They also bristled with defensive armament, carrying up to 12 x .50 caliber heavy machine guns and up to 10,000 rounds of ammunition. The US planes usually flew in cells, designed to provide maximum overlapping defensive firepower against German fighters. The bombers often flew alone, with no long-range fighter escorts to accompany them. Both planes were equipped with the Norden bomb sight, developed by Dutch engineer Carl Norden to enable US Navy aircraft to hit enemy warships from 20,000 feet! The navy abandoned the Norden when it discovered that it was virtually impossible to hit a maneuvering ship from that altitude and went over to dive-bombing.

The Norden was the first 'black box' piece of equipment, and the origin of the term. The sight was kept secured away from the plane and then carried in a black box by an armed bombardier to the aircraft prior to the mission. Its supporters claimed that the Norden could drop 'a bomb into a pickle barrel at 20,000 feet.' But in order to achieve accuracy the bombardier had to enter a great many variables, such as wind drift, and a period of sustained level flight was necessary in the approach to the target. The Norden accompanied the more skilled bombardiers in the lead aircraft. Trailing bombers would drop their own bomb loads on the cue of the lead aircraft, producing a salvo effect. Weather played a key role in bombing operations. Often it was terrible, halting operations altogether or rendering them very difficult. Bombardiers using the Norden had to see the target in order to hit it, and often the target area was obscured by cloud or haze, and later by German smoke pots.

German fighter pilots were alerted to the Allied raids well in advance. As the big bombers took off from their bases and joined their formations, the keying of their radios provided ample warning. Forming up, often in foggy conditions, was in itself dangerous, particularly in an aircraft carrying thousands of pounds of bombs and aviation fuel. The close, dense bomber 'box' formations massed machine gun defensive firepower, but they also resulted in some planes being lost to friendly fire. Long contrails high in the sky identified the bombers' location for the intercepting German fighters. The bombers were also on their own, without fighter protection, most of the way to their targets and back home. Because of their limited range, escorting fighters could only accompany the bombers as far as France.

Once the attacking German aircraft located the bombers they would occupy a 'stand off' position, employing their longer-range 20mm cannon to fire into the box. The Bf 110 and FW 190 were excellent bomber interceptors. Like the later USAAF P-47 Thunderbolt, the FW 190 was a tough aircraft with a big radial engine. Favored attack positions were either directly ahead or astern of the bombers where there was no deflection problem in aiming. The frontal attack and slightly high ('12 o'clock high') allowed the interceptors to take the bomber box as they passed. The defending German fighters did their best to break up the bomber formations and then pick off crippled strays. Anti-aircraft fire was a major threat and pilots especially feared it. Guns on the ground often threw skyward a thick carpet of shell bursts, through which the bombers had to fly. Of bombers lost to hostile causes, just about half were destroyed by fighters; the remainder succumbed to anti-aircraft fire.[35]

As with the British, the shift in US targeting to include cities – and ultimately to focus on them – had its origins in pragmatism rather than military dogma. The costly daylight bombing of heavily defended German industrial targets abandoned by the British in late 1940 was subsequently given up by the Americans as well. Precision daylight bombing did not work. It was not the fault of the air crews but the circumstances under which they operated, including bad weather and the lack of fighter protection. Harassment from fighters and anti-aircraft fire made level bomb runs prohibitively expensive. Thus the Americans no less than the British bought into the Douhetian argument that the way to win the war was to shatter civilian morale by area bombing of cities.

The British tried to get the US to abandon the B-17, which carried 3 tons of bombs, in favor of the Lancaster, which could deliver 9 tons; and to abandon efforts at precision daylight bombing in favor of nighttime area bombing. But the Americans persisted, although in reality US 'precision daytime bombing' and British nighttime 'area bombing' became one and the same. In at least some instances, American commanders resorted to the same sort of rationalization used by their British counterparts to justify the mounting toll of German non-combatants. The 'way to stop the killing of civilians,' suggested General Arnold in 1943, 'is to cause so much damage and destruction and death that civilians will demand that their government cease fighting.'[36]

The strain on bomber crews was incredible. The Ploesti raid of August 1 and the Schweinfurt-Regensburg raid of August 17, 1943, were good examples. These strikes were part of the bomber offensive initiated by the Combined Chiefs of Staff (CCS) in June 1943. USAAF leaders were determined, despite concerns about the effectiveness of largely unescorted daylight bombing raids, to prove that bombers could win the war.

The Ploesti raid in Romania was mounted to destroy the dozen oil refineries ringing the city that were providing Germany with more than a third of its oil. Ploesti had first come under attack on June 12, 1942, when 12 B-24s flying from Egypt inflicted minimal damage, but without loss. Operation TIDAL WAVE of August 1, 1943, carried out by Brigadier General Uzal G. Ent's IX Bomber Command of Major General Brereton's Ninth Air Force, was quite a different proposition. Ent was ordered, over his objections and those of his group leaders, to carry out a low-level attack.

Early on August 1, 178 B-24s took off from their North African bases. Thirteen planes were lost before the target was reached. The Germans and Romanians had 300 fighters available and had ringed Ploesti with 237 anti-aircraft guns and some 2000 smoke pots. The Germans tracked the American air armada all the way from North Africa to Ploesti. Then a navigational error led the lead bombers to attack from the wrong direction, confusing trailing groups in their bomb runs. Some bombers flew so low that their gunners actually fired up at the flak towers. Some were scorched by ground fires and had branches caught in their bomb-bay doors. Anti-aircraft fire and Axis fighters downed more than 40 bombers; another 50 were damaged. Only three aircraft were considered ready for an immediate mission. Five officers were awarded the Medal Of Honor for this raid, the most ever for a single action. Although it temporarily reduced oil output, the refineries were soon back in full production.[37]

Two weeks later Eaker's Eighth Air Force carried out its deepest large long-range mission into Germany, simultaneously attacking the ball-bearing plants at Schweinfurt and the Messerschmitt aircraft complex at Regensburg. Both targets were far beyond normal B-17 range: Regensburg, to be attacked by 3rd Bombardment Group, was more than 500 miles from the English coast while Schweinfurt, to be struck by 1st Bombardment Group, was nearly 400 miles away. German fighters would thus have ample opportunity to attack the bomber streams both coming and going. The Regensburg attack force was to fly on to North Africa. Eighteen squadrons of P-47s and 16 squadrons of RAF Spitfires could provide protection only about 40 percent of the way.

Early morning fog on August 17 disrupted the plan for simultaneous attacks. Of the 3rd Bombardment Group's 146 B-17s, 122 reached the target and dropped 250 tons of bombs. Four hours later, 184 of its original 230 bombers dropped 380 tons of bombs on Schweinfurt. Of the total of 376 B-17s, 60 (36 over Regensburg and 24 over Schweinfurt) were shot down, but more than 25 percent of the 306 bombers that returned were damaged beyond repair. Eighth Air Force lost 601 airmen killed, wounded, or captured. US air crews claimed 208 German fighters downed; the Germans admitted to 25. The raid did have some success. Nearly half of the machine tools in the Regensburg assembly plant were destroyed. Although the plant was back in production in less than four weeks, fighter production losses were 800 to 1000 planes. Unknown at the time, the raid also destroyed the jigs for the fuselage of the Me 262 jet fighter. German managers later speculated that this loss delayed the production of jets by a critical four months. At Schweinfurt ball-bearing production suffered a temporary 50 percent drop off.

A belated attempt to renew the assault on Schweinfurt on October 14, so-called 'Black Thursday,' cost the Americans 60 of 291 aircraft and more than 600 air crew, and again had only limited success. This raid left 133 planes so badly damaged that it took four months to bring Eighth Air Force back to anything approaching full strength. The Germans lost perhaps 35 fighters. The attacks proved to Allied leaders that deep raids were impossible without long-range fighter escort.[38]

Albert Speer believed the Allies could have won the war in 1944 had they continued raids against the ball-bearing industry. 'Thus, the Allies threw away success when it was already in their hands. Had they continued the attacks . . . we would quickly have been at our last gasp.' Speer believed that raids such as that at Schweinfurt could well have proven fatal if continued at a high level.[39]

But the USAAF could not sustain such raids, which were simply too costly. The Eighth Air Force was suffering a loss rate of some 30 percent a month, insuring that few crews made it to the 25 missions necessary for rotation back to the United States. The Schweinfurt-Regensburg raid did force the USAAF to address a host of long-standing problems, including navigation and bombing procedures, but also a crash program for mass production of a long-range fighter, hitherto inexplicably low on the list of military priorities.

This aircraft appeared in the North American Aviation P-51 Mustang. Developed by North American in response to a British order, the initial 1940 model was underpowered. Fitted with the high-performance Rolls Royce Merlin 61 engine in May 1942, it emerged in June 1943 as the P-51B, probably the best all-around piston-engine fighter of the war. Mounting 6 x .50 caliber machine guns and capable of 440 mph, it outclassed the Bf 109 in maneuverability and in speed by at least 50 mph. It could also carry 2000 lbs of bombs. The British and Americans were slow to utilize drop tanks. An obvious range-extender for fighter aircraft, they had been utilized by the Japanese early, in operations against the Philippines. The P-51's range was 810 miles, but with two 75-gallon drop tanks it had a round trip range of 1200 miles; a further 85-gallon internal tank extended this to 1474 miles, and even with two drop tanks it could reach 400 mph and more. The Allies now had an aircraft with the range of a bomber and the speed and maneuverability of a fighter. The North American P-51 and the Republic P-47 Thunderbolt, another fine fighter and rugged ground support aircraft, arrived in the European Theater at the end of 1943. With drop tanks they could protect the bombers to and from their targets.[40]

The air war now turned dramatically. In February 1944 the Allies carried out a series of massive raids against German aircraft factories and strikes against Berlin, forcing the German fighters aloft so they could be destroyed. In 'Big Week,' beginning on February 20, 1944, Eighth Air Force sent out, for the first time in the war, a thousand four-engined bombers escorted by hundreds of fighters to strike a dozen targets, most of them aircraft factories. Although losses were heavy, they were within acceptable limits, and the bombers drew up many German fighters, which were then destroyed by the American fighter escorts.

In March new Eighth Air Force commander Major General Doolittle ordered his fighters to stage low-level attacks against German fighter fields. These early 1944 attacks were punishing to both sides, but they destroyed the bulk of the German Air Force and gave the Allies air superiority over Europe, a necessary prerequisite for the bomber and fighter-bomber offensive in northern France prior to the Normandy invasion. On the night of March 30/31, 1944, the 'Black Night' of the RAF, Bomber Command sent 795 planes against Nuremberg; 95 of the bombers failed to return (nearly 12 percent of the force); 71 others were badly damaged. Fortunately for Bomber Command, this marked the end for such losses, which could not have been sustained.[41]

The Allies continued making improvements to their aircraft and techniques. The addition of a chin turret on the B-17G provided better protection for the bomber box and impeded frontal attacks. The H$_2$S airborne radar also proved a big asset, as did the presence of long-range fighter protection.

In April the Allies shifted priority to strikes in support of Operation OVERLORD, the long-awaited cross-Channel invasion of France. Eisenhower's deputy commander Tedder, with advice from scientist Sully Zuckerman, originated the so-called 'Transportation Plan' by which the Allies would isolate northern France. Despite opposition from Air Marshal Harris, who wanted to continue striking cities, and commander of the USAAF in Europe Lieutenant General Spaatz, who sought concentration against the German aviation and oil industries, the top commanders finally agreed that OVERLORD would have priority. A number of heavy bombers were diverted to join the medium bombers and fighter bombers of General Brereton's US Ninth Air Force and Vice-Air Marshal Sir Arthur Coningham's British Second Tactical Air Force.

Allied aircraft went after railroad marshaling yards, bridges, trains, and other communications targets, all to make it extremely difficult for the Germans to reinforce Normandy or to shift artillery and armor assets there once the invasion had begun. The attacks proved highly success-ful. Only four of the 80 main transportation targets in France were not damaged, and rail traffic within France declined by 70 percent. The campaign was one of the major air power contributions to Allied victory in the war.[42]

Not only did the Allied planes provide cover during OVERLORD itself, but they provided invaluable ground support afterward. Major General Elwood 'Pete' Quesada, commander of the IX Tactical Air Command under Brereton, implemented techniques already worked out in North Africa and Sicily that revolutionized aerial support of ground troops. Among these were the absolute necessity of air superiority over the battlefield; the co-equal status of ground and air commanders; centralized command of tactical air assets to take advantage of the changing tactical situation; and the introduction of FM radios and the placement in tanks of compatible radio equipment to provide instant communication between ground forces and supporting aircraft.[43]

At the same time in the summer of 1944 the Germans effected a major technological leap when they introduced the first jet aircraft. Germany, Italy, Britain, Japan, and the United States all flew jets during the war, but the German twin-turbojet engine Messerschmitt Me 262 *Schwalbe* (Swallow) was the first to enter combat. It underwent trials in 1942 and might have entered service the next year had it not been for delayed deliveries of its Junker jet engines. General Galland protested this decision but to no avail. Seventy mph faster than the speediest Allied aircraft, the Me 262 made aviation history when on July 25, 1944, one attacked, but failed to destroy a British de Haviland Mosquito. The Me 262 was only marginally successful as a ground attack aircraft but it was a superb interceptor. As USAAF General Spaatz reported, 'These deadly German fighters could make Allied bombing attacks impossible in the near future.'[44]

The Me 262 arrived too late to have any real effect on the outcome of the struggle for air supremacy over Germany. The Germans also were developing the Arado Ar 234 *Blitz* (Lightning), intended as a reconnaissance aircraft and light bomber. The second jet aircraft to go into service and the first bomber, the Ar 234 took to the air for the first time in June 1943 and entered service a year later. A total of 274 were assembled. It conducted a series of unstoppable pinprick raids at the end of the war, the most noteworthy of which helped collapse the Remagen Bridge over the Rhine on March 17, 1945. Armed with 2 x 20mm cannon and capable of carrying 23,307 lbs of bombs, it had 460-mph speed and a range of 684 miles. Had it been produced earlier, the *Blitz* would undoubtedly have had a major impact. The British responded with their Gloster Meteor. In service only the last two months of the war, it was the only Allied jet aircraft to fly in combat during the war. The American Lockheed P-80 Shooting Star, the prototype of which flew in January 1944, saw no combat in the war.[45]

The introduction beginning in mid-June 1944 of Hitler's 'vengeance weapons,' the V 1 buzz-bomb and the V 2 rocket, did force the Allies to divert heavy-, medium-, and light-bomber assets to destroy launch sites. These were difficult to locate, and the Allied attacks were only partially successful. The V 1 was basically a pilotless pulse-jet aircraft with a one-ton explosive warhead. Beginning in mid-June 1944 the Germans launched thousands of these against London and English coastal cities. The buzz-bomb took its name from its sputtering sound as it flew. Not an accurate weapon, it simply dropped when its fuel was cut off after a predetermined distance. The V 1 moved at sufficiently low speed that intercepting pilots could on occasion use their own plane's wing tips to lift a V 1's wing and cause it to spin out of control. However, the V 2 was a proper rocket and much more formidable. It also carried a one-ton warhead, could reach the stratosphere and be targeted far more accurately. At 3600 miles an hour, it was impossible to intercept. Hitler hoped these V weapons would tip the balance; but although they killed nearly 12,000 people and injuring another 53,000, they also came too late in the war to affect the course of events.

The first strike launched on the V 2 test site at Peenemünde on the Baltic was carried out on the basis of intelligence provided by the Polish underground. It fell on August 17, 1943, the same day that the Americans were striking Schweinfurt and Regensburg. Bomber Command dispatched 596 heavy bombers – 324 Lancasters, 218 Halifaxes, and 54 Stirlings – on this mission. A total of 560 bombers reached the target, dropping 1800 tons of bombs. Although losses were heavy – 40 aircraft shot down – the raid was successful, delaying the V 2's entry into service by three months. The first V 2s did not fall on Britain until September 1944.[46]

It was during this raid that the Germans first used the *Schragmusik* (slang for jazz) cannon. Capitalizing on the fact that the British bombers lacked a belly or 'ball' turret along the lines of the B-17, the Germans mounted two 20mm cannon on an Bf 110 in an upward firing position. They would use Lichtenstein radar, approach the bomber from underneath, position themselves at a distance of 50–100 meters, and match the bomber's speed, then fire on its belly and wing fuel tanks. Usually a single burst of cannon fire from the German plane would be sufficient to wreck the bomber above. The Germans probably shot down six of the Peenemünde raiders in this fashion.[47]

Speer achieved near-miracles, demonstrating what might have transpired had German industry been properly organized for war from its onset. Although fighter production fell off at the beginning of 1944, in September Germany produced 3538 new aircraft and returned another 776 damaged aircraft to service, twice the January rate. Of 113,514 aircraft produced by Germany during the war, 40,593 were introduced in 1944, of which 25,285 were fighters. Even in the last four months of the war Germany produced nearly 5000 fighters. Although the Germans could manufacture the planes, they could not replace the trained pilots lost combatting American bombers escorted by swarms of fighters, because fuel shortages sharply limited training time.[48]

By the summer of 1944 British and American bombers were flying in broad daylight virtually unopposed, save for anti-aircraft fire, over all Germany, including Berlin. Allied bomb tonnages went up dramatically. In one month of 1944 the USAAF was dropping more bombs than in all the months of 1942; similarly, Bomber Command in the last three months of 1944 carried bomb loads four times as heavy for the same period as 1943, and 20 times as heavy for that period in 1942.[49]

Strikes against oil storage and synthetic oil production facilities had a dramatic impact on *Luftwaffe* operations. The fuel shortage also severely impacted pilot training. Speer noted that on one visit to a

Luftwaffe training facility in July 1944 he was told that there was only sufficient fuel for student pilots to fly for one hour a week. In July 1944 a survey of *Luftflotte* 3 pilots revealed that with but few exceptions only wing and squadron commanders had more than six months' operation fighter experience. The bulk of the pilots had between eight and 30 days' combat service. The declining skill of the pilots pushed up the level of attrition, with growing losses from accidents.[50]

All parties recognized the importance of such attacks, and in November 1944 the British and Americans made oil refineries their primary target with communications second. Attacks against German cities also continued. On August 10, 17, 18, and 19, 1944, the US Fifteenth Air Force mounted its final raids on Ploesti, finally halting oil production there. Twenty-four separate attacks against Ploesti cost the Fifteenth 305 heavy bombers and 3000 men. Success would not have been possible in these operations without the reduction of Germany's fighter defenses and the escorting P-51 fighters. By December 1944 oil was in such short supply that Hitler's panzers in the Ardennes Offensive had only enough fuel for three days of operations, sufficient only to reach the Meuse. The Germans were reduced to capturing the stocks they needed from the Americans.[51]

By early 1945 the Germans were hardly able to mount any effective air defense. They had not only lost their network of early warning radar stations in northern France, but Allied tactical air forces were now based in France against the Reich. In these circumstances, Tedder sought a concentration on the German transportation system. Harris called these 'panacea targets' and continued to cling to area bombing of German cities, while Spaatz wanted the USAAF to concentrate on oil production. Spaatz did agree, however, that when targeting would allow, his planes would go after lines of communication.[52]

The direction of significant tactical air assets against transportation paid handsome dividends. This campaign reduced the flow of raw materials and industrial products and gradually strangled the economy. By February the Allies had virtually cut off the Ruhr from the rest of the country. This marked the most effective use of strategic bombing in the European Theater during the war.

Terror bombing of German cities continued until the end, however, and the USAAF was very much involved. On February 3, 1945, the USAAF mounted a large raid, designed in part to show the Soviets that the United States had recovered from the setback of the Battle of the Bulge and was determined to assist the Soviet drive to Berlin. Nearly 1000 USAAF B-17s went after the German capital, while 400 B-24s struck Magdeburg. Perhaps as many as 25,000 people died in Berlin alone. The deaths of so many people would indicate that this was an area rather than a precision attack. But, in contrast to Harris, the US commanders continued to claim they were attacking industrial and transportation targets rather than conducting area bombing of cities. Queried as to whether this marked a shift in US priorities in favor of the indiscriminate bombing of cities, Spaatz noted that 'the Americans were not bombing cities indiscriminately, but attacking transportation facilities inside cities in missions which the Russians had requested and seemed to appreciate.'[53]

That same month of February 1945 the Allies mounted against the Saxon city of Dresden one of the most destructive air raids of the entire war. Carried out in response to a Soviet request to help bring about a more rapid collapse of the German front in the east, the raid became the locus of arguments regarding the strategic bombing campaign and specifically the area bombing of German cities. Harris did not shrink from taking responsibility. He wrote in his memoirs,

> In February 1945, with the Russian army threatening the heart of Saxony, I was called upon to attack Dresden; this was considered a target of the first importance for the offensive on the Eastern Front. . . . I know that the destruction of so large and splendid a city at this stage of the war was considered unnecessary even by a good many people who admit that our earlier attacks were as fully justified as any other operations of war. Here I will only say that the attack on Dresden was at the time considered a military necessity by much more important people than myself . . . .[54]

Dresden was a major communications and industrial center. It was also known as the 'Florence of the Elbe,' being one of Europe's most beautiful cities; it was also largely composed of wooden structures. Dresden was the capital of Saxony and the largest German city as yet untouched by bombers. Its prewar population was 650,000 people, but in February 1945 the city was choked with refugees from the fighting in the east and from other bombed German cities. Bomber Command struck on the night of February 13/14.

Harris planned the attack carefully. It consisted of two waves of Lancasters, the first of 244 planes and the second, three hours later, of 529. As a consequence of the long distance the planes would have to fly to attack the target and return, bomb loads were minimal: about 7000 lbs versus 12,000–13,000 lbs per plane carried for attacks on the much shorter range strikes against the Ruhr. Most planes carried one 'cookie' or thin-walled blast bomb, which was in sections and could be up to 6000 lbs, with the remainder in incendiaries. Then, over the next two days 527 USAAF B-17s attacked in daylight. Over a three-day period 1299 Allied planes dropped 2431 tons of high explosives (HE) and 1476 tons of incendiaries.[55]

The raging inferno of firestorms at Dresden was visible 200 miles away. Much of the city was laid waste, particularly the *Altstadt*, or 'Old Town,' the non-industrial part of the city. Estimates of dead vary widely, from 8200 to a wildly exaggerated 250,000. The figure will never be known with certainty because of the number of refugees and the fact that many bodies were completely incinerated. It was certainly one of the most destructive air raids in history. German novelist Gerhart Hauptmann wrote of it, 'Those who had forgotten how to weep learned again when Dresden fell.'[56]

On May 8, 1945, the war in Europe came to an end. The Strategic Bombing Survey, conducted by the Eighth Air Force after the war, showed that bombing – while important in the war – was not the decisive element believed previously. Strategic bombing was important in the European theater in many ways – in disrupting the German transportation system, in isolating the Normandy invasion site, and in destroying Germany's capacity to produce key industrial components. But Speer's work in fully mobilizing the German economy for war, German inventiveness, and dispersal of industry all meant that Germany actually increased its production of armaments, including aircraft, at the height of the Allied bombing. But the Germans lacked both the fuel to fly their new planes and trained pilots for the new jet aircraft. Another point must also be made: without these raids, Germany's armaments production would have been far greater in all areas, perhaps by a third in aircraft alone. The strategic bombing program forced Germany to redefine its production priorities, taking assets from other needed areas, to increase the production of anti-aircraft artillery for example.

The Allies had destroyed the German Air Force. During the war the *Luftwaffe* trained about 30,000 fighter pilots. Of these 18,000 died in combat or in training. Others were wounded or captured, and at the end of the war only 5500 *Luftwaffe* pilots remained, making this branch second only to German submariners in terms of percentage losses. Allied bombing of the pre-1939 Reich killed perhaps 305,000 Germans and injured 780,000. Some 7,500,000 Germans had been rendered homeless. By way of comparison, 60,595 British civilians died under German air attacks.[57]

The strategic bombing campaign had been an immense effort. In the European theater alone it accounted for nearly one-third of Britain's industrial effort in the war, and 11 percent of the total war cost to the United States. At peak strength the British and Americans deployed 1,335,000 men and 28,000 aircraft. During the war in Europe the USAAF flew 754,818 sorties; RAF Bomber Command, 687,462. These dropped on Germany and occupied Europe a combined 2,790,000 tons of bombs. Of this amount 85 percent came after June 1, 1944. But the bombing was costly. The United States lost 9949 bombers; Bomber Command 10,045. Counting fighters and transport aircraft, the air effort in Europe cost the British and Americans nearly 40,000 aircraft. Personnel losses were also heavy: including fighter personnel, nearly 159,000 men killed – 79,265 US and 79,253 RAF – the great majority of these in the bombing effort.[58]

The air war in the Pacific theater

As the Allied air forces were counting their losses and assessing the damage inflicted in the European theater, air operations were coming to a climax against Japan. Aviation, both naval and land-based, played a key role in the defeat of Japan, although in the Pacific theater the air effort was largely waged by the United States. Thus the chief differences in approach were between the US Army and Navy, such as the reluctance of General Arnold and Major General Curtis LeMay to see B-29s of XXI Bomber Command utilized in mine-laying activities, which nonetheless turned out to be a highly successful enterprise. At least a half million tons of shipping was sunk in this fashion, and hundreds of ships were paralyzed in their harbors.[59]

Air power was vital in the wide expanse of the Pacific. Fast carrier task forces protected surface fleets and covered amphibious assaults and resupply efforts. Aviation ashore provided protection against assaults from the sea and enabled strikes against enemy naval forces and merchant shipping. The new truism of naval war was the need to control the skies above the sea. As it turned out, the United States was able to employ its vastly superior manufacturing capability to overwhelm the Japanese in the air, both in numbers and in quality of aircraft. One major Japanese failing was the lack of an effective pilot training/rotation system. The United States rotation system provided much more training time before combat. In contrast, Japanese training time steadily diminished during the conflict, and the best Japanese pilots were consumed at the Battle of Midway and in fighting for the Solomons.

New US aircraft also appeared in the Pacific Theater. The rugged Grumman F6F Hellcat replaced the F4F Wildcat as an air superiority fighter. The Hellcat was superior to the Zero in everything save turning radius. The gull-winged Vaught F4U Corsair was a superbly versatile aircraft (it continued in production until 1952) and the Lockheed Air Force P-38 Lightning an excellent long-range fighter. Other new aircraft included the Grumman TBF Avenger, probably the best torpedo-bomber of the war.

The USAAF in the Pacific also had a superb leader in Major General George C. Kenney, who took over Fifth Air Force and all US air assets throughout the South Pacific in September 1942. He provided air support to General MacArthur's Southwest Pacific campaigns from New Guinea to the Philippines. Promoted to full general in March 1945, Kenney then commanded all Allied air forces in the Pacific theater. No ideologue in the employment of air assets, Kenney worked to provide effective support to land and naval operations. He inherited an ineffec- tive organization and conducted a thorough house-cleaning, sacking five generals among other officers, but Kenney's chief accomplishment was in operations. Among his tactical innovations were the modification of the B-25 Mitchell light bomber with 8 x .50 caliber nose-mounted machine guns and twin gun turrets to suppress flak, and using these planes for low-level strafing and bombing. Kenney also instituted the highly effective skip-bombing technique, employing 500-lb bombs, to attack Japanese ships.

The devastating effectiveness of Kenney's innovations was revealed in the March 2–5, 1943, Battle of the Bismarck Sea, part of the long Solomons Islands campaign. Made aware by 'Magic' (breaking of Japan's naval codes) that Japan was attempting a major reinforcement of New Guinea, Kenney on March 3 sent a dozen B-25s against the Japanese ships. Already successfully employed by the RAF, this was the first use of skip-bombing by the USAAF. The bomb fuses were set to detonate at five seconds delay, and the bombs bounded like flat rocks across the water to the ships, then exploded at or near their waterlines. By the end of the battle the Japanese had lost all 8 of their transports and 4 destroyers. In total the United States lost 5 aircraft; Japan lost 62 aircraft, 12 ships, and more than 3700 men.[60]

American air attacks destroyed much of Japan's South Pacific avia- tion on the ground. One such attack, at Wewak on August 17, 1943, destroyed 100 planes. Heavy air combat occurred over the principal

Japanese base of Rabaul on New Britain Island in October and November. Both sides suffered heavily in this air combat, but the United States could make its losses good while Japan could not. US control of the skies as a consequence of both carrier- and land-based aviation was essential in some of the big naval battles of the Pacific theater, including the Philippine Sea and Leyte Gulf, for it insured the success of US amphibious assaults against Japanese-held islands.

The strategic bombing of Japan

Strategic bombing of the Japanese home islands began in June 1944 with the 4-engine Boeing B-29 Superfortress flying from bases in China. The B-29 was ordered in August 1940, first flew in September 1942, and entered service in 1944. It had a ten-man crew and was protected by 10 x .50 caliber machine guns and a 20mm cannon in the tail. Capable of carrying 10 tons of bombs, its usual load was 4 tons, because of the fuel necessary for the distance to be covered. The B-29 was a revolutionary aircraft. Unlike the B-17 or B-24, it was fully pressurized, its ceiling was 31,850 feet, and it had a phenomenal range of 4100 miles. Fast for a bomber, its maximum speed was 358 mph.[61]

Basing the B-29s in China was unsatisfactory for a number of reasons. All supplies for the planes, including bombs and even fuel, had to be flown in from India over 'the Hump' (a series of mountain ranges). This was extremely difficult and time consuming. Then, too, Chinese Nationalist troops were unable to protect the B-29 airfields. No sooner were they in operation, than Japanese troops attacked and took them. Another solution was at hand. In July and August US forces captured Saipan, Guam, and Tinian in the Marianas Group. Even as these were being cleared of their last Japanese defenders, naval construction crews (Seabees) were at work building runways and support facilities for Brigadier General Haywood S. 'Possum' Hansell's XXI Bomber Command – soon his B-29s were striking Japan.

The initial B-29 raids from the Marianas were of 150–200 planes per strike, with the 1200-mile flight to Tokyo and return taking up to 16 hours in the air. USAAF planners had called for precision bombing (from 30,000 feet!), but this proved impossible. Jet streams threw the planes off course and ice forming on windshields and wings reduced aircraft performance. The B-29s also flew unescorted, and Japan controlled the island of Iwo Jima, over which the bombers would twice have to pass. By December 1944 the B-29 loss rate per mission was averaging 6 percent (the maximum permissible was 5 percent), lowering both morale and crew efficiency. The raids were having an effect on Japan, however. The strain of frequent air alerts reduced Japanese worker efficiency and lowered the morale of the entire population. Concentration of US bombing attacks on aircraft factories also forced their dispersal, bringing about a decline in actual production.

XXI Bomber Group, nominally under Lieutenant General Nathan Twining's Twentieth Air Force, actually answered to General Arnold and the Joint Chiefs in Washington, and Arnold was displeased with XXI's progress. In January 1945 he replaced Hansell with General LeMay, who had enjoyed success commanding XX Bomber Command in India. LeMay was determined to repeat his performance in the Marianas. Arnold's staff in Washington instructed LeMay to give first priority to attacks upon cities rather than industrial targets. During Arnold's visit to the Marianas in June 1945, he asked LeMay when he thought the war would be over. LeMay's staff quickly calculated that the B-29s – which were attacking a Japanese city a day by the spring of 1945 – would run out of targets by October 1. LeMay reasoned, that if there were no targets left in Japan, certainly there wouldn't be much war left.[62]

In February and March 1945 LeMay had developed new tactics. He decided to replicate 'Bomber' Harris' strategy of area bombing at night, taking advantage of the Japanese failure to develop an effective night fighter. The B-29s would fly low, stripped of all armament save the tail gun, in order to increase payloads. Incendiaries rather than HE would be used and the bombers would drop their loads from only 5000–8000 feet. His first great firebomb raid was against Tokyo, the Japanese capital, on the night of March 9/10; it was the single most destructive raid in the history of warfare. A total of 334 B-29s flying at 7000 feet dropped 1667 tons of incendiary bombs on a city largely of wooden structures. Widespread firestorms destroyed 15 square miles of central Tokyo, including 267,171 houses. Japanese sources cite 83,793 confirmed dead and 40,918 injured. More than 100,000 people were rendered homeless. The success of the Tokyo raid was repeated four times over the next ten nights. The profusion of wooden buildings had always made fires in Tokyo a problem, but this was something quite different.[63]

Over the next months B-29s hit the largest Japanese cities, one after the other: of 64 major cities, 63 were struck; only the cultural center of Kyoto was spared. Up to 300,000 Japanese died. B-29 losses dropped dramatically, to 1.4 percent, in part because of the US capture of Iwo Jima and its use as a fighter field and emergency landing point for crippled B-29s.[64]

Not only did the Japanese lack an effective night fighter, they also lagged behind the British, Americans, and Germans in radar development, although in November 1943 the Germans gave the Japanese the plans for their Freya and Würzburg systems. In the Pacific theater the Americans employed four squadrons of B-24s and B-29s specifically outfitted for radar jamming, while B-25s equipped with radar homing-signal devices attacked Japanese radar sites and destroyed them with their nose-mounted .50 caliber machine guns.[65]

By August 1945 Japan's cities were blackened shells. With targets scarce, the big US bombers were used to drop mines in the Inland Sea, shutting down what was left of Japanese shipping and helping to bring the Japanese nation to starvation levels. Under these conditions, and with the dropping of the atomic bombs on Hiroshima and Nagasaki (discussed in Chapter 11), Japanese leaders decided to surrender.

Air power had played a key role in the war. Despite the failure of strategic bombing to achieve the goals of its advocates, it was certainly an essential complement to operations on land and sea. Strategic bombing, however, reached its maximum effectiveness only towards the end of the war. The strategic bombing campaigns against Germany and Japan also demonstrated an axiom of war; rarely are conflicts won by one branch or service, but by all working in tandem.

10

The Allies Victorious in Europe

The Eastern Front, 1943

Despite the débâcle of Stalingrad, by early 1943 German forces had reestablished their lines. During mid-May to mid-June 1943 both sides observed an informal cease-fire. When fighting resumed, the Red Army held options it had not before possessed. The Soviet Union were aided considerably by Hitler's insistence that Germany retain all captured territory as long as possible. His refusal to authorize timely withdrawals to consolidate meant that each ensuing defeat would be at higher cost because retreat was delayed too long.

The Germans and their allies fielded 240 to 260 divisions, while the Soviets had 250 to 275. More importantly, Soviet manufacturing was registering solid gains, and they now enjoyed a clear advantage in *matériel*, as well as in manpower. Soviet factories, many of which had literally been picked up and moved east beyond the Urals and the range of German bombers, were producing increasingly greater quantities of armaments. Then, too, US Lend-Lease aid, including aircraft, tanks, and trucks, was arriving in the Soviet Union in substantial quantities. At the same time the Anglo-American strategic bombing campaign was helping to reduce Germany's output of aircraft, which in turn affected the close relation between aircraft and tanks so vital to early *Wehrmacht* success.

The Battle of Kursk

In surveying the Eastern Front in the spring of 1943 Hitler knew that he no longer had the resources for one short, victorious campaign. Faced with that situation, he planned to mount a series of punishing blows against the Soviet lines, first in the south-central part of the front at the

Kursk pocket and then north at Leningrad. Hitler expected these offensives to reduce Soviet reserves and allow him to hold the Eastern Front with fewer men.

Both sides now prepared for a showdown. Stalin's generals, above all Zhukov, persuaded him to let the Germans take the offensive while the Red Army prepared defenses in depth. The Germans also delayed. Their original plan was to attack once the spring weather allowed solid ground for tanks to maneuver, but German positions north and south of the Kursk salient remained vulnerable to counter-attack and a delay would allow these to be strengthened and time to bring up Tiger and new Panther tanks. Manstein, however, favored maintaining a flexible defense to wear down the Red Army 'to such an extent that it would tire of its already excessive sacrifices and be ready to accept a stalemate.' That would mean only a spoiling attack and counter-attack of a forthcoming Soviet spring offensive. It also involved yielding some territory, at least temporarily.[1]

Hitler refused to consider such a plan, however, demanding that the army cling to all territory it had taken. Manstein then planned a preemptive 'blow of limited scope' before the Red Army could recover from its losses of the previous winter campaign. Hitler recast this into an all-out offensive.[2]

This offensive, codenamed Operation CITADEL, was to be a classic double envelopment mounted against both shoulders of the salient. Army Group Center's Ninth Army would push south against the salient from near Orel, while Army Group Center drove north from near Belgorod. The two were to meet well to the east, behind Kursk, cutting off the salient entirely and destroying Soviet forces trapped in the pocket. Hitler sought a smashing psychological victory, one that would restore German prestige. Victory at Kursk, he said, 'must be a signal to all of the world.'[3]

Scheduled to begin in the first half of May, Hitler then delayed its start until June in order to strengthen the panzer divisions with new tanks. A number of German generals disagreed with this decision, including Colonel General Kurt Zeitzler, who had replaced Halder as army chief of staff and largely planned CITADEL. The two army group commanders involved, Günther von Kluge and Manstein, strongly opposed delay, which gave the Soviets additional time to fortify. Guderian opposed any such operation at all.[4]

Unfortunately for the Germans, 'the Red Orchestra,' the Soviet spy apparatus in Berlin, knew all about the German plans. The Soviets had learned of the basic outline of CITADEL in April and they made extensive preparations to meet it. The front-line defensive belt was two to three miles in depth. Secondary and tertiary defenses reached back up to 25 miles. The entire area was studded with bunkers and strong points, supported by massive amounts of heavy artillery and anti-tank guns, up to a million mines, and 5128 tanks and self-propelled guns. More than a million troops were in position. Four Soviet armies held the northern shoulder and six the south. Five armies remained in reserve. Five additional Soviet armies were north and south of the salient and could be shifted there as a last resort.[5]

The Germans had been able to make up many of their equipment losses, but their resources were still inferior to those of the Soviets. Field Marshal Model's Army Group in the north consisted of Ninth Army (four panzer and one army corps) and Second Army; while Manstein's Army Group South consisted of Fourth Panzer Army (three panzer corps) and Army Detachment Kempf. Altogether the Germans had available 780,900 men and 2928 tanks and assault guns.

When CITADEL finally began on July 5 it thus came up against heavily defended, well-prepared Soviet positions. The German offensive lasted from July 5 to 17, but if one considers the subsequent Soviet elimination of the Orel and Kharkov salients (beginning on July 10 and August 3 respectively) as part of the battle, it was actually the largest battle of the Second World War, lasting some 50 days. Kursk ultimately involved nearly 3.5 million men and 12,000 aircraft. With more than 10,600 tanks involved, it also saw the largest armor battles in history.[6]

Model's Ninth Army in the north enjoyed initial success, reaching the second Soviet defensive belt at the end of the first day. On July 6 the Soviet commander in the north, Marshal Rokossovsky, was forced to bring up reserves, and on the third day the German drive stalled well short of the final Soviet line. German attempts to break through were unsuccessful, and fighting then settled down to slow-moving attrition warfare. This played to Soviet defensive strength and minimized the chief German asset of mobility.

To the south Manstein's assaulting formations suffered heavy losses as they moved to their assembly areas in the pre-dawn hours of July 5. Fully informed of the German plans, Soviet commander General Nikolai F. Vatutin ordered a massive pre-emptory artillery bombardment that caught the German troops still deploying. Despite this setback, the German drive from the south enjoyed initial success. Manstein's troops broke through the first Russian defensive belt in a matter of a few hours, but were temporarily halted by a great thunderstorm that impeded tank movement. When the attack resumed, the Germans quickly realized the full extent of the Soviet defensive preparations. But, despite a heavy cost in men and equipment, Manstein's forces drove forward. By July 11 they had gone 25 miles, and on the next day the largest tank battle of the entire war occurred, at Prokhorovka. In it the Germans lost 300 tanks. The Soviets lost more, 400, but they managed to hold on. Their IL 2 Sturmovik aircraft proved invaluable; flying at very low altitude and firing rockets, they knocked out large numbers of the Tigers. The Germans called the IL 2 *Schwartz Tod* (Black Death).[7]

At this point other events influenced the battle. The British and Americans landed in Sicily and Mussolini's regime tottered on the verge of collapse. With the Soviets also threatening their own offensives north and south of Kursk, Hitler broke off the attack on July 13 to shift resources elsewhere, including reinforcing the Mediterranean. Manstein argued for continuation of the attack. He was so confident he could break through that he was prepared to commit his reserves, but Hitler refused. The German offensive was over. Two weeks of fighting cost the Russians 177,847 men out of 1,910,261 engaged and 1614 tanks of 4128 committed; the Germans had lost 49,822 of 780,900 men and an unknown number of their 2928 tanks. The extended Battle of Kursk cost the Soviets 863,303 out of 2,500,000 men engaged and 6064 tanks out of 7360. German losses in the extended battle are unknown. Key factors in the battle's outcome included Soviet foreknowledge of German plans, Hitler's postponement of the operation, the German failure to understand the extent of Soviet defensive preparations, harassment of supply lines by Soviet partisans, and the T-34 tank.[8]

Kursk proved the graveyard of the German panzer armies, and its outcome left the Soviets with the military initiative. The Red Army would now mount attacks all along the front – north, central, and south. Instead of using the German method of deep penetrations on a limited front with the aim of double envelopments, the Soviets mounted a series of wide-front offensives designed to push the Germans back. These, while lacking in imagination, were less risky and took advantage of superior Soviet resources in men and *matériel*. Stalin would utilize his 2.5:1 advantage in air power in a ground support role and his massive numbers of artillery pieces to push the Germans out of one position after another.

American Lend-Lease equipment now was arriving in the Soviet Union in prodigious quantities. A steady stream of planes, guns, vehicles, clothing, and food made its way to the Soviet Union through the Arctic Ocean and the Persian Gulf. Shipping losses via the Arctic remained prohibitive, so that the bulk of the aid came by ship via the Persian Gulf to Abadan and then by rail to Azerbaijan. The Red Air Force ultimately received 22,000 planes. The Red Army received 12,000 tanks; its soldiers moved in 375,000 US trucks and 51,000 jeeps, wore 34,000,000 uniforms and marched in 15,000,000 pairs of US boots. The Soviets received over $1 billion in US food, amounting to one half-pound per soldier per day.

The Soviets accepted this aid but provided no information to the West about their own industrial situation or war plans. When the Americans inquired, they found themselves treated more like German spies than allies. The Soviets also refused to grant the United States air bases on Soviet soil. This was in part not to alarm Japan, but it is also true that Stalin was far more wary of the Western powers than he ever was with Hitler. Even as he fought for survival against Germany, Stalin's preoccupation was with the West.

The Allied contribution to the Soviet war effort was indispensable but Soviet losses in the Second World War were tremendous. The leaders in the Kremlin never forgot that they lost more men in the Battle of Stalingrad than the United States lost during the entire war in all theaters combined. From June 1941 the Soviets had to contend most of the time with four-fifths of the German Army and never less than three-quarters of it.

The Soviet counter-offensive

Following the Battle of Kursk the Soviets held the initiative. The Red Army employed massed artillery fire and made excellent use of ground support aviation. It also effectively utilized an estimated 250,000 partisans behind German lines, a consequence of the brutal German occupation policies. Partisans attacked the lengthy German communication lines to the front, tied down large numbers of German troops away from the front, and over a two-year period, inflicted perhaps 300,000 casualties.[9]

The Soviet counter-offensive itself actually began on July 12 with a drive against the northern side of the Orel salient north of Kursk, although Model was able to prevent a Soviet breakthrough even though Hitler had authorized a German withdrawal from the salient. South of the Kursk salient, the situation soon became desperate for the Germans once the Red Army opened a drive there. Manstein warned Hitler that he must either provide substantial reinforcements or abandon the Donets Basin. Hitler refused either to reinforce or to authorize a withdrawal to the Dnieper, 150 miles to the west, where the Germans might have made a strong stand. The northern flank of Army Group South soon collapsed, and the Red Army retook Belgorod on August 5. Kharkov changed hands for the last time when it fell to the Soviets on August 21. Not until August 30 did Hitler authorize Manstein to withdraw, and ultimately the Germans were at the Dnieper. The Soviets had recovered an area some 150 miles deep by 650 miles wide, severed contact between German Army Groups South and Center, and secured much of Ukraine's valuable agricultural lands east of the Dnieper, as well as a strong bridgehead over that river, which could be used to resume their advance.

Soviet forces also cut off Axis forces in the Crimea. On October 9 the Soviets employed 45 infantry divisions, 3 tank corps, 2 mechanized corps, and 400 batteries of artillery against only 13 German and 2 Romanian divisions there. Kleist and Romanian dictator Ion Antonescu pleaded with Hitler to abandon the Crimea and allow Seventeenth Army to withdraw. Hitler refused and, by November, the Red Army had isolated the Crimean Peninsula. Steady Soviet military pressure prevented the Germans from stabilizing their front, and Kiev fell. Only the arrival of heavy rains saved the Germans in the south.

By now the heavily outnumbered German forces on the Eastern Front were in dire straits. The massive and constant Soviet attacks hammering one section after another the length of the front had depleted the defending infantry. The panzer divisions, rushed about to shore up gaps in the lines, soon were likewise a shambles, their equipment spent.

The Mediterranean

The Allied invasion of Sicily

In early July 1943, meanwhile, British, Canadian, and American troops invaded Sicily. At the Casablanca Conference in January 1943, US military leaders, most notably Army Chief of Staff General Marshall, attempted to secure British approval for a cross-Channel invasion in 1943. Churchill demurred and convinced Roosevelt to pursue operations in the Mediterranean against Italy. Attacking there would have the advantages of securing the Mediterranean, obtaining bomber bases closer to Germany, and perhaps driving Italy from the war. The Americans agreed on condition that such operations only involve those forces already in the theater. Then, at the TRIDENT Conference in Washington in May 1943, the Western Allies agreed to begin planning for a cross-Channel invasion to take place in May 1944, but the British continued pressing for operations in the eastern Mediterranean. They had important interests in the region, most notably the Suez Canal, and Churchill wanted to meet the Soviets as far east as possible and vindicate his failure at Gallipoli in 1915.

The Allied landings on Sicily were greatly assisted by an elaborate deception, Operation MINCEMEAT, orchestrated by British intelligence. A man who had died of pneumonia was identified as a fictitious 'Major William Martin.' A briefcase locked to his wrist carried a number of fictitious documents. The body, transported by submarine, was allowed to wash up on the Spanish coast and, as the British hoped, Spanish authorities turned it over to the Germans, who believed that Martin was a courier who had drowned when his plane had gone down at sea. German intelligence carefully studied the documents and concluded (the British did not want it to be too obvious) that the next Western targets would be Sardinia and islands in the eastern Mediterranean. Hitler then shifted resources to these two locations, thereby facilitating the invasion of Sicily.[10]

US General Eisenhower had overall command of Allied forces in the Mediterranean: British General Alexander, commander of Fifteenth Army Group, had command of the ground forces; British Admiral Andrew B. Cunningham commanded the naval forces; while Air Chief Marshal Tedder had charge of the supporting Allied air forces. British and US forces would participate in the invasion, code-named HUSKY, in almost equal numbers in the largest amphibious operation of the war. The operation involved 180,000 Allied troops and 2590 ships. Montgomery's British Eighth Army would come ashore in southeastern Sicily. It was then to advance along the coast, with the port of Messina on the northeastern tip of the island as its final objective. Patton's US Seventh Army would come ashore to the southwest, between Licata and Cape Scaramia, then move inland to protect Montgomery's left flank. Alexander assigned the newly formed Seventh Army the supporting role because he believed that Montgomery's veteran troops were better suited for the chief offensive role. The Allies enjoyed a 2:1 air superiority over the Axis, with 3700 aircraft as opposed to 1600.

For the defense of Sicily, Italian General Alfredo Guzzoni's Sixth Army had seven static coastal divisions and four maneuver divisions. Despite Hitler, German Mediterranean commander Field Marshal Kesselring believed that the Allies intended to attack Sicily, and he reinforced there. The Germans had Lieutenant General Hans Hube's XIV Panzer Corps of two divisions, and when the invasion began on July 10,

Kesselring committed two other divisions. Altogether, Axis forces on the island totaled between 300,000 and 365,000 men.

The invasion of Sicily was preceded by naval and air bombardment. The actual invasion began on the night of July 9/10, 1943, with the first large Allied deployment of airborne forces. A shortage of transport aircraft meant that only about 400 were available for both the British and Americans and only one US regiment (Colonel James Gavin's 505th) could be dropped initially, rather than the two Patton had wanted. High winds and faulty navigation resulted in widely scattered drops. Gavin claimed that only 425 of 3405 men in his total force actually landed as planned. Most of the men simply assembled as *ad hoc* units. Meanwhile, the British 1st Airborne Brigade departed Tunisia. Jumpy pilots receiving anti-aircraft fire released many early, and a large number of gliders crashed into the sea; of 137 gliders that left Tunisia, just 54 landed on Sicilian soil. Only slightly more than 100 men out of the initial force of 2075 were able to reach their objectives. Remarkably these few were able to accomplish the tasks assigned to the larger force.

The second airborne drop, on July 11, met with disaster. The Allied invasion fleet, despite having been warned, opened up on the second wave of transport aircraft in the mistaken belief that they were part of a German air attack a few minutes before. Sixty of the 145 C-47s in the second wave were hit, and 23 went down. In all the Allies had committed 9,163 paratroopers and gliderists to the invasion. Many were casualties but the effort had paid dividends. The airborne forces created confusion among the Axis defenders, who assumed that the total force was much larger than was actually the case. The paratroopers cut Axis lines of communications, and, despite light weapons, prevented German armor units, particularly the Hermann Göring Division, from reaching the beaches and pushing the Allies into the sea.[11]

On July 10 the seaborne invasion forces came ashore. Montgomery's plan had British forces driving due north to the port of Messina and accorded them the honor of entering it first. The Allied conquest of the island was eased considerably by previous Axis losses in Tunisia. Nonetheless, the defenders fought well, aided by hilly terrain and the command rivalry between Montgomery and Patton as they raced to Messina. A major controversy erupted when Montgomery expropriated an inland road that had been assigned to the Americans. This shift delayed the advance for two days and prolonged the campaign. Patton now swung west and captured Palermo before heading north in a series of short, costly, but well-executed amphibious flanking attacks along the north coast east of San Stefano.

Kesselring was determined to avoid a repetition of the heavy losses that befell the Axis in Tunisia, and early on he ordered plans drawn up for evacuation across the narrow strait to Italy. The evacuation began on August 4. Altogether the Germans evacuated 54,723 men, 9789 vehicles, and many tons of supplies. The Italians got off approximately 62,000 men and 227 vehicles. It was thus something of a hollow victory when, on August 17 Patton's forces reached Messina just hours after the last Germans had evacuated. Later that same day elements of the British Eighth Army entered the city.[12]

The conquest of Sicily cost the Allies 22,383 casualties. The Germans suffered some 5000 killed and perhaps 6000 captured; Italian losses are estimated at 2000 killed and 137,000 captured, most of the latter taken by Seventh Army. The Axis also lost up to 1850 aircraft against only 375 for the Allies.[13]

Although it had taken longer than anticipated and too many Axis troops had escaped, the Allied conquest of Sicily was both the first assault by the Western Allies upon Fortress Europe and their first real experience with coalition planning. As such, it established important precedents that would bear fruit a year later at Normandy. It also helped bring an end to Operation CITADEL in the Soviet Union, and it achieved its goal of driving Italy from the war. On July 24 the fascist Grand Council voted to remove Mussolini from office. The fascist era had ended, and a new government was established under Marshal Pietro Badoglio that secretly sought peace with the Allies. On September 3 the Badoglio government signed a secret armistice with the Allied powers, to go into effect five days later. Then on September 12, in a daring raid, German commandos under Captain Otto Skorzeny rescued Mussolini, and Hitler then installed his comrade-in-arms as nominal leader of German-controlled north Italy.

Invasion of Italy

In early September Alexander's 15th Army Group invaded Italy. On September 3 the British Eighth Army came ashore at Calabria, across the Straits of Messina from Sicily. Kesselring, unaware of the impending armistice, began an Axis delaying action. On September 8 the armistice went into effect. The Germans reacted quickly, disarming and imprisoning most Italian troops. They also secured the Italian ports, where some ships were scuttled by their own crews. These included 2 cruisers, 8 destroyers, 22 destroyer escorts, 10 submarines, 9 corvettes, and 215 minor and auxiliary units. By far the most serious loss was the battleship

Roma on September 9. The Italian fleet was steaming west of Corsica when it came under attack by German aircraft from southern France. The crews thought the attackers were Allied planes and were thus slow to take defensive measures. The *Roma* took a hit by a glide bomb in her forward magazine. The crew tried to fight the fire but, after 20 minutes, the magazine exploded and the ship was lost. The battleships *Doria* and *Duilio*, two cruisers and a destroyer, reached Malta on December 10, where they joined the main body of the Italian fleet from La Spezia.[14]

On September 9 the Eighth Army carried out a secondary landing at Taranto, and the Fifth Army commanded by US Lieutenant General Mark Clark came ashore at Salerno. The Allies wanted to take Salerno, located on the west coast of Italy, in order to secure the prize of Naples, just to the north. Clark and other Allied generals expected a short campaign – Italy having capitulated the day before, they expected to encounter no opposition. Clark planned to secure the beachhead, race to Naples and quickly secure it, then throw a line across the Italian peninsula from west to east, catching German forces in the south between the Fifth Army and Montgomery's Eighth Army moving north after its landings in the extreme south of the peninsula.

Virtually nothing went right for the Allies at Salerno. Only the weather was favorable. Indeed, the Italian campaign witnessed some of the fiercest fighting of the war. Allied staff planning was woefully inadequate, and Clark failed to weld his army (one British and one US corps) into a cohesive fighting force. The complacent Allies assumed they would meet only Italians. One of the leading divisions – the American 36th from Texas – had never seen combat and the Germans held the two British divisions of X Corps in low regard. The Germans also correctly divined Allied intentions and the exact location for the landing, and they easily took over the Italian defenses. The biggest mistake at Salerno was the decision to forego a preliminary naval bombardment. Clark wanted surprise, but this meant that the German defenses were virtually undisturbed when the Allies came ashore. Both sides then raced to bring up reinforcements. The Allies sought to build up strength so they might expand their front into the surrounding hills, but they were hampered by a shortage of landing craft. The Germans had the advantage of a shorter, overland, distance to travel, but they were slow to exploit Allied weakness, in part because of Allied air power.

Kesselring assembled six divisions and, on September 12, he launched an all-out attack on the center of the beachhead. The next day only intense land artillery, in some cases at point-blank range, and naval gunfire saved the beachhead. In this desperate situation three battalions of the 82nd Airborne Division were dropped onto the beachhead. Air support and naval gunfire were also increased. Montgomery, meanwhile, failed to apply maximum pressure from the south and stretch German resources. Despite orders from Alexander, Montgomery moved the Eighth Army forward at only a snail's pace, enabling the Germans to divert resources to Salerno, around which desperate fighting followed, but the Germans lacked the strength to push the Allies back into the sea. Nonetheless, it was October 2 before the Fifth Army took Naples, suffering 12,000 casualties along the way. German forces not only escaped the Allied trap but later established a heavily fortified line to the north across the Italian peninsula. Salerno was a harbinger of how much more heavy fighting lay ahead.[15]

The Italian campaign soon turned into a disheartening stalemate. Weather and geography (the narrowness of the peninsula and its high mountains and narrow passes) played their part, as did the skill of the defenders, above all Kesselring. The Germans also made a major investment of troops in Italy; indeed, in the winter of 1944 their numbers actually exceeded those of the Allies. By then the British and Americans were, on US insistence, concentrating troops in Britain for the approaching cross-Channel invasion.

Until early October the Allies consolidated their control over southern Italy. On September 27 the Eighth Army took Foggia and its large air base, then advanced to Termoli on the Adriatic, which fell on October 3. Meanwhile, Free French troops, assisted by the Resistance, took Corsica during the period September 11 to October 4.

The Germans briefly held up the Fifth Army at the Volturno by blowing the bridges over that rain-swollen river. Skilful German delaying actions bought time to bring up reinforcements and consolidate behind a formidable defensive line, known as the 'Winter Line' or the Gustav Line. Some ten miles deep, it ran from the mouth of the Garigliano River on the Gulf of Gaeta west along its swift-running tributary, the Rapido River, then over the mountains to the Adriatic north of the Sangro River. General Heinrich von Vietinghoff's Tenth Army held the Gustav Line.

The Fifth Army eventually got across the Volturno, but it soon found itself crowded into a small attack zone along the Rapido. The Allies registered some progress, but German resistance, difficult terrain, constant rain or snow, and a morass of mud all conspired to produce a stalemate by year's end. Given the location of the defensive zone, it was inevitable that Cassino would be its hub. It lay astride Route 6, the principal road from Naples to Rome, 80 miles to the north through the Liri Valley.

Allied landings at Anzio

On January 22, 1944, the Allies attempted to outflank the Gustav Line by landing north of it at Anzio on the west coast of Italy, just 25 miles from Rome. They hoped that this operation would divert German units from the Gustav Line, allowing a breakout and permitting the two Allied pincers to converge on Rome. Anzio was in fact an incredible opportunity thrown away. Codenamed Operation SHINGLE, and pushed by Churchill, the invasion proceeded virtually unopposed. Two days before it took place, the Allies launched a diversionary strike against Cassino and Kesselring had rushed two reserve divisions south from Rome. Consequently, when the Anzio invasion occurred there were no German reserves to meet a swift Allied thrust to Rome.

Clark had overall command of the Anzio operation, while Major General John Lucas led the actual invasion force. Lucas did get valuable amounts of supplies ashore quickly, which enabled the Allies to beat back subsequent German counter-attacks, but he was overly cautious and failed to take advantage of the temporary German weakness to secure the critical nearby Alban Hills. Although the US 504th Parachute Regiment was available for that purpose, Clark had vetoed its use.

The chief reason for the failure at Anzio was insufficient resources in the initial assault. This was owing to an agreement releasing landing craft and other assets from Italy to prepare for the upcoming Normandy Invasion. Lacking adequate resources at Anzio, the Allies would have been better off by mounting a decisive operation along the Gustav Line. The Anzio Beachhead soon developed into a precarious situation whereby the Allied forces were in danger of being hurled into the sea. The most famous comment on the situation was provided by Winston Churchill: 'I had hoped that we were hurling a wild cat onto the shore, but all we got was a stranded whale.'[16]

The bombing of Monte Cassino

Meanwhile, the Fifth Army was also held up outside Cassino. The elite German 1st Parachute Division held the high ground of Monte Cassino overlooking the valley. At the top of this 1700-foot peak, the last bastion of the Apennine Mountains, loomed the great monastery founded by St Benedict in 529. Regarded as the mother of all Christian monasteries, it had been destroyed many times over the centuries but repeatedly rebuilt. A powerful structure with 15-foot-thick walls and itself a work of art, the monastery housed many artistic treasures.

Allied troops stalled in the freezing mud of the valley below Monte Cassino became obsessed by the monastery and were absolutely certain the Germans were using it as an observation post. Although they were definitely entrenched farther down the slopes below the monastery, the Germans emphatically denied that their troops were using the building. In February 1944, in what came to be known as the First Battle of Cassino, troops of the US 34th and 36th divisions of the Fifth Army attacked at Cassino and managed to secure high ground northeast of the monastery, only to be driven out by February 11. When relieved by the 4th Indian Division, the two US divisions had taken between them 3900 casualties. The task of breaking the German line then fell to General Freyberg's New Zealand Corps, and Freyberg insisted on a preliminary aerial bombardment of the monastery.

In mid-February the monastery housed perhaps 800 civilians, five of them monks. Conditions were desperate; food and water were in short supply and typhoid had broken out. On February 14 the Allies dropped leaflets warning that the monastery would be bombed, but few heeded it, partly because the interval between the leaflet and bombing was short, the Allies not wishing to allow the Germans time to move out equipment presumed to be in the monastery. Just before 9:30 a.m. on February 15, 1944, the first of some 144 B-17 Flying Fortresses arrived over the monastery; it was the first time heavy bombers had been used in such close support of infantry. Later that day 112 medium bombers, Martin B-26s and North American B-25s, followed. The attacks killed about 300 people and destroyed the basilica.[17]

The bombing of Monte Cassino stunned the Roman Catholic world and provided a propaganda windfall for the Germans. Later Clark, who had authorized the bombing, said it was a mistake but placed the blame on Freyberg. The bombing also failed to turn the battle in favor of the Allies. If anything, it was a defensive bonanza for the Germans, who immediately moved into the rubble. They were soon subjected to another bombing attack, by 59 fighter bombers dropping another 23 tons of bombs.

The destruction of the monastery made no difference to the outcome of the Second Battle of Cassino, February 15–19. The main infantry attack did not occur until three days after the bombing, and the Gurkhas and New Zealanders were driven back. Subsequent massive Allied bombing of Cassino town made no difference either in what is known as the Third Battle of Cassino, March 15–25. This Allied air strike was followed by a heavy artillery barrage. New Zealand troops then entered the town's ruins, but poor communication, caused in part by sheets of rain, stalled the advance.

General Eaker's Mediterranean Allied Air Forces then undertook an interdiction campaign known as Operation STRANGLE to cut supplies to the German forces south of Rome, while a masterful Allied deception feigning an amphibious attack north of Rome led Kesselring to weaken the Cassino line. As a result, Allied troops there enjoyed a 3:1 advantage in manpower by May. Employing 2000 guns, they launched their assault on May 11. In Operation DIADEM British, Canadian, French, Polish, and US units smashed through a 20-mile zone between Cassino and the sea. The Poles occupied Monte Cassino monastery on May 18, shortly after the Germans abandoned it. At the same time the Allied strength in artillery, including naval gunfire support and air superiority, led to the break-out from the beachhead at Anzio on May 23.

Kesselring regrouped his forces north of Rome and declared it an open city. Alexander ordered VI Corps from the Anzio beachhead to cut off the Tenth Army's retreat, but Clark wanted Rome and thought the plan was a ruse by Alexander to let the British Eighth Army take Rome first. After the Anzio break-out, he changed the direction of the thrust so that he would have the glory of liberating the Eternal City and that this would occur before the Normandy Invasion grabbed the headlines. This decision, which dumbfounded subordinate commanders and was one of the most controversial of the war, allowed the Americans to enter Rome on June 4, but it also permitted the German Tenth Army to escape from the Gustav Line north to what became the Gothic Line. The subsequent Italian campaign tied down large German resources, but fighting there continued until May 2, 1945.[18]

Western Europe

The Normandy Invasion

Meanwhile, resources that might have gone to the Italian front were steadily drained off in preparation for the invasion of France. At the Teheran Conference in November 1943, Churchill, Roosevelt, and Stalin had agreed to a major cross-Channel invasion as well as a landing in southern France and a major offensive by the Soviets on the Eastern Front.

Fortress Europe and its coasts of Holland, Belgium and France bristled with all manner of German fortifications and booby traps. Organization Todt (named for Fritz Todt, the German civil engineer responsible for the autobahn system and the Siegfried Line, who had preceded Speer at the Ministry of War Production and Armaments and died in 1942) began erecting the Atlantic defenses in mid-1942. Over the next two years the Germans expended some 17,300,000 cubic yards of concrete and 1.2 million tons of steel in thousands of fortifications. They also strongly fortified the Channel ports, which Hitler ordered turned into fortresses. All this was for nought for, as Speer noted, the Allies came over the beaches and 'brought their own port with them . . . . Our whole plan of defense had proved irrelevant.'[19]

In what one author has called 'the greatest military engineering achievement since the Persian crossing of the Dardanelles by a bridge of boats in 480 BC, thousands of men labored in Britain for months to build two large artificial harbors known as 'Mulberries.' Hauled across the Channel from Britain and sunk in place, the Mulberries were designed to ease resupply. Their importance to the Allied cause may be seen in that by the end of October, 25 percent of stores, 20 percent of personnel, and 15 percent of vehicles had passed through Mulberry B.[20]

The Allies worked out precise and elaborate plans for the mammoth cross-Channel invasion to occur on the Cotentin peninsula in Normandy. British Admiral Bertram H. Ramsay had overall command of the naval operation, codenamed NEPTUNE, while Montgomery exerted overall command of the land forces. The object of the operation was 'to secure a lodgement on the continent, from which further offensive operations can be developed.'[21]

Prior to the landing, Allied air forces would carry out a massive bombing campaign to isolate Normandy. The landing itself would be preceded by a night drop of paratroops. General Marshall, an enthusiastic supporter of airborne forces, urged employment of five airborne divisions, but Eisenhower had his doubts and, as it worked out, only three were employed: the British 6th, and the US 82nd and 101st. The lightly armed paratroopers, operating in conjunction with the French Resistance, had the vital task of securing the flanks of the lodgement and destroying key transportation choke points in order to prevent the Germans from reinforcing the beaches. The German 21st Panzer and 12th SS Panzer divisions were stationed just outside Caen. If they reached the beaches, they could strike the amphibious forces from the flank and roll them up.

The amphibious assault would occur early the next morning after the airborne assault with five infantry divisions wading ashore along the 50-mile stretch of coast, divided into five sectors. The designated beaches were, from west to east, the US 4th Infantry Division (Utah), the US 1st Infantry (Omaha), the British 50th Infantry (Gold), the Canadian 3rd Infantry (Juno), and the British 3rd Infantry (Sword). It proved a vast undertaking. The airborne forces alone would require 1340 C-47 transports and 2500 gliders. Ten thousand aircraft would secure the skies, while naval support for the invasion would come from 138 bombarding warships, 221 destroyers and other convoy escorts, 287 minesweepers, 495 light craft, and 441 auxiliaries. In addition there were 4000 landing ships and other craft of various sizes.

Invasion commander General Eisenhower faced a difficult decision, given terrible weather in the days leading up to the planned landing. Informed by his chief meteorologist that a break in the weather should occur, Eisenhower decided to proceed. This decision also worked to the Allies' advantage, for the Germans did not expect a landing in such poor weather. The French Resistance was informed by radio code and the airborne forces took off. The drops occurred on schedule on the night of June 5/6, but thick cloud banks over Normandy that caused pilots to veer off course to avoid mid-air collisions, German anti-aircraft fire, jumpy flight crews, and Pathfinders who were immediately engaged in fire-fights on the ground and unable to set up their beacons, all led to premature drops and to paratroopers being scattered all over the peninsula. Some were even dropped into the English Channel, where they were dragged down by their heavy equipment. Gliders crashed into obstacles, and they and the paratroopers came down in fields that had been deliberately flooded by the Germans as a defensive measure. Much equipment was thus lost. Nonetheless, the wide scattering of forces caused confusion among the defenders as to the precise Allied objectives. Officers collected as many men as they could, and improvised units were soon moving on the objectives, most of which were secured.[22]

Success was likely if the Allies could establish a bridgehead large enough to build up their strength and overcome the German defenders. Once they broke out, the Allies would have the whole of France for maneuver, because their armies were fully mechanized and the bulk of the defending German forces were not. Rommel, who had charge of the coastal defenses, well understood that the German defense was doomed unless it could destroy the invaders on the beaches. He told Hitler, 'If we don't manage to throw them back at once, the invasion will succeed in spite of the Atlantic Wall.'[23]

Hitler did not understand this, and in fact he welcomed the invasion as a chance to get at and destroy the British and US forces. In Britain the Allied armies could not be touched; in France they could be destroyed. Hitler was convinced that the Allied effort would result in another Dieppe. Let them come, he said, 'They will get the thrashing of their lives.'[24]

The only possibility of German success was rapidly to introduce panzer reserves, but this step was fatally delayed by two factors. The first was Allied air superiority of 30:1 over Normandy, including large numbers of ground-support aircraft, especially the P-47 Thunderbolt and the P-51 Mustang. The second factor was Hitler's failure immediately to commit resources available elsewhere. Hitler was convinced that the invasion at Normandy was merely a feint and that the main thrust would come in the Pas de Calais sector. Allied intelligence played a key role in deluding him. The 'Double-Cross System' worked to perfection. Every German agent in Britain was either dead, jailed, or working for British intelligence. The British actually controlled the entire German spy network in the United Kingdom and used it to feed disinformation to the Germans.[25]

In Operation FORTITUDE the British orchestrated two deceptions prior to the Normandy Invasion. FORTITUDE NORTH suggested an invasion of Norway by a bogus British 'Fourth Army' headquartered at Edinburgh, Scotland. To convince the Germans the British employed radio nets, but they also created large numbers of decoy barges of canvas, wood, and wire; dummy gliders; and inflatable rubber tanks and trucks. Some German reconnaissance aircraft were then permitted to fly over them. This deception and perceived threat to his northern flank caused Hitler to shift some 400,000 men to Norway.

FORTITUDE SOUTH, on the other hand, was designed to convince Hitler that the landing at Normandy was only a diversion and that the major invasion would indeed occur later in the Pas de Calais. To this end the Allies created the 'First US Army Group' under Patton, still without command following an incident in which he had slapped soldiers suffering from combat fatigue in Sicily. The Germans expected the aggressive Patton would command any Allied invasion of the Continent. First US Army Group, a formation of 18 divisions and four corps headquarters, contributed nothing to OVERLORD.

Both deceptions involved feeding small bits of information to the Germans, some of it through the 'Double-Cross System,' and then letting the Germans draw the proper conclusions. The British plan worked to perfection. Not until late July did Hitler authorize the movement of the Fifteenth Panzer Army from the Pas de Calais to Normandy. In effect the deception totally immobilized 19 German divisions east of the Seine. Although units of Fifteenth Army were moved west to Normandy before that date, this was done piecemeal and hence they were much easier for the Allies to defeat. As Eisenhower reported to the Combined Chiefs of Staff:

> Lack of infantry was the most important cause of the enemy's defeat in Normandy, and his failure to remedy this weakness was due

primarily to the Allied threats levelled against the Pas de Calais. This threat, which had already proved of so much value in misleading the enemy as to the true objectives of our invasion preparations, was maintained after 6th June, and it served most effectively to pin down the German Fifteenth Army east of the Seine while we built up our strength in the lodgment area to the west. I cannot over-emphasize the decisive value of this most successful threat, which paid enormous dividends, both at the time of the assault and during operations of the two succeeding months. The German Fifteenth Army, which if committed to battle in June or July, might possibly have defeated us by sheer weight of numbers, remained inoperative throughout the critical period of the campaign, and only when the breakthrough had been achieved were its infantry divisions brought west across the Seine – too late to have any effect upon the course of victory.[26]

Meanwhile, the Normandy Invasion began. Some 2700 vessels, manned by 195,000 men were on the move. They transported 130,000 troops, 2000 tanks, 12,000 other vehicles, and 10,000 tons of supplies. At about 5:30 a.m. on June 6, 1944, the bombardment ships opened up against the 50-mile-long invasion front, engaging the German shore batteries. The first US assault troops landed 30 to 40 minutes later, while the British landing craft were ashore two hours later.

The landing was in jeopardy only on Omaha Beach where, because of rough seas, only 5 of 32 amphibious DD (duplex drive) tanks reached the shore. Support artillery was also lost when DUKWs amphibious trucks were swamped by the waves. Some landing craft were hit and destroyed, and those troops of the 1st Infantry Division who gained the beach were soon pinned down by a withering German fire. US First Army Commander Lieutenant General Bradley even considered withdrawal. At 9:50 a.m. the gunfire support ships opened up against the German shore batteries. Destroyers repeatedly risked running aground to provide close-in gunnery support; indeed, several destroyers actually scraped bottom. It was nearly noon before the German defenders began to give way. The 1st Infantry Division overcame German opposition with sheer determination reinforced by the knowledge that there was no place to retreat. The landings on the other beaches were much easier, and the Allies suffered surprisingly light casualties overall for the first day, of 10,000–12,000 men.[27]

A recent study suggests that a nighttime landing would have produced fewer casualties. The Allies had employed these with great success in the Mediterranean, but Montgomery believed that over-whelming Allied air and naval power would make a daytime landing preferable.[28]

The Allies put ashore a million men within a month. Eventually the United States committed 60 divisions to the battle for the Continent. The British and Canadians never had more than 20, and as the disparity grew so too did US influence over military and political strategy. No wonder Churchill was insistent that Montgomery exercise prudence and not sacrifice his men needlessly, which would reduce British influence even further.

Unfortunately for the Allies, during June 19–20 a Force 6–7 storm blew out of the northwest and severely damaged Mulberry A in the American sector. It also sank well over 100 small craft and drove many more ashore, bringing to a halt the discharge of supplies. Vital ammunition stocks had to be flown in. Mulberry A was abandoned, but a strengthened Mulberry B provided supplies to both armies until the end of the war.[29]

The Allied ground offensive, meanwhile, proceeded slower than expected. By ordering his armies to fight for every inch of ground rather than a withdrawal along phase lines as his generals wanted, Hitler at first delayed the Allied timetable. But this decision also greatly speeded it up at the end and ensured that the resultant defeat would be costly. Complete Allied air superiority devastated the Germans by day, forcing them to move largely at night.

The Normandy countryside proved ideal defensive terrain. Over the centuries the dividing lines between individual fields had been allowed to grow up into tangled hedgerows. This *bocage* resisted passage and slowed the Allied advance to a crawl. On June 17 and 18 the Germans blocked Montgomery's efforts to take the city of Caen. Major General J. Lawton Collins's US VII Corps had more success on the Allied right, gradually pushing across the base of the Cotentin peninsula. On June 18 it turned north to liberate the important port of Cherbourg, while the remainder of Bradley's army maintained an aggressive defense. Cherbourg fell on June 27, but its German defenders destroyed the harbor facilities, and it took Major General Lucius Clay six weeks to get them back in operation.

Not until the end of July were the Allies able to break out. In Operation COBRA (July 25–31) Bradley's US First Army forced the German line west of St-Lô, with Collins's VII Corps making the main effort. The attack, originally scheduled for July 24, was postponed until the next day, although some bombers could not be recalled in time and dropped their loads, costing Bradley the element of surprise. The rescheduled attack began at 9:40 a.m. on July 25 with a tremendous air attack. A total of 1900 heavy bombers, 400 medium bombers, and 440 fighter-bombers dropped more than 5000 tons of explosives to blast a gap in the German lines. Despite extra precautions with 'shorts' in bombing the day before, 35 heavy bombers and 24 medium bombers dropped their ordnance on US positions, killing 111 and wounding 490. Among those who died was Commander of US Army Ground Forces Lieutenant General Lesley J. McNair, present as an observer. After the bombing, Collins's tanks and infantry rolled through the German left flank. Patton had arrived in France on July 6, and two days after the start of COBRA Bradley ordered him to take command of VIII Corps headed toward Avranches. Moving two armored divisions into the lead side-by-side, Patton reached Avranches on July 31.[30]

On August 1 the US command was reorganized. Bradley moved up to command 12th Army Group, Lieutenant General Courtney H. Hodges assumed command of the First Army, and Patton's Third Army was activated. In the British zone of operations Montgomery's mostly British Commonwealth 21st Army Group consisted of Lieutenant General D. G. Crerar's Canadian First Army and Lieutenant General Miles C. Demsey's Second British Army. Patton's Third Army scored the greatest success, although he was fortunate to arrive in command at just the right time. The static warfare of the previous two months had finally passed into the mobile warfare at which he excelled. The weather was also dry and the flat terrain of northern France was ideal tank country. Patton took full advantage of circumstances. He was certainly the outstanding general of the campaign for France. Third Army displayed instant efficiency and soon had parlayed the local breakthrough of COBRA into a theater-wide breakout. Patton took risks but made them pay off. After the breakout Patton's Third Army turned west to clear out the Brittany peninsula, then turned back to the east after taking Brest. In a single month the Third Army liberated most of France north of the Loire River.

Operation DRAGOON

Meanwhile, the Allies launched Operation DRAGOON on the Côte d'Azur near Cannes in southern France. The operation had been planned largely to secure the large French Mediterranean ports for a rapid Allied build-up in France. Originally codenamed ANVIL and planned to coincide with D-Day, it had to be postponed because of a shortage of landing craft as a consequence of OVERLORD priorities and British reluctance to divert assets from Italy. On August 15, 4000 aircraft provided support while 860 Allied ships and 1370 smaller craft put ashore some 86,000 men and 12,000 vehicles on a 30-mile front 20 miles east of the French naval base of Toulon. The initial invasion force consisted of the three divisions of Major General Lucian Truscott's VI Corps. General Alphone Juin's I French Corps followed. The only British force was a 2000-man parachute brigade.

German Colonel General Johannes Blaskowitz had seven divisions to defend the Mediterranean coast but they were thinly spread and supported by only 130 aircraft and 600 artillery pieces. German resistance was weak and the Allies continued landing additional men and supplies. Lieutenant General Alexander Patch's Seventh Army ultimately consisted of seven US divisions and three French divisions. The invaders then pushed up the Rhône River Valley. By the time of the link-up with Bradley's 12th Army Group near the Swiss border in the fall of 1944, the southern Allied force had grown into the 6th Army Group under Lieutenant General Jacob Devers: 23 divisions in Patch's First Army and General Jean de Lattre de Tassigny's First French Army.

Some questioned DRAGOON's utility, but Eisenhower had no such doubts. It provided him two large, intact French ports that could be used to help supply the expanding Allied build-up in France. The operation was also successful for the Allies in terms of casualties. They sustained only 13,800 casualties while capturing 79,000 Germans.[31]

Paris was liberated at the end of August, a task wisely left to the French. Units of Major General Jacques Philippe Leclerc's French 2nd Armored Division entered the capital on the night of August 24. Paris was spared the fate of Rotterdam and Warsaw because the commander of greater Paris, General Dietrich von Choltiz, refused to use heavy weapons or air power to defend the city or to destroy it as Hitler ordered. Choltiz surrendered the city to Leclerc on August 25.

The Falaise-Argentan gap

The Allies now squandered a golden opportunity. Montgomery was making little progress, while Patton and his Third Army swung wide in an enormous enveloping movement that prevented German forces from consolidating along the Seine. Patton's rapid movement made possible the trapping of large numbers of two German field armies, including seven Panzer divisions, in the so-called Falaise Pocket. The destruction of these German forces was within the Allied grasp. To do so the Allied armies would have to span a 15-mile-wide gap between Argentan and

Falaise. Argentan had been assigned as a British objective but the Canadian First Army advanced very slowly. Near midnight on August 12 Patton learned that his forces had arrived at Argentan, and he sought permission from Bradley to drive north and close the ring on the Germans in the pocket. Bradley refused and ordered Patton to build up on the Argentan shoulder. All during August 13 Patton tried to secure authority to move north, link up with the British and Canadians and cut off the Germans, but he was not allowed to do so.

The pocket was finally closed on August 18. Although 60,000 Germans were killed or captured in the pocket, along with substantial amounts of arms and equipment, some 100,000 Germans escaped. Without Bradley's imposition of a delay, which gave the Germans from August 13 to 18 to extract their forces, the Allies might have bagged the lot and brought the war to an end in 1944. German forces in France now fought their way homeward under Allied pursuit. By August 31 Patton's Third Army reached the Meuse at Verdun, and the following day it gained the Moselle River. In the north Montgomery drove into Belgium, all the while complaining of shortages of supplies and fuel and pressing for a single thrust under his command into Germany itself.

Between the two Allied spearheads there was virtually nothing. Facing Patton's six strong divisions were five weak German divisions with few tanks or anti-tank guns. Facing the British was the hastily assembled German First Parachute Army, a scratch force of some 18,000 men, boys, and walking wounded. In the sector between Aachen and Metz the Germans had only eight infantry battalions. On the whole front the Germans had only some 100 tanks and 570 aircraft. In tanks and in aircraft the Allies had a 20:1 advantage.

Yet the Allied advance stalled. Their supply lines were lengthening while those of the Germans were contracting. The original Allied plan had been to consolidate on the Seine while opening the Brittany ports and establishing a sound logistical base, but that had been nullified by their unanticipated rapid advance after the St-Lô break-out. Much of the French railroad system had been destroyed by Allied air strikes, and the bulk of the supplies had to move from the Normandy beaches by road to the front. Despite the best efforts of the 6000 trucks of the US 'Red Ball Express,' supplies were simply insufficient for the broad-front strategy that Eisenhower insisted upon. The supply situation was made even worse by the needs of essential services for liberated French cities and towns, including Paris, which alone required 4000 tons of supplies daily. There were natural obstacles as well in the Vosges Mountains, the Ardennes, and the Hürtgen Forest.[32]

Another difficulty was the failure of the United States to field a heavy tank to match those of its German adversaries. US armor formations had to take on superior German tanks with the M-4 Sherman medium. While it had a power turret and was much more reliable than the German tanks, the M-4 was grossly inferior to them in two critical respects: it was both under-gunned and thinly armored. Dubbed by its crews the 'Ronson' for its tendency to catch fire easily (the Ronson cigarette lighter was sold with the motto 'Lights every time'), the M-4 had only a 75mm gun and 3.5 inch armor; the German tanks had heavier frontal armor and a much higher velocity gun; the Tiger, for example, mounted an 88mm gun. The German *Panzerfaust* anti-tank weapon could easily knock out the Shermans, whereas the US 2.36-inch Bazooka was only effective against German side armor. Also the Sherman tread mark was 14 inches; the Germans tanks had a much wider track of 30–36 inches and were not as easily bogged down. In the course of 1944–45 the 3rd Armored Division alone lost 648 Sherman tanks completely destroyed and another 700 knocked out, repaired, and put back into operation – a loss rate of 580 percent. The US lost 6000 tanks in Europe in World War II. The Germans never had more than 1500 tanks in the west.[33]

The M-26 Pershing heavy tank was not available until after the Battle of the Bulge. Patton was in part to blame; he insisted on concentrating on high production of M-4 Shermans, because the army needed a fast, medium tank and because he believed that 'tanks do not fight other tanks.' Patton counted on tank destroyers to protect the tanks. The US M-36 tank destroyer's 90mm gun had a muzzle velocity of 2850 feet per second, making it less powerful than the German PzKpfw VIb King Tiger's 88mm; nor could the M-36 shell penetrate the Tiger's 6-inch frontal armor. The M-36 also had only 1.5 inches of frontal armor and only 1 inch on its side. Its gun was also mounted in the open without a turret, making it vulnerable to artillery air bursts.[34]

Antwerp

By the end of August the German Army had suffered more casualties than at Stalingrad, roughly 500,000 soldiers and 1600 tanks in what was one of the greatest defeats in the history of warfare. One daring thrust through the north, south, or center might have proved decisive, but the Allies hesitated, bickered, and threw the chance away. In the view of German General Westphal, who in September 1944 became chief of staff on the Western Front:

The over-all situation in the West was serious in the extreme. A heavy defeat anywhere along the front, which was so full of gaps that it did not deserve this name, might lead to catastrophe, if the enemy were to exploit his opportunity skillfully. A particular source of danger was that not a single bridge over the Rhine had been prepared for demolition, an omission which took weeks to repair . . . . Until the middle of October the enemy might have broken through at any point he liked with ease, and would then have been able to cross the Rhine and thrust deep into Germany almost unhindered.[35]

There were two competing schools of Allied operational strategy: the narrow front and the broad front. Montgomery and Patton were the two leading proponents of the narrow front, provided it was for their own forces; Eisenhower wanted the broad front. Eisenhower, of course, had control over the flow of supplies and would make the ultimate decision.

By the end of August Allied logistics capabilities were stretched to their limit and beyond. Arguing that there were only sufficient resources for one major thrust, Montgomery pressed Eisenhower to halt Patton's Third Army and concentrate resources behind his troops and the US First Army. Montgomery believed he could make a quick end to the war, and he wanted the British to lead the charge and take Berlin. Patton wanted above all else to beat Montgomery to that prize. If anything, pressure on Eisenhower increased after September 1, when Churchill promoted Montgomery to field marshal. Technically, he now outranked Eisenhower (five stars to four).

While this discussion was in progress, Montgomery missed a golden opportunity to shorten the war. British tanks rolled into Brussels on September 3 and took Antwerp the next day, so rapidly that the Germans were unable to destroy its port facilities. Only the opening of the 45-mile-long Scheldt estuary stood between the Allies and relief of their growing supply difficulties. But Montgomery preferred to concentrate his troops for a thrust across the Rhine into northern Germany, over-looking the enormous logistical implications of Antwerp. The British were well positioned to bag the German Fifteenth Army. That sizable force had guarded the Pas de Calais and was now fleeing northeastward up the coast. An advance of less than ten miles beyond Antwerp would have sealed off the Walcheren and South Beveland peninsula, bottling up the Fifteenth Army. But Montgomery halted at Antwerp. Consequently, the Germans ferried the Fifteenth Army across the

Scheldt at night. It escaped to Walcheren Island and then back into Holland.

Operation MARKET-GARDEN

Eisenhower, who on September 4 assumed direct command of ground operations, restricting Montgomery to 21st Army Group, now had to decide between concentrating upon a narrow front or a broad-based attack in which the Allies would attack, regroup, and then attack again. While rejecting the narrow-front approach as too risky, Eisenhower nonetheless allowed Montgomery to proceed with a bold plan to end the war in one stroke.

Eisenhower biographer Stephen Ambrose believes this was one of the great mistakes of the war and perhaps the only real chance of ending the war in 1944. Ambrose concluded that, although Allied headquarters had always known that no major thrust could be made into Germany until Antwerp had been secured as a supply base, Eisenhower allowed Montgomery to ignore opening Antwerp in favor of getting a bridgehead across the Rhine. Ambrose is not alone in noting that the supreme commander of Allied Forces manifested an 'eagerness to be well liked, coupled with his desire to keep everyone happy.'[36]

But Eisenhower agreed to Montgomery's plan because he too wanted to get across the Rhine before the offensive's momentum was entirely spent. Also affecting the plan was pressure to use the three Allied Airborne divisions that had participated in the Normandy Invasion and were now recuperating in Britain. Unfortunately, Montgomery failed to carry out the detailed staff planning to make the plan work.

The plan was MARKET-GARDEN. MARKET was the airborne segment and involved three paratroop divisions: the US 82nd and 101st, and the British 1st. GARDEN, the ground portion, was centered in the British Second Army. The airborne forces were to secure key bridges over the Maas (Meuse), Waal, and Lek (Lower Rhine) rivers, then Second Army, led by XXX Corps, would race up a corridor from Belgium along a 60-mile long narrow causeway, over marshy ground, cross the rivers, and secure Arnhem on the lower Rhine.

Montgomery and his airborne commander, Lieutenant General Frederick Browning, selected the inexperienced British 1st Airborne to secure the farthest bridge, at Arnhem. The US 82nd and 101st received the easier tasks of securing the bridges at Nijmegen and Eindhoven respectively. The plan involved a high degree of risk, but the prize of outflanking the Siegfried Line (called the West Wall by the Germans) and entry into northern Germany, enabling 21st Army Group either to circle the Ruhr or proceed on to Berlin, seemed worth it. Success hinged on the 60-mile carpet of airborne troops, and the surprise was that it came from the conservative Montgomery.

In MARKET-GARDEN the dominant theme was over-confidence. In September 1944 many senior commanders including Montgomery saw Germany as tottering on the brink of defeat. Other factors in the failure of the operation include the refusal to modify the hastily developed plan. The Allies also failed to coordinate with the Dutch underground and simply ignored warnings by the Dutch as well as Ultra intercepts and late photographic evidence of the presence of the German 9th and 10th SS Panzer Divisions. These two battle-hardened divisions had recently transferred from the Eastern Front and were reconstituting and reequipping around Arnhem. Model, one of Hitler's best generals, was also there.

The actual land attack was along one narrow road, and the entire operation suffered from insufficient men and logistical support. Eisenhower might have helped solve the latter problem at least by halting Patton on the Meuse. But the greatest tactical mistake was to drop Major General Robert Urquhart's 1st Airborne Division 7–8 miles from the highway bridge at Arnhem, allowing German panzers to isolate it. Only about 500 men of the 10,000 men ultimately sent to Arnhem succeeded in reaching that bridge. (The Germans destroyed the railroad bridge.) In an airborne drop, paratroops must be landed on their target in order to control it, despite possible losses.

MARKET-GARDEN began on September 17 when the British 1st Airborne Division dropped beyond that 'bridge too far' at Arnhem, and the US 82nd and 101st Airborne floated out of the skies at Nijmegen and Eindhoven. It was the largest airborne attack of the war. In all, 34,000 paratroops were carried in 1400 planes (20,000 men on the first day), but three lifts over three days were necessary. Unfortunately, despite stringent prohibitions, an American officer carried a complete set of plans aboard one of the gliders. It crashed, killing him and the other occupants. Soon the plans were in the hands of General Kurt Student, commander of German paratroopers who happened to be in the area.

The 82nd and 101st achieved their goals, but the Germans delayed the advance of Lieutenant General Brian Horrocks's XXX Corps across Holland. The airborne troops at Arnhem, reinforced by the Polish 1st Parachute Brigade, which was dropped too late, had been expected to hold only two to three days. But only one battalion made it to Arnhem bridge before the Germans sealed the drop zone. Still, the British managed to hold out for nine days before evacuating across the Rhine at night. The operation ended on September 26. MARKET-GARDEN, which Montgomery later termed as '90 percent successful,' was, in fact, a failure. This operation to secure a salient that led nowhere and harder to defend than it was worth cost the Allies more than 17,000 casualties. The British suffered the most: 13,266 men, 7576 of whom were in the 10,005-man Arnhem force that included the Poles and glider pilots. German casualties were 7500–10,000, while the Dutch lost perhaps 10,000.[37]

By mid-September the Allied opportunity had been lost and the Germans had recovered sufficiently to slow the advance almost to a standstill. The task of forcing the Germans from the Scheldt fell chiefly to Lieutenant General Guy Simonds's First Canadian Army. To clear the estuary took two months of hard fighting and claimed nearly 13,000 Allied casualties, half of the them Canadian. Patton was also held up in a month of bloody fighting before the fortress of Metz. With the onset of bad weather, any chance for the Allies to win the war in 1944 was gone. The German lines now ran from the North Sea to the Swiss border and were centered on the old West Wall. The Germans not only managed to rebuild their shattered divisions but they brought new ones into the battle, so that they actually enjoyed a manpower advantage over the Allied Expeditionary Forces, although they were inferior to the Western Allies in numbers of tanks, artillery, and, above all, air power.[38]

Central Europe

The destruction of Army Group Center

While the Western Allied armies were pushing their way east through France in the summer of 1944, the Red Army was also advancing. In March and April 1944 the Soviets unleashed their own *Blitzkrieg*, first pushing the Germans back across the Bug, then across the Dniester and Prut rivers. During June to September they overran Byelorussia, destroying much of German Army Group Center in the process. This was a considerable achievement, largely ignored by Western historians of the war. As Jeremy Black notes, 'The Germans were outgeneraled and outfought, with the Soviets using effective deception to disguise their plans and also skilful infantry tactics.' In less than two-and-a-half years the Soviets had pushed the Germans back from the Volga to the Elbe, 'a greater distance than that achieved by any European force for over a century, and one that showed that a war of fronts did not preclude one of frequent movement of those fronts.'[39]

In their offensive operations the Soviets employed massive amounts of conventional artillery. They also utilized the BM 13 *Katyusha* multiple rocket launcher, Known as the 'Stalin Organ,' and mounted on rails in the back of a truck, it could fire a ripple salvo of 16 fin-stabilized 132mm rockets and be reloaded within 6–10 minutes. The Red Army also enjoyed a tremendous advantage in numbers of tanks and aircraft over its enemy, and its US-supplied trucks gave it great mobility. The few German aircraft available were simply unable to halt the Soviet ground advance or even provide adequate intelligence of Soviet intentions.

In their great Byelorussian Offensive the Soviets deployed the 1st, 2nd, and 3rd Byelorussian Fronts, supported by the Dnieper Flotilla and the First Polish Army attached to the 1st Byelorussian Front. Enjoying a great superiority in numbers, the Soviets smashed through the German defenses and carried out deep penetrations of the rear areas before the Germans could bring up reserves. During the period June 23 to August 29, 1944, along a more than 600-mile-wide front, the Soviets defeated Army Group Center and advanced from 300 to 360 miles. In the process the Soviets destroyed 17 German divisions and three brigades; 50 German divisions lost over half their strength. The OKW's official figure of losses was about 300,000 men or 44 percent of those engaged, but this figure may be low. Soviet losses were also high, more than 178,000 dead and missing alone (8 percent of the total force involved) and more than 587,000 sick and wounded.[40]

In the summer of 1944, the Soviets reached the Vistula River opposite Warsaw. Warsaw, a city of more than a million inhabitants scattered over 54 square miles, was vital to Russians and Germans alike. Seven main arteries traversed it, crossing the 600-foot wide Vistula River over three main road and two railway bridges. Soviet Army leaders encouraged the Poles to rise up against the Germans and promised aid. In response, on August 1, the secret Polish Home Army rose in rebellion and forced the Germans out of the city. Until October 3 General Taduesz Bor-Komorowski's embattled forces fought the Germans, while the Soviets did nothing to help. Perhaps 10,000 Germans and up to 300,000 Poles died in the abortive revolt, after which the Germans razed large areas of Warsaw. The city for which its people had fought no longer existed. The Soviets maintained that a pause in their advance was necessary because of supply shortages, but the convenient fact was that the Germans smashed the core of national Polish resistance, destroying the apparatus that was awaiting liberation to take over. This was of tremendous assistance in the imposition of a communist-sponsored regime later. Warsaw fell to the Soviets in January 1945, when they finally resumed their advance, and by early February most of Poland had been cleared of the Germans.

The Soviet advance was not simply on one axis. By the end of 1944 the Red Army had taken most of the Baltic states. It forced the capitulation of Romania in August, and of Finland and Bulgaria in September. Steady Soviet pressure all along the front prevented the Germans from launching meaningful counter-attacks. In October Soviet forces invaded Slovakia and went on to take most of eastern Hungary. Budapest fell on February 13, 1945, following a 49-day siege. In December 1944 Soviet forces actually crossed the German frontier.

In late autumn 1944, Hitler sought to encourage the German people to undertake one last major effort to win the war. Taking advantage of the temporary halt in military operations in the west, Hitler endeavored to create large new forces that might halt and then defeat the invaders closing on the Reich from both east and west. He also placed great store in military inventions, such as new submarines, jet aircraft, and the 'vengeance weapons' of the V 1 buzz bomb and the V 2 rocket, but they came too late to affect the outcome of events.

The Western Front

The Battle of the Hürtgen Forest

In the West, meanwhile, the US Army suffered one of its worst defeats in the September 12 to December 16, 1944, Battle of the Hürtgen Forest in the center of the West Wall. Even before the start of MARKET-GARDEN, Hodges's First Army of eight veteran divisions had breached the Siegfried Line in two places, including Aachen just north of the Hürtgen Forest. Hodges intended to attack north of the forest across the flat open Rhine plain, closing to that river at Köln (Cologne). But he also believed that not securing the Hürtgen Forest would leave his right flank dangerously exposed. With its deeply wooded ravines, the Hürtgen Forest was ideal defensive terrain, and by releasing water from dams along the Roer River in the middle of the forest, the Germans could flood the Rhine plain and halt military movement for weeks. Field Marshal Model, overall German commander for the campaign, fought a brilliant battle and the Germans, who were now defending their own homeland, resisted with great tenacity.

On December 16 the Germans launched their Ardennes Offensive immediately to the south, bringing the Hürtgen Forest Campaign to a close. US forces had suffered 33,000 casualties and had nothing to show for their sacrifice. Although the Germans probably sustained more casualties than the Americans in the Hürtgen Forest fighting, they had held the vastly better equipped attackers in place for three months.[41]

The Battle of the Bulge

Hitler now readied an offensive in the West. With the Eastern Front static for several months and the Allied offensive in the West gaining ground, in September 1944 Hitler conceived of a sudden offensive to take the Allies by surprise, break their front, and recapture Antwerp. He hoped at the very least to buy three to four months to deal with the advancing Soviets. Western Front commander Field Marshal von Rundstedt thought the plan was unrealistic, as did other high-ranking officers. But Hitler refused to change his mind and substantial German forces were transferred from the Eastern Front to the west for what would be the biggest battle fought on the Western Front in World War II and the largest engagement ever fought by the US Army.

On December 16, 1944, in pre-dawn darkness and fog, the Germans began their counter-offensive. Hitler could not have selected a better location than the Ardennes. Allied forces in the area were weak, as Eisenhower had deployed most of his strength northward and southward, and bad weather restricted the use of Allied air power. In an exceptional achievement the Germans marshaled, without Allied knowledge, 250,000 men, 1420 tanks and assault guns, and 1920 rocket and artillery pieces, along with 2000 planes.

The attack took the Allies completely by surprise. They had assumed that only they could launch an offensive. Initially, Bradley and Patton did not assess the offensive as major. Eisenhower did, and on its second day he ordered the battle-weary 82nd and 101st Airborne divisions out of a reconstitution camp in France up to the front. Traveling in trucks, the 101st arrived at midnight December 18 near Bastogne, Belgium, a small town but an important road hub. The German force of 24 divisions pushing against three divisions of Hodges's First Army soon drove a 'bulge' in the American defenses, which gave the battle its name. The German penetration eventually extended 50 miles deep and 70 miles wide.

The invaders flowed around Bastogne, heading northwest toward the Meuse. Model correctly sought to have Fifth Panzer Army make the main effort, but Hitler, ignorant of the situation on the ground, insisted that this go to SS General Josef 'Sepp' Dietrich. On the north shoulder of the bulge, the 1st Infantry Division dug in. The Americans massed 348 artillery pieces that shattered the German attack. In the center, groups in mostly isolated formations stood firm, further impeding the German advance. Meanwhile, Patton's Third Army rushed to the rescue from the south. Patton had anticipated the German attack and ordered his staff to prepare for just such a contingency. He told an unbelieving Eisenhower that he could wheel his army 90 degrees and strike north into the bulge with three divisions in only two days. He accomplished this feat in one of the most memorable mass maneuvers of that or any war.[42]

Other Allied resources were also diverted to the Ardennes, and on December 23 a weather change moved over the front, clearing the sky and freezing the ground, making the terrain passable for armor. Allied planes filled the skies and transports dropped supplies to Bastogne, which was down to only ten rounds per gun. On Christmas Day, the German panzers ground to a halt, out of fuel, while 2nd Armored Division gunners had a turkey shoot at Celles, almost at the Meuse, destroying 82 German tanks. On December 26 Lieutenant Colonel Creighton Abrams's tanks of the 37th Tank Battalion of the 4th Armored Division lifted the siege of Bastogne.

Unfortunately, Montgomery had decided to stay on the defensive, overruling US General Collins's plan to cut off the bulge by striking from each shoulder. Finally, the Allies attacked midway up the salient, passing up the chance to surround the Germans. Patton believed that timidity on the part of Eisenhower and Montgomery allowed most of the Germans to escape. Said Patton, 'The only way you can win a war is to attack and keep on attacking . . . .'[43]

Patton noted, 'Monty is so slow and timid that he will find a German build-up in front of him and stall.' Montgomery portrayed the battle as an Anglo-American affair and implied that the British had saved the Americans. Winston Churchill set this right in a speech to the House of Commons on January 18 when he said that 'United States troops have done almost all the fighting, and have suffered almost all the losses.'[44]

On January 1, 1945, the Germans mounted a surprise attack on Allied air bases in Belgium. Operation BODENPLATTE (base plate) destroyed 500–800 Allied aircraft, most of them on the ground, but it also resulted in about 300 German aircraft shot down and 214 trained pilots lost, many of them to German anti-aircraft fire. The Allies could replace their losses; the Germans could not. The Battle of the Bulge dragged on to the middle of January. Prior to that point Hitler ordered part of the panzer divisions transferred back to the east. Before the Germans could switch these resources, the Soviets launched their last great offensive. In effect the Ardennes Offensive hastened the end of the war.

By the end of January the American First and Third Armies had reached the German frontier and reestablished the line of six weeks before. The Battle of the Bulge had been fought and won largely by American forces. Of the 600,000 US troops involved, 19,000 were killed, about 47,000 were wounded, and 15,000 were prisoners. Among 55,000 British engaged, casualties totaled 1400, of whom 200 were killed. The Germans, employing nearly 500,000 men in the battle, sustained nearly 100,000 casualties killed, wounded, and captured. Both sides suffered heavy equipment losses, about 800 tanks on each side, and the Germans lost virtually all their aircraft committed. But again the Western Allies could quickly make good their losses, while the Germans could not.[45]

Deaf to all reason, Hitler categorically forbade retreat. If it was unavoidable, then everything that could be of use to the enemy had to be destroyed. The fate of his people was irrelevant, for Hitler concluded that if the Germans were unable to win, then they did not deserve to survive.[46]

On March 7, 1945, in an important move, Bradley's forces captured intact a German bridge across the Rhine at Remagen and immediately exploited the opportunity. In the west the Germans now had fewer than 60 understrength and poorly equipped divisions to oppose 85 well-equipped Allied divisions. On March 23 Patton pushed his 5th Division across the Rhine at Oppenheim, a surprise move that cost only eight American lives. With both Patton and Hodges making solid progress, Eisenhower now ordered Bradley's 12th Army Group to make the main thrust, pushing through central Germany and ignoring Berlin, on which the Soviets were advancing. The Ninth Army would encircle the Ruhr while the remainder of Montgomery's 21st Army Group covered Bradley's drive by moving northeast to secure the German North Sea provinces of Schleswig-Holstein and the Baltic port of Lübeck, cutting off German forces in Denmark and Norway. Lieutenant General Devers's 6th Army Group, meanwhile, provided right-flank security for Bradley, advancing down the Danube to secure the so-called *Alpenfestung* or National Redoubt. The Ruhr was encircled on April 1 when elements of the Ninth and First Armies met at Paderborn. The Ninth Army then reverted to Bradley's control and he sent it eastward. On April 11 the Ninth reached the Elbe near Magdeburg.

Meanwhile, early in 1945 Soviet forces had entered Czechoslovakia and Hungary, and began driving into Germany. Stalin was convinced the

British and Americans wanted Berlin, and he was determined that the German capital would be taken by Soviet forces. While telling Eisenhower that he considered the German capital of no importance, Stalin concentrated his resources and goaded his commanders toward that very end.[47]

US forces might have taken both Berlin and Prague, and airborne forces were poised for an assault on the German capital, but Bradley estimated that taking Berlin would have cost the United States 100,000 casualties. Berlin was deep inside the designated Soviet zone of occupation and would, in accordance with previous agreement, soon pass to their control. Bradley's estimate of the cost of taking Berlin was not off the mark. According to one important study, The 'Berlin Strategic Offensive,' lasting from April 16 to May 8 and involving the 1st Byelorussian, 2nd Byelorussian, and 1st Ukrainian Fronts, produced the staggering total of 352,475 casualties (78,291 dead), an average of 15,325 a day.[48]

The end was fast approaching, and the Allied effort might best be characterized, despite hard fighting, as a mopping-up operation. Stalin ordered Zhukov's 1st Byelorussian Front to make the final drive on Berlin. On April 22 the Soviets entered the German capital and three days later surrounded it. That same day, April 25, elements of Bradley's 12th Army Group linked up at Torgau on the Elbe with Soviet Marshal Ivan Konev's 1st Ukrainian Front forces, which Stalin had diverted to prevent a possible push by the Western Allies into eastern Germany. On April 28, as they attempted to flee the country, Mussolini and his mistress were captured in north Italy by the anti-Fascist resistance and shot. Later their bodies were hung upside down in a public square in Milan. That same day Hitler married his mistress, Eva Braun, in the Berlin command bunker. Two days later, on April 30, they committed suicide. Berlin surrendered on May 2. The next day US elements of Montgomery's 21st Army Group linked up with Marshal Rokossovsky's 2nd Byelorussian Front at Wismar. Rodion Malinovsky's 2nd Ukrainian Front moved from Hungary into Austria and Czechoslovakia and was preparing to link up with Patton's advance down the Danube near Linz. On May 7 Hitler's designated successor as chief of state, Admiral Dönitz, surrendered all German forces unconditionally to the Allies, with a formal ceremony the next day. After nearly six years of fighting, the guns fell silent. The war in Europe was over.

11

The Defeat of Japan

Although the Japanese advance had been halted in the Solomons in February 1943, Tokyo regarded this as merely shifting from the offensive to the defensive in accordance with prewar planning. Losses on Papua and Guadalcanal had been unexpectedly heavy but these could be replaced. Midway was another matter; the sinking of four fleet carriers was a heavy blow. Equally serious was the loss of so many well-trained carrier pilots there and in the air battles over Guadalcanal. Tokyo hoped to make good these shortfalls while American forces themselves suffered heavily in attempting to capture the fortified islands constituting the Japanese defensive ring. Tokyo anticipated that casualties from a prolonged campaign would cause the American public to lose heart and pressure Washington to recognize the Japanese conquests.

There was utterly no sentiment in the United States, or in Britain, for a negotiated settlement with Japan or any of the Axis powers. The Allies sought total victory and toward that end had agreed that their principal focus would be Germany. But unexpected early successes against Japan and the fact that, for the time being at least, no invasion of the European continent was possible, meant that additional naval resources and also troops were available for use in the Pacific. Among Allied military leaders, US Admiral Ernest King was especially determined to increase the momentum of Pacific operations. Thus there was a partial deviation from the original Allied strategy of concentrating against Germany. That the United States was able to step up its Pacific timetable was proof positive of its incredible industrial capacity.

The China-Burma-India theater

The China-Burma-India theater (CBI), which was under overall British command from India by Field Marshal Sir Archibald Wavell (promoted

279

to that rank in February 1943), remained a major theater of war, although the United States was little interested in it. Actually the bulk of the Japanese Army was committed to the Asian mainland in this area.

The Japanese anchored the western frontier of their empire in the mountains and jungles of Burma. In India, Brigadier General Orde Wingate obtained Wavell's permission to use a brigade to carry out his plan of 'long-range penetration.' Wingate believed that small British ground forces, supplied by air, could operate for extended periods deep behind Japanese lines, cutting lines of communications, destroying supplies and creating confusion. During February–May 1943 Wingate's 77th Indian Brigade, known later as the 'Chindits' (their emblem was a *chinthe*, a mythical Burmese beast resembling a lion, and they operated beyond the Chindwin River), conducted a raid behind Japanese lines in Burma, then fought its way out again. While not accomplishing much militarily, the raid embarrassed the Japanese and raised Allied morale in a theater heretofore characterized by defeat.

Promoted to major general and securing Churchill's full support, Wingate planned an even more audacious raid. This included three brigades supported logistically by the USAAF. The operation involved 25,000 men, of whom 3000 were Americans (led briefly by Brigadier General Frank Merrill, the US force was known as 'Merrill's Marauders'). The March 1944 raid began with high promise, but the whole venture was doomed from the start since its success rested on the active participation of Chinese divisions. These forces were being husbanded by Chinese leader Jiang Jieshi, who drove his chief of staff, US Lieutenant General Stilwell, who also commanded all US forces in the CBI, to distraction. In secret instructions to his generals, Jiang sharply limited Chinese military involvement, which in any case proved to be ineffectual. Another factor in the raid was the death of Wingate in a plane crash in India on March 24, whereupon Stilwell controlled operations. Wingate and Stilwell were much alike – both eccentric and dynamic – but they seldom disclosed their intentions and as a result there were serious failures in planning and staff work. Stilwell, in fact, did not like the British and did not use the Chindits effectively. Nor did he understand the difficulties facing guerrilla forces while dependent on aerial resupply but operating as conventional units.

The Japanese, heavily outnumbered in the air and lacking other modern weapons, fought back with considerable tenacity. Finally, the monsoon rains that began in mid-May slowed the offensive and brought more malaria. By June the chief enemy was not the Japanese, but exhaustion, malnutrition, and disease. Although the raid inflicted 50,000

Japanese casualties against only 17,000 for the British, Allied forces were obliged to withdraw from Burma in July. Since it was ultimately not successful, the 1944 Burma campaign has remained controversial. Unfortunately for all involved, it had no practical effect on the outcome of the war.[1]

The lack of Chinese support in this operation displeased US leaders, who had hoped that Nationalist armies would tie down the Japanese forces. But Jiang seemed more preoccupied with building up his own strength so that he could do battle with his domestic opposition, the Chinese communists, after the war. Washington's realization that it could not count on Jiang to fight the Japanese meant increased support for forces under Nimitz in the Central Pacific and MacArthur in the Southwest Pacific.

In the spring of 1944 Japanese forces actually invaded India. After much hard fighting, Lieutenant General Slim's Fourteenth Army halted Lieutenant General Mutaguchi Renya's U-GO offensive before Kohima and Imphal during March–July 1944. Slim was one of the best generals of the war. He warned his officers that they must tend to the needs of their men or they would be broken in front of their regiments. Slim was a tough commander and would not allow units to surrender. In central Burma Slim effectively utilized aerial resupply to mount an offensive in December 1944 that brought success in the Irrawaddy Valley. By January 1945 Allied troops reopened the Burma Road. Slim's forces took Mandalay in March and Rangoon in May 1945. Terrain and climate, as well as disease, remained formidable obstacles in the CBI theater of war.

Central Pacific naval operations

Meanwhile, the Americans were building up their Pacific naval strength. By the end of 1943 Nimitz had seven Essex-class aircraft carriers in commission. Ultimately, 24 were built, three of which were commissioned after the war. Displacing 27,200 tons, they were 820 feet long, 87.2 feet wide, and capable of 32.7 knots. Cruising range was 15,000 miles at 15 knots. The Essex-class ships mounted 12 x 5-inch guns along with 32 x 40mm and 46 x 20mm anti-aircraft guns. Designed to carry an air complement of 91 aircraft (36 fighters, 37 dive-bombers, and 18 torpedo-bombers), the Essex-class carriers in fact frequently operated as many as 100 planes in combat. The US Navy traded armor – its carriers had wooden flight decks – for speed. British carriers of the same size with steel decks could absorb great punishment, as they demonstrated time and again, but they carried fewer planes. The four British Illustrious-class carriers displaced 23,000 tons, were 673 feet long, and carried only 36 planes.[2]

Nimitz also acquired new fast battleships. These performed valuable roles as anti-aircraft platforms to protect the carriers and in shore bombardment, even while being held ready for possible fleet actions. The slow battleships did shore bombardment exclusively, save in the Battle of Leyte Gulf. The fast battleships carried three spotter aircraft each and could thus assist in reconnaissance. They also served as oilers, being able to keep up with the carriers.

At the May 1943 TRIDENT Conference, held in Washington, the Combined Chiefs of Staff worked out a three-phase strategy for defeating Japan. The first phase was to cut Japan off from the oil resources of South Asia; the second was to open a strategic bombing campaign against the Japanese home islands; and the third consisted of an outright invasion.

Admiral King in Washington and Nimitz at his Pearl Harbor Headquarters now worked out a plan for a Central Pacific offensive. Carrier task forces would take the lead in striking Japanese-held islands, which would then be secured by marine and army amphibious forces. This would be carried out in a methodical approach on a definite timetable and at the smallest possible cost in American lives. Japan's material resources were fast diminishing, but Japanese determination appeared to increase with every island-hopping step towards the home islands. Typically, these island strongholds would first receive bombardment by surface ships and carrier aircraft, and if possible, from land-based aviation. Marine assault forces, supported by army troops, would then go ashore and secure possession. Despite careful planning and the fleet train concept, logistical problems were staggering and governed strategy because of the need to first secure bases.

Admiral Spruance's US Fifth Fleet consisted of a number of task forces supported by fleet trains and landing craft. By mid-1943 it had become an armada of more than 200 ships and 1500 aircraft. The smaller escort ('jeep') carriers proved invaluable in getting reinforcements forward much earlier than otherwise would have been the case. (Designated CVE, their crews claimed this stood for 'Combustible, Vulnerable, and Expendable.') The Pacific build-up was rapid, and by the end of 1943 nearly two million American military personnel were in the Pacific, more than in the European theater.

The year 1943 saw the effective end of Japan's fine naval air arm. The trained pilots were consumed at Midway and in Operation CARTWHEEL in the Solomons, and replacements received but little training. The Japanese also continued to rely on the old Zero, once superior to any Allied fighter in the Pacific, including the US Navy F4F Wildcat. But in 1943 the United States began deploying the new Grumman F6F Hellcat, the gull-winged Vought F4U Corsair, and the Lockheed P-38 Lightning, all generally superior to the Zero and other aircraft in the Japanese arsenal.

On April 18, 1943, after codebreaking revealed Admiral Yamamoto's inspection-tour itinerary, long-range P-38s intercepted and shot down two Japanese bombers carrying him and his staff from Rabaul to Bougainville. Admiral Koga Mineichi succeeded him as commander-in-chief of the Combined Fleet.

With Allied victories on Guadalcanal and New Guinea, the great Japanese base of Rabaul in northern New Britain Island seemed the next objective. Rabaul anchored the southeastern portion of the Japanese defensive ring. Admiral Halsey's forces of the South Pacific Area, designated the US Third Fleet, were then shifted from Nimitz to MacArthur for a two-pronged Allied offensive against Rabaul. Halsey's forces would push northwest through the Solomons, while General Walter Krueger's US Sixth Army, under MacArthur's supervision, would advance northward through northeast New Guinea and New Britain toward Rabaul. Halsey, while under MacArthur, was nonetheless dependent upon Nimitz logistically to conduct operations. All cooperated to make this campaign work effectively.

Leapfrogging

A system of 'island hopping' was begun, but the pace of the advance was slow for both MacArthur in New Guinea and Halsey in the Solomons. At that rate it would have taken the Allies ten years to reach Japan and the Japanese strategy of wearing them out might have worked. But in July 1943 'leapfrogging' was substituted, designed to hit the Japanese where they were not in force. Since Rabaul had always been MacArthur's objective, it shocked him when in late July 1943 Marshall suggested that he leapfrog Rabaul instead of assaulting it. Then the next month the Combined Chiefs of Staff at the Quebec meeting directed Halsey and MacArthur to do just that. This major leap proved to be fortunate, as Rabaul had 100,000 defenders and stockpiles of supplies for various invasions that had not taken place. It thus had ample provisions and weapons and would have been costly to secure. Now, Rabaul would simply be isolated and allowed to wither on the vine. MacArthur's naval forces were also reorganized in January 1943 as the Seventh Fleet under Vice-Admiral Arthur S. Carpenter, replaced in August by Vice-Admiral Kinkaid. It and its subordinate VII Amphibious Force played a key role in supporting MacArthur's subsequent amphibious operations.

The marines took the lead. In the 1920s the Corps had come under attack. Many, especially in the army, thought it superfluous and wanted it disbanded. The largest amphibious operation of World War I, the Allied invasion of Gallipoli in Turkey in 1915, had been a failure, and many observers concluded that assaults of fortified positions from the sea were over. But others, particularly Marine Lieutenant Colonel Earl H. Pete Ellis, saw that the key to winning a Pacific war would be base seizure and defense. A war with Japan meant, *ipso facto*, that the marines would end up fighting their way back across the Pacific, retaking the outpost bases. Ellis believed that the marines should prepare to 'execute opposed landings and attacks on denial positions . . . with the greatest rapidity.'[3]

By 1921 Ellis had outlined the problems of conducting assaults in the Marshall and Caroline Islands, but he was also confident that with proper training the Marine Corps could storm defended beachheads. Opposed landings could succeed if ship-to-shore movement by assault craft was rapid and supported by concentrated naval gunfire and air power. Securing the beach would be the key. Assault troops would require high-firepower weapons but also new landing craft or amphibious vehicles armed with machine guns and light cannon. Close-in naval gunfire could help neutralize enemy shore positions. Ellis disagreed with those who advocated night assaults to minimize casualties. He believed attacks would have to occur in the daytime, in order to minimize confusion. To be successful the assaults would require careful planning, preparation, and coordination.[4]

Ellis had provided the doctrine. All that was now required was the will to implement it, proper training, and some new equipment. The marines began experimenting with amphibious operations, and they contracted for specialized landing craft. These latter eventually included the incredibly successful LSTs (landing ship, tank) and LSIs (landing ship, infantry) and smaller LCIs (landing craft, infantry) that were so important in the war, especially in the Pacific. The marines also utilized LVTs (landing vehicle, tracked, or amtrac), true amphibians, to carry their forces and supplies from troop ships across the beaches of Japanese-held islands. Amphibious operations became the *raison d'être* of the US Marine Corps, which became the world's greatest practitioner of them.

Isolation of Rabaul

In early October 1943 the Japanese strongholds in eastern New Guinea fell, paving the way for an invasion of New Britain. On December 15 VII Amphibious Force landed elements of the US 1st Cavalry Division in southern New Britain. On December 26 the 1st Marine Division came ashore at Cape Gloucester on the northwestern part of the island and, in four days of heavy fighting, secured it and two airfields. Seizure of Kavieng in New Ireland, Manus in the Admiralties, and the St Mathias Islands north of New Britain Island during February–March 1944 completed the isolation of Rabaul.

East of Rabaul, in the Central and North Solomons, in July 1943 US infantry and marines landed on New Georgia Island, taking it the next month. In August they leapfrogged Japanese-held Kolombangara to land on Vella Lavella, which they secured by October. Japanese control in the Solomons was now limited to the islands of Bougainville and Choiseul. On November 1, after feinting an attack on Choiseul, marines landed on Bougainville and established a major naval base on Empress Augusta Bay, complete with three airfields. In November US carriers launched two air strikes on Rabaul and inflicted heavy damage to the port, sinking and damaging a number of ships. Throughout this period US land-based and naval aircraft continued hammering away at Japanese air bases around Rabaul and inflicting heavy losses in air combat as well.

In April 1944 the US 24th and 41st Infantry Divisions landed near Hollandia and Aitape on New Guinea. This brilliantly planned and executed operation encircled Lieutenant General Imamura's Japanese Second Area Army and, at a cost of about 100 Americans dead and 1000 wounded, killed more than 5000 Japanese. In May US forces took Wakde but its soil proved unsuitable for heavy bomber operations so, during May and June, in a hard-fought action that claimed 2700 American casualties and nearly 10,000 Japanese, the 41st Infantry Division secured the island of Biak. In July the island of Noemfoor also fell to the Americans, providing additional air bases. During this period MacArthur pressed the offensive on New Guinea, and by July 1944 Japanese forces there had been routed.

Meanwhile, Fifth Fleet was readying strikes throughout the central Pacific. Admiral Spruance assembled the largest US naval task force to date: 8 carriers, 7 battleships, 10 cruisers, and 34 destroyers. Its subordinate Fifth Amphibious Force under Rear-Admiral Turner lifted the V Amphibious Corps commanded by Marine Major General Holland M. ('Howlin' Mad') Smith. Supporting this were land-based aircraft of Major General Willis A. Hale's Seventh USAAF. Nimitz also worked out a system whereby staffs rotated in command of the fleet. When Spruance and his staff were in place, it was designated Fifth Fleet; when Halsey had command it was Third Fleet. This system worked perfectly, giving staffs some down time and the opportunity to plan the next strike, which they would then execute.

The Gilberts

Nimitz's initial target was the Gilbert group, consisting of 16 atolls straddling the equator, just across the international date line. The Japanese defense centered on the two atolls of Tarawa and Makin. About 100 miles apart, both atolls are ringed with coral reefs. The Japanese had constructed a small airfield on Betio, Tarawa's biggest island. From there their planes could threaten vital Allied shipping lanes between the United States and Australia. Conversely, US airfields in the Gilberts would ease the capture of Nimitz's next target, the Marshall Islands. For the invasion 7000 army troops were allocated to Makin and 18,000 marines to Tarawa.

The offensive against the Gilberts began on November 13, 1943, with a heavy USAAF bomber attack followed by naval gunfire. During November 20–23 the US Army 27th Infantry Division secured Makin, which was defended by only 284 marines and 693 air logistics personnel and airfield construction workers. The four days claimed 214 US casualties, but this short operation was too slow for the navy. On November 24 Japanese submarine *I-175*, dispatched from Truk as soon as the invasion began, torpedoed the escort carrier *Liscombe Bay*. A terrific explosion blew off the entire aft third of the carrier, which went down with 640 crewmen.

Concurrently, on November 20 the 2nd Marine Division invaded Betio Island, the key to Tarawa Atoll. Reconnaissance failed to reveal coral reefs just below the surface of the water. Although most of the amphibious tractors carrying the first wave of attackers made it to the beach, the landing craft that followed got hung up. The marines were then forced to wade through several hundred yards of water to reach the beach, under heavy Japanese fire, and with little naval gunfire support available for fear of hitting them. Tarawa comprised only 300 acres, yet had 400 concrete bunkers and strong points. Of 5000 marines landed the first day, 1500 were killed or wounded by nightfall. Supplies came ashore that night and the floating reserve landed the next day. Tarawa was finally secured on November 24. Of Rear-Admiral Shibasaki Keiji's defenders, 4690 were dead; the marines took only 17 prisoners, along with 129 Korean laborers. The marines in turn suffered 984 killed, 88 missing, and 2162 wounded, the costliest few days of the war to that date for the United States. In terms of ratio of casualties to force engaged, it was one of the bloodiest battles in US military history. Writers referred to it as 'tragic Tarawa' or 'terrible Tarawa' and compared it to the Crimean War charge of the Light Brigade. There were even calls for a Congressional investigation.[5]

The first amphibious landing against a heavily defended coast since Gallipoli during World War I, Tarawa actually provided valuable lessons for subsequent US amphibious operations. Improvements included better reconnaissance, navy underwater demolition teams to remove obstacles in advance of landings (something recommended by Colonel Ellis 20 years before), more effective naval gunfire support (especially plunging fire to destroy fortifications), and improved communications. The number of amphibious tractors was increased. After Tarawa each marine division had 300 amtracs to transport troops ashore and 25 others to carry cargo. Infantry firepower was also augmented. Within six months the number of BARs increased from one per squad to three; each platoon received a special assault squad armed with a bazooka, demolition charges, and two flamethrowers. The number of long-range flamethrowers per division rose from 24 to 243 and each division was provided with 24 tank-mounted flamethrowers. The number of medium tanks also increased. In the months ahead the marines would fight more costly battles in terms of total casualties, but Tarawa became a symbol of Marine Corps gallantry.[6]

The Marshalls

Because of lessons learned on Tarawa the next assaults, against Kwajalein and Eniwetok islands in the Marshall Islands, proved less costly. By now the Navy had set up floating logistical bases. On January 29 the offensive opened against Kwajalein with a three-day naval and air bombardment. Then on February 1 the US 7th Infantry Division and 4th Marine Division of V Amphibious Corps went ashore. The island was secured on February 7 with relatively light losses: 1372 casualties out of 41,000 troops landed. Out of 7230 Japanese defenders, only 265 survived, but this figure included Korean laborers.

On February 17–18 Spruance's Task Group 50.9 completed a swing around the Japanese base at Truk before the arrival of Vice-Admiral Marc Mitscher's Carrier Task Force (TF) 58. Fifty merchant ships were in the harbor, along with 365 aircraft huddled on runways. In one of the most successful carrier raids of the war, American ships and aircraft destroyed 70 Japanese planes in the air and destroyed or damaged 200 on the ground. They also sank 200,000 tons of shipping, including 10 combatants and 20 transports; 9 other ships were damaged. Truk was then bypassed, the Japanese withdrawing their naval strength to the Philippine Sea. On February 17 army and marine forces went ashore on the islands of Eniwetok Atoll. It was secured four days later.

The Marianas

The Marianas Islands were the next target in the central Pacific. Securing these would provide bases from which long-range B-29 bombers could strike Japan. Following the death of Admiral Koga in an aircraft accident, new commander of the Combined Fleet Toyoda Soemu ordered Vice-Admiral Ozawa Jisaburo to prepare a plan to lure US warships, once they moved west against the Marianas, into a battle in the Philippine Sea. This operation, code-named A-GO, was designed to allow the Japanese to employ land-based aviation.

Steaming from Eniwetok 1000 miles to the east, V Amphibious Corps of 530 warships and auxiliaries, lifting more than 127,000 men, arrived off Saipan on June 15, 1944. Mitscher's ships and aircraft were already pounding the island, destroying 200 Japanese aircraft and a dozen or more cargo vessels. On June 15 the 2nd and 4th Marine Divisions went ashore on Saipan. A few days later Mitscher's carriers and then all warships departed for the Battle of the Philippine Sea, depriving the troops ashore of badly needed naval gunfire and air support. Lieutenant General Saito Yoshitsugo had command of the defenders, who included Admiral Nagumo, commander of the Pearl Harbor attack in December 1941, and 15,164 sailors. The Japanese put up a skilful defense and mostly fought to the death. The pace of the US advance was too slow for Marine General Holland Smith, who removed Army General Ralph Smith from command of the 27th Infantry Division, creating a storm of controversy that still rages between the army and marines.[7]

Saipan was secured by July 13 at a cost of 3126 Americans killed and 13,160 wounded. The Japanese lost 39,134 military and 8000–10,000 civilian dead. Many civilians committed suicide rather than fall into

American hands. The US seizure of Saipan so shocked Japanese leaders that the cabinet resigned on July 18. Guam was taken during the period July 21 to August 10 and Tinian over the period July 25 to August 2, both after heavy Japanese resistance.

The liberation of the Philippines

The Battle of the Philippine Sea

Meanwhile, a major battle had been fought at sea. Upon learning of the US assault on Saipan, Vice-Admiral Ozawa immediately moved his ships into the Philippine Sea. Spruance, warned of this development by US submarines, concentrated Fifth Fleet under Mitscher's tactical command on June 18 some 160 miles west of Tinian. In the resulting battle the Japanese had 55 ships (5 fleet and 4 light carriers, 5 battle-ships, 11 heavy and 2 light cruisers, and 28 destroyers) while the Americans had 112 (7 fleet and 8 light carriers, 7 battleships, 8 heavy and 13 light cruisers, and 69 destroyers). In the air there were 476 Japanese aircraft to 956 for the Americans. The Japanese expected partially to offset the US advantage in naval aircraft by utilizing 110 land-based planes on Guam, Rota, and Yap. Ozawa also hoped to engage the Americans at longer range, then land planes at Guam in shuttle bombing.

The resulting Battle of the Philippine Sea, June 19–21, 1944, was the first fleet battle between the United States and Japan in two years and turned out to be pivotal. Events went badly for the Japanese early on as Ozawa's dispositions exposed his carriers to submarine attack, and fleet carriers *Taiho* and *Shokaku* succumbed to attacks by USS *Albacore* and *Cavalla*. Still, Ozawa managed four massive air attacks against the US ships, but Mitscher's fighters and anti-aircraft fire downed most of them. The Americans called the battle the 'Great Marianas Turkey Shoot.' The Japanese carriers launched 324 planes but recovered only 56. Other Japanese planes were shot down over Guam or crash landed there. US losses were only 30; no US ships were sunk and only a few sustained damage. Meanwhile, Mitscher's planes attacked Guam and Rota to neutralize the Japanese airfields there. By 6:45 p.m. the battle was over.

The Japanese now hauled off, and Mitscher pursued. He sent 216 planes against Ozawa's ships, sinking the carrier *Hiryu* and two tankers, and damaging some other vessels. The attack cost the Americans 20 planes, but the Japanese lost 21. The US attack was launched late in the day, which meant that the homeward-bound US planes were forced to find their carriers in the dark. Mitscher took the risky decision to light his carriers. Still, 80 aircraft ran out of gas and either ditched or crash-landed. Destroyers later picked up most of the air crews, leaving US personnel losses for the day at only 16 pilots and 33 crewmen.

The Battle of the Philippine Sea was a major defeat for Japan. Air combat and operational losses cost the Japanese approximately 450 aviators. Unable to replace either the carriers or the trained pilots, the vaunted Japanese naval air arm ceased to be a factor in the war. In the Battle of Leyte Gulf that October, the remaining carriers, bereft of aircraft, served as decoys.[8]

The Battle of Leyte Gulf

In July 1944 President Roosevelt met with his two Pacific commanders, MacArthur and Nimitz, at Pearl Harbor. MacArthur insisted that the next US move be the liberation of the Philippines; Nimitz, supported by CNO Admiral King, sought Formosa instead. The former made political sense, the latter military sense. In any case, Roosevelt agreed with MacArthur that the Philippines should be retaken. This shifted Nimitz's operations further north to Okinawa, planned as the staging point for an eventual invasion of the Japanese home islands. Retaking the Philippines, then, was probably unnecessary. It may even have prolonged the war and increased US casualties; but it was US territory, and MacArthur had vowed, 'I shall return.' Both plans, it should be noted, pursued the same goal of cutting off Japan from strategic resources, especially oil, from the Netherlands East Indies. The resulting plan of operations called for MacArthur's forces to land on Mindanao while Nimitz secured Yap. The two would then combine to attack Leyte. MacArthur's troops would then invade Luzon while Nimitz moved against Iwo Jima and Okinawa.

At the conclusion of operations against the Marianas, Nimitz gave Spruance and his Fifth Fleet staff the task of planning the operations against Iwo Jima and Okinawa. Halsey and Third Fleet Staff were given charge of the invasions of Yap and Leyte. One problem, over-looked at the time, loomed large. Leyte would be the first landing to involve two entire US fleets and the first without unity of command. Kinkaid's Seventh Fleet was operating under MacArthur's Southwest Pacific Command, while Halsey's Third Fleet fell under Nimitz at Pearl Harbor. Halsey had multiple tasks: to secure and maintain air superiority over the landing area; to support Kinkaid and the landings ashore; and to engage and destroy the Japanese fleet should that opportunity present itself. This divided command would have unfortunate consequences.

The Japanese had long realized that US seizure of the Philippines, Formosa, or the Ryukus Islands would split their empire and separate the Southern Resources Area from the home islands. As early as July 21, 1944, the naval general staff in Tokyo had issued a directive for subsequent 'urgent operations.' The combined fleet was to maintain the strategic status quo, and take advantage of tactical situations 'to crush the enemy fleet and attacking forces.' On July 26 the naval general staff informed Combined Fleet Commander Toyoda that the 'urgent operations' would be known by the *SHŌ* (victory) code name. The Japanese had four *Shō* plans to meet any US move. *SHŌ ICHI GO* (Operation Victory One) covered defense of the Philippine archipelago and involved the entire Combined Fleet. Toyoda knew it would be a gamble risking the entire fleet. But if the Americans retook the Philippines, the lines of communications from Japan to the south would be cut and Japan denied its resources. If the fleet were to return to Japanese waters, 'there would not be a drop of fuel for the ships.' If it remained in southern waters with the Philippines lost, the fleet would not be able to receive supplies and would suffer 'self-destruction through malnutrition.' Thus it made no sense to try to save the fleet at the expense of the Philippines.[9]

On October 20 Second Fleet commander Vice-Admiral Kurita Takeo called together his division commanders and told them that they had been given a 'glorious opportunity' and that there were 'such things as miracles. What man can say that there is no chance for our fleet to turn the tide of war in a decisive battle?'[10]

The success of the Japanese plan rested on sufficient air support. This had been severely reduced in the Battle of the Philippine Sea, but the Japanese worked hard to reconstitute their strength. During October 7–16, however, US carrier planes and army B-29s – Fifth USAAF from New Guinea and Seventh USAAF from Guam – struck every Japanese airfield within reach, including Formosa, Okinawa, and the Philippines. These strikes destroyed more than 650 Japanese planes; US losses were two cruisers badly damaged and 75 planes lost. This probably doomed the *SHŌ-1* Plan, but Toyoda hoped that land-based planes in the Philippines might make up this deficiency. The Japanese did add extra anti-aircraft guns to their ships in an attempt to offset the lack of air power, but offensively they had to rely on naval gunnery and some 335 land-based planes in the Luzon area.

The Japanese hoped to destroy sufficient US shipping to break up the amphibious landing. There were four elements in the plan. A decoy force was to draw the American fleet north while two elements struck from the west on either side of Leyte to converge simultaneously on the landing area in the Leyte Gulf and destroy the Allied shipping there. At the same time shore-based aircraft would inflict maximum damage on US forces assisting the landings. On October 17, upon receiving intelligence that US warships were off Suhuan Island, Toyoda alerted his forces. The next day the Japanese intercepted American messages regarding the approaching Leyte landings and Toyoda initiated *SHŌ-1*. The original target for the fleet engagement was October 22, but logistical difficulties delayed it to October 25.

The resulting battle of Leyte Gulf was history's largest naval engagement. The 282 vessels involved (216 American, two Australian, and 64 Japanese) outnumbered the 250 ships in the 1916 Battle of Jutland. The battle engaged nearly 200,000 men and covered an area of more than 100,000 square miles of sea. It included all aspects of naval warfare – air, surface, submarine, and amphibious – and witnessed employment of the largest guns ever at sea, the last clash of the dreadnoughts, and the introduction of *Kamikazes*. Ozawa's decoy Northern Force (Third Fleet) consisted of 1 fleet carrier, 3 light carriers, 2 hybrid battleship-carriers, 3 cruisers, and 8 destroyers. Ozawa had only 116 planes flown by half-trained pilots. His force sortied from Japan on October 20 and on the evening of the 22nd it turned south toward Luzon.

The strongest element of the Japanese attack was the 1st Division Attack Force. Its Center Force under Kurita had the bulk of Japanese attack strength: 5 battleships (including super battleships *Musashi* and *Yamato*), 12 cruisers, and 15 destroyers. Center Force steamed up the west coast of Palawan Island and then turned eastward through the waters of the Central Philippines to gain San Bernardino Strait. Meanwhile, Vice-Admiral Nishimura Shoji's Southern Force (C Force) of 2 battleships, 1 heavy cruiser, and 4 destroyers struck eastward through the Sulu Sea in an effort to force its way through Surigao Strait between the islands of Mindanao and Leyte. It was trailed by Vice-Admiral Shima Kiyohide's Second Diversion Attack Force with 2 heavy cruisers, 1 light cruiser, and 4 destroyers. Shima's force was late joining Nishimura and followed it into Surigao Strait.

On the US side, Kinkaid's Seventh Fleet was split into three task groups. The first consisted of Rear-Admiral Jesse Oldendorf's 6 old battleships, 16 escort carriers, 4 heavy and 4 light cruisers, 30 destroyers, and 10 destroyer escorts. The other two were amphibious task groups carrying out the actual invasion. As most of Halsey's amphibious assets had been loaned to Kinkaid, Third Fleet consisted almost entirely of TF-38: 14 fast carriers (more than 1000 aircraft) organized into four task groups also containing 6 battleships, 8 heavy and 13 light cruisers, and 57 destroyers.

Both western Japanese attacks were detected early, and the Battle of Leyte Gulf was actually a series of battles, the first of which was the October 23–24 Battle of the Sibuyan Sea. Early on the 23rd, US submarines *Darter* and *Dace* discovered Kurita's Center Force entering Palawan Passage from the South China Sea and alerted Halsey, whose ships guarded San Bernardino Strait. The submarines sank two Japanese heavy cruisers, including Kurita's flagship, and damaged a third. Kurita transferred his flag to the *Yamato* and his force continued east into the Sibuyan Sea where, beginning on the morning of the 24th, TF-38 launched five air strikes against it. The first wave of carrier planes arrived at 10:25 and concentrated on the *Musashi*. She took 11 torpedoes and ten bombs (and six near hits) before finally sinking. Only half of her nearly 2200-man crew survived. All-day US air attacks also damaged several other Japanese vessels. In mid-afternoon Kurita reversed course and headed west; Halsey incorrectly assumed that this part of the battle was over. He issued a preliminary order detailing a force of battleships known as TF-34 to be commanded by Vice-Admiral Willis A. Lee. Aware of that signal, Kinkaid assumed TF-34 had been established. Meanwhile, Japanese land-based planes from the Second Air Fleet harassed a portion of TF-38. Most were shot down, but they did sink the light carrier *Princeton* and badly damaged the cruiser *Birmingham*. Moreover, unknown to Halsey, with the cessation of US air strikes in the Sibuyan Sea, Kurita's force reversed course again and headed for San Bernardino Strait.

Aware of the initial approach of the Japanese Combined Fleet, Kinkaid had placed Oldendorf's six old Seventh Fleet fire-support battleships (all but one a veteran of Pearl Harbor), flanked by eight cruisers, across the mouth of Surigao Strait. He also lined the strait with 39 patrol torpedo (PT) boats and 28 destroyers. The resulting October 24–25 Battle of Surigao Strait was a classic example of 'crossing the T' in naval warfare, during which Nishimura's force was annihilated. While the battleships often get the credit for the Surigao Strait victory, it was US destroyers that inflicted most of the damage. Two converging torpedo attacks sank a battleship and three destroyers. The Japanese then ran into the line of Oldendorf's battleships and all Japanese warships save one destroyer were sunk. Nishimura went down with his flagship, the battleship *Yamashiro*.

Shima's force, bringing up the rear, was hit 30 minutes later by PT boats, which crippled a light cruiser. Shima then attempted an attack, but his flagship collided with one of Nishimura's sinking vessels. Oldendorf's ships pursued the retreating Japanese. Another Japanese cruiser succumbed to attacks by land-based planes and those from Admiral Thomas L. Sprague's escort carriers. The rest of Shima's force escaped when Oldendorf, knowing his ships might be needed later, turned back. By the morning of October 25 the southern Japanese pincer had ceased to exist.

Meanwhile, during the night of October 24–25 Kurita's force, hoping to join Nishimura in Leyte Gulf, moved through San Bernardino Strait, issued from it unopposed, and headed south. In the most controversial aspect of the battle, near midnight Halsey left San Bernardino Strait unprotected to rush with all available units of Third Fleet after Admiral Ozawa's decoy fleet, sighted far to the north. Several of Halsey's subordinates registered reservations about his decision, but the admiral was not deterred. Compounding his error, Halsey failed to inform Kinkaid, who in any case assumed TF-34 was protecting the strait. Halsey's decision left the landing beaches guarded only by Seventh Fleet's Taffy 3 escort carrier group, one of three such support groups off Samar. Rear-Admiral Clifton A. F. Sprague's Taffy 3 had 6 light escort carriers, 3 destroyers, and 4 destroyer escorts.

Fighting off Samar erupted about 6:30 a.m. on October 25 as Taffy 3 found itself opposing Kurita's 4 battleships (including the *Yamato* with her 18.1-inch guns), 6 heavy cruisers, and 10 destroyers. Aircraft from all three Taffies now attacked the Japanese. Unfortunately, the planes carried fragmentation bombs for use against land targets. Nonetheless, the planes put up a strong fight, dropping bombs, strafing, and generally harassing the Japanese. Sprague's destroyers and destroyer escorts also joined the fight at close quarters. Their crews skilfully and courageously attacked the much more powerful Japanese warships, launching torpedoes and laying down smoke to try to obscure the escort carriers. These combined attacks forced several Japanese cruisers to drop out of the battle.

Kurita now lost his nerve. By 9:10 his warships had sent to the bottom the CVE *Gambier Bay*, the only US carrier ever lost to gunfire, and had also sunk two destroyers and a destroyer escort. But Kurita believed he was being attacked by aircraft from TF-38 and at 9:11, just at the point when he might have had a crushing victory, he ordered his forces to break off the attack, his decision strengthened by word that the southern attacking force had been destroyed. After the war Kurita said, 'The conclusion from our gunfire and anti-aircraft fire during the day had led me to believe in my uselessness, my ineffectual position, if I proceeded into Leyte Gulf where I would come under even heavier air attack.' Several days of incessant attacks may also have frayed the exhausted Kurita's nerves. He hoped to join Ozawa's force to the north, but changed his mind and exited through San Bernardino Strait. Sprague later noted that the failure of Kurita's force 'to completely wipe out all vessels of this Task Unit can be attributed to our successful smoke screen, our torpedo counterattack, continuous harassment of the enemy by bomb, torpedo, and strafing air attacks, timely maneuvers, and the definite partiality of Almighty God.' The four ships lost by Taffy 3 were the only US warships sunk by Japanese surface ships in the Battle of Leyte Gulf.[11]

At 9:40 p.m. Kurita's ships reentered San Bernardino Strait. As the Japanese withdrew they came under attack by aircraft from Vice-Admiral John S. McCain's TG-38.1 of Halsey's fleet, which sank a destroyer. Meanwhile, Admiral Sprague's escort carriers and Oldendorf's force returning from the Battle of Surigao Strait came under attack from Japanese land-based Kamikaze aircraft, the first such attacks of the war. These sank the escort carrier St-Lô and damaged several other ships.

Earlier, at about 2:20 a.m. on October 25, Mitscher's search planes from Halsey's force located Ozawa's northern decoy force. At dawn the first of three strikes were launched in what became known as the Battle of Cape Engaño. Ozawa had sent most of his planes ashore to operate from bases there and thus had only anti-aircraft fire with which to oppose the US air strike. While engaged against Ozawa, Halsey learned of the action off Samar when a signal came in from Kinkaid at 8:22, followed by an urgent request eight minutes later for fast battleships. Finally, at 8:48 Halsey ordered McCain's ships to make 'best possible speed' to engage Kurita's Center Force. With more carriers and planes than any of the three other task groups in Halsey's force, it made good sense to detach them. Several minutes later Halsey was infuriated by a query from Nimitz at Pearl Harbor: 'WHERE IS RPT WHERE IS TASK FORCE THIRTY-FOUR.' At 10:55 Halsey ordered all six fast battle-ships and TG 38.2 to turn south and steam at flank speed, but they missed the battle.

After the war Kurita freely admitted his error in judgment; Halsey never did. In fact, he sought to make Kinkaid the scapegoat for allowing his Taffey 3 ships to be attacked by Kurita. Halsey said his decision to send the battleships south to Samar was 'the greatest error I committed during the Battle of Leyte Gulf.' Historian Thomas Cutler believes that if Halsey had left part of his force behind instead of taking the entire Third Fleet north, 'all other errors would have been canceled out.'[12]

By nightfall US aircraft, submarines, and surface ships had sunk all four Japanese carriers of Ozawa's force as well as five other ships. In effect this blow ended Japanese carrier aviation in the war. Although the battle of annihilation that would have been possible with the fast battleships eluded Halsey, only two converted battleship-carriers, two light cruisers, and a destroyer of Ozawa's force escaped.

Including retiring vessels sunk on October 26 and 27, Japanese losses in the Battle of Leyte Gulf came to 30 warships (3 battleships, 4 carriers, 6 heavy and 4 light cruisers, 12 destroyers, and a submarine) and more than 700 aircraft. Japanese personnel losses totalled 10,500 seamen and aviators dead. The US Navy lost six ships (1 light carrier, 2 escort carriers, 2 destroyers, and 1 destroyer escort) and more than 200 aircraft. About 2800 Americans were killed and another 1000 wounded. Put succinctly, the Battle of Leyte Gulf ended the Japanese fleet as an organized fighting force.

Reconquest of the Philippines

The US landings on Leyte that had precipitated the battle began on October 20, with 132,000 men of Krueger's Sixth Army put ashore the first day. MacArthur landed with the third wave, accompanied by members of the Philippine government and press. General Yamashita, the conqueror of Malaya, had overall command of Japanese defenses. Although some 350,000 Japanese Army troops garrisoned the islands, only its 16th Division of 16,000 men was on Leyte. The invaders had an accurate picture of Japanese strength and dispositions, thanks to Filipino guerrillas. Their general support was a morale-booster for US forces.

The Japanese did not fight for the beaches, choosing instead to contest the advance inland and away from naval gunfire. The US drive was slowed by heavy rains, skilful Japanese delaying actions, and rugged terrain. Yamashita also reinforced Leyte with some 45,000 additional troops sent from the big island of Luzon and the Visayas. US aircraft and ships gradually cut off this supply line, and the US 77th Infantry Division also went ashore on the west coast of Leyte. Organized Japanese resistance ended on December 25. The United States had suffered 15,584 casualties; Japan's losses were more than 70,000. There were no survivors from the Japanese 16th Division, which had conducted the infamous Bataan Death March. On December 15 Americans seized the island of Mindoro in the northern Visayas, just south of Luzon, for use as an advance air base for the strike against Luzon.

Yamashita had 250,000 troops on Luzon, but an Allied deception caused him to withdraw most of them south toward Manila. Meanwhile, Kamikaze pilots took a heavy toll of Admiral Oldendorf's gunfire support group in the Lingayen Gulf, sinking an escort carrier and damaging 1 battleship, 1 escort carrier, 1 heavy and 4 light cruisers, and other vessels. Nonetheless, on January 9, 1945, Krueger was able to land 68,000 men of his Sixth Army almost unopposed from the Lingayen Gulf in northern Luzon. Then, when Yamashita had committed his forces to the northern threat, Lieutenant General Eichelberger's Eighth Army landed in southern Luzon and struck north. Handicapped by shortages of equipment, transport, and air support, Yamashita organized his forces on Luzon into three main groups and settled in for a static defense.

Rear-Admiral Iwabuchi Sanji received Yamashita's order too late to be able to withdraw from Manila and ordered his 17,000-man Manila Naval Defense Force to hold the capital to the last. The Battle for Manila (February 3 to March 4, 1945) saw the destruction of much of the city and an estimated 100,000 civilian casualties. Afterwards the United States held Yamashita responsible for Japanese atrocities committed in Manila and executed him as a war criminal. At least 16,655 Japanese were killed in the battle. Most of Luzon was secured by July.

With no hope of victory or rescue, most Japanese stoically fought on. With his force down to 50,000 men, on August 15 Yamashita surrendered. The US campaign for the Philippines was skilfully fought with proportionally few US casualties. The Battle for Luzon cost Japan more than 192,000 killed and 9700 captured. US losses were 7933 killed and 32,732 wounded. The high ratio of losses for the Japanese to the Americans is an exception to the general rule that attackers suffer heavier casualties in battle and a tribute to the skill of the American commanders.

Meanwhile, from February to August Eichelberger's Eighth Army liberated the Visayas and southern Philippine Islands. Simultaneously, Australian troops took the remaining Japanese strongholds on New Guinea and in the Bismarck and Solomon Islands.

The campaign against the Japanese home islands

Iwo Jima

In February and March 1945 some of the most bitter fighting of the entire war occurred in the capture of the island of Iwo Jima. It remains a classic example of an assault operation and the ultimate test for the US

Marine Corps after 20 years of amphibious training and three years of war. The capture of the island was an essential step in the US plan to invade Japan. Okinawa and Iwo Jima were the islands desired, and Iwo Jima was selected first because it was thought to be the easier of the two to capture and because, unlike Okinawa, it was beyond the range of Kamikazes. Iwo Jima lies half-way between the Marianas and Japan, only 700 miles from Tokyo. In Japanese hands it was a threat to B-29s raiding Japan; US control would end this and the island could also serve as an emergency stopping point for B-29s and an air base for long-range US fighters.

Iwo Jima is the central island of the Volcano Group of the Nanpo Shoto, or Bonin, Islands. Of pork-chop shape, it is only about 4.5 miles long and 2.5 miles across at its widest point. Its most distinctive feature is Mount Suribachi, a 548-foot-high extinct volcano at the narrow, southern end. Also at that end, just north of Suribachi and extending from its base for more than two miles to the north and east, are beaches of thick beds of light volcanic ash and cinders. The Japanese correctly assumed the beaches would be the invasion site, as the northern part of the island is a plateau 350 feet high with inaccessible rocky sides. The invasion was originally planned for October 1944, but delay in taking the Philippines caused the attack to be postponed, resulting in heavier casualties for the attacking marines, as the Japanese had time to turn the island into a formidable defensive bastion.

Beginning in August 1944 and accelerating over the next several months, Iwo Jima was subjected to air attack by heavy bombers from the Marianas. After December 8 it came under daily attack. Cruisers also bombarded the island three times in December and twice in January. In all, 6800 tons of bombs and 22,000 rounds of 5- to 16-inch shell were hurled at Iwo Jima prior to the invasion in the heaviest preliminary bombardment in the Pacific war. Even so, it was less than called for by General Holland Smith.

The Japanese had long been aware of the inevitability of a US invasion. They evacuated the small civilian population from Iwo and assigned to its defense some 14,000 army and 7000 navy personnel. With six months to prepare, Lieutenant General Kuribayashi Tadamichi, the island's commander, oversaw construction of an elaborate system of subterranean fortifications and worked to turn this obscure bit of volcanic rock into what one writer has called 'probably the most ingenious fortress the world had ever seen.'[13]

The Japanese dug caves with angled entrances and constructed command posts and concrete pillboxes, some with 6-foot-thick walls.

Many of the defenses were interconnected by tunnels. The defenders also buried tanks up to the turrets as instant pillboxes and converted bombs into rockets, launched electronically along 45-degree slanted wooden ramps. Mount Suribachi became a fortress. The defenders were prepared to defend the island to the last and they did.

Kuribayashi assumed that the Americans would get ashore and prohibited the futile *banzai* charges that satisfied honor but wasted manpower. He ordered his men to stay in their defensive positions and inflict maximum casualties on the attackers. General Holland Smith later referred to Kuribayashi as the 'most redoubtable' of all his Pacific war adversaries.[14]

The battle for Iwo Jima witnessed a Japanese attempt to use human-guided torpedoes, known as *Kaiten* (Divine Fate), launched from *I*-boats. Kaiten were directed by individual swimmers who 'rode' the torpedoes. Although US Navy Hunter-Killer anti-submarine units intercepted all *Kaiten* successfully, they signalled the extent to which the Japanese were prepared to resist the American advance toward Tokyo.

Spruance had overall command while Turner took charge of the invasion. Lieutenant General Holland Smith, commanding the new Fleet Marine Force, exercised authority ashore with Major General Harry Schmidt heading the V Amphibious Corps. For three days prior to the invasion, 8 battleships, 5 heavy cruisers, and a number of destroyers rained shells on Iwo Jima. Turner was later criticized by some for failing to extend the bombardment by another day, especially as poor weather had obscured many targets and all ammunition had not been expended. Holland Smith did not oppose Turner's decision, but he had wanted the bombardment begun earlier, not end later. A longer naval bombardment would have lengthened the time the ships would be exposed to suicide attack, and in any case the bombing and shelling had only mixed results on the island's subterranean defenses.

At 6:45 a.m. on February 19 the landing operation began. The initial assault was by the 4th and 5th Marine Divisions; 3rd Division was kept in floating reserve. The 5th Marine Division went ashore at the most southerly narrow point of the island, just north of Mount Suribachi; the 4th Division was on their right flank. The first wave of 68 LVT amtrac tanks hit the beaches at 9:00. The remaining assault waves landed in the next half-hour, followed by 12 LSMs transporting medium tanks. The landing, accompanied by a rolling barrage from the ships off-shore, was easy, and optimists predicted Iwo Jima would be secured in a few days. But most Japanese defenders, deep in their caves, had survived the bombs and shells. When the marines landed and crowded onto the invasion beaches the Japanese opened a withering fire, pinning them down. The troops found movement difficult in the volcanic ash, and they were easily visible from observation posts on Mount Suribachi.

Close naval gunfire support and strikes by naval aircraft allowed the marines to establish a beachhead. By nightfall the 5th Marine Division had pushed across the island's most narrow point north of Suribachi. Marines had also reached the southernmost of two Japanese airstrips. The day had been costly: of 30,000 marines sent ashore, 600 lay dead and another 1600 were wounded. For the combatants, Iwo Jima was truly an experience in hell. Fighting was bloody and foot by foot. There was little room for maneuver, and the Japanese fought from concealment.

On the morning of February 23 the marines successfully scaled Mount Suribachi and planted a US flag on its summit. The photograph by AP photographer Joe Rosenthal – one of the most famous of the war and the inspiration for the Marine Corps memorial in Arlington, Virginia – was not staged and was taken under combat conditions, but it was actually the second raising of a US flag on Suribachi. Meanwhile, the battle for the island, expected to take only ten days, dragged on for another month. By the beginning of March the Japanese had retreated to the northern part of the island. On March 4 the first B-29, short on fuel from a raid on Japan, landed on an airfield hastily reactivated by the Seabees. On March 16 General Schmidt announced Iwo Jima secured, although some Japanese resistance continued past that date. Iwo Jima was the first territory under direct Tokyo administration captured by the Americans in the war.

Through March 26 the marines and navy sustained 6812 killed and 19,189 wounded. Battle casualties totalled 30 percent of the entire landing force and 75 percent in the infantry regiments of the 4th and 5th Divisions. The battle also produced an incredible 27 Medals of Honor. Most of the Japanese fought to the end. Kuribayashi was one of the last to die, and of the Japanese garrison only 216 men were taken alive. Marines counted 20,703 Japanese dead. Through May the US Army's 147th Infantry Regiment, which took over from the marines, netted an additional 1,602 Japanese dead and 867 prisoners.

There was also a cost at sea. Some Kamikaze aircraft succeeded in penetrating the US defensive fighter screen and struck the carrier *Saratoga*, resulting in the loss of 42 aircraft, as well as the death of 123 and the wounding of 192 crewmen. The escort carrier *Bismarck Sea*, hit by Kamikazes, exploded and sank with the loss of 218 men. Another escort carrier, a cargo ship, and an LST were also damaged by Kamikazes.

Was the battle worth the high cost in American lives? US airmen certainly thought so. From March to August 2,251 B-29s made forced landings on the island; many of these planes would have otherwise been lost. Iwo Jima also served as an important part of elaborate air-sea rescue operations to retrieve B-29 crews forced to ditch at sea. VII Fighter Command soon moved to the island and long-range P-47 Thunderbolts and P-51 Mustangs began flying from Iwo Jima, accompanying the B-29s to Japan and back. Their presence enabled the big bombers to carry out mid-level daytime raids in addition to the low-level night attacks. With the American fighters along, losses of Japanese planes mounted rapidly, while those of the B-29s continued to decline.

The invasion of Okinawa

The final preliminary to an invasion of the Japanese mainland was Operation ICEBERG, the capture of Okinawa in the Ryukyu group of islands between Formosa and Kyushu, southernmost island of Japan. Okinawa is about 60 miles long and at most 18 miles wide. The island is mountainous in the north and south and level and cultivated in the central portion. Japan had taken the island in 1875. Securing Okinawa would sever Japanese communications with south China, but the principal reason for taking it was to secure a staging area for the projected invasion of Japan. Okinawa offered suitable air bases, anchorages, and staging grounds for such a vast undertaking.

Execution of ICEBERG fell to Admiral Spruance's Fifth Fleet. The lifting force involved 1213 vessels of 45 different classes and types in Vice-Admiral Turner's TF-51. The vessels ranged from 179 attack transports and cargo ships to 187 LSTs. This does not include the covering force of 88 ships of Mitscher's TF-58 and the 22 ships of TF-57, a British component commanded by Vice-Admiral H. B. Rawlings. The land assault force for the Pacific theater's largest and most complicated amphibious operation was US Army Lieutenant General Simon Bolivar Buckner's Tenth Army of some 180,000 men. It consisted of Major General Roy S. Geiger's III Marine Amphibious Corps (1st, 2nd, and 6th Marine Divisions) and Major General John R. Hodge's XXIV Army Corps (7th, 27th, 77th, and 96th Infantry Divisions).

Tokyo had begun strengthening Okinawa at the end of March 1944 with the activation of Thirty-Second Army (Ryukus). By October 1944 it comprised four divisions (9th, 24th, 62nd, and the 28th on Sakishima) plus other units. Altogether, the Japanese commander on Okinawa, Lieutenant General Ushijima Mitsuru, had about 130,000 men, including the 20,000-man Okinawan Home Guard. The Japanese had constructed a formidable defensive system, particularly on the southern part of the island.[15]

In the second half of March 1945, US forces sought to isolate Okinawa by striking Japanese air bases on Kyushu and the Sakishima island group between Formosa and Okinawa. Army heavy bombers also hit Formosa and the Japanese home island of Honshu. During these operations the ships, especially the aircraft carriers, came under heavy Japanese Kamikaze attacks.

Kamikazes

Named for the 'divine wind,' a thirteenth-century typhoon that saved Japan from invasion by Kublai Khan's fleet, Kamikazes were first proposed to the First Air Fleet by Vice-Admiral Onishi Takijiro during the Battle of Leyte Gulf. The Kamikaze Special Attack Corps first entered battle on October 25, 1944, when Lieutenant Seki Yukio, flying a Zero armed with a 550-lb bomb, struck and badly damaged the escort carrier *Santee*. Other CVEs were also struck, including the *St-Lô*, which suffered internal explosions, broke apart, and sank [16]

Impressed by these early results, the Japanese expanded Kamikaze operations. The army began preparations for the Kamikaze units, and more types of aircraft were adapted for suicide missions, including dive-bombers and medium bombers. On November 25, 1944, eight Kamikazes damaged several US carriers, including the *Essex*. Kamikazes participated in the defense of Luzon, but failed to prevent the US landings there. The Japanese First Air Fleet then transferred to Formosa, and on January 21, 1945 Formosa-based Kamikazes seriously damaged the aircraft carrier *Ticonderoga*.

On March 18–19, 1945, Allied ships off Okinawa came under a heavy Kamikaze attack. Carrier *Franklin* took two bomb hits on her flight deck that virtually incinerated the upper decks. Heroic efforts by the crew saved the carrier, but the attacks led to the loss of 724 men, the highest casualty rate of any surviving US Navy vessel in any war. Carrier *Wasp* was also hit by a Kamikaze and saved only by new fire-fighting techniques.

In August 1944 the Japanese Navy had begun experiments with a specialized, piloted glide-bomb. This single-seat craft, named *Oka* (Cherry Blossom) II carried a 2640-lb warhead and was designed to be carried to its target by a twin-engine Betty bomber – the Americans dubbed it the *Baka* (Fool). A new volunteer unit, the *Jinrai Butai* (Corps of Divine Thunder), manned the Oka IIs, which were to operate from bases in the Philippines, Formosa, and Okinawa. The Kamikaze effort was dealt a serious blow when 50 Okas were lost in the November 29 sinking of the giant Japanese aircraft carrier *Shinano* by the US submarine *Archerfish*.

The first major Oka assault occurred in the preliminaries for the Battle of Okinawa. On March 21, 1945, 16 Betty bombers, each carrying a single Oka, and two conventionally armed Bettys, all escorted by 30 Zero fighters were intercepted by US Navy F6F Hellcats 300 miles south of Kyushu. The F6Fs downed all the Japanese bombers and 15 of the Zeros. A second and final raid against American warships at Okinawa incorporated 74 Okas. Although some found targets, most Okas were shot down still attached to their mother planes.

On April 7, shortly after the initial landings on Okinawa, some 121 Kamikazes and 117 additional orthodox aircraft swept in on the amphibious force. The Americans claimed 383 of the attackers shot down, but two US destroyers and four smaller ships were sunk, and an additional 24 other vessels damaged. The Allies sought to counter these attacks by extending their destroyer screen up to 95 miles from Okinawa. The destroyers provided early warning of the attacks but also became easy targets for the Kamikazes. From April 6 until July 29 the destroyer screen was pounded by suicide attacks, and 14 destroyers were sunk. Through June 10 the Japanese launched nearly a dozen mass Kamikaze raids of between 50 and 300 planes each against the invasion fleet. During the two months the US Navy was off Okinawa it underwent 2482 Kamikaze attacks (1298 army and 1184 navy). The Kamikazes were eventually defeated by new defensive formations that provided maximum anti-aircraft fire protection to the carriers and by crushing Allied air superiority.

Although never operational, other piloted-bomb Kamikaze prototypes were in development at war's end: the jet-engine powered Oka Model 22, the turbo-jet *Kikka* (Mandarine Orange Blossom), the pulse-jet *Baika* (Plum Blossom), and the *Shinryu* (Divine Dragon) glider launched by solid fuel rockets. The Japanese Army also produced the *Tsurugi* (Sword), similar to the navy's reciprocating engine-powered *Toka* (Wisteria Blossom). In all, some 3940 crewmen died during the war in 2443 army and navy aircraft involved in Kamikaze missions. Although their effectiveness declined because of Allied countermeasures, Kamikazes inflicted heavy losses on Allied ships and crews. They also influenced the US decision to employ the atomic bomb.[17]

The largest Kamikaze was battleship *Yamato*. Departing Japan on
April 6 on a one-way mission to Okinawa with the aim of attacking the
invasion fleet and then being beached as a stationary fort, the giant
battleship and her escort force of a cruiser and eight destroyers was intercepted on April 7 by 180 US carrier aircraft 200 miles from Okinawa and
sunk in a furious assault of nearly four hours. Only 269 officers and men
were rescued; 3063 aboard *Yamato* died. The US planes also sank a light
cruiser and four escorting destroyers, killing another 1187 officers and
men. US losses came to ten aircraft and 12 men. Had remaining Japanese
air power been concentrated to provide fighter cover for the battleship
until she reached Okinawa, *Yamato* might have inflicted serious damage
to the amphibious force before her end came.[18]

The land battle for Okinawa

During March 14–31 air attacks and naval shelling proceeded against
Okinawa. Then, beginning on March 23, the 77th Infantry Division
secured the outlying Kerama Islands. This provided anchorages and
artillery positions for the invasion force and led to the destruction of
some 300 small Japanese suicide boats. On Easter Sunday morning,
April 1, the Americans went ashore on Okinawa proper, landing on the
west coast Kadena beaches. Some 16,000 troops landed in the first hour
and 50,000 by the end of the day. Once again the initial assault was
deceptively easy, as the Japanese did not contest the beaches, but chose
to fight in the more populous interior.

The Marine III Amphibious Corps on the left (1st and 6th Divisions)
now turned north. It met relatively little opposition in clearing the northern
area (by April 13) and nearby Ie Shima Island (April 16–20). The US Army
XXIV Corps swung south. The main landing was facilitated by a demonstration against the southern end of the island by the 2nd Marine Division.
The 27th and 77th Infantry Divisions were held in reserve. Ushijima now
had the majority of his 24th and 62nd Divisions in the rugged southern end
of the island where they could mount a determined defense. It was at this
point, beginning on April 7, that the Japanese launched their first major
Kamikaze assault with the intent of driving the Allied fleet from Okinawa.
The XXIV Corps met stiff resistance in the south. Japanese defenders were
well dug-in along a series of east–west ridge lines across the island, and
they incorporated Okinawan burial caves in their successive, mutually
supporting positions. The advance soon ground to a halt.

On April 22 the 1st Marine Division took up position on the right of
the line and was joined there later by the 6th Marine Division. The

marines then came up against the main Japanese defensive line with the heart of its defense at Shuri Castle. On May 4 the Japanese mounted a desperate counter-attack that made some headway before it was blunted. On May 18 the marines took Sugar Loaf Hill, the western portion of the Shuri Line. Four days later, the Japanese withdrew seven miles south to a new line. Final operations occurred in June, but on June 18 Buckner was killed by a Japanese shell while at a forward observation post; he thus became the highest-ranking US officer lost to hostile fire in the war. Geiger then took command, the only US marine ever to command a field army, and he directed the final days of fighting.

Although pockets of resistance remained, Geiger declared the island secure on June 21. The Americans took only 7400 Japanese prisoners. General Ushijima committed ritual suicide. The Japanese suffered 92,000–94,000 military dead. Okinawa was a bloodbath for both sides, the costliest battle for the Americans in the Pacific theater. The army lost 12,520 dead and 36,631 wounded. The marines suffered 2938 dead and 13,708 wounded. The navy lost 4907 men killed and 4874 wounded, the only service in the battle in which the dead exceeded the wounded and a total higher than all the other wars fought by the US Navy put together. The navy also lost 38 ships sunk and 368 damaged. In the campaign for Okinawa the Japanese lost to all causes 6810 aircraft. Civilians on Okinawa especially suffered. Of the 450,000 pre-invasion population, perhaps 94,000 died.[19]

The atomic bomb

In light of Iowa Jima and Okinawa, it is easy to see why the Joint Chiefs were reluctant to invade Japan. The Japanese military had available in its home islands a million troops, 3000 Kamikaze aircraft, and 5000 suicide boats. With a US invasion scheduled for November 1, 1945, and well aware of the high cost of such an enterprise, the Joint Chiefs of Staff had pressed Roosevelt at the February 1945 Yalta Conference to get the Soviet Union into the war against Japan at any cost.

After the successful test firing of an atomic bomb at Alamogordo, New Mexico, on July 16, 1945, sharp debate arose among advisors to US President Harry S. Truman (who had succeeded Roosevelt as president on the latter's death on April 12, 1945) whether to employ the new weapon. Admiral William Leahy demurred, recalling after the fact, 'in being the first to use it, we had adopted an ethical standard common to the barbarians of the Dark Ages. I was not taught to make war in that fashion, and wars cannot be won by destroying women and children.'[20]

Was it a matter of degree? The terror threshold had already been passed in the fire-bombing of Japanese cities. The bomb also was not then viewed as the threat to all mankind as it as seen today. Material for only two bombs was immediately available; others were several months away. Thus dropping one bomb in a remote location as a warning would leave only one other, of a different type, available. Also, this was total war. It was always assumed that the bomb would be used if it became available. Employing the bomb would, in all likelihood, bring the war to a speedy end, saving many American lives. It would also mean the United States would not have to share occupation of Japan with the Soviet Union, and hopefully it would deter Stalin from future aggression. The atomic bomb was essentially a psychological weapon, the use of which was designed to influence Japanese political leaders, rather than a military tool. President Truman never regretted the decision, which was certainly supported by the great majority of the American people at the time.

Revisionist historians have held that the Japanese government was trying desperately to leave the war and that employing the bomb was unnecessary. Recently available intercepts of diplomatic messages indicate, however, that Japan had not yet reached the decision to surrender when the first bomb was dropped. Emperor Hirohito and his principal advisers had concluded that Japan could not win the war, but they also hoped for a negotiated settlement and that a last 'decisive battle' would force the Allies to grant more favorable peace terms.[21]

Historian Ray Skates has concluded that the first phase of the invasion of Japan, the conquest of the island of Kyushu planned for November 1945, would have taken two months and resulted in 75,000 to 100,000 US casualties. Such losses, while they would not have affected the outcome of the war, might indeed have brought the political goals sought by the Japanese leaders.[22]

But even if the bomb had not been employed, an invasion of Japan might not have been necessary. In all likelihood the United States would have continued the strategic bombing campaign. By August 1945 it had largely burned out the Japanese cities and the nation was close to starvation. Caloric intake had fallen to an average of 1680 daily, and even this reduced food supply was highly dependent on railroad distribution. Destruction of the railroads might well have been the final straw leading the emperor to conclude peace, even without the bomb.[23]

Not employing the bomb would have delayed the surrender and thus have meant a significantly higher cost in Japanese lives than those actually killed in the atomic bombs. In the war the Japanese lost 323,495 dead on the 'home front,' the vast majority of them from air attack. In continued strategic bombing, this total would have swelled; many others would simply have died of starvation. In effect, dropping the bomb resulted in a net saving of lives, both Japanese and American.[24]

The first bomb fell on Hiroshima on August 6. This city of 300,000 people was an important military headquarters and supply depot and had not yet suffered severely in the bombing offensive. Early that morning an air-raid alert sounded and most people took cover. Realizing that there were only a few planes overhead, most people then came out in the open and were without protection when the bomb detonated. The resulting blast destroyed two-thirds of Hiroshima; about 100,000 people perished outright or died later from radiation effects; another 40,000 were injured, and most of the remaining population suffered some long-term radiation damage. This was, however, less carnage than that inflicted in the fire-bombing of Tokyo in March.

On August 8 the Soviet Union declared war on Japan, Stalin honoring to the day his pledge at Yalta to enter the war against Japan 'two or three months after the defeat of Germany.' On August 9 a second atomic bomb fell. The primary target of Kokura was obscured by smoke and haze, so the bomb was dropped on the secondary target of Nagasaki, a seaport and industrial city of 230,000 people. Hills protected portions of Nagasaki so less than half the city was destroyed. The blast here claimed about 70,000 dead, either killed outright or dying later from radiation, and injured as many more.[25]

The day they declared war, the Soviets invaded Manchuria in force. The Japanese defenders, largely caught off guard, found themselves heavily outnumbered in terms of both men and equipment; the Red Army committed 1.5 million men, 4370 aircraft, 5500 tanks, and 28,000 artillery pieces. Soviet commanders planned bold operations and carried them out well. Their armored columns sliced through the Greater Khingan Range, and the Soviets employed airborne forces to take Japanese positions well to the rear. In the fighting the Soviets lost more than 12,000 killed and nearly 25,000 wounded. They claimed to have killed 84,000 Japanese, while capturing 594,000. Japanese historians claim they lost 60,000 killed in combat as well as 185,000 subsequently dead in Manchuria. They also claim about 600,000 Japanese soldiers and civilians were taken to prison camps, where most worked until 1947–50 and 55,000 died of illness or malnutrition. The last prisoners were not released until 1956.[26]

After prolonged meetings with his advisers, Emperor Hirohito made the decision for peace. Braving possible assassination by fanatics determined to fight to the end, Hirohito communicated this decision over radio on August 15, the first time the Japanese people had heard his voice. On September 2 the final terms of surrender were signed aboard the battleship *Missouri* in Tokyo Bay; the emperor remained as head of state, but the Japanese islands were placed under the rule of a US army of occupation.[27]

What were the chief factors in the defeat of Japan? For one thing, its early successes spread Japan's resources thin and allowed the United States to hit wherever it wanted. Vastly superior US manufacturing resources were another key. The sea blockade of Japan was an immense success, US submarines in the Pacific accomplishing what the Germans had hoped to achieve in the Atlantic. And, finally, in the last year of the war, Japan was devastated by strategic bombing, both conventional and nuclear.

12

Wartime Diplomacy and the Peace Settlement

World War II was, by virtually any measurement, the most costly war in history. In economic and financial terms alone it cost perhaps five times that of World War I. In human terms it was half again as costly in military dead (15 million versus 10 million). The Soviet Union sustained the most killed, 7,500,000. Other totals for the major combatants were as follows: Germany, 4,000,000; China, 500,000; Japan, 1,506,000; United Kingdom, 397,762; Romania, 300,000; United States, 292,100; and France, 210,762. Total deaths from the war, including civilians, came to 41–49 million people, a figure that would have been much higher without new sulfa and penicillin drugs and blood plasma transfusions.[1]

When the war finally ended, vast stretches of Europe and Asia lay in ruins; large numbers of people were utterly exhausted and millions, uprooted from their homes, were displaced. In France 2.5 million people had been sent to Germany to work as slave laborers; 200,000 of them died there. Transport, especially in parts of western and central Europe and Japan, was at a standstill, with bridges blown, rail lines destroyed, and highways cratered and blocked. Ports were especially hard hit and many would have to be rebuilt. Most of the large cities of Germany and Japan were devastated, the bulk of the buildings mere shells. Some countries had fared reasonably well. Damage in Britain was not too extensive, and Denmark and Norway escaped with little destruction. The rapid Allied advance had largely spared Belgium, although the port of Antwerp was badly damaged. The Netherlands, however, sustained considerable destruction, and portions of the population were starving. The situation in Greece was also dire.

All of the world was touched by the war to some degree. France emerged from the German occupation in terrible shape economically. Allied bombing and fighting on land had claimed half a million buildings destroyed. Transportation was paralyzed, and the vast majority of locomotives and trucks were inoperative. Industrial production stood at 40 percent of its 1938 level and, thanks to German financial plundering through exaggerated occupation costs, the franc was disastrously inflated.[2]

Germany appeared even worse off. Its cities were piles of rubble and, as late as 1946, industrial production was only one-third the volume of a decade earlier. Large numbers of Germans were homeless and out of work. The immediate problems for several years centered on food, housing, and employment. As it turned out the damage was not as extensive as initially thought, and many machines were still operative once the rubble was removed. In one perverse sense, Germany and Japan benefitted from the bombing in that they rebuilt with the most modern techniques and systems.

Among major powers, the USSR was the hardest hit. Its 27 million dead in the war dramatically affected national demographics to the present. In 1959 Moscow announced that the ratio of males to females in the Soviet Union was 45:55. Aside from the catastrophic human costs, the Germans had occupied the USSR's most productive regions and the 'scorched earth' policy practiced by both the Soviets and the Germans resulted in the total or partial destruction of 1700 towns, 70,000 villages, 6,000,000 buildings, and 84,000 schools. The Soviet Union also lost 71 million farm animals, including 7 million horses. There was widespread destruction in the great cities such as Kiev, Odessa, and Leningrad. Perhaps a quarter of the property value of the USSR was lost in the war and tens of millions of Soviet citizens were homeless. Simply feeding the Soviet population became a staggering task. All of this goes a long way to explaining the subsequent policies, both internal and external, of the Soviet Union.[3]

The long war greatly stimulated colonial unrest around the world, especially the defeat of France and the Netherlands and the preoccupation of Britain. Where the colonial powers sought to hold on to their empires after August 1945, there was often fighting. The French government, determined to maintain the nation as a great power, insisted on retaining its empire. This led to the long (1946–54) Indo–China War. Fighting also erupted in many other places around the world, including Malaya and the Netherlands Indies. Even where the European powers chose to withdraw voluntarily, as in the case of Britain in Palestine and on the Indian subcontinent, there was fighting as competing nationalities sought to fill the vacuum.

The war was over, but winning the peace would be difficult. Although the conflict had decided the shape of European affairs for the next half-century, this did not suddenly occur in 1945, but rather evolved over the course of the long war. Following the conquest of Poland, Hitler had offered peace to Britain and France on a forgive-and-forget basis, but the Western democracies rejected it. Following his victories over Norway, the Low Countries, and France, Hitler had again expected the British to sue for peace. Even though Britain and its empire were then fighting Germany alone, Churchill absolutely rejected negotiations and pledged himself and his nation to see the conflict through to final Allied victory. Hitler had then decided to attack the Soviet Union, certain this would bring Britain around. His June 1941 invasion of Russia had stunned Stalin, who for some reason had reposed more trust in Hitler than he extended to any other national leader. Meanwhile the Soviet Union survived the terrible autumn of 1941 and in the winter mounted a counter-offensive. Then, thanks to the Japanese decision, the United States entered the war.

Even before the Japanese attack on Pearl Harbor, President Roosevelt and Prime Minister Churchill met aboard ship off the coast of Newfoundland. These talks produced the Atlantic Charter of August 14, 1941. Here the two leaders eschewed any territorial aggrandizement and agreed to support the principle of self-determination of peoples. They also pledged to work for world economic prosperity and freedom from 'fear and want,' and to seek disarmament and international security. Churchill hoped for a statement about an international peace-keeping organization but Roosevelt, mindful of US isolationist sentiment, balked at the suggestion. Later Moscow announced its support for the Atlantic Charter's principles.

Even this early in the war, however, there were sharp differences between the Anglo-Saxon powers and the Soviet Union over the post-war composition of Europe. British Foreign Secretary Anthony Eden soon reported from Moscow that the Kremlin wanted Germany dismembered, to retain Finnish territory, and to incorporate the Baltic states and Bessarabia. Stalin also insisted on the Curzon Line, the boundary drawn by the Allied commission after World War I, as the western boundary for the Soviet Union. This would enable the USSR to incorporate its 1939 gains at the expense of Poland. On January 1, 1942, representatives of 26 nations signed the United Nations declaration by which they pledged to support the principles of the Atlantic Charter and not to sign a separate peace or armistice until the Axis powers were defeated.

During January 14–24, 1943, following successful Allied landings in North Africa and the Eighth Army's break-out at El Alamein, Roosevelt, Churchill, and the Combined Chiefs of Staff met in Casablanca,

Morocco. Stalin was invited but declined to attend. The main topic of discussion was setting the next military objective once North Africa had been cleared of Axis troops. The British, who were better prepared than the Americans, made a strong case for invasions of Sicily and then Italy, and the Americans reluctantly acceded. Casablanca is chiefly remembered, however, for Roosevelt's surprise announcement that the Allies would insist on 'unconditional surrender.' Churchill, who had not been informed ahead of time that the announcement would be made, nonetheless immediately supported it. Some believe that this decision precluded negotiations with the German resistance that might have led them to topple Hitler's regime and that it needlessly prolonged the war. If Allied leaders had been wise enough to provide some assurance as to their peace terms, Hitler's hold on the German people might have been released before May 1945. After the Casablanca announcement Hitler repeatedly told his subordinates: 'Don't fool yourself. There is no turning back. We can only move forward. We have burned our bridges.'[4]

Certainly, the declaration was a windfall for the German propaganda machine. In making his announcement, Roosevelt had in mind World War I and the way the German right had utilized the November 1918 armistice to spread the myth that Germany had not been defeated militarily. The 'stab in the back' myth had been of powerful assistance in Hitler's rise to power.

Another aspect of the Casablanca Conference concerned relations with France. Charles de Gaulle, leader of the Free French, was not informed of the meeting beforehand; Churchill simply ordered him to Morocco – still a French protectorate. Roosevelt and Churchill pushed de Gaulle into a partnership with General Henri Giraud, who had been spirited out of France by submarine. De Gaulle eventually elbowed aside the politically inept and equally stubborn Giraud, but the whole affair affected de Gaulle's attitude toward the Anglo-Saxon powers. He was already upset by the British undermining of the French position in Syria and Lebanon. Relations between de Gaulle and the two chief Western leaders remained tense, especially with Roosevelt.[5]

In August 1943 Roosevelt, Churchill, and their military staffs met at Quebec. The principal topic of discussion was planning for the cross-Channel invasion of France, now codenamed OVERLORD and projected for May 1, 1944. Churchill had argued for concentration upon the Balkans, which the US military chiefs strongly opposed. Roosevelt and Churchill agreed on the cross-Channel attack and that it would constitute the major Anglo-American effort against Germany. Because it was increasingly obvious that the Americans would be providing the bulk of the manpower, Churchill suggested that an American appointed by Roosevelt command the invasion.[6]

Stalin notified the Western leaders that he was interested in further talks, and in October 1943 US Secretary of State Cordell Hull and British Foreign Secretary Eden traveled to Moscow to meet with Foreign Minister Molotov and Stalin. This meeting was intended to pave the way for a meeting of the three heads of state. Although this conference is usually overlooked, a number of important decisions were taken there, and it deserves to rank in importance with the meetings at Teheran, Yalta, and Potsdam. At Moscow the three foreign ministers decided that Austria was the first 'victim of Hitlerite aggression,' which allowed its restoration to full independence. They also called for the complete destruction of Fascism in Italy and encouraged the Italians to form a new government. They set up the European Advisory Commission to meet in London and work out plans for the subsequent occupation of Germany and Austria. A similar group was set up for Italy. The Allies also issued a specific warning that those guilty of crimes against humanity would be 'brought back to the scene of their crimes and judged on the spot by the people whom they have outraged . . . most assuredly the three allied Powers will pursue them to the uttermost ends of the earth and will deliver them to their accusers in order that justice may be done.'[7]

The three governments further iterated their pledge not to sign a separate peace, and they agreed to consult one another on issues of peace and security until the establishment of an organization to handle such matters. With Nationalist Chinese leader Generalissimo Jiang Jieshi threatening to sign a separate peace in order to extract more aid from the United States, a representative of China was induced to sign the document, which became known as the Declaration of Four Nations on General Security. Finally, Stalin assured Hull that the USSR would declare war on Japan after Germany had been defeated.

In November 1943 Roosevelt and Churchill, on their way to meet with Stalin at Teheran, stopped off in Cairo to see Jiang Jieshi. Churchill had his doubts, but Roosevelt hoped to see China as a fourth great power after the war. At Cairo all three leaders restated their determination to fight on until victory was achieved. They also decided that after the war Japan would be reduced to her home islands. China would regain Manchuria, the Pescadores Islands, and Formosa; Korea would also be restored, 'in due course,' to independence. The mandated Japanese islands would in all probability pass to US control, and it was implied that the USSR would regain South Sakhalin Island (lost in the

Russo–Japanese War) and secure the Kuriles, which had never been Russian. Stalin also pressed for a warm-water port for the Soviet Union, probably at Dairen.

From November 28 to December 1, 1943, Roosevelt, Churchill, and Stalin met at Teheran. Stalin claimed that his wartime responsibilities would not allow him to travel far, and certainly he did not have to do so to attend the conference, but it was his first trip abroad since 1912. It was also the first time that Stalin and Roosevelt met and the American president, convinced that Stalin was 'getable,' turned on all his formidable charm to try and win Stalin's confidence. To this end, at both Teheran and the subsequent conference at Yalta, Roosevelt deliberately distanced himself from Churchill. The British prime minister was shocked, not believing that the democracies would take separate paths.

At Teheran the Western leaders labored under disadvantages. The first was the strategic situation. British and US troops were fighting the Germans on the ground only in Italy with 14 divisions; the Soviet Union had 178 divisions in combat. If the Teheran Conference marked the beginning of the Soviet empire, it also reflected the reality of forces on the ground. The two Western leaders feared that the Soviet Union and Germany might yet seek diplomatic accommodation, and Roosevelt wanted to secure Soviet assistance in the war against Japan. At Teheran Stalin pressured the West on OVERLORD. Soviet Ambassador to Moscow Ivan Maisky had counseled Stalin to press for an immediate second front, which he knew was impossible, in order to secure additional Lend-Lease assistance. Stalin insisted on learning the name of the commander as proof that the Western allies were serious about OVERLORD. Shortly after the conference Roosevelt named Eisenhower to that post.

There was also much discussion on Germany and its possible future division. Roosevelt suggested splitting it into five states and internationalizing the Ruhr and other areas. Churchill, worried about possible Soviet expansion into Europe, thought that Prussia might be detached from the rest of Germany. Discussions over Poland were more controversial. All three leaders agreed on the Oder River as the future boundary of Poland with Germany. There was, however, no agreement by the West for a tributary of the Oder, the Western Neisse River, as the southern demarcation line. Nor did the West sanction Poland securing the important port of Stettin on the west bank of the Oder. The three did agree that Poland would get most of East Prussia, although the Soviet Union claimed the Baltic port of Königsberg and land to the northeast. There was no major opposition from Western leaders to the Curzon Line as the eastern boundary of Poland. The British did object, however, to the Soviet seizure of the predominantly Polish city of Lvov.

Churchill pointed out to Stalin that Britain had gone to war over Poland, but Stalin insisted that the Soviet Union needed security against a future German attack. Obviously a Poland that would be compensated for the loss of eastern territory to the USSR by being given German territory in the west would necessarily have to look to the Soviet Union for security. Churchill had the difficult task of having to sell all these arrangements to the Polish government-in-exile in London. Stalin refused normal diplomatic relations with the so-called London Poles – and not because of Moscow's false charge that they were stirring up trouble for the Red Army. No independent Polish government would ever concede changes that put the country at the USSR's mercy. But a Polish government subservient to Moscow proved inevitable.

Stalin also demanded that the Soviet Union be allowed to keep its 1939–40 acquisitions of Bessarabia, the Karelian Isthmus, and the Baltic states. Although these were clear violations of the Atlantic Charter, the siege of Leningrad gave Stalin a strong argument for a security zone there. Stalin also demanded that Finland cede its Arctic port of Petsamo, pay heavy reparations, and provide space for a base to protect sea approaches to Leningrad. In return he promised to respect Finnish independence, pending 'proper behavior' by that country.

Stalin reassured Roosevelt that the Soviet Union would enter the war against Japan after the defeat of Germany. The three leaders also agreed that after the war Iran, which was serving as a supply corridor to the Soviet Union and occupied by Allied troops, would be restored to full territorial integrity and sovereignty, and all troops would be withdrawn.[8]

In September 1944 Roosevelt and Churchill again met at Quebec. Stalin was invited but declined on the claim of heavy wartime responsibilities. The conference was primarily devoted to war plans against Japan. The one important development regarding Europe was the vengeful and ill-advised Morganthau Plan. Developed by US Secretary of the Treasury Henry Morganthau, it envisioned turning Germany into an agricultural state. Wisely, the suggestion was scrapped.

In October 1944, as the Red Armies steadily pushed the Germans west, Churchill flew to Moscow to meet with Stalin. The high point in their talks was an agreement suggested by Churchill and approved by Stalin without dissent over spheres of influence in Eastern Europe: Romania (90 percent Soviet influence), Bulgaria (USSR 75 percent), Greece (Britain with the United States, 90 percent), and Yugoslavia and Hungary (50–50). The two men also reached agreement on Austrian occupation zones.[9]

Poland proved more difficult, and the premier of the London Poles, Stanislaw Mikolajczyk, traveled to Moscow to confer with Stalin. The Soviet dictator insisted that a majority of any Polish government come from the Soviet-sponsored Union of Polish Patriots. Mikolajczyk was prepared to compromise, but his government in London was not. Unable to persuade his colleagues, Mikolajczyk resigned at the end of November. Demanding all or nothing, in the end the London Poles got nothing.

Meanwhile, the European Advisory Commission on Germany had begun meeting in London in January 1944. It decided that Germany's postwar government would be an Allied Control Council in Berlin composed of commanders of the occupying forces of the various powers. It still needed clarification from the Big Three on other matters. From August 21 to October 10, 1944, delegates at Dumbarton Oaks in Washington had been at work drafting proposals for a postwar United Nations international organization, which was much desired by Roosevelt. Churchill and Stalin were alike in that they felt comfortable with the establishment of spheres of influence. Roosevelt, however, wanted world rule of law and felt the smart of the United States never having joined the League of Nations following World War I. The result was a meeting at Yalta.

This second and last meeting of the Big Three of Churchill, Roosevelt, and Stalin took place during February 4–11, 1945, at Yalta in the Crimea. The most controversial of all World War II conferences, Yalta decided far less than that for which it is usually credited or blamed; at the time there was general satisfaction with its outcome. It was only with the Cold War and realization that Soviet help had not been necessary in the Pacific that Yalta became a fractious issue in US politics, with Republican Party leaders charging a Democratic Party 'giveaway' to the communists. At Yalta the two Western leaders found themselves in an awkward position. Their bargaining stance had not appreciably improved since the Teheran Conference. Indeed, they had just suffered a humiliating rebuff by the Germans in the Battle of the Bulge. The Red Army, on the other hand, was just 50 miles from Berlin.

Another factor at Yalta was Roosevelt's determination to bring the Soviet Union into postwar cooperation. As a result, he went out of his way to accommodate Stalin. It did not help the Western bargaining position for Roosevelt to announce that US troops were unlikely to remain long in Europe, and he continued distancing himself from Churchill, most especially in colonial issues. A third factor at work was that Roosevelt and the Americans had waged the war to bring it to the speediest possible conclusion with the least expenditure of American lives. In contrast, Stalin was waging war to make the world safe for the Soviet Union. After World War I the Western Allies had sought to construct a *cordon sanitaire* against Bolshevism. Stalin's goal was the reverse, a belt of East European satellite states to keep the West out. This was to provide security against another German invasion, but also to protect a severely wounded Soviet Union against the West and its influences. Roosevelt did secure Soviet agreement to the Declaration on Liberated Europe. In it the leaders pledged that the provisional governments of liberated areas would be 'representative of all democratic elements' and that there would be 'free elections . . . responsive to the will of the people.' But such lofty phrases were, of course, subject to different interpretations.

Regarding Germany, the Big Three set German occupation zones and Stalin agreed that France might have a zone, although he insisted it be carved from territory already assigned to Britain and the United States. The three leaders also agreed on steps to demilitarize Germany, dissolve the National Socialist party, and punish war criminals. The Soviets also insisted on heavy reparations. The Western Allies, remembering the trouble caused by reparations after World War I and fearful they would be subsidizing Soviet exactions, balked at setting a specific amount but they did agree to a talking figure of $20 billion, with the Soviet Union to receive half of any reparations payments.

Particularly important to Roosevelt was the establishment of a post-war United Nations organization. Well aware of Roosevelt's concern and not much interested in the proposed organization himself, Stalin used it to gain concessions elsewhere. The Big Three adopted recommendations from the Dumbarton Oaks conference that the UN have a General Assembly, a Security Council, and a Secretariat. It also set the composition of the Security Council. The most difficult matter to resolve was the veto in the Security Council, although the US Senate would have insisted on it in any case, and it became an issue only later when the Soviet Union exercised it liberally.

Poland was a particularly vexing matter for the two Western leaders but Stalin held all the cards, for the Red Army already occupied the country. As Poland's eastern border Stalin demanded and won the Curzon Line, with slight modifications. The Allies were more strenuous in objecting to the Oder–Neisse line as its western boundary, and there was no agreement on this matter at Yalta. Regarding the Polish government, Moscow had, only a month before Yalta, recognized the Lublin Poles as the official government of Poland. Stalin agreed to broaden this puppet government on a 'democratic basis,' and he pledged to hold 'free and unfettered elections as soon as possible on the basis of universal suffrage and secret ballot.' The Western Allies secured the same concessions for Yugoslavia, Romania, and Bulgaria.[10]

The most controversial actions taken at Yalta concerned the Far East. Stalin had already made it clear that the Soviet Union would enter the war against Japan sometime after the defeat of Germany; this was never in doubt. The problem was in the timing; here Stalin was in the same position enjoyed by the Allies before the Normandy Invasion. Late Soviet entry into the Pacific war might mean horrendous US casualties in an invasion of the Japanese home islands. No one knew whether the atomic bomb would work and, even if it did, whether it would be decisive in bringing about Japan's defeat.

In return for a Soviet pledge to enter the war against Japan 'two or three months' after the defeat of Germany, Russia was to receive South Sakhalin Island, concessions in the port of Dairen, the return of Port Arthur as a naval base, control over railroads leading to these ports, and the Kurile Islands. Outer Mongolia would continue to be independent of China, but China would regain sovereignty over Manchuria. In effect these concessions sanctioned the replacement of Japanese imperialism with Soviet, but the Western leaders thought they were necessary to secure the timing of the Soviet entry into the Pacific War. What really bothered Americans most about Yalta in future years was that these concessions need not have been made.[11]

The final wartime conference was held at Potsdam, near Berlin, during July 17 to August 2, 1945. Its codename TERMINAL signalled both the end of the war and the end of the wartime alliance. Roosevelt had died in April 1945 and President Harry S. Truman, assisted by Secretary of States James F. Byrnes, represented the United States. The results of British elections were announced in the midst of the conference and, in one of the most stunning electoral upsets in British history, the Conservatives were ousted. Labor Party leader Clement Attlee became prime minister with Ernest Bevin as foreign minister, replacing Churchill and Eden respectively.

At Potsdam there were sharp disagreements over many issues, including German reparations. Stalin held out for a firm figure whereas Truman would agree only to the Soviet Union receiving a set percentage of a whole to be determined on the German capacity to pay. The US delegation also disagreed with the Soviets over their very loose interpretation of 'war booty,' goods that could be confiscated without reference to reparations. Agreement was reached that the Soviets would receive 25 percent of plants and industrial equipment removed from the Western zones. In return the Soviets were to repay 15 of the total 25 percent in food and raw materials from their zone. The Soviets also secured permission to seize German assets in Bulgaria, Hungary, Finland, Romania, and their zone of Austria. No agreement on reparations was ever reached, but it is estimated that the Russians probably took about $20 billion (or the total sum discussed at Yalta) from their zone of Germany alone. The Allies also reached agreement on the 'three Ds' of democratization, denazification, and demilitarization; German industrial production was to be limited to a level no higher than the average for Europe as a whole.[12]

No peace treaty was signed between the Allies and Germany, so further 'temporary' arrangements sanctioned by Potsdam became permanent. East Prussia was divided according to agreements at Teheran. The Soviet Union annexed Königsberg (renamed Kaliningrad), Memel (Klaipeda), and northern East Prussia, while the remainder of East Prussia went to Poland. The 'orderly and humane' transfer of the German population from this region, agreed to at Potsdam, did not occur. Perhaps 16 million Germans were displaced from their homelands in Poland, Czechoslovakia and elsewhere in Central and Eastern Europe, and more than 2 million may have lost their lives in the forced repatriations and exodus that followed.[13]

In the weeks following Potsdam US and Soviet negotiators delineated areas of responsibility for the surrender of Japanese forces in Korea. The Soviets were to be responsible for their surrender north of the 38th parallel and the Americans south of that line. In Indo-China, Chinese Nationalist troops were to take the surrender of the Japanese north of the 17th parallel, British troops south of it. These two decisions, not considered important at the time, had profound implications in the postwar period.[14]

Finally, the leaders at Potsdam set up a Council of Foreign Ministers to plan the preparation of peace treaties. Their discussions produced increasingly bitter exchanges reflecting the arrival of the Cold War. Not until several years later was the final complexion of postwar Europe hammered out in a series of treaties arranged at Paris. These ratified the Soviet annexation of Bessarabia from Romania and the Karelian Isthmus and Arctic seaport of Petsamo from Finland. In the meantime, without formal treaty, the Soviet Union annexed the Baltic states of Estonia, Latvia, and Lithuania.

In other developments Italy's frontiers were slightly redrawn to reflect more closely lines of nationality. Yugoslavia seemed determined to secure not only Venezia Giulia, which was largely Yugoslav in population, but also the port of Trieste, which was heavily Italian. Initially declared a 'free territory,' Trieste was incorporated into Italy in 1954.

One of the supreme ironies of World War II is that Germany had waged the conflict with the stated goal of destroying Communism. Far from eradicating his ideological adversary, however, Hitler had strengthened it. In 1945 the USSR was one of the two leading powers of the world, its international prestige was at an all-time high, and in France and Italy there were powerful communist parties seemingly poised to take power. In 1949 the communists did come to power in China and they almost did so in Greece. Indeed, far from destroying the Soviet Union and containing the United States, Germany and Japan had enhanced the international position of both. The year 1945 saw the emergence of a bi-polar world and the Soviet Union and the United States poised to embark on a new and different struggle, known as the Cold War.

Notes

1 The road to war, 1931–1939

1. J. W. Wheeler Bennett, *Brest Litovsk: The Forgotten Peace, March 1918* (London, 1938), pp. 270–1, 273, 392–408.
2. On the League see Elmer Bendiner, *A Time for Angels: The Tragicomic History of the League of Nations* (New York, 1975).
3. John Maynard Keynes, *The Economic Consequences of the Peace* (New York: Harcourt, Brace and Howe, 1920), Étienne Mantoux, *Le Paix calominiée, ou les conséquences economiques de M. Keynes* (Paris: Gallimard, 1946).
4. Carl H. Pegg, *Contemporary Europe in World Focus* (New York: Henry Holt, 1956), p. 15.
5. Inflation figures are from Fritz K. Roger, *The German Inflation of 1923* (New York: Oxford University Press, 1969), p. 79.
6. Jean-Jacques Becker, *The Great War and the French People*, trans. Arnold Pomerans (Oxford: Berg Publishers, 1985), p. 330; also 'Casualties Table,' *The European Powers in the First World War, An Encyclopedia*, ed. Spencer C. Tucker (New York: Garland, 1996), p. 173.
7. See Anthony Kemp, *The Maginot Line: Myth & Reality* (New York, 1982).
8. John Terraine, *A Time for Courage: The Royal Air Force in the European War, 1939–1945* (New York: Macmillan, 1985), p.13.
9. Adolf Hitler, *Mein Kampf*, trans. Ralph Manheim (Boston, MA: Houghton Mifflin, 1943), p. 140.
10. Robert Conquest, *The Great Terror: A Reassessment* (rev. edn, New York: Macmillan, 1973), pp. 450, 485–6.
11. See Herbert P. Bix, *Hirohito and the Making of Modern Japan* (New York: HarperCollins, 2000).
12. Bendiner, *A Time for Angels*, pp. 266–7.
13. See Walter B. Maass, *Assassination in Vienna* (New York: Charles Scribner's Sons, 1972).
14. Denis Mack Smith, *Mussolini's Roman Empire* (New York: Viking Press, 1976), p. 65.

15. Barton Whaley, *Covert German Rearmament, 1919–1939: Deception and Misrepresentation* (Frederick, MD: University Publications of America, 1984), p. 79.

16. William Evans Scott, *Alliance against Hitler: The Origins of the Franco-Soviet Pact* (Durham, NC: Duke University Press, 1962), pp. 265–7.

17. Pierre Renouvin, *World War II and Its Origins: International Relations* (New York: Harper & Row, 1969), p. 81; See James T. Emmerson, *The Rhineland Crisis, 7 March 1936: A Study in International Diplomacy* (Ames: Iowa State University Press in Association with the London School of Economics and Political Science, 1977).

18. Albert Speer, *Inside the Third Reich*, trans. Richard and Clara Winston (New York: Macmillan, 1970), p. 72.

19. Raymond L. Proctor, *Hitler's Luftwaffe in the Spanish Civil War* (Westport, CT: Greenwood Press, 1983), pp. 251, 257; Brian R. Sullivan, 'Fascist Italy's Military Involvement in the Spanish Civil War,' *The Journal of Military History*, Vol. 59, No. 4, pp. 713–15.

20. On the arms aid see Gerald Howson, *Arms for Spain: The Untold Story of the Spanish Civil War* (New York: St Martin's Press – now Palgrave Macmillan, 1999). On the war itself see Hugh Thomas, *The Spanish Civil War* (New York: Harper & Brothers, 1961), still valuable despite its age; and Herbert Matthews, *Half of Spain Died: A Reappraisal of the Spanish Civil War* (New York: Charles Scribner's Sons, 1973). Casualty figures after the war are from Michael Richards, *A Time of Silence: Civil War and the Culture of Repression in Franco's Spain, 1936–1945* (Cambridge: Cambridge University Press, 1998), pp. 11, 46.

21. Statistics on the Rape of Nanjing vary widely. In the 1960s and 1970s two Japanese researchers, Hora Tomio, a university professor, and Honda Katsuichi, a journalist, each concluded that Japanese soldiers had killed some 300,000 Chinese in Nanjing between 1937 and 1938. They immediately came under attack by Japanese revisionists. Iris Chang, in *The Rape of Nanking: The Forgotten Holocaust of World War II* (New York: BasicBooks, 1997), supports the 300,000 figure, but her work has been widely disputed. Masahiro Yamamoto, a Japanese scholar now teaching in the United States, concluded in *Nanking, Anatomy of an Atrocity* (Westport, CT: Praeger, 2000) that the massacre lasted for six weeks and claimed 15,000 to 50,000 lives, most of them adult males.

22. Chang, *The Rape of Nanking*, pp. 199–214.

23. Anthony Cave Brown and Charles B. MacDonald, *On a Field of Red: The Communist International and the Coming of World War II* (New York: G. P. Putnam's Sons, 1981), p. 455.

24. Evan Burr Bukey, *Hitler's Austria: Popular Sentiment in the Nazi Era* (Chapel Hill, NC: University of North Carolina Press, 2000), p. 32.

25. Between 1945 and 1948 Austrian tribunals convicted 10,694 people of war crimes, most on Austrian soil, sentencing 43 to death. Ibid., p. 228.

26. Beck, frustrated in his efforts to bring others to his point of view, resigned on August 18. Harold C. Deutsch, *The Conspiracy against Hitler in the Twilight War* (Minneapolis: University of Minnesota Press, 1968), pp. 30–1.
27. William L. Shirer, *Berlin Diary* (New York: Alfred A. Knopf, 1941), pp. 142–3.
28. Gene Smith, *The Dark Summer: An Intimate History of the Events that led to World War II* (New York: Macmillan, 1987), pp. 104–5; Keith Eubank, *Munich* (Norman: University of Oklahoma Press), p. 1963.
29. Winston Churchill, *The Gathering Storm* (Boston, MA: Houghton Mifflin, 1948), pp. 336–9. See also Robert Boyce, ed., *French Foreign and Defense Policy, 1918–1940: The Decline and Fall of a Great Power* (New York: Routledge, 1998).
30. Ibid., pp. 338–9.
31. William Shirer, *The Rise and Fall of the Third Reich: A History of Nazi Germany* (New York: Simon and Schuster, 1960), p. 427; David Irving, *Göring: A Biography* (New York: William Morrow, 1989), p. 245.
32. Churchill, *Gathering Storm*, p. 337.
33. Alan Bullock, *Hitler, A Study in Tyranny* (rev. edn, New York: Harper & Row, 1962), pp. 509–10.
34. Ibid., p. 510.
35. Most notably Yevgeny Gnedin and Davyd Kandelaki.
36. R. C. Raack, *Stalin's Drive to the West, 1938–1945: The Origins of the Cold War* (Stanford, CA: Stanford University Press, 1995), pp. 25–8, and 52.
37. Shirer, *Rise and Fall of the Third Reich*, p. 423.
38. Galeazzo Ciano, *The Ciano Diaries, 1939–1943* (Garden City, NY: Doubleday, 1946), Entries for Aug 20–27, 1939, pp. 124–30.
39. Ibid., August 27, 1939, p. 130; Klaus P. Fischer, *Nazi Germany: A New History* (New York: Continuum, 1995), p. 440.

2   The Axis triumphant, 1939–1940

1. De Gaulle's book was translated into English as, *The Army of the Future*. Guderian recalled the impact of these Western reformers, 'It was principally the books and articles of the Englishmen, Fuller, Liddell Hart and Martel, that excited my interest and gave me food for thought.' Heinz Guderian, *Panzer Leader* (New York: Dutton, 1952), p. 20.
2. Terraine, *A Time for Courage*, p. 56.
3. Enzo Angelucci, *The Rand McNally Encyclopedia of Military Aircraft, 1914–1980* (New York: Crown Publishers, 1983), pp. 256, 259, 282.
4. I. C. B. Dear and M. R. D. Foot, *The Oxford Companion to World War II* (Oxford: Oxford University Press, 1995), p. 38.

5. Guderian, *Panzer Leader*, pp. 38–46.

6. Basil H. Liddell Hart, *History of the Second World War* (New York: G. P. Putnam's Sons, 1970), p. 22.

7. Harold Faber, ed., *Luftwaffe: A History* (New York: Times, 1978), pp. 65–6.

8. Statistics for other leading fighter aircraft are: Yak 1, 30,000; Supermarine Spitfire, 20,351; Folke Wolfe FW 190, 20,001; Polikarpov I 16, 20,000; North American P-51 Mustang, 15,686; and Republic P-47 Thunderbolt, 15,683. The largest production run Japanese fighter was the A6M Reisen, with only 10,449 produced. Angelucci, *Rand McNally Encyclopedia of Military Aircraft*, p. 246.

9. Siegfried Westphal, *The German Army in the West* (London: Cassell, 1951), p. 70.

10. Ibid.

11. Friedrich Wilhelm von Mellenthin, *Panzer Battles: A Study of the Employment of Armor in the Second World War*, trans. H. Betzler (Norman, OK: University of Oklahoma Press, 1956), p. 3.

12. Westphal, *The German Army in the West*, p. 71.

13. Ibid.

14. Alistair Horne, *To Lose a Battle: France 1940* (Boston, MA: Little Brown, 1969), p. 97; John Terraine, *A Time for Courage: The Royal Air Force in the European War, 1939–1945* (New York: Macmillan, 1985), p. 96. On the French Rhineland campaign see Jon Kimche, *The Unfought Battle* (London: Weidenfelds, 1968).

15. M. K. Dziewanowski, *War at Any Price* (2nd edn, Englewood Cliffs, NJ: Prentice-Hall, 1991), pp. 69–70; Horne, *To Lose a Battle*, p. 97.

16. Casualty figures vary for this and other campaigns. See Steven Zaloga and Victor Madej, *The Polish Campaign, 1939* (New York: Hippocrene Books, 1991), p. 156; Dziewanowski, *War at Any Price*, p. 68; Dear and Foot, *The Oxford Companion to World War II*, p. 906; G. F. Krivosheev, ed., *Soviet Casualties and Combat Losses in the Twentieth Century* (London: Stackpole Books, 1997), p. 58.

17. Shirer, *Rise and Fall of the Third Reich*, pp. 660 and 944.

18. J. K. Zawodny, *In the Forest: The Story of the Katyn Forest Massacre* (South Bend, IN: University of Notre Dame Press, 1962), pp. 5, 15, 77.

19. See F. W. Winterbotham, *The Ultra Secret* (New York: Harper & Row, 1974); see also Ronald Lewin, *Ultra Goes to War* (New York: McGraw Hill, 1978), pp. 17–18.

20. R. V. Jones, *Most Secret War: British Scientific Intelligence, 1939–1945* (London: Hamish Hamilton, 1978), pp. 443–5.

21. Shirer, *Rise and Fall of the Third Reich*, pp. 641–3.

22. David M. Glantz, *Stumbling Colossus: The Red Army on the Eve of World War* (Lawrence, KS: University Press of Kansas, 1999), pp. 9, 24.

23. William R. Trotter, *A Frozen Hell: The Russo-Finnish Winter War of*

1939–40 (Chapel Hill, NC: Algonquin Books of Chapel Hill, 1991), pp. 15–16.

24. Ibid., p. 34.
25. Ibid., p. 263.
26. See Roger R. Reese, *Stalin's Reluctant Soldiers: A Social History of the Red Army, 1925–1941* (Lawrence: University Press of Kansas, 1996).
27. Trotter, *A Frozen Hell*, pp. 264–8.
28. Shirer, *Rise and Fall of the Third Reich*, pp. 656–8; Bullock, *Hitler, A Study in Tyranny*, pp. 568–9.
29. Ibid.
30. Horne, *To Lose a Battle*, p. 108; Shirer, *The Rise and Fall of the Third Reich*, p. 34. See also Tom Shachtman, *The Phony War, 1939–1940* (New York: Harper & Row, 1982).
31. Anthony J. Trythall, *'Boney' Fuller: The Intellectual General, 1878–1966* (London: Cassell, 1977), pp. 198; R. A. C. Parker, *The Second World War: A Short History* (New York: Oxford University Press, 1989), p. 285.
32. Shirer, *Rise and Fall of the Third Reich*, pp. 644–9.
33. François Kersaudy, *Norway 1940* (New York: St Martin's Press, 1987), p. 15.
34. Ibid., p. 42.
35. Ibid., pp. 54–6.
36. Ibid., pp. 59–60.
37. Ibid., pp. 59, 62, 69, 71–2.
38. S. K. Roskill, *White Ensign: The British Navy at War, 1939–1945* (London: William Collins Sons, and Co., 1960), pp. 62–3.
39 Ibid., p. 65.
40 Roskill, *White Ensign*, pp. 69–71.
41. Ronald L. Tarnstrom, *The Sword of Scandinavia* (Limdsberg, KS: Trogen Books, 1996), p. 148; Berit Nokleby, 'Adjusting to Allied Victory,' in Henrick S. Nissen, ed., *Scandinavia during the Second World War* (Minneapolis: University of Minnesota Press, 1983), p. 318.
42. Briand Bond, *France and Belgium, 1939–1940: The Politics and Strategy of the Second World War* (Newark: University of Delaware Press, 1975), p. 63.
43. A recent study suggests that under the old plan the Germans would have met defeat. See Ernest R. May, *Strange Victory: Hitler's Conquest of France* (New York: Hill & Wang, 2000).
44. R. H. Barry, 'Military Balance,' *Purnell's History of the Second World War*, Vol. 1, No. 7 (London: Purnell, 1966), pp. 169–77. It should be noted that order of battle figures vary widely , depending on source.
45. Estimates of the number of tanks vary widely, but all sources concede an Allied advantage. Guderian puts German armored strength at the beginning of the campaign at 2800 vehicles, including armored reconnaissance cars, and notes that only 2200 were actually available for the operation.

Guderian, *Panzer Leader*, p. 94. Guy Chapman, *Why France Fell: The Defeat of the French Army in 1940* (New York: Holt, Rinehart and Winston, 1969), p. 44; Alistair Horne, *To Lose A Battle*, pp. 182–4; Christer Jorgensen and Chris Mann, *Strategy and Tactics: Tank Warfare* (Osceola, WI: MBI Publishing, 2001), p. 43; Liddell Hart, *History of the Second World War*, p. 143.

46.   Norman Gelb, *Dunkirk: The Complete Story of the First Step in the Defeat of Hitler* (New York: William Morrow, 1989), pp. 98–100.

47.   A total of 775 De 520s were produced to the end of the war. Angelucci, *Rand McNally Encyclopedia of Military Aircraft*, pp. 214, 222; John C. Fredriksen, *International Warbirds* (Oxford, UK; Denver, CO: ABC-CLIO, 2001), pp. 49, 94.

48.   Horne, *To Lose a Battle*, pp. 84–5.

49.   Kemp, *The Maginot Line*, pp. 37, 113.

50.   Horne, *To Lose a Battle*, pp. 197, 242–3.

51.   Liddell Hart, *The Second World War*, 67–8.

52.   Ibid., pp. 68–9; James E. Mrazek, *The Fall of Fort Eben Emael* (New York: David McKay, 1971), p. 183.

53.   Gelb, *Dunkirk*, 117–22.

54.   Cited in Walter Warlimont, *Inside Hitler's Headquarters, 1939–45*, trans. R. H. Berry (New York: Frederick A. Praeger, 1964), p. 95.

55.   Faber, *Luftwaffe: A History*, p. 40.

56.   Gelb, *Dunkirk*, pp. 232–3.

57.   Ibid., pp. 309–11.

58.   Joseph P. Lash, *Roosevelt and Churchill, 1939–1941: The Partnership that Saved the West* (New York: W. W. Norton, 1976), p. 149.

59.   Gelb, *Dunkirk*, p. 303.

60.   Robert Wright, *The Man Who Won the Battle of Britain* (New York: Charles Scribner's, 1969), pp. 111–17.

61.   Denis Mack Smith, *Mussolini's Roman Empire* (New York: Viking, 1976), p. 175.

62.   *Jane's Fighting Ships of World War II*, foreword by Antony Preston (London: Bracken Books, 1989), pp. 162–278; Marc' Antonio Bragadi, *The Italian Navy in World War II*, trans. Gale Hoffman (Annapolis, MD: Naval Institute Press, 1957), pp. 5, 8; James Sadkovich, *The Italian Navy in World War II* (Westport, CT: Greenwood Press, 1994), p. 20.

63.   Smith, *Mussolini's Roman Empire*, p. 243. On the Italian military's efforts to modernize see John J. T. Sweet, *Iron Arm: The Mechanization of Mussolini's Army, 1920–1940* (Westport, CT: Greenwood Press, 1980).

64.   Ciano, *The Ciano Diaries, 1939–1943*, July 2, 1940, pp. 271–2.

65.   Ibid., p. 267.

66.   Geoffrey Warner, *Pierre Laval and the Eclipse of France* (New York: Macmillan, 1968), p. 217.

67.   On Vichy see Robert O. Paxton, *Vichy France: Old Guard and New Order,*

1940–1944 (New York: Alfred A. Knopf, 1944); Philippe Burrin, *France under the Germans: Collaboration and Compromise*, trans. Janet Lloyd (New York: The New Press, 1996).

68. Guy Chapman, *Why France Fell: The Defeat of France in 1940* (New York: Holt, Rinehart and Winston, 1969), p. 18.

69. Mellenthin, *Panzer Battles*, pp. 24–5.

70. D. R. Dorondo, 'CATAPULT, Operation,' *The Encyclopedia of Naval Warfare*, ed. Spencer C. Tucker (Denver, CO: ABC-CLIO, 2002), pp. 199–201; Jack Greene and Alessandro Massignani, *The Naval War in the Mediterranean, 1940–1943* (London: Chatham Publishing, 1998), pp. 56–61. See also Warren Tute, *The Deadly Stroke* (New York: Coward, McCann & Geoghegan, 1973).

71. Terry Hughes and John Costello, *The Battle of the Atlantic* (New York: The Dial Press, 1977), p. 120.

72. The latter phrase was actually provided by Jean Monnet. Jean Monnet, *Memoirs* (New York: Doubleday, 1978), p. 160.

73. Ronald Lewin, *Churchill as Warlord* (New York: Stein and Day, 1982), p. 37.

74. Lash, *Roosevelt and Churchill*, pp. 196–7, 207.

75. Thomas A. Bailey and Paul B. Ryan, *Hitler vs. Roosevelt: The Undeclared Naval War* (New York: The Free Press, 1979), pp. 169–84, 206–8.

3 The limits of German power

1. Gelb, *Dunkirk*, p. 311; Roger Parkinson, *Summer, 1940: The Battle of Britain* (New York: David McKay, 1977), p. 5; Churchill, *The Second World War*. Vol. 2: *Their Finest Hour* (Boston, MA: Houghton Mifflin, 1949), pp. 144–5.

2. Ronald Wheatley, *Operation Sea Lion* (London: Oxford University Press, 1958), p. 39; Parkinson, *Summer, 1940*; Liddell Hart, *The Second World War*, pp. 89–90.

3. David Irving, *The Rise and Fall of the Luftwaffe: The Life and Death of Field Marshal Erhard Milch* (Boston, MA: Little, Brown, 1974), pp. 91–2.

4. Parkinson; *Summer, 1940*, p. 14; John Terraine, *A Time for Courage: The Royal Air Force in the European War, 1939–1945* (New York: Macmillan, 1985), p. 181.

5. Irving, *The Rise and Fall of the Luftwaffe*, p. 294; R. S. Overy, *The Air War, 1919–1945* (New York: Stein and Day, 1980), p. 31.

6. Richard Hough and Denis Richards, *The Battle of Britain: The Greatest Air Battle of World War II* (New York: W. W. Norton, 1989), p. 121.

7. Adolf Galland, *The First and the Last* (New York: Henry Holt, 1954), p. 34.

8. David E. Fisher, *A Race on the Edge of Time: Radar – the Decisive*

Weapon of World War II (New York: McGraw-Hill, 1988), ix–xi. See also Louis Brown, *A Radar History of World War II: Technical and Military Imperatives* (Bristol: Institute of Physics Publishing, 1999).

9. Seymour Reit, *Masquerade: The Amazing Camouflage Deceptions of World War II* (New York: Hawthorn Books, 1978), pp. 58–9.

10. Liddell Hart, *History of the Second World War*, p. 91; Faber, *Luftwaffe*, p. 192.

11. Faber, *Luftwaffe*, p. 39; Churchill, *The Gathering Storm*, p. 338.

12. Parkinson, *Summer, 1940*, pp. 168–9; 209; Liddell Hart, *History of the Second World War*, p. 92.

13. Faber, *Luftwaffe*, p. 191; Parkinson, *Summer of 1940*, pp. 85, 136.

14. John Killen, *A History of the Luftwaffe* (New York: Doubleday, 1968), p. 80.

15. Peter Townsend, *Duel of Eagles* (London: Butler and Tanner, 1991), p. 348; Parkinson, *Summer. 1940*, p. 150.

16 Leonard Mosely, *The Reich Marshal: A Biography of Hermann Goering* (Garden City, NY: Doubleday, 1974), p. 259; Wright, *The Man Who Won the Battle of Britain*, p. 184.

17. Whatley, *Operation Sea Lion*, p. 79.

18. Churchill, *The Second World War. Vol. 3: Their Finest Hour*, p. 343; On Dowding see Wright, *The Man Who Won the Battle of Britain*, 1969.

19. Mack Smith, *Mussolini's Roman Empire*, pp. 230–1.

20. Lewin, *Ultra Goes to War*, pp. 97–103; Robin Neillands, *The Bomber War: The Allied Air Offensive Against Nazi Germany* (New York: The Overlook Press, 2001), pp. 46–7.

21. Churchill, *The Second World War. Vol. 3. The Grand Alliance*, pp. 46–7.

22. Wheatley, *Operation Sea Lion*, pp. 96–7.

23. Parkinson, *Summer, 1940*, pp., 207–8.

24. Warlimont, *Inside Hitler's Headquarters*, p. 116.

25. Ciano, *The Ciano Diaries, 1939–1943*, October 12, 1940, p. 300.

26. Robert Cecil, *Hitler's Decision to Invade Russia, 1941* (New York: David McKay, 1976), pp. 94–5.

27. Raeder, *Struggle for the Sea*, pp. 194–5.

28. Mosley, *The Reich Marshal*, pp. 269–70.

29. Warlimont, *Inside Hitler's Headquarters*, p. 133; Guderian, *Panzer Leader*, p. 139.

30. John Toland, *Adolf Hitler* (New York: Doubleday, 1976), p. 671.

31. Shirer, *The Rise and Fall of the Third Reich*, p. 798.

32. Alan Bullock, *Hitler and Stalin: Parallel Lives* (New York: Alfred A. Knopf, 1992), pp. 677–9.

33. Glantz, *Stumbling Colossus*, pp. 116–17.

34. Michael Bloch, *Ribbentrop, A Biography* (New York: Crown Publishers, 1992), pp. 313–15.

35. Ibid., pp. 315–16.

36. Misha Glenny, *The Balkans: Nationalism, War, and the Great Powers, 1804–1999* (New York: Viking Penguin, 2000), p. 474; Cecil, *Hitler's Decision to Invade Russia 1941*, p. 132.

37. Glenny, *The Balkans*, p. 476.

38. On this see David Martin, *The Web of Disinformation: Churchill's Yugoslav Blunder* (New York: Harcourt Brace Jovanovich, 1990); and Michael Lees, *The Rape of Serbia: The British Role in Tito's Grab for Power, 1943–1944* (New York: Harcourt Brace Jovanovich, 1990). For a memoir of the struggle against the Germans, see Milovan Djilas, *Wartime*, trans. Michael B. Petrovich (New York: Harcourt Brace Jovanovich, 1977).

39. Callum MacDonald, *The Lost Battle: Crete 1941* (New York: The Free Press, 1993), pp. 297–301.

40. Ibid., p. 297. Greene and Massignani, *The Naval War in the Mediterranean, 1940–1943*, pp. 170–2. On the subsequent German occupation see G. C. Kiriakopoulos, *The Nazi Occupation of Crete, 1941–1945* (Westport, CT: Praeger, 1995).

41. Guderian, *Panzer Leader*, p. 151.

42. Anthony Cave Brown and Charles B. MacDonald, *On a Field of Red: The Communist International and the Coming of World War II* (New York: G. P. Putnam's Sons, 1981), pp. 568–9.

43. See Carl Boyd, *Hitler's Japanese Confidant: General Ōshima Hiroshi and Magic Intelligence, 1941–1945* (Lawrence: University Press of Kansas, 1993).

44. Bullock, *Hitler and Stalin*, p. 719.

45. Lash, *Roosevelt and Churchill*, p. 354.

46. Christopher Andrew and Vasili Mitrokhin, *The Sword and the Shield: The Mitrokhin Archive and the Secret History of the KGB* (New York: Basic Books, 1999), p. 94; Gordon W. Prange, *Target Tokyo: The Story of the Sorge Spy Ring* (New York: McGraw-Hill, 1984), pp. 337–41.

47. Andrew and Mitrohhin, *The Sword and the Shield*, p. 94.

48. Albert Seaton, *Stalin as Military Commander* (New York: Praeger, 1976), p. 95; Henry Kissinger, *Diplomacy* (New York: Simon and Schuster, 1994), p. 364; Raack, *Stalin's Drive to the West, 1938–1945*, p. 46.

49. Cecil, *Hitler's Decision to Invade Russia 1941*, pp. 132–3; Guderian, *Panzer Leader*, p. 151.

50. Antony Beevor, *Stalingrad, The Fateful Siege: 1942–1943* (New York: Viking, 1998), pp. 21, 28.

51. Ibid., pp. 150–1; Glantz, *Stumbling Colossus*, pp. 24, 293–4.

52. Cecil, *Hitler's Decision to Invade Russia 1941*, pp. 118–19; Glantz, *Stumbling Colossus*, pp. 21, 155. Glantz's figures are based on archival calculations by M. I. Mel'tiukhov in 1991.

53. Fredriksen, *International Warbirds*, p. 175.

54. Glantz, *Stumbling Colossus*, p. 119.

55. Beevor, *Stalingrad*, pp. 21, 28.
56. Bullock, *Hitler and Stalin*, p. 729; David M. Glantz, *Barbarossa: Hitler's Invasion of Russia, 1941* (Stroud, UK: Tempus, 2001), p. 61,
57. Aleksander A. Maslov, *Captured Soviet Generals: The Fate of Soviet Generals Captured by the Germans, 1941–1945*, trans. David M. Glantz and Harold S. Orenstein (Portland, OR: Frank Cass, 2001), p. 184; Beevor, *Stalingrad*, pp. 84–5.
58. Guderian, *Panzer Leader*, p. 225; Beevor, *Stalingrad*, p. 29.
59. Nicholas V. Riasanovsky, *A History of Russia* (5th edn, New York: Oxford University Press, 1993), p. 518; on the siege see Harrison E. Salisbury, *The 900 Days: The Siege of Leningrad* (New York: Harper & Row, 1969).
60. Beevor, *Stalingrad*, p. 31; Guderian, *Panzer Leader*, p. 256.
61. Beevor, *Stalingrad*, p. 13; Martin K. Sorge, *The Other Price of Hitler's War: German Military and Civilian Losses Resulting from World War II* (Westport, CT: Greenwood Press, 1986), p. 7; Martin van Creveld, *Supplying War: Logistics from Wallenstein to Patton* (Cambridge: Cambridge University Press, 1977), p. 161.
62. Guderian, *Panzer Leader*, p. 247.
63. Liddell Hart, *History of the Second World War*, p. 149; Glantz, *Stumbling Colossus*, pp. 154, 293.
64. Guderian, *Panzer Leader*, pp. 182–3, 185; Bevor, *Stalingrad*, p. 33.
65. Prange, *Target Tokyo*, pp. 401, 408.
66. Cecil, *Hitler's Decision to Invade Russia*, p. 121.
67. Barrie Pitt, 'General Sir Richard O'Connor,' in *Churchill's Generals*, ed. John Keegan (New York: Grove Weidenfeld, 1991), pp. 196–7
68. Greene and Massignani, *Rommel's North African Campaign*, pp. 33–5.
69. Ian Beckett, 'Field Marshal Earl Wavell,' in *Churchill's Generals*, p. 80; Correlli Barnett, *The Desert Generals* (New York: Viking Press, 1961), p. 72.
70. Jeremy Black, *Warfare in the Western World, 1882–1975* (Bloomington, IN: Indiana University Press, 2002), p. 112.
71. Ibid., p. 113.

4   Japanese successes

1. Dear and Foot, *Oxford Companion to World War II*, pp. 606 and 1180.
2. Monnet, *Memoirs*, p. 159; H. P. Willmott, *The Great Crusade: A New Complete History of the Second World War* (New York: The Free Press, 1989), p. 293.
3. See Warren Kimball, *The Most Unsordid Act: Lend Lease, 1939–1941* (Baltimore, MD: Johns Hopkins Press, 1969); also Churchill, *Their Finest Hour*, p. 569.
4. Spencer C. Tucker, 'Lend Lease,' *Naval Warfare: An International Encyclopedia*, 3 vols (Denver, CO: ABC-CLIO, 2002), II: 619; Michael S.

Neiberg, *Warfare in World History* (London: Routledge, 2001), p. 79; David Zimmerman, *Top Secret Exchange: The Tizard Mission and the Scientific War* (Montreal: McGill-Queen's University Press, 1996).

5. Geoffrey Perret, *There's A War to be Won: The United States Army in World War II* (New York: Random House, 1991), pp. 30–1.

6. Mauer Mauer, *Aviation in the US Army, 1919–1939* (Washington, DC: Office of Air Force History, 1987), p. 436; John Ellis, *World War II: A Statistical Survey* (New York: Facts on Files, 1993), pp. 277, 231.

7. Perret, *There's A War to be Won*, pp. 12–18, 26.

8. Ibid., p. 32.

9. Max Hastings, *Overlord: D-Day, June 6, 1944* (New York: Simon and Schuster, 1984), pp. 50, 166–7; Shelby L. Stanton, *Order of Battle: US Army, World War II* (Novato, CA: Presidio Press, 1984), p. 4.

10. Ibid., pp. 83–5.

11. See George F. Hofmann and Donn A. Starry, *Camp Colt to Desert Storm: The History of the US Armored Forces* (Lexington: The University Press of Kentucky, 1999).

12. Ibid., pp. 86–8.

13. Dear and Foot, *Oxford Companion to World War II*, p. 1192.

14. Ibid., p. 1198.

15. Ibid., pp. 1198–9.

16. Ibid., p. 1060.

17. Theodore Roscoe, *Destroyer Operations in World War II* (Annapolis, MD: Naval Institute Press, 1953), pp. 33–40.

18. On the Japanese Army see Meirion and Susie Harries, *Soldiers of the Sun: The Rise and Fall of the Imperial Japanese Army* (New York: Random House, 1991).

19. Gordon W. Prange with the assistance of Donald M. Goldstein and Katherine V. Dillon, *At Dawn We Slept: The Untold Story of Pearl Harbor* (New York: McGraw Hill, 1981), p. 4.

20. January 24, 1941; Prange, *At Dawn We Slept*, p. 5; Lash, *Roosevelt and Churchill, 1939–1941*, p. 220.

21. Michael Bloch, *Ribbentrop, A Biography* (New York: Crown Publishers, 1992), p. 304.

22. Thomas A. Bailey, *A Diplomatic History of the American People* (New York: Appleton-Century-Crofts, 1958), pp. 733–4.

23. Harries, *Soldiers of the Sun*, p, 288; Prange, *At Dawn We Slept*, p. 143.

24. Prange, *At Dawn We Slept*, pp. 208–9.

25. Dear and Foot, *Oxford Companion to World War II*, p. 622; Harries, *Soldiers of the Sun*, pp. 348–52.

26. Ibid., pp. 346–7.

27. Janusz Skulski, *The Battleship Yamato* (Annapolis, MD: Naval Institute Press, 1988).

28. On the *Iowas* see Malcolm Muir, *The Iowa Class Battleships* (Poole, UK:

Blandford Press, 1987). The US taxpayers got their money's worth; the *Wisconsin* and *Iowa* remain in reserve status.

29. A total of 33 battleships were sunk in World War II, two of them three times so the actual total is 37. One French, two American, and two British battleships were recovered. Nineteen were sunk after the issue of defeat and victory had been decided. Figures supplied by Ned Willmott to the author.

30. Richard Connaughton, *MacArthur and Defeat in the Philippines* (New York: The Overlook Press, 2001), p. 200; Carl Boyd and Akihiko Yoshida, *The Japanese Submarine Force in World War II* (Annapolis, MD: Naval Institute Press, 1995), pp. 37, 168.

31. Angelucci, *The Rand McNally Encyclopedia of Military Aircraft*, pp. 224–5, 230–1, 286–8.

32. Fredriksen, *International Warbirds*, pp. 230–2; Angelucci, *The Rand McNally Encyclopedia of Military Aircraft*, pp. 246, 251, 264.

33. Totals include ships other than in service. Figures are from H. P. Willmott, *Empires in the Balance: Japanese and Allied Pacific Strategies to April 1942* (Annapolis, MD: Naval Institute Press, 1982), p. 116.

34. H. P. Willmott, *The Second World War in the East* (London: Cassell, 1999), p. 76.

35. *The United States Strategic Bombing Surveys* (Maxwell Air Force Base, AL: Air University Press, 1987; reprint of report of September 30, 1945), p. 54.

36. Prange, *At Dawn We Slept*, p. 10.

37. Roskill, *White Ensign*, pp. 110–11; Marc' Antonio Bragadin, *The Italian Navy in World War II*, trans. Gale Hoffman (Annapolis, MD: Naval Institute Press, 1957), pp. 44–7.

38. Prange, *At Dawn We Slept*, pp. 168–270

39. H. P. Willmott, *Pearl Harbor* (New York: Sterling Publishing, 2001), p. 63.

40. Ibid., pp. 341, 495–7.

41. Ibid., pp. 499–501.

42. Ibid., pp. 485–6; 489–90; 493–4.

43. Ibid., p. 412.

44. Connaughton, *MacArthur and Defeat in the Philippines*, p. 162.

45. Prange, *At Dawn We Slept*, pp. 541–3.

46. Willmott, *Pearl Harbor*, pp. 155–7.

47. Boyd, *Hitler's Japanese Confidant*, p. 35; Weitz, *Hitler's Diplomat*, p. 277; Thomas A. Bailey and Paul B. Ryan, *Hitler vs. Roosevelt: The Undeclared Naval War* (New York: The Free Press, 1979), pp. 250–5.

48. Prange, *At Dawn We Slept*, pp. 402–13.

49. The conspiracy theory has been advanced by John Toland in *Infamy: Pearl Harbor and Its Aftermath* (Garden City, NY: Doubleday, 1982) and, more recently, by Robert B. Stinnett, *Day of Deceit: The Truth about FDR and Pearl Harbor* (New York: The Free Press, 2000).

50. Connaughton, *MacArthur and Defeat in the Philippines*, p. 49.
51. Ibid., p. 135. The author is sharply critical of MacArthur's leadership.
52. Ibid., p. 143.
53. Ibid., p. 149.
54. Ibid., pp. 164–273.
55. D. Clayton James, *The Years of MacArthur*. Vol. 2: *1941–1945* (Boston, MA: Houghton Mifflin, 1975), p. 36.
56. Ibid., p. 293.
57. Ibid., p. 296. For an extraordinary memoir on the Bataan Death March, see Preston J. Hubbard, *Apocalypse Undone: My Survival of Japanese Imprisonment during World War II* (Nashville, TN: Vanderbilt University Press, 1990).
58. Stephen Roskill, *Churchill and the Admirals* (London: William Collins, 1977), pp. 197–200; Stanley L. Falk, *Seventy Days to Singapore* (New York: G. P. Putnam, 1975), pp. 101–18,
59. Falk, *Seventy Days to Singapore*.
60. Harries, *Soldiers of the Sun*, p. 309.
61. Ted Ferguson, *Desperate Siege: The Battle of Hong Kong* (Garden City, NY: Doubleday, 1980).
62. Louis Allen, *Burma, the Longest War, 1941–45*. New York: St Martin's Press, 1984.
63. Tominaga Kengo, *Teihon Taiheiyosenso* [Standard History of the Pacific War] (Tokyo: Tosho Kanko-Kai, 1986), pp. 509, 522.

5   Japan checked

1. On this see David Day, *The Great Betrayal: Britain, Australia & the Onset of the Pacific War, 1939–1942* (New York: W. W. Norton, 1988).
2. Perret, *There's A War to be Won*, pp. 58–60.
3. Harries, *Soldiers of the Sun*, p. 316.
4. Carroll V. Glines, *The Doolittle Raid: America's Daring First Strike against Japan* (New York: Orion Books, 1988), p. 62.
5. Ibid., pp. 139–40.
6. Mitsuo Fuchida and Masatake Okumiya, *Midway: The Battle that Doomed Japan* (Annapolis, MD: Naval Institute Press, 1955), pp. 71–2.
7. Ibid., pp. 100–1.
8. Bernard Millet, *The Battle of the Coral Sea* (Annapolis, MD: Naval Institute Press, 1974); and Samuel Eliot Morison, *History of United States Naval Operations in World War II*. Vol. 4: *Coral Sea, Midway and Submarine Actions, May 1942–August 1942* (Boston, MA: Little, Brown, 1947).
9. Fuchida and Okumiya, *Midway: The Battle that Doomed Japan*, pp. 242–3.

10. Ibid., pp. 80–4.
11. Ibid., pp. 245–6.
12. Walter Lord, *Incredible Victory* (New York: Harper & Row, 1967), p. 256.
13. Fuchida and Okumiya, *Midway: The Battle that Doomed Japan*, pp. 249–50.
14. Eric Bergerud, *Touched with Fire: The Land War in the South Pacific* (New York: Viking, 1996), pp. 266–7.
15. Ibid., pp. 33, 143.
16. Ibid., pp. 33–5, 438–9.
17. Ibid., p. 26. A classic first-hand account of the early fighting is Richard Tregaskis, *Guadalcanal Diary* (New York: Random House, 1943). The most recent, and comprehensive account, is Richard B. Frank, *Guadalcanal: The Definitive Account of the Landmark Battle* (New York: Random House, 1990).
18. Bruce Loxton with Chris Coulthard-Clark, *The Shame of Savo: Anatomy of a Naval-Disaster* (Annapolis, MD: Naval Institute Press, 1994), pp. 254–70.
19. For the United States 49,445 aircraft to only 8861 for Japan. Frank, *Guadalcanal*, p. 615.
20. See Eric Hammel, *Guadalcanal, Decision at Sea: The Naval Battle of Guadalcanal, November 13–15, 1942* (Pacifica, CA: Pacifica Press, 1988).
21. Frank, *Guadalcanal*, pp. 613–14; Hatsutori Takushiro, *Daitoa Senso Zenshi* [Complete History of the Greater East Asian War] (Tokyo: Hara Shobo, 1965), p. 384.
22. Tominaga, *Teihon Taiheiyosenso*, pp. 491–2.

6   The tide turns in Europe

1. Brian Villa, *Unauthorized Action: Mountbatten and the Dieppe Raid, 1940* (New York: Oxford University Press, 1990).
2. Winston S. Churchill, *The Second World War*. Vol. 4. *The Hinge of Fate* (Boston, MA: Houghton Mifflin, 1950), p. 603.
3. George F. Howe, *The United States Army in World War II. Northwest Africa: Seizing the Initiative in the West* (Washington, DC: US Government Printing Office, 1957). E. H. Jenkins, *A History of the French Navy* (Annapolis, MD: Naval Institute Press, 1973), p. 336. Although 77 ships sunk is the figure generally cited, another source gives 90 ships totalling 250,000 tons.
4. Jean Meyer and Martine Acerra, *Histoire de la Marine Française: des origines à nos jours* (Rennes: Éditions Ouest-France, 1994), pp. 377–8.
5. Orr Kelly, *Meeting the Fox: The Allied Invasion of Africa, from Operation Torch to Kasserine Pass to Victory in Tunisia* (New York: J. Wiley, 2002).
6. Martin Blumenson, 'Rommel,' in Correlli Barnett, ed., *Hitler's Generals* (New York: Grove Weidenfeld, 1989), pp. 307–8.

7. David Rolf, *The Bloody Road to Tunis* (Mechanicsburg, PA: Stackpole Books, 2001); Bruce A. Watson, *Exit Rommel: The Tunisian Campaign, 1942–1943* (Westport, CT: Praeger, 1999).

8. Erich von Manstein, *Lost Victories*, ed. and trans. Anthony G. Powell (Chicago, IL: Henry Regnery, 1958), pp. 275, 284. For Manstein's critique of Hitler as supreme military commander, see pp. 273–88.

9. Manstein, *Lost Victories*, pp. 293–4; Field Marshal Lord Calver, 'Manstein,' in Barnett, ed., *Hitler's Generals*, p. 230.

10. Guderian, *Panzer Leader*, pp. 280–1.

11. Antony Beevor, *Stalingrad, The Fateful Siege: 1942–1943* (New York: Viking, 1998), p. 106.

12. Joel S. A. Hayward, *Stopped at Stalingrad: The Luftwaffe and Hitler's Defeat in the East, 1942–1943* (Lawrence, KS: University Press of Kansas, 1998), pp. 225, 234, 237, 244, 279, 284–5, 291.

13. Beevor, *Stalingrad*, pp. 428, 430, 439.

14. Manstein, *Lost Victories*, p. 424.

15. Ibid., p. 438.

16. Ibid., p. 443.

17. David Glantz, *Zhukov's Greatest Disaster: The Red Army's Epic Disaster in Operation Mars, 1942* (Lawrence, KS: University Press of Kansas, 1999).

7   Home Fronts and Axis occupation tactics

1. Speer, *Inside the Third Reich*, p. 182.

2. Dear and Foot, *Oxford Companion to World War II*, p. 459; James H. Doolittle with Carroll V. Glines, *I Could Never Be So Lucky Again* (New York: Bantam Books, 1991), p. 380.

3. See Albert Speer, *Infiltration: How Heinrich Himmler Schemed to Build an SS Industrial Empire* (New York: Macmillan, 1981).

4. Jeremy Black, *Warfare in the Western World, 1882–1975* (Bloomington, IN: Indiana University Press, 2002), p. 117.

5. Warner, *Pierre Laval and the Eclipse of France*, p. 217.

6. Gordon Craig, *The Germans* (New York: G. P. Putnam's Sons, 1982), p. 166.

7. Dear and Foot, *Oxford Companion to World War II*, p. 1060.

8. Douglas Botting, *From the Ruins of the Reich: Germany, 1945–1949* (New York: Crown Publishers, 1985), pp. 25, 150; Speer, *Infiltration*, p. 35.

9. Botting, *From the Ruins of the Reich*, p. 155; Beevor, *Stalingrad*, p. 59.

10. Botting, *From the Ruins of the Reich*, pp. 155–8.

11. Callum MacDonald, *The Killing of SS Obergruppenführer Reinhard Heydrich* (New York: The Free Press/Macmillan, 1989), pp. 184–9.

12. Leni Yahil, *The Holocaust: The Fate of European Jewry, 1932–1945* (Oxford: Oxford University Press, 1990), pp. 256–7; 344.

13. Lucy S. Dawidowicz, *The War Against the Jews, 1933–1945* (New York: Holt, Rinehart and Winston, 1975), p. 129; Gerald Fleming, *Hitler and the Final Solution* (Berkeley: University of California Press, 1982).

14. On this see Daniel J. Goldhagen, *Hitler's Willing Executioners: Ordinary Germans and the Holocaust* (New York: Alfred A. Knopf, 1996).

15. Dawidowicz, *The War Against the Jews*, p. 148. On I. G. Farben see Joseph Borkin, *The Crime and Punishment of I.G. Farben* (New York: Free Press, 1978).

16. Dawidowicz, *The War Against the Jews*, p. 403.

17. See Israel Gutman, *Resistance: The Warsaw Ghetto Uprising* (Boston, MA: Houghton Mifflin, 1994).

18. On the colonel see Joachim Kramarz, *Stauffenberg* (New York: Macmillan, 1962).

19. On the various plots against Hitler see Herbert M. Mason, Jr, *To Kill the Devil: The Attempts on the Life of Adolf Hitler* (New York: W. W. Norton, 1978).

20. Department of History, Kyoto University, *Nihon Kindaishi Jiten* [Encyclopedia of Modern Japanese History] (Tokyo: Toyokeizaishinpo-Sha, 1958), pp. 839, 866–7; Dear and Foot, *Oxford Companion to World War II*, p. 1062.

21. Yamada Akira, *Gunbi Kakucho no Rekish* [History of Armaments Production] (Tokyo: Yoshikawakobundo, 1997), p. 10; Mark Harrison, ed., *The Economics of World War II* (Cambridge: Cambridge University Press, 1938), p. 21.

22. Prange, *Miracle at Midway*, p. 361.

23. Ronald H. Spector, *Eagle Against the Sun* (New York: The Free Press, 1985), p. 486; Hansegeorg Jentschura and Dieter Peter Mickel, *Warships of the Imperial Japanese Navy, 1869–1945* (Annapolis, MD: Naval Institute Press, 1978), p. 61.

24. Dear and Foot, *Oxford Companion to World War II*, p. 1060.

25. Japanese and French sources claim far fewer deaths from starvation, but the official Vietnamese figure is 2 million. Nguyen Khac Vien, *Vietnam, A Long History* (Hanoi: Gioi Publishers, 1993), pp. 227–8.

26. Bergen Evans, ed., *Dictionary of Quotations* (New York: Avenel, 1978), p. 196.

27. Much has been written on Churchill and the military. Two fine books are Ronald Lewin, *Churchill as Warlord* (New York: Stein and Day, 1982); and Richard Lamb, *Churchill as War Leader* (New York: Carroll & Graf, 1991).

28. Robert Paxton, *Europe in the Twentieth Century* (New York: Harcourt Brace, 1997), pp. 484–6.

29. Dear and Foot, *Oxford Companion to World War II*, p. 1060.

30. Ibid., p. 1060.

31. Black, *Warfare in the Western World*, p. 119.

32. Dear and Foot, *Oxford Companion to World War II*, p. 1216.
33. Riasanovsky, *A History of Russia*, p. 528.
34. Botting, *From the Ruins of the Reich*, p. 156.
35. Dear and Foot, *Oxford Companion to World War II*, pp. 610, 1060, 1181–3, Angelucci, *The Rand McNally Encyclopedia of Military Aircraft*, pp. 165, 167.
36. Perret, *There's A War to be Won*, p. 109.
37. Figures vary. Dear and Foot, *Oxford Companion to World War II*, pp. 471, 623; John Ellis, *World War II: A Statistical Survey* (New York: Facts on File, 1995), pp. 115–41.
38. Dear and Foot, *Oxford Companion to World War II*, p. 1273.
39. Ibid., p. 1182.
40. Perret, *There's a War to be Won*, p. 124.
41. See Michael J. Bennett, *When Dreams Came True: The GI Bill and the Making of Modern America* (Washington, DC: Brassey's, 1996).
42. Dear and Foot, *Oxford Companion to World War II*, p. 1180.

8   The war at sea

1. Strength figures for individual navies vary widely, depending on source. I have relied especially on Robert Gardiner, ed., *Conway's All the World's Fighting Ships, 1922–1946* (London: Bracken Books, 1989; Conway Maritime Press, 1980); but also *Jane's Fighting Ships of World War II*; Siegfried Breyer's *Battleships and Battlecruisers, 1905–1970: Historical Development of the Capital Ship*, trans Alfred Kurti (West Chester, PA: Schiffer, 1889); and James L. George, *History of Warships: From Ancient Times to the Twenty-First Century* (Annapolis, MD: Naval Institute Press, 1998); as well as correspondence with naval historians H. P. Willmott, Malcolm Muir Jr, and Eric Osborne.
2. Roger Chesneau, *Aircraft Carriers of the World, 1914 to the Present: An Illustrated Encyclopedia* (London: Arms and Armour Press, 1984), pp. 101–3.
3. It is hard to come up with precise figures as different accounts vary greatly. In arriving at these, I have utilized the following: Erich Raeder, *Struggle for the Sea* (London: William Kimber, 1959), pp. 62–3, 137; John Creswell, *Sea Warfare, 1919–1945* (Berkeley, CA: University of California Press, 1967), p. 15; *Jane's Fighting Ships of World War II* (London: Bracken Books, 1939); Dear and Foot, *The Oxford Companion to World War II*, pp. 403; 905; H. P Willmott, *Warships: Sea Power since the Ironclad* (London: Octopus Books, 1975), p. 72.
4. Raeder, *Struggle for the Sea*, pp. 121, 128–9.
5. Ibid., pp. 83–92, 136–7; Dönitz, *Memoirs*, p. 46.
6. Ship totals are from Roger Chesneau, ed., *Conway's All the World's*

Fighting Ships, 1922–1946 (London: Conway Maritime Press, 1980), p. 320.

7   Raeder, *Struggle for the Sea*, pp. 135–6; Dönitz, *Memoirs*, pp. 46, 48.

8.   Gerhard L. Weinberg, *A World at Arms: A Global History of World War II* (Cambridge: Cambridge University Press, 1994), p. 70; Dönitz, *Memoirs*, p. 57.

9.   Dönitz, *Memoirs*, pp. 67–9; S. W. Roskill, *The War at Sea, 1939–1945*, Vol. 2 (London: Her Majesty's Stationery Office, 1954–61), p. 615.

10.   Dudley Pope, *The Battle of the River Plate* (London: W. Kimber, 1956).

11.   Dönitz, *Memoirs*, p. 112.

12.   See Ernle Bradford, *Siege: Malta, 1940–1943* (New York: William Morrow, 1986).

13.   William H. Garzke, Jr and Robert O. Dulin, Jr, *Battleships: Axis and Neutral Battleships in World War II* (Annapolis, MD: Naval Institute Press, 1985), p. 246. Robert J. Winklareth, *Bismarck Chase: New Light on a Famous Engagement* (Annapolis, MD: Naval Institute Press, 1998).

14.   Ernest McNeill Eller, *The Soviet Sea Challenge: The Struggle for Control of the World's Oceans* (New York: Cowles, 1971), pp, 86–9.

15.   Emory S. Land, 'Winning the War with Ships: Land, Sea and Air – Mostly Land,' in Peter Elphick, ed., *Liberty: The Ships that Won the War* (Annapolis, MD: Naval Institute Press, 2001), p. 64; Peter Elphick, 'Lifeline: The Merchant Navy at War, 1939–1945', ibid., p. 67; Terry Hughes, *The Battle of the Atlantic: The First Complete Account of the Origins and Outcome of the Longest and Most Crucial Campaign of World War II* (New York: The Dial Press, 1977), p. 216; Peter Kemp, *The Encyclopedia of Ships and Seafaring* (New York: Crown Publishers, 1980), p. 216; Dear and Foot, *Oxford Companion to World War II*, p. 1182.

16.   Perhaps the best description of the Battle of the Atlantic is Martin Middlebrook, *Convoy* (New York: William Morrow, 1977).

17.   Peter Padfield, *Dönitz: The Last Führer: Portrait of a Nazi War Leader* (New York: Harper & Row, 1984), pp. 484–5; Middlebrook, *Convoy*, p. 15.

18.   Dönitz, *Memoirs*, pp. 84–99.

19.   On the RCN see Tony German, *The Sea Is at Our Gates: The History of the Canadian Navy* (Toronto, ON: McClelland and Stewart, 1990).

20.   William T. Y'Blood, *Hunter-Killer: US Escort Carriers in the Battle of the Atlantic* (Annapolis, MD: Naval Institute Press, 1983), pp. 272–3,

21.   Chesneau, *Aircraft Carriers of the World*, pp. 108–110; see also Y'Blood, *Hunter-Killer*.

22.   Middlebrook, *Convoy*, p. 324.

23.   Dan van der Vat, *The Atlantic Campaign: World War II's Great Struggle at Sea* (New York: Harper & Row, 1998), p. 382.

24.   Garzke, and Robert Dulin, *Battleships: Axis and Neutral Battleships in World War II*, p. 273; John Sweetman, *Hunting the Beast: Air Attacks on*

the German Battleship Tirpitz, 1940–1944 (Annapolis, MD: Naval Institute Press, 2000).

25. On the evacuation see Christopher Dobson, John Miller, and Ronald Payne, *The Cruelest Night* (Boston, MA: Little, Brown, 1979).

26. Ibid.

27. Numbers of submarines in service on December 7, 1941, and built during the war differ, depending on source. The US tally is from Clay Blair, Jr, *Silent Victory: The US Submarine War against Japan* (Philadelphia, PA: J. B. Lippincott, 1975), p. 877; Japanese figures are from Nihon Sensuikan Shi Hensan Iinkai [Japanese Submarine History Committee], *Sensuikan Senshi* [History of Japanese Submarines] (Tokyo: Sensuikan Senshi Hensan Iinkai, 1979), pp. 892–5.

28. Tominaga Kengo, *Teihon Taiheiyosenso*, pp. 532, 540.

29. *The United States Strategic Bombing Surveys*, pp. 72–3; Blair, *Silent Victory*, p. 877.

30. H. P. Willmott, 'World War II at Sea: Pacific Theater,' *Naval Warfare: An International Encyclopedia*, ed. Spencer C. Tucker, III: 1120.

9   The war in the air: the strategic bombing of Germany and Japan

1.   Peter Calvocoressi and Guy Wint, with John Pritchard, *Total War: Causes and Courses of the Second World War* (rev. 2nd edn, New York: Pantheon Books, 1989), p. 514.

2.   Anthony John Trythall, *'Boney' Fuller: Soldier, Strategist, and Writer, 1878–1966* (Baltimore, MD: The Nautical & Aviation Publishing Co. of America, 1977), p. 198.

3.   Harold Faber, ed., *Luftwaffe: A History* (New York: Times Books, 1977), p. 160.

4.   Spencer C. Tucker, *Who's Who in Twentieth-Century Warfare* (London and New York: Routledge, 2001), p. 226.

5.   John Terraine, *A Time for Courage: The Royal Air Force in the European War, 1939–1945* (New York: Macmillan, 1985), pp. 100–4.

6.   Neillands, *The Bomber War*, p. 58; Terraine, *A Time for Courage*, pp. 292–4.

7.   Alan J. Levine, *The Strategic Bombing of Germany, 1940–1945* (Westport, CT: Praeger, 1992), p. 25.

8.   Arthur Harris, *The Bomber Offensive* (London: Collins, 1947), pp. 220–4.

9.   Ibid., p. 147.

10. Speer, *Inside the Third Reich*, p. 300.

11. Neillands, *The Bomber War*, p. 117.

12. Harris, *Bomber Offensive*, p. 105; Terraine, *A Time for Courage*, pp. 473–8.

13. Neillands, *The Bomber War*, pp. 120–3.
14. Churchill, *The Second World War*, Vol. 4: *The Hinge of Fate*, p. 480.
15. Fredriksen, *International Warbirds*, p. 212.
16. Terraine, *A Time for Courage*, pp. 516–7, 649.
17. Neillands, *The Bomber War*, pp. 229–34.
18. Fredriksen, *International Warbirds*, p. 37; *Jane's Fighting Aircraft of World War II* (London: Jane's, 1946), pp. 105–6; 210.
19. Terraine, *A Time for Courage*, p. 515
20. Craig A. Hannah, *Striving for Air Superior: The Tactical Air Command in Vietnam* (College Station, TX: A&M University Press, 2002), pp. 74–5.
21. Neillands, *The Bomber War*, pp. 23–243; Terraine, *A Time for Courage*, pp. 546–8.
22. Terraine, *A Time for Courage*, pp. 551–2.
23. Ibid., p. 552.
24. Ibid., p. 554.
25. Calvocoressi and Wint, with Pritchard, *Total War*, p. 525.
26. Speer, *Inside the Third Reich*, pp. 407–9.
27. Daniel Ford, *Flying Tigers: Claire Chennault and the American Volunteer Group* (Washington, DC: Smithsonian Institution Press, 1991).
28. Williamson Murray, *Luftwaffe* (Baltimore, MD: Nautical & Aviation Publishing Co. of America, 1985), p. 292.
29. Neillands, *The Bomber War*, pp. 157–8.
30. Thomas M. Coffey, *Hap: The Story of the US Air Force and the Man Who Built it, General Henry H. 'Hap' Arnold* (New York: The Viking Press, 1982), p. 251.
31. Ibid., p. 285; James Parton, *'Air Force Spoken Here': General Ira Eaker and the Command of the Air* ((Bethesda, MD: Adler & Adler, 1986), p. 191.
32. Neillands, *The Bomber War*, pp. 200–2.
33. Roger A. Freeman, *The Mighty Eighth War Manual* (Osceola, WI: Motor Books, 1991, pp. 305–13.
34. Angelucci, *Rand McNally Encyclopedia of Military Aircraft*, pp. 269, 291.
35. Roger Freeman, *The US Strategic Bomber* (London: Macdonald and Janes, 1975), p. 157.
36. Coffey, *Hap*, pp. 293–4; Conrad C. Crane, *Bombs, Cities, and Civilians: American Airpower Strategy in World War II* (Lawrence: University Press of Kansas, 1993), p. 33.
37. Neillands, *The Bomber War*, pp. 244–7.
38. Ibid., pp. 248–55. On these raids see also Martin Middlebrook, *The Schweinfurt-Regensburg Mission* (New York: Charles Scribner's Sons, 1983).
39. Speer, *Inside the Third Reich*, p. 286.
40. Angelucci, *Rand McNally Encyclopedia of Military Aircraft*, p. 201; Terraine, *A Time for Courage*, pp. 555–6.

41. Terraine, *A Time for Courage*, p. 557.
42. Neillands, *The Bomber War*, pp. 314–16.
43. Thomas A. Hughes, *Overlord* (New York: The Free Press, 1995), p. 249.
44. Hannah, *Striving for Air Superiority*, pp. 34–5.
45. Angelucci, *The Rand McNally Encyclopedia of Military Aircraft*, p. 293; Fredriksen, *International Warbirds*, p. 28.
46. Neillands, *The Bomber War*, pp. 257–60.
47. Ibid., pp. 261–2.
48. Calvocoressi and Wint, with Pritchard, *Total War*, pp. 525–6.
49. Ibid., p. 526.
50. Faber, *Luftwaffe: A History*, p. 249; Speer, *Inside the Third Reich*, p. 406; Williamson Murray, *Luftwaffe* (Baltimore, MD: The Nautical & Aviation Publishing Company of America, 1985), p. 241.
51. Neillands, *The Bomber War*, p. 326.
52. Ibid., p. 355.
53. Alexander McKee, *Dresden 1945: The Devil's Tinderbox* (New York: E. P. Dutton, 1982), pp. 104–5.
54. Harris, *Bomber Offensive*, p. 242.
55. McKee, *Dresden*, pp. 113–14.
56. Ibid., pp. 243, 274. A recent air power study puts German losses at Dresden at upwards of 100,000 killed. John Buckley, *Air Power in the Age of Total War* (London: UCL Press, 1999), p. 163.
57. Neillands, *The Bomber War*, p. 380; *The United States Strategic Bombing Surveys* (reprint; Maxwell Air Force Base, AL: Air University Press, 1987), p. 36; Tom Harrisson, *Living through the Blitz* (New York: Schocken Books, 1976), p. 266.
58. Terraine, *A Time for Courage*, p. 682; Neillands, *The Bomber War*, p. 379; Levine, *The Strategic Bombing of Germany*, pp. 189–90.
59. Thomas M. Coffey, *Iron Eagle: The Turbulent Life of General Curtis LeMay* (New York: Crown Publishers, 1986), p. 169.
60. Samuel Eliot Morison, *History of United States Naval Operations in World War II*, Vol. 6: *Breaking the Bismarcks Barrier, 22 July 1942–1 May 1944* (Boston, MA: Little, Brown, 1950), pp. 54–60.
61. Angelucci, *The Rand McNally Encyclopedia of Military Aircraft*, p. 273.
62. Coffey, *Iron Eagle*, p. 174.
63. Hata Ikuhiko, Sase Morimasa and Tuneishi Keiichi, eds, *Sekai Senso Hanzai Jiten* [Encyclopedia of Crimes in Modern History] (Tokyo: Bungei-Shunju, 2002), p. 199.
64. Johoji Asami, *Nihon Boku Shi* [History of Japanese Air Defense] (Tokyo: Hara Shobo. 1981), p. 386; On this campaign see E. Bartlett Kerr, *Flames over Tokyo: The US Army Air Forces' Incendiary Campaign Against Japan, 1944–1945* (New York: Donald I. Fine, 1991).
65. Hannah, *Striving for Air Superiority*, pp. 74–5.

10   The Allies victorious in Europe

1. Manstein, *Lost Victories*, p. 443–7.
2. Ibid., pp. 446–7.
3. David M. Glantz and Jonathan M. House, *The Battle of Kursk* (Lawrence: University Press of Kansas, 1999), p. 23.
4. Manstein, *Lost Victories*, p. 446; Kenneth Macksey, *Guderian, Creator of the Blitzkrieg* (New York: Stein and Day, 1975), p. 174.
5. Glantz and House, *The Battle of Kursk*, pp. 536–7.
6. Ibid., p. 345.
7. Fredriksen, *International Warbirds*, p. 175.
8. Glantz and House, *The Battle of Kursk*, pp. 218 and 345.
9. Robert A. Doughty, Ira D. Gruber, et al., *World War II: Total Warfare Around the Globe* (Lexington, MA: D. C. Heath, 1996), p. 119.
10. See Ewen Montagu, *The Man Who Never Was* (Philadelphia: Lippincott, 1954).
11. Clay Blair, *Ridgway's Paratroopers: The American Airborne in World War II* (Garden City, NY: Doubleday, 1985), pp. 84–107.
12. Carlo D'Este, *Bitter Victory: The Battle for Sicily, 1943* (New York: E. P. Dutton, 1988), p. 504; Greene and Massignani, *Naval War in the Mediterranean*, p. 297.
13. D'Este, *Bitter Victory*, pp. 552, 560, 597, 606–9.
14. Marc' Antonio Bragadin, *The Italian Navy in World War II*, trans. Galo Hoffman (Annapolis, MD: Naval Institute Press, 1957), pp. 317–18.
15. Eric Norris, *Salerno: A Military Fiasco* (New York: Stein and Day, 1983).
16. Carlo D'Este, *Fatal Decision: Anzio and the Battle for Rome* (New York: HarperCollins, 1991); Raleigh Trevelyan, *Rome '44: The Battle for the Eternal City* (New York: Viking Press, 1982), p. 144.
17. Wesley F. Craven and James L. Cate, eds, *The Army Air Forces in World War II* (Washington, DC: Office of Air Force History, 1983), III: 363.
18. Trevelyan, *Rome '44*, p. 291.
19. Speer, *Inside the Third Reich*, pp. 352–3.
20. Guy Hartcup, *Code Name Mulberry: The Planning, Building and Operation of the Normandy Harbours* (London: David and Charles, 1977), pp. 136, 140.
21. Colin F. Baxter, 'OVERLORD, Operation,' *Naval Warfare: An International Encyclopedia*, II: 778–9.
22. On the airborne role in the invasion see Blair, *Ridgway's Paratroopers*, pp. 206–97.
23. Speer, *Inside the Third Reich*, p. 353.
24. John Keegan, *Six Armies in Normandy: From D-Day to the Liberation of Paris, June 6th–August 25th, 1944* (New York: The Viking Press, 1982), p. 143.
25. J. C. Masterman, *The Double-Cross System in the War of 1939–1945* (New Haven, CT: Yale University Press, 1972), p. 3.

26. Roger Hesketh, *Fortitude: The D-Day Deception Campaign* (New York: The Overlook Press, 2000), p. 1.

27. Baxter, 'OVERLORD, Operation,' II: 779.

28. Adrian R. Lewis, *Omaha Beach: A Flawed Victory* (Chapel Hill, NC: University of North Carolina Press, 2001).

29. Hartcup, *Code Name Mulberry*, pp. 123–30.

30. Kevin Dougherty, 'Saint Lô Breakout,' *World War II in Europe: An Encyclopedia*, ed. David T. Zabecki (New York: Garland, 1999), II: 1658.

31. Alan F. Wilt, *The French Riviera Campaign of August 1944* (Carbondale, IL: Southern Illinois University Press, 1981).

32. Stephen E. Ambrose, *Eisenhower: Soldier, General of the Army, President-Elect, 1890–1952* (New York: Simon & Schuster, 1983), p. 348.

33. See Belton Y. Cooper, *Death Traps: The Survival of an American Armored Division in World War II* (Novato, CA: Presidio Press, 1998).

34. Ibid., pp. 161–2.

35. Westphal, *The German Army in the West*, pp. 172 and 174.

36. Ambrose, *Eisenhower*, pp. 344, 348–9.

37. Cornelius Ryan, *A Bridge Too Far* (New York: Simon & Schuster, 1974), p. 599; the title of Ryan's book is drawn from General Browning's verdict of the battle.

38. Ambrose, *Eisenhower*, p. 355.

39. Paul Adair, *Hitler's Greatest Defeat: The Collapse of Army Group Center* (London: Brockhampton Press, 1998); Walter S. Dunn, *Soviet Blitzkrieg: The Battle for White Russia, 1944* (Boulder, CO: Lynne Rienner, 2000); Black, *Warfare in the Western World, 1882–1975*, p. 114.

40. Adair, *Hitler's Greatest Defeat*, pp. 171–2; Krivosheev, *Soviet Casualties*, p. 145.

41. David T. Zabecki, 'Hürtgen Forest, Battle of,' *Encyclopedia of American Military History*, ed. by Spencer C. Tucker (New York: Facts on File, 2003), II: 411–12. See also Robert Sterling Rush, *Hell in Hürtgen Forest* (Lawrence: University Press of Kansas, 2001); and Edward G. Miller, *A Dark and Bloody Ground: The Hürtgen Forest and the Roer River Dams, 1944–1945* (College Station: Texas A&M University Press, 1995).

42. Martin Blumenson, *Patton: The Man Behind the Legend, 1885–1945* (New York: William Morrow, 1985), pp. 246–50.

43. Ibid., p. 252.

44. Stanley P. Hirshson, *General Patton: A Soldier's Life* (New York: HarperCollins, 2002), p. 599; Winston S. Churchill, *The Second World War*, Vol. 6: *Triumph and Tragedy* (Boston, MA: Houghton Mifflin, 1953), pp. 281–2.

45. MacDonald, *A Time for Trumpets*, p. 618.

46. Speer, *Inside the Third Reich*, pp. 435, 456.

47. Anthony Read and David Fisher, *The Fall of Berlin* (New York: W. W. Norton, 1992), pp. 280–1.

48. James M. Gavin, *On to Berlin: Battles of an Airborne Commander, 1943–1945* (New York: Viking, 1978), pp. 298, 300; Krivosheev, *Soviet Casualties*, pp. 158–9.

11 The defeat of Japan

1. See Shelford Bidwell, *The Chindit War: Stilwell, Wingate, and the Campaign in Burma, 1944* (New York: Macmillan, 1980).
2. Chesneau, *Aircraft Carriers*, pp. 103, 220–2.
3. Allan R. Millett, *Semper Fidelis: The History of the United States Marine Corps* (New York: Macmillan, 1980), p. 325. On Ellis see Dirk A. Ballendorf and Merrill L. Bartlett, *Pete Ellis: An Amphibious Warfare Prophet, 1880–1923* (Annapolis, MD: Naval Institute Press, 1997).
4. Ibid., p. 326.
5. Charles T. Gregg, *Tarawa* (New York: Stein and Day, 1984), p. 167.
6. Ibid., p. 176. See Leo J. Dougherty, *Fighting Techniques of a US Marine, 1942–1945: Training, Techniques, and Weapons* (Osceola, WI: MBI Publishing, 2000).
7. See Harry A. Galley, *'Howlin' Mad' vs the Army: Conflict in Command, Saipan, 1944* (Novato, CA: Presidio Press, 1986).
8. William T. Y'Blood, *Red Sun Setting: The Battle of the Philippine Sea* (Annapolis, MD: Naval Institute Press, 1981), p. 221.
9. Edwin P. Hoyt, *The Battle of Leyte Gulf: The Death Knell of the Japanese Fleet* (New York: Weybright and Talley, 1972), p. 168.
10. Thomas J. Cutler, *The Battle of Leyte Gulf, 23–26 October 1944* (New York: HarperCollins, 1994), p. 93.
11. Ibid., pp. 262–4; 286–7.
12. Ibid., pp. 261, 288–93.
13. Richard Wheeler, *Iwo* (New York: Lippincott & Crowell, 1980), p. 42.
14. Ibid., p. 205.
15. Ian Gow, *Okinawa, 1945: Gateway to Japan* (Garden City, NY: Doubleday, 1985), pp. 28–41.
16. Cutler, *The Battle of Leyte Gulf*, pp. 266–73.
17. Jeff Kinard, 'Kamikazes,' *World War II in the Pacific: An Encyclopedia*, ed. Stanley Sandler (New York: Garland, 2001), pp. 293–4; Hara Takeshi, ed., *Nihon Rikukaigun Jiten* [Encyclopedia of the Japanese Army and Navy] (Tokyo: Shinjinbutsuoraisha, 1998), pp. 146–7. See also Rikihei Inoguchi and Tadashi Nakajima, with Roger Pineau, *The Divine Wind: Japan's Kamikaze Force in World War II* (New York: Bantam Books, 1978); and Bernard Millot, *Divine Thunder: The Life and Death of the Kamikazes*, trans. Lowell Blair (New York: McCall, 1970).

18. Russell Spurr, *A Glorious Way to Die: The Kamikaze Mission of the Battleship Yamato, April 1945* (New York: Newmarket Press, 1981), p. 308.
19. Gow, *Okinawa, 1945*, p. 195.
20. Richard B. Frank, *Downfall: The End of the Japanese Empire* (New York: Random House, 1999), p. 333.
21. Ibid., pp. 126–7.
22. John Ray Skates, *The Invasion of Japan: Alternative to the Bomb* (Columbia: University of South Carolina Press, 1998), p. 256.
23. Frank, *Downfall*, pp. 350–1.
24. Ibid., p. 334.
25. Hata et al., *Sekai Senso Hanzai Jiten*, pp. 234–5.
26. Black, *Warfare in the Western World, 1882–1975*, p. 114; Frank, *Downfall*, p. 325. The Soviet figure of Japanese casualties includes Manchurian and Mongolian auxiliaries and many Japanese civilians.
27. Leonard Mosley, *Hirohito, Emperor of Japan* (Englewood Cliffs, NJ: Prentice-Hall, 1966), p. 330.

12 Wartime diplomacy and the peace settlement

1. R. Ernest Dupuy and Trevor N. Dupuy, *The Harper Encyclopedia of Military History: From 3500 BC to the Present* (New York: HarperCollins, 1993), p. 1309.
2. Gordon Wright, *France in Modern Times* (Chicago, IL: Rand McNally, 1960), p. 532.
3. Riasanovsky, *A History of Russia*, p. 528.
4. Liddell Hart, *History of the Second World War*, pp. 712–13; Speer, *Inside the Third Reich*, p. 293.
5. On relations between de Gaulle, Roosevelt, and Churchill see François Kersaudy, *Churchill and De Gaulle* (New York: Atheneum, 1982); and Milton Viorst, *Hostile Allies: FDR and De Gaulle* (New York: Macmillan, 1965).
6. Winston S. Churchill, *The Second World War*, Vol. 5: *Closing the Ring* (Boston, MA: Houghton Mifflin, 1951), pp. 82–5.
7. Richard Breitman, *Official Secrets: What the Nazis planned, What the British and Americans Knew* (New York: Hill and Wang, 1998), p. 215.
8. Louis Fischer, *The Road to Yalta: Soviet Foreign Relations, 1941–1945* (New York: Harper and Row, 1972), pp. 116–42.
9. Winston S. Churchil, *The Second World War*, Vol. 6: *Triumph and Tragedy* (Boston, MA: Houghton Mifflin, 1953), pp. 227–8.
10. For the minutes of the Yalta Conference, see Robert Beitzell, ed., *Teheran, Yalta, Potsdam: The Soviet Protocols* (Hattiesburg, MI: Academic International, 1970), pp. 48–126; the communiqué is on pp. 127–40.

11. Ibid., p. 139.
12. For the minutes of the Potsdam Conference, see ibid., pp. 141–310; the communiqué is on pp. 311–35.
13. Botting, *From the Ruins of the Reich*, p. 179.
14. Sherman Pratt, 'Korea, History, 1945–1947,' *Encyclopedia of the Korean War: A Political, Social, and Military History*, ed. Spencer C. Tucker (Santa Barbara, CA: ABC-CLIO, 200), I: 347.

Selective Bibliography

General histories

Doughty, Robert A., Ira D. Gruber, et al., *World War II: Total Warfare Around the Globe*. Lexington, MA: D. C. Heath, 1996.

Dziewanowski, M. K. *War at Any Price*. 2nd edn. Englewood Cliffs, NJ: Prentice-Hall, 1991.

Liddell Hart, Basil H. *History of the Second World War*. New York: G. P. Putnam's Sons, 1970.

Murray, Williamson, and Allan R. Millett. *A War to be Won: Fighting the Second World War*. Cambridge, MA: The Belknap Press of Harvard University Press, 2000.

Weinberg, Gerhard L. *A World at Arms: A Global History of World War II*. Cambridge: Cambridge University Press, 1994.

Willmott, H. P. *The Great Crusade: A New Complete History of the Second World War*. New York: The Free Press, 1989.

The background

Bendiner, Elmer. *A Time for Angels: The Tragicomic History of the League of Nations*. New York: Alfred A. Knopf, 1975.

Kemp, Anthony. *The Maginot Line: Myth & Reality*. New York: Stein & Day, 1982.

Mack Smith, Denis. *Mussolini's Roman Empire*. New York: Viking Press, 1976.

Read, Anthony and David Fisher, *The Deadly Embrace: Hitler, Stalin and the Nazi–Soviet Pact, 1939–1941*. New York: W. W. Norton, 1988.

Whaley, Barton. *Covert German Rearmament, 1919–1939: Deception and Misrepresentation*. Frederick, MD: University Publications of America, 1984.

Wheeler Bennett, J. W. *Brest-Litovsk: The Forgotten Peace, March 1918.* London, 1938.

The war in Europe and North Africa

Ambrose, Stephen E. *D-Day, June 6, 1944: The Climactic Battle of World War II.* New York: Simon & Schuster, 1994.

Atkinson, Rick. *An Army at Dawn: The War in North Africa, 1942–1943.* New York: Henry Holt, 2002.

Barnett, Correlli. *The Desert Generals.* New York: Viking Press, 1961.

Beaufre, André. *1940: The Fall of France.* Trans. Desmond Flower. New York: Alfred A. Knopf, 1968.

Beevor, Antony. *The Fall of Berlin, 1945.* New York: Viking, 2002.

——. *Stalingrad, The Fateful Siege: 1942–1943.* New York: Viking Penguin, 1998.

Bond, Brian. *France and Belgium, 1939–1940: The Politics and Strategy of the Second World War.* Newark: University of Delaware Press, 1975.

Bradford, Ernle. *Siege: Malta, 1940–1943.* New York: William Morrow, 1986.

Chapman, Guy. *Why France Fell: The Defeat of France in 1940.* New York: Holt, Rinehart and Winston, 1969.

D'Este, Carlo. *Decision in Normandy.* New York: E. P. Dutton, 1983.

——. *Bitter Victory: The Battle for Sicily, 1943.* New York: E. P. Dutton, 1988.

——. *Fatal Decision: Anzio and the Battle for Rome.* New York: HarperCollins, 1991.

Dunn, W. S. *Soviet Blitzkrieg: The Battle for White Russia, 1944.* Boulder, CO: Lynne Rienner, 2000.

Gelb, Norman. *Dunkirk: The Complete Story of the First Step in the Defeat of Hitler.* New York: William Morrow, 1989.

Glantz, David M. *Zhukov's Greatest Disaster: The Red Army's Epic Disaster in Operation Mars, 1942.* Lawrence, KS: University Press of Kansas, 1999.

——. *Barbarossa: Hitler's Invasion of Russia, 1941.* Stroud, UK: Tempus, 2001.

Glantz, David M. and Jonathan M. House, *The Battle of Kursk.* Lawrence: University Press of Kansas, 1999.

Horne, Alistair. *To Lose a Battle: France 1940.* Boston, MA: Little, Brown, 1969.

Keegan, John. *Six Armies in Normandy: From D-Day to the Liberation of Paris, June 6th–August 25th, 1944.* New York: Viking Press, 1982.

Kersaudy, François. *Norway 1940.* New York: St Martin's Press, 1987.

MacDonald, Charles B. *A Time for Trumpets: The Untold Story of the Battle of the Bulge.* New York: William Morrow, 1985.

May, Ernest R. *Strange Victory: Hitler's Conquest of France.* New York: Hill & Wang, 2000.

Mellenthin, Friedrich Wilhelm von. *Panzer Battles: A Study of the Employment of Armor in the Second World War.* Trans. H. Betzler. Norman: University of Oklahoma Press, 1956.

Moorehead, Alan. *The March to Tunis: The North African War, 1940–1943.* New York: Harper & Row, 1967.

Parkinson, Roger. *Summer, 1940: The Battle of Britain.* New York: David McKay, 1977.

Ryan, Cornelius. *A Bridge Too Far.* New York: Simon & Schuster, 1974.

Terraine, John. *A Time for Courage: The Royal Air Force in the European War, 1939–1945.* New York: Macmillan, 1985.

Trevelyan, Raleigh. *Rome '44: The Battle for the Eternal City.* New York: Viking Press, 1982.

Trotter, William R. *A Frozen Hell: The Russo-Finnish Winter War of 1939–40.* Chapel Hill, NC: Algonquin Books of Chapel Hill, 1991.

Warlimont, Walter. *Inside Hitler's Headquarters, 1939–45.* Trans. R. H. Berry. New York: Frederick A. Praeger, 1964.

Werth, Alexander. *Russia at War, 1941–1945.* New York: E. P. Dutton, 1964.

Westphal, Siegfried. *The German Army in the West.* London: Cassell, 1951.

Wilt, Alan F. *The French Riviera Campaign of August 1944.* Carbondale, IL: Southern Illinois University Press, 1981.

The war in Asia

Allen, Louis. *Burma: The Longest War, 1941–1945.* New York: St Martin's Press, 1984.

Bergerud, Eric. *Touched with Fire: The Land War in the South Pacific.* New York: Viking, 1996.

Connaughton, Richard. *MacArthur and Defeat in the Philippines.* Woodstock, NY: Overlook Press, 2001.

Day, David. *The Great Betrayal: Britain, Australia & the Onset of the Pacific War, 1939–1942.* New York: W. W. Norton, 1988.

Drea, Edward J. *New Guinea*. Washington, DC: US Army Center of Military History, 1993.

Falk, Stanley J. *Seventy Days to Singapore*. New York: G. P. Putnam's Sons, 1975.

Ferguson, Ted. *Desperate Siege: The Battle of Hong Kong*. Garden City, NY: Doubleday, 1980.

Frank, Richard B. *Guadalcanal: The Definitive Account of the Landmark Battle*. New York: Random House, 1990.

——. *Downfall: The End of the Japanese Empire*. New York: Random House, 1999.

Gow, Ian. *Okinawa, 1945: Gateway to Japan*. Garden City, NY: Doubleday, 1985.

Gregg, Charles T. *Tarawa*. New York: Stein and Day, 1984.

Harries, Meirion and Susie. *Soldiers of the Sun: The Rise and Fall of the Imperial Japanese Army*. New York: Random House, 1991.

James, D. Clayton. *The Years of MacArthur*. Vol. 2: *1941–1945*. Boston. MA: Houghton Mifflin, 1975.

Loxton, Bruce, with Chris Coulthard-Clark. *The Shame of Savo: Anatomy of a Naval-Disaster*. Annapolis, MD: Naval Institute Press, 1994.

Prange, Gordon W., with the assistance of Donald M. Goldstein and Katherine V. Dillon. *At Dawn We Slept: The Untold Story of Pearl Harbor*. New York: McGraw Hill, 1981.

——. *Miracle at Midway*. New York: McGraw-Hill, 1982.

Spector, Ronald H. *Eagle against the Sun: The American War with Japan*. New York: Free Press, 1985.

Willmott, H. P. *The Second World War in the East*. London: Cassell, 1999.

——. *Pearl Harbor*. New York: Sterling Publishing, 2001.

The war at sea

Bekker, Cajus D. *Hitler's Naval War*. Garden City, NY: Doubleday, 1974.

Belote, James H., and William M. Belote. *Titans of the Seas: The Development and Operations of Japanese and American Carrier Task Forces during World War II*. New York: Harper & Row, 1975.

Blair, Clay, Jr. *Silent Victory: The US Submarine War against Japan*. Philadelphia, PA: J. B. Lippincott, 1975.

Boyd, Carl, and Akihiko Yoshida. *The Japanese Submarine Force in World War II*. Annapolis, MD: Naval Institute Press, 1995.

Bragadin, Marc' Antonio. *The Italian Navy in World War II*. Trans. Gale Hoffman. Annapolis, MD: Naval Institute Press, 1957.

Chesneau, Roger. *Aircraft Carriers of the World, 1914 to the Present: An Illustrated Encyclopedia*. London: Arms and Armour Press, 1984.

Culter, Thomas J. *The Battle of Leyte Gulf, 23–26 October 1944*. New York: HarperCollins, 1994.

Dönitz, Karl. *Memoirs: Ten Years and Twenty Days*. Trans. R. H. Stevens. London: Weidenfeld and Nicolson, 1958.

Dull, Paul S. *The Battle History of the Imperial Japanese Navy*. Annapolis, MD: Naval Institute Press, 1978.

Evans, David C., and Mark R. Peattie. *Kaigun: Strategy, Tactics, and Technology in the Imperial Japanese Navy, 1887–1941*. Annapolis, MD: Naval Institute Press, 1997.

Fuchida, Mitsuo, and Masatake Okumiya, *Midway: The Battle that Doomed Japan*. Annapolis, MD: Naval Institute Press, 1955.

Greene, Jack, and Alessandro Massignani. *The Naval War in the Mediterranean, 1940–1943*. London: Chatham Publishing, 1998.

Middlebrook, Martin. *Convoy*. New York: William Morrow, 1977.

Morison, Samuel Eliot. *History of United States Naval Operation in World War II*. 15 vols. Boston, MA: Little, Brown, 1947–62.

Muir, Malcolm Jr. *The Iowa Class Battleships*. Poole, UK: Blandford Press, 1987.

Raeder, Erich. *Struggle for the Sea*. London: William Kimber, 1959.

Reynolds, Clark G. *The Fast Carriers: The Forging of an Air Navy*. Annapolis, MD: Naval Institute Press, 1992.

Roscoe, Theodore. *On the Seas and in the Skies: A History of the US Navy's Air Power*. New York: Hawthorn Books, 1970.

Roskill, S. K. *The Navy at War, 1939–1945*. 3 vols. Ware, UK: Wordsworth Editions, 1960.

———. *White Ensign: The British Navy at War, 1939–1945*. London: William Collins Sons, 1960.

Sawyer, L. A., and W. W. Mitchell, *The Liberty Ships*. London: Lloyd's of London Press, 1985.

Skulski, Janusz. *The Battleship Yamato*. Annapolis, MD: Naval Institute Press, 1988.

Van der Vat, Dan. *The Atlantic Campaign: World War II's Great Struggle at Sea*. New York: Harper and Row, 1988.

Y'Blood, William T. *Red Sun Setting: The Battle of the Philippine Sea*. Annapolis, MD: Naval Institute Press, 1981.

———. *Hunter-Killer: US Escort Carriers in the Battle of the Atlantic*. Annapolis, MD: Naval Institute Press, 1983.

The air war

Boyne, Walter J. *Clash of Wings: World War II in the Air*. New York: Simon & Schuster, 1993.

Buckley, John. *Air Power in the Age of Total War*. London: UCL Press, 1999.

Hayward, Joel S. A. *Stopped at Stalingrad: The Luftwaffe and Hitler's Defeat in the East, 1942–1943*. Lawrence, KS: University Press of Kansas, 1998.

Inoguchi, Rikihei, and Tadashi Nakajima, with Roger Pineau. *The Divine Wind: Japan's Kamikaze Force in World War II*. New York: Bantam Books, 1978.

Kerr, E. Bartlett. *Flames over Tokyo: The US Army Air Forces' Incendiary Campaign Against Japan, 1944–1945*. New York: Donald I. Fine, 1991.

Levine, Alan J. *The Strategic Bombing of Germany, 1940–1945*. Westport, CT: Praeger, 1992.

Neillands, Robin. *The Bomber War: The Allied Air Offensive Against Nazi Germany*. New York: The Overlook Press, 2001.

Terrain, John. *A Time for Courage: The Royal Air Force in the European War, 1939–1945*. New York: Macmillan, 1985.

United States Strategic Bombing Surveys. Maxwell Air Force Base, LA: Air University Press, 1987. Reprint of September 30, 1945, summary reports.

Home fronts

Barber, John, and Mark Harrison. *The Soviet Home Front, 1941–1945: A Social and Economic History of the USSR in World War II*. London: Longman, 1991.

Burrin, Philippe. *France under the Germans: Collaboration and Compromise*. Trans. Janet Lloyd. New York: The New Press, 1996.

Dawidowicz, Lucy S. *The War Against the Jews, 1933–1945*. New York: Holt, Rinehart and Winston, 1975.

Paxton, Robert O. *Vichy France: Old Guard and New Order, 1940–1944*. New York: Alfred A. Knopf, 1972.

Salisbury, Harrison E. *The 900 Days: The Siege of Leningrad*. New York: Harper & Row, 1969.

Yahil, Leni. *The Holocaust: The Fate of European Jewry, 1932–1945*. Oxford: Oxford University Press, 1990.

Diplomacy

Bailey, Thomas A., and Paul B. Ryan, *Hitler vs. Roosevelt: The Undeclared Naval War*. New York: The Free Press, 1979.
Lash, Joseph P. *Roosevelt and Churchill, 1939–1941: The Partnership that Saved the West*. New York: W. W. Norton, 1976.

Intelligence and deception

Boyd, Carl. *Hitler's Japanese Confidant: General Ōshima Hiroshi and Magic Intelligence, 1941–1945*. Lawrence: University Press of Kansas, 1993.
Drea, Edward J. *MacArthur's ULTRA: Codebreaking and the War against Japan, 1942–1945*. Lawrence: University of Kansas Press, 1992.
Hesketh, Roger. *Fortitude: The D-Day Deception Campaign*. New York: The Overlook Press, 2000.
Lewin, Ronald. *Ultra Goes to War*. New York: McGraw Hill, 1978.
——. *The American Magic: Codes, Ciphers and the Defeat of Japan*. New York: Farrar Straus Giroux, 1982.
Masterman, J. C. *The Double-Cross System in the War of 1939–1945*. New Haven, CT: Yale University Press, 1972.
Reit, Seymour. *Masquerade: The Amazing Camouflage Deceptions of World War II*. New York: Hawthorn Books, 1978.

Miscellaneous

Creveld, Martin van. *Supplying War: Logistics from Wallenstein to Patton*. Cambridge: Cambridge University Press, 1977.
Dear, I. C. B., and M. R. D. Foot, eds. *The Oxford Companion to World War II*. Oxford: Oxford University Press, 1995.
Perret, Geoffrey. *There's A War to be Won: The United States Army in World War II*. New York: Random House, 1991.
Zabecki, David, ed. *World War II in Europe: An Encyclopedia*. 2 vols. New York: Garland, 1999.

Index

355